UNDE

✳ THE ✳

SOUTHERN

CROSS

UNDER
✳ THE ✳
SOUTHERN
CROSS

The rebels, martyrs, exiles and
activists who shaped Australia

GEOFF HOCKING

The Five Mile Press

The Five Mile Press Pty Ltd
1 Centre Road, Scoresby
Victoria 3179 Australia
www.fivemile.com.au

First published as *Rebel Chorus* in in 2007
This revised and reformatted edition published 2012
Reprinted 2012

Printed in China

Cover and page design by Shaun Jury
Cover image:
   Unknown Maker
   Eureka Flag, 1854
   wool, cotton
   Collection: Art Gallery of Ballarat, Gift of the King Family, 2001

National Library of Australia Cataloguing-in-Publication entry
   Hocking, Geoff
   Under the Southern Cross : the rebels, martyrs, exiles
   and activists who shaped Australia / Geoff Hocking.
   ISBN: 9781743007952 (pbk.)
   Australia–History.
   994

CONTENTS

Map of Eastern Australia showing the colonies as they were in 1852

(National Library of Australia)

INTRODUCTION

From the very first day in 1788 when Captain Arthur Phillip stepped onto the shore at Botany Bay and raised the flag of Queen Anne against a sunny blue sky, there was another class of new arrivals who were not invited to his party. On board the convict transport ships that lay at anchor in the harbour were several hundred of the outcasts of British society who were never going to find a place in the new colony of New South Wales equal to the elevated status of their masters.

To cope with the status of the permanent outsider the new Australians developed a technique that has lasted up until the present day: it is the ability to see their masters as a joke, to be suspicious of authority and find humour in adversity.

This attitude, which persisted across the generations, so incensed English officers charged with command of the Australian forces in World War I that they complained of the lack of respect shown to them by the common Australian soldier. The Australian soldier may have been common but he was never anyone's lackey, and only saluted any man who had earned his respect; gold braid and polished boots were to him symbols of privilege, rarely earned, and therefore unworthy of deference.

Australian society grew rapidly apart from its roots in old England; the bastard child may have thumbed its nose at its 'mother' but it never lost its sense of heritage. Australians are descended from bog-poor Irish, homeless Scots, the street urchins of Dickensian London and the dispossessed labourers of the English heartlands. Steeped in the revolutionary fervour of the nineteenth century agitators, they retained little respect for authority, nurturing the belief that their world could change; that there was plenty enough for all, if only the system were made fair for all.

For most it was the cry of democracy that flamed their rebel hearts. The Chartists' ideals, which inspired so many to stand together against the ruling classes in the mid-nineteenth century, saw many a bright young man arrive in Botany Bay in chains.

England sent the firebrands, the unionists, the democrats, the rebels, rural warriors and street fighters to the Australian colonies and wondered why they stood tall under the sun and demanded that which had been denied them at home.

The Rights of Everyman

The following editorial comment, published in the *Illustrated London News* on 26 June 1852, came after three-quarters of a century of colonial rule over Australia from Westminster.

> The mind of the nation has been awakened to the full consciousness and appreciation of the fact that our Colonies are not alone magnificent in extent and resources, but that they have been grossly neglected by the people, as well as by our rulers; and that in the times in which we live, while other nations are making such rapid advances towards an equality with us in the arts that extend and maintain the power of States and Governments, it is not wise on the part of Great Britain to suffer those splendid possessions to be alienated, either by misgovernment or by neglect. We remember, at last, that we have a duty to ourselves to perform, as well as towards them—and that this double duty demands a closer and more cordial intercourse between ourselves and those trans-oceanic regions, where our language is spoken, and where our children live, than we have yet found it convenient to establish.
>
> Australia, that has long had cause for complaint, has for the present forgotten most of her grievances, in gratulations over the abundant wealth that has recently been dug out of her streams and mountains . . . though for the moment she has forgotten her old sources of complaint, will, sooner or later, remember and insist upon them again; and, with such treasures in her hands, she will not, in future, suffer herself to remonstrate as vainly as she has formerly done against the injustice which she must suffer under a system by which an official in Downing-street, often entirely ignorant even

of the very geography of the Colony, is permitted to control her affairs.
– *The* Illustrated London News, *26 June 1852*

Tools of imprisonment and punishment
In its desire to dominate trade in the southern oceans Britain had discovered a fertile land in Australia and turned it into a brutal prison.
(National Library of Australia)

The discovery of gold in the Australian colonies in September 1851 had made the mother country sit up and take notice, ever fearful that the Australians could follow the lead set by the United States and declare themselves free of her colonial apron-strings. While the writer has given the British government of his day what in hindsight would appear to be some good advice, it is obvious that Britain took little notice. Only a few months after this publication in England, diggers in Victoria refused to obey the governor's demands for increased taxation via the licence fee to dig for gold.

Dissatisfaction with the colonial representative of the Crown in Victoria at that time was running at such a head of steam that one newspaper even ran a daily headline, which read: 'Wanted! A Governor. Apply to the people of Victoria'. The following year insurrection was afoot as diggers led by an Irishman, with family links to Vinegar Hill and the failed rebellion of 1845, supported by scores of Americans–Californian freemen who had little love for the English queen–stood firm against the colonial government.

The Governor of the Colony of Victoria had warned the British Parliament that his colony was in danger of becoming 'another California', where 'revolutionaries, chartists, socialists, red republicans and others' were enjoying 'a growing sense of importance and independence arising from unexampled prosperity, emancipation from old ties and obligations, and powers of self-support and self-government'. He was correct in his belief that this prosperity would bring about social and political change that neither he, nor the British Government, had prepared themselves for—democracy.

Currency vs Sterling

Australian society has among its many charms the following two well-established social norms: a cavalier disregard for authority; and the tall poppy syndrome, a desire to cut down to size anyone who gets too big for his, or her, boots.

The first stems from the days of convict transportation to the colony when the difference between the gaoler, the convict and the law was usually only the uniform each man wore. The overseer and the flogger were more often than not 'favoured' convicts selected by the authorities to undertake a brutalising task. Although most of those selected relished the opportunity to punish, and control, the old lags they had left behind in their chains, few paid any respect to any so-called high office assumed by one of their own kind.

The second is a time-honoured tradition of the rejection of class distinction, and aristocracy, in an egalitarian Australian society. Colonial Australians, whether convict or free, sought to create a new society in their new world, and cut down anyone who would seek to rise above the motley crew. They rejected those who believed they were born to rule, honouring only those they deemed worthy of calling 'mate'. No matter how grand their station or noble their achievement, to remain a true mate any Aussie must have their feet firmly on the ground, their head not in the stars, and never forget from whence they came.

This is not to say that colonial Australia did not nurture those who sought to improve their lot. Australian society did not dumb down in the pursuit of social equality. Australians made their own heroes and built a pantheon of colonial stars of their own kind, all mates, who made a lasting impact on the Australian way of life. However, this impact did not always coincide with the administrative desires of the colonial masters abroad.

The ambivalence of ordinary Australians towards political authority, coupled with an embarrassing convict past, has led to obsequious fawning before monarchy, and a desperation to adopt any new idea percolating in the rest of the world. This has been described as 'the cultural cringe', a syndrome suggesting that Australian achievement will always be second-rate, that the rest of the western world, Britain in particular, will always be first-rate. This was an attitude so entrenched in the early years of the colony that those born in Australia were dubbed 'currency' while English-born colonists were known as 'sterling', a discriminating acknowledgement of the superiority of old-country Englishmen. The problem for 'currency' Australians was that most bore the convict stain. Although born free, few would ever be considered the equal of a true-blue Englishman.

The English did their utmost to maintain their position of superiority in Australia, just as they had done in the American colonies, until the revolution led by George Washington finally called them to account. The *Illustrated London Times* continued:

> Had we been a wiser nation and a wiser Government seventy years ago, the Queen of Great Britain might now have been the Queen of North America, and Victoria the First might have held her court in New York as well as in London.
>
> ... if we do not succeed in governing them [the colonies] more to their own satisfaction than we have hitherto done, it is likely that one by one they will imitate the example set by the United States of America, and declare themselves independent. With independence may come rivalry; with rivalry, that worst of all evils, war between nations of the same stock, language, and religion. In such a war, or series of wars, we might be defeated with shame; but we could scarcely conquer with glory.

Britain certainly continued to reinforce cultural supremacy over her other possessions a little closer to home in the domination of Ireland, Scotland and Wales.

While the Celts and the Gaels battled against the Anglo-Saxons for centuries the English Crown amassed a vast empire. Having conquered the territory close to home, the English then took the Middle

East, most of Asia, Canada, a large portion of southern Africa, bits of southern America, Australia, New Zealand and countless little islands and archipelagos in between. At one time the globe was coloured predominantly red—the colour of the British Empire.

It was a very brave Briton who took on the dominance of this mighty empire, but many did, and millions suffered for their rebellious causes.

In the declining years of the eighteenth century, Britain was at the centre of a world increasingly hostile to colonial expansion. In all its dominions Britain was faced with insurrection, nascent independence movements or open rebellion—and did little to appease its subjects. The Crown ruled with an iron glove and would brook no entreaty from its common people.

Even in the face of this international movement towards political freedom for the individual and government by consensus, and with the approval of an enlightened citizenry, the English monarch and the merry lords of Westminster resisted the ever-increasing demand for constitutional change. The English ruling classes were simply not interested in democracy, which was, after all, something that the French were toying with, and the Americans were creating far too much of a fuss over individual rights.

In England dissenting Protestants, of all stripes, denied the supremacy of the Anglican church, and even the common labouring classes, particularly in the newly industrial north, were organising themselves in defiance of their masters, rallying to the cry of a fair go for all.

The Trouble with Ireland

The English had been in Ireland from as early as the twelfth century. However, it was the decision to fully colonise the fertile, green land, taken in the time of King Henry VIII, when 'plantations' of selected Englishmen were granted vast tracts of land upon which they could build their grand houses, creating hugely profitable agricultural estates while dispossessing the native Irish of their own homeland.

Protestants also flocked to Ireland where they could worship without interference from Henry VIII's church; as a result the

Catholic Irish were pushed further into the background of social, civil and political affairs.

In the time of Elizabeth I the colonisation of Ireland was all but complete when the indigenous, but landless, Irish were forced to rent their own country back from their English conquerors. However, the Irish sought almost incessantly to force the English to abandon Ireland—but to no avail. The overt Catholic James II failed in his attempt to take the English throne from William of Orange when his forces were soundly defeated at the battle of the Boyne (a river to the north of Dublin) on 1 July 1690. Three weeks later his Irish army was forced to retreat from Derry in the north, where he had trapped 30,000 Protestants loyal to King William for 105 days within the walled city. After his defeat the Irish lost their champion in England and the Protestants secured their domination of Ireland.

The Protestant English then began a slow process of gradually stripping away all the rights of the Catholic Irish in their own land. By the end of the eighteenth century Catholics had been disbarred from practising law; they were not allowed to hold public office, purchase land or even own horses or property valued at more than £5. Catholic education was outlawed and forced underground, and it is there that the seeds of sedition would be deeply sown.

With the loss of the American colonies to the Republican Army of George Washington, and the success of the revolutionary French just across the channel, the English had much to fear from the rumblings of dissent heard from across the Irish Sea.

There were many among the English, and several Irish parliamentary representatives including Henry Grattan and Charles James Fox, who believed that the penal laws subjugating the Catholic Irish were too harsh; that reform was necessary to stave off open rebellion. They argued that Ireland be granted free-trade terms and legislative independence, but it was already too late.

A war with revolutionary France had all but bankrupted England, while Austria, Russia and Prussia made peace with Napoleon, leaving England without allies on the continent. Buoyed by the success of the American revolution, an Irish Volunteer Army formed by the Protestant ruling class as protection against a French invasion

The conflict at Ballinhassig, sketched by Mr Mahony, Cork
Illustration published in *The Illustrated London News*, 12 July 1845
Police can be seen shooting at rioters from a dispensary in Ballinhassig, County Cork.
Any fight with the authorities was an uneven one; firearms were rare among the
peasantry and they always seemed to come off second best.
(National Library of Ireland)

demanded greater autonomy from England, while threatening their own Irish War of Independence.

England caved in and in 1782 granted the Irish parliament equality with Westminster. While they had, albeit temporarily, staved off a revolution, the decision to hand political control of Ireland to the Protestants simply exacerbated the exclusion of the Catholics from all areas of decision making in their own country. The seeds of revolution were germinated and it was not long before they were in full flower.

The Irish rebels were, by and large, elegant, well-educated, middle-class gentlemen; much the same class that was pressing for reform right across western Europe, had already tasted success in America, and were keen to import that kind of success to Ireland.

The Seeds of Sedition Transported to the Colony

Throughout the early years of the nineteenth century there was also discontent among the transported Irish already in the colonial penal settlements. They saw their banishment from Ireland, and incarceration in Australia, as proof of the desire of the British to crush their homeland, its culture and its national religion–Catholicism. They believed that England was trying its best to rid their country of its own heroes and subjugate the people in virtual slavery to the service of the English Crown. There was no place in England's Ireland for the sentiment of Irish nationalism. Be killed or be buried alive in a far-flung colonial outpost–this was the fate of those who stood against the might of the Union flag.

The Irish had taken their lead from the Americans and the French and had risen up against the English in the ill-fated revolutionary war of 1798. The eventual defeat of the Irish rebels by the might of the English army at the battle of Vinegar Hill in County Wexford on 21 June 1798 gave the transported Irish convicts a catchword to remind them of the spirit of all those who had tried, yet failed, to stand tall in their own land.

The Irish transported to Australia were well versed in the stories of their own nation's demise. They well knew the horrible punishments meted out to those who dared defy the English Crown. They mourned the execution of the inspirational rebel leader Robert Emmett, a fine young man, beheaded in public, humiliated by the crowing English on the scaffold in front of Dublin gaol. They resented the brutal treatment of rebel leader Father Patrick Murphy, who upon capture was stripped, flogged, hanged, beheaded and burned in a barrel. His head was placed upon a spike opposite the Catholic church in Tullow, County Carlow, where he had been captured, and all those living in the village were forced to open their windows and allow the 'holy smoke' from his pyre to billow through their humble cottages.

If they weren't executed at home the heroes of old Ireland were transported abroad, and the English by default sent to its colonies some of the cleverest, ardently political, most erudite and charismatic of its foes. Just the sort with whom to start a new nation.

However, it was the memories of the troubles at home that under-pinned the behaviour of the insurrectionist abroad.

The Vinegar Hill catchword was used time and again as a rally-ing cry when Irishman stood alongside Irishman in defiance of the English on Australian shores.

There is a blood-red thread that runs directly from Vinegar Hill to Toongabbie; from the riot at Castle Hill to the battle at the Eureka Stockade; from the muddied trenches of the Great War to the excesses of the Old Guard; from 'New Australia' to 'Waltzing Matilda'—it is the legacy of Vinegar Hill, where each person stands beside their mate fighting for their right to determine their own fate.

Vinegar Hill stands for everyman. This legacy defies the notion of a class born to rule, as it celebrates the unassailable 'rights of man'.

'Common Sense' of Tom Paine

While it may seem that the Irish had been the most persistent in their demands for freedom from the yoke of old England, there were plenty of thinking men in Great Britain who were also making demands for social change. Following the publication of Thomas Paine's *The Rights of Man* the floodgates of liberal thought were opened. Britain saw the genesis of home-grown insurrection, partic-ularly among the Scots and the working class of the industrial midlands.

Born in Thetford, Norfolk, on 29 January 1737, Thomas Paine, son of a Quaker corset maker, was educated at the local grammar school and was himself apprenticed to a corset maker in Kent. At thirty-one years of age, after some time working in London as an exciseman and a school teacher, he moved to Lewes where he also worked as an excise officer, but was dismissed from this post after he asked for higher wages. While in Lewes he had became active in local politics, served on the local council and formed a local debating club. He returned to London where he was to meet Benjamin Franklin and it was Franklin's influence that convinced him to emigrate to America in 1774.

In Pennsylvania Paine worked as a journalist and had several articles published in the *Pennsylvania Journal*, including one on the abolition of slavery. He was convinced that America should be able to stand alone and wrote a pamphlet titled 'Common Sense', which attacked the British monarchy, while outlining his demands for American Independence. 'Common Sense' shone like a beacon into all the shadowy corners of the British Empire inhabited by agitators for political and social reform.

Thomas Paine

Engraving by A Easton, after George Romney, c.1810

Paine's book *The Rights of Man* was a profound influence on the 'rebel heart' wherever British subjects felt aggrieved by the state of the Empire. In his lifetime the book had sold more than 1,500,000 copies in Europe alone.

(Rex Nan Kivell Collection NK3595, National Library of Australia)

Paine joined with Washington's forces in the 'War of Independence' against Britain, even travelling to France in 1871 to raise funds for the American cause. He played no part in the new government after the war and returned to England in 1787.

In response to Edmund Burke's *Reflections on the Republic in France*, in 1791 Paine published his most influential work *The Rights of Man*, in which he attacked hereditary government and argued for equal political rights for all. In *The Rights of Man* he sought a constitutional guarantee of the civil rights of all individuals. He sought the franchise for all men over the age of twenty-one, the creation of a House of Commons, progressive taxation, family allowances, old-age pensions, maternity grants and the abolition of the House of Lords.

Paine's book was immediately banned in England, he was charged with seditious libel, and in fear of his life fled to the Republic of France.

Paine's influence on the push for democratic reforms across all of the colonies and territories where allegiance was demanded by the British Crown is undeniable. His ideas had opened the floodgates and the British did their best to stem the tide that would wash over them

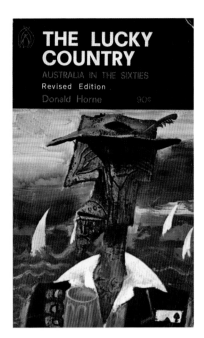

The Lucky Country: Australia in the Sixties by Donald Horne
Jacket illustration by Albert Tucker
Published by Penguin Books in 1964, the title of this book entered the Australian vernacular as soon as it hit the bookstores. Although Horne intended the term to be ironic, 'The Lucky Country' suited the Australians' view of themselves—maybe they were cast away on the far side of the world, but they truly believed they had been cast into paradise.

for the better part of the ensuing century-and-a-half.

From the transportation of the Tolpuddle Martyrs to the battle at the Eureka Stockade, the English fought against the desire for fairness and democracy, but the colonists, whether in chains or free to roam, continued to demand a 'fair go'.

The rebel heart flourished in the sun, and even after the dust had settled over the Ballarat battleground and democratic principles became the established way of social organisation in Australia, the Aussies still never buckled under. What became known as the 'larrikin spirit' was far too entrenched, and even until the present day Australians revere those who stand up for the mob, who take on the bosses, have a go at the nobs and demand 'a fair go' for his, or her, mates.

Under the Southern Cross takes a look at those who have bucked the system, from the transported Irish rebels to those who took part in the Eureka Stockade; from the Wild Colonial Boy to Ned Kelly; from Billy Lane and the Free Australia Movement to 'Kangaroo' and the New Guard. *Under the Southern Cross* celebrates all those who have made a difference in the way life in Australia is lived today.

Geoff Hocking, 2012

Patriot's Memorial, New Ross, County Wexford, Ireland
(Author's photograph)

The Wearing of the Green

(TRADITIONAL)

O Paddy dear, and did ye hear the news that's goin' round?
The shamrock is by law forbid to grow on Irish ground!
No more Saint Patrick's Day we'll keep, his colour can't be seen
For there's a cruel law ag'in the Wearin' o' the Green.

I met with Napper Tandy, and he took me by the hand,
And he said, 'How's poor ould Ireland, and how does she stand?'
She's the most distressful country that ever yet was seen,
For they're hanging men and women there for the Wearin' o' the Green.

So if the colour we must wear be England's cruel red
Let it remind us of the blood that Irishmen have shed;
And pull the shamrock from your hat, and throw it on the sod
But never fear, 'twill take root there, though underfoot 'tis trod.

When laws can stop the blades of grass from growin' as they grow
And when the leaves in summer-time their colour dare not show,
Then I will change the colour too I wear in my caubeen;
But till that day, plaise God, I'll stick to the Wearin' o' the Green.

The first parliament of Botany Bay in high debate

Engraving published in the *Hibernian* magazine, 1786

Transported rebels continued passionate political debate
on Australian soils. Even exile could not shut them up.

(Rex Nan Kivell Collection NK1345, National Library of Australia)

THE YEARS
~ of ~
EXILE

And, oh, Britannia! Should she cease to ride
Despotic Empress of the Ocean's tide–
May this, thy last-born infant then arise
To glad thy heart, and greet thy parent's eyes
And Australia float, with flag unfurled,
A new Britannia in another world!
— WILLIAM WENTWORTH c.1823

THE SCOTTISH EXILES
Thomas Muir and the Scottish Rebels

The best and noblest privilege in Hell
For souls like ours, is, Nobly to renell,
To raise the standard of revolt and try
The happy fruits of lov'd Democracy.

– *written by Thomas Muir while in exile in Sydney*

The writings of Thomas Paine had a profound influence on the movement for reform in England and was in fact cited in one of the charges brought against the Scottish martyr Thomas Muir in 1793.

In 1794 four Scottish gentlemen were found guilty of sedition and sentenced to be transported to the Australian penal colonies for fourteen years. The most prominent among them was Thomas

Martyr's keepsake
(Mitchell Library, State Library of New South Wales)

Muir, a young Glasgow lawyer, convicted for the heinous crime of handing out copies of Paine's work. On hearing of his sentence Muir stood up in the court and declared that he had 'engaged in a grand, a just, and a glorious cause, which, sooner or later, must and *will* prevail'.

Lord Braxfield, in the prosecution of charges against the Scottish Martyrs, told the court, 'The British constitution is the best that ever was since the creation of the world, and it is not possible to make it better.' He accused Muir of going 'among the ignorant country people and [telling] them Parliamentary Reform was absolutely necessary for preserving their liberty'.

Those in the seat of power had no inclination to change; they persisted in maintaining their birthright to power and to rule over all the land. They were prepared to dispose of any man, woman or child who stood in their way. Laws were created that attempted to stifle any move towards democratic reform and those who did challenge the law were quick to suffer its retribution.

Writers, thinkers, political activists, debaters, factory workers and farm labourers were picked up, arrested, transported or hanged, drawn and quartered, all for seeking to bring about change to the established pattern of English social structure.

At what point was the English government prepared to consider that the harshness of the penalties handed down, time after time, to a large number of well-educated men was simply not working? It didn't seem to matter what was done to curb the push for democratic reform; revolutionaries continued to step forward and take up the 'rebel' cause. Time and again convicted men stood before the courts and proclaimed the justice of their cause, never recanting, prepared for banishment or for death as martyr to their beliefs.

The Transportation of Thomas Muir

Thomas Muir was born in Glasgow in 1765. He attended Glasgow Grammar School and enrolled in Glasgow University at the age of ten. His Calvinist parents wanted him to study divinity but he abandoned this in 1782 when he began to attend classes held by John Millar, one of Britain's first sociologists. A republican and

Illustrious Martyr in the glorious cause
Of truth of freedom and of equal laws.

Thomas Muir

Etching by James Kay, 1793

Muir (1765–98) was transported to the Australian colonies, sentenced to fourteen years for sedition.

(Mitchell Library, State Library of New South Wales)

parliamentary reform advocate, Millar had a profound influence on the young Thomas Muir.

After graduation Muir joined the Faculty of Advocates and soon developed a reputation as a lawyer, showing a readiness to appear for poor clients who were unable to pay his fee. This pro bono representation was an expression of his belief that the legal system was constructed to favour the wealthy and disenfranchise the poor.

After the success of the French Revolution, organisations of free thinkers sprouted up all over England. The Society of the Friends of the People was formed in London and Thomas Muir and William Skirving established the Scottish Association in July 1792. Eighty-seven branches of the Society of the Friends were formed across Britain by the end of that year. The government became concerned about Muir and the activities of the Society and with the intelligence gained by the use of spies soon felt that they had enough evidence to have Muir convicted of sedition. Accordingly, he was arrested on 2 January 1793, but after several hours of interrogation was released on bail.

Not fazed by his arrest, Muir then travelled to London. Concerned by the violence that consumed post-revolutionary France, he agreed to travel to Paris to meet with Thomas Paine and to petition the Directorate for the life of Louis XVII. Their representation was unsuccessful and Muir returned to Scotland. The day after his arrival he was once again placed under arrest, once again charged with sedition. Among the charges laid against Muir this time was that he 'exhorted three people residing in Cadder, to buy and read Paine's *Rights of Man*'; that he 'had circulated Paine's work, "A Declaration of Rights", to the friends of reform in Paisley'; and that 'he had delivered speeches in which he seditiously endeavoured to represent the government as oppressive and tyrannical'.

Muir was sentenced to fourteen years' transportation, and although sympathisers in the House of Commons began a campaign to save Muir and others also under sentence from their fate, they sailed from Portsmouth aboard the *Surprise* on 2 May 1794, bound for Botany Bay. As a political prisoner Muir was afforded better treatment than common criminal transportees. On arrival in the penal settlement he was allowed to purchase a small farm near Sydney Cove and lived therewith almost the same freedom as any settler.

The Americans learned of Muir's banishment to the Australian colony and with the help of the chief mate of an American ship he was able to escape on the *Otter of Boston*, bound for Vancouver Island, after only two years in Port Jackson. He was offered a passage back to Europe on a Spanish ship, the Ninfa, but was arrested once again. En route for Cadiz the Ninfa was attacked by the seventy-four-gun British warship *Irresistible*. In the attack Muir was struck in the face by a cannonball, which shattered his cheekbone and caused the loss of his left eye. He was so severely injured that he was not expected to survive. He did eventually recover but suffered permanent facial disfigurement.

On his arrival back in Spain the French, hearing of Muir's arrest and the severity of his injuries, sought his freedom from the Spanish authorities. Muir went back to live in Paris where he once again joined with Thomas Paine as they continued the fight to bring democratic reform to Britain.

Muir never fully recovered from his injuries and gradually deteriorated over the following years, passing away in Chantilly on 26 January 1799. Muir was the first foreign national to have been granted full citizenship in republican France.

Thomas Fyshe Palmer

Born in August 1747, son of a Bedfordshire landowner, Unitarian preacher Thomas Fyshe Palmer was also transported to Australia, convicted of having been found guilty of writing and publishing pamphlets on the subject of parliamentary reform.

Like Muir he also formed a 'Friends' society, called the Friends of Liberty in Dundee. He published a pamphlet titled 'Dundee Address to the Friends of Liberty' and it was this that brought him to the attention of the authorities. He was arrested, and charged with writing a seditious pamphlet and distributing 100 copies of the 'Dundee Address' to fellow conspirator William Skirving. Labelled by the trial judge as 'the most determined rebel in Scotland', Palmer was convicted and sentenced to seven years in the colonies.

He was taken to the hulks laying at anchor on the Thames, and it was there he waited until he was transferred to Portsmouth and the *Surprise*. On the long journey to Botany Bay, Palmer and Skirving, who was being transported with him, along with a group of convicts, were accused of plotting to kill the captain and crew. Palmer always believed that it was another transportee, Maurice Margarot, who had exposed the plot to the Captain, but no evidence was brought forward to confirm this. However, Margarot remained estranged from the other Scottish rebels for the rest of his days. Ship's captain Patrick Campbell wrote a memo to the Commissioners of the Navy in 1794 accusing Palmer and Skirving of leading the ring of convicts in the plot against him. Muir was not implicated at all. Captain Campbell commended Margarot for his honourable behaviour 'throughout the whole business' and remarked that he had been 'not only pleasing but serviceable to us'.

Thomas Fyshe Palmer
(Mitchell Library, State Library of New South Wales)

Once in Sydney Palmer also enjoyed a degree of freedom because of his status as a political prisoner. He was allowed to establish a business in Sydney, transporting goods between New South Wales and Norfolk Island. Once his sentence was complete Palmer set himself up as a boatbuilder. He had no previous experience in this type of work but he was fortunate enough to have the only copy of the *Encyclopedia Britannica* in the colony and simply looked up the entry under 'Ships'—after having first looked up 'beer', and then 'soap'.

In 1801 Palmer attempted to sail a refurbished Spanish warship back to England but his ship sank in a violent storm off the coast of Guam. Palmer was marooned there, held by the Spanish as a prisoner of war, until his death from cholera in January 1802.

Once they were made aware of Palmer's reforming zeal the Spanish refused him the dignity of a Christian burial and he was buried among pirates in a common grave on the beach. Two years later, an American ship's captain sympathetic to Palmer's beliefs retrieved his body and took him back to America where was laid to rest in a Boston church.

Joseph Gerrald

Born in the West Indies on 9 February 1763, Joseph Gerrald was the son of a wealthy planter. He was educated in England and returned to the West Indies after inheriting his father's property.

After some financial difficulties, and the death of his wife, he took his two young children and migrated to America. It was in America that he met Thomas Paine and was deeply influenced by his ideas. He returned to England in 1788 and soon joined the London Corresponding Society. In 1793 he published the pamphlet 'A Convention is the Only Means of Saving Us from Ruin'.

At a meeting in the London district of Chalk Farm on 24 October 1793, Gerrald and Maurice Margarot were elected as its delegates to the Edinburgh Convention to be held the following month. Before they left London they learned that Muir and Palmer had been arrested and charged with sedition. However, the delegates continued to Edinburgh and were themselves arrested, as was William Skirving.

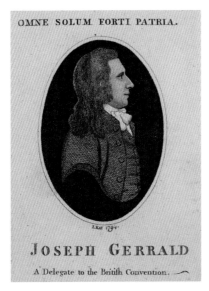

Left: Joseph Gerrald
Mezzotint by Samuel Reynolds, after Charles Smith, 1795
Right: William Skirving
(Mitchell Library, State Library of New South Wales)

Gerrald did not enjoy the best of health and was released on bail. Believing that he would not survive the long trip to Australia, Gerrald's friends urged him to flee the country, but he refused. He was committed to face his accusers. When he stood in the dock, his long hair loose and unpowdered in the French style, he did not defend himself but used the dock as a platform for the expression of his desire for parliamentary reform.

He angered Judge Lord Braxfield with his opinion that even 'Jesus Christ was a radical reformer' and finished his speech by stating that 'what ever may become of me my principles will last forever...' The judge sentenced him to fourteen years' transportation as well.

Gerrald did not last long in the colony; he suffered badly on the journey out and died of tuberculosis only five months after landing on 16 March 1796. Thomas Fyshe Palmer had cared for him during that time and was with him when he died. His last words to Palmer were, 'I die in the best of causes and, you witness, without repining'. Gerrald was a true believer to his last breath.

William Skirving

Skirving was the son of a prosperous farmer from Midlothian. Educated at Edinburgh University, he spent some years as tutor to a prominent family in Prestonville. He also published a book on farming practice titled *The Husbandman's Assistant* in 1792.

Skirving became interested in politics and joined the Scottish Association of the Friends of the People, becoming its secretary in 1792. Skirving, Joseph Gerrald and Maurice Margarot were arrested at the same meeting in Edinburgh on 2 December 1793. Accused of being a member of the Friends, he was also accused of distributing political pamphlets written by Thomas Palmer, and of imitating the French by calling other members of the Friends by the title of 'citizen'. He was charged and convicted of treason, sentenced to fourteen years' transportation and also awaited his fate in the hulks on the Thames, until he too walked up the gang-plank to the *Surprise*. He left a wife and eight children behind in Scotland, and was never to return home.

Although he was also able to enjoy his freedom in the colonies– Governor Hunter described him as 'a very decent, quiet and industrious man, who had purchased a farm, and was indfatigable in his attentions to its improvement'–life was harsh in the largely undeveloped settlement and he died of dysentery on 19 March 1794.

Maurice Margarot

The only member of the group of five who had once stood proudly among the Friends to live out a full life was the shadowy figure of Devon-born Maurice Margarot.

Margarot was born in 1745. The son of a wine importer from France, he was educated in Geneva and had lived in France at the time of the French Revolution. Back in England, he joined the London Corresponding Society and was elected its chairman in 1792. Accompanied by the novelist Thomas Hardy, Maurice Margarot attended a National Convention in France where he argued that an 'alliance of the great free nations America, France and Britain could bring peace and prosperity to all of Europe, and to the rest of the world'–if only Britain would herself agree to constitutional reform.

He was arrested in Scotland in 1793 alongside Gerrald and Skirving, as they attended meetings of the Association of the Friends. He joined the others on board the *Surprise* and sailed from Portsmouth, bound for Botany Bay.

Margarot was arrested again after the failed insurrection of Irish prisoners in August 1804 near Castle Hill. Governor King believed that the well-known political agitator had been preaching rebellion and had urged the prisoners to rise up against the government. Margarot was deported to Van Diemen's Land where, although he had been flogged, he continued to make political speeches.

Margarot was seen as a double-dealer who slipped between the various cliques in the colony. Hunter's successor Philip Gidley King was convinced that Margarot was reporting on him to the Colonial Office in London. He wrote on 23 January 1806:

> Margarot is well known as a troublesome character. [His] body cannot bear the punishment he has so often merited, and the contagious principles he disseminates are so destructive ...

Soon after arriving in the colony Margarot was joined by his wife and family; in many ways he seemed quite content to serve out his term. It was well after his time was up, seventeen years in fact, before he attempted to return to England in 1812. Unable to stay away from political intrigue he joined the campaign to end transportation and gave evidence to the Parliamentary Committee in London, which was looking into the manner in which transportation was executed– and the effectiveness of this mode of punishment. Having suffered the lash across his back more than once, Margarot was perfectly placed to refute the effectiveness of the harshness of transportation. He was never deterred from the struggle for reform, even publishing a pamphlet titled 'Thoughts on Revolution' on his return to England.

Margarot spent the remaining few years of his life in extreme poverty. Thomas Hardy, along with other members of his former Friends, attempted to raise funds to assist him but he died in a hospital for the poor at St Pancras, London on 11 November 1815.

Although his double-deal-ing had distanced him from his former compatriots and he never again shared the stimulation of their company, Margarot was remembered by the *The Examiner* on 1 December 1815 as a man 'of middle stature, [who] had been handsome in his youth, well-pro-portioned, full of pleasantry and anecdote, with elegant manner— a scholar and a gentleman. Age and care had made havoc with his appearance, but the lively and intelligent spirit still shone through … and [although] on the verge of the grave, was meditating on a history of his life'.

Maurice Margarot
'A Brave Man Struggling in the Storms of Fate
A great Man falling with a falling state!!'
(Mitchell Library, State Library of New South Wales)

The Martyr's Memorial

In the Old Calton Cemetery in the Scottish city of Edinburgh stands a ten-metre-tall obelisk honouring the Scottish Political Martyrs. Chiselled into the five-sided plinth at the base is the following inscription:

SCOTTISH POLITICAL MARTYRS MEMORIAL.
AD MDCCCLI.
Erected with funds collected at a public meeting in London on XX Feby.
MDCCCXXXVII Joseph Hume MP Chairman.
To the memory of Thomas Muir, Thomas Fyshe Palmer, William Skirving, Maurice Margarot and Joseph Gerrald.
Condemned in Scotland AD MDCCXCIII-IV
to transportation for advocating, with fearless energy, the principles of parliamentary reform.

An Irish Hug alias A Fraternal Embrace.
The Dearest Friends must Part.

VINEGAR HILL

1798: The Transported Legacy of the Defeated Irish Rebels

Encouraged by the writings of English-born Thomas Paine, whose pamphlet titled 'Common Sense', published in 1776, had argued for complete independence of the American colonies and an 'end to executive tyranny, through the "virtue" and common good of representative democratic republican government', Irish dissidents soon abandoned the philosophy of change through moral pressure and parliamentary debate and steered a course of direct and forceful action.

The Society of United Irishmen was formed and the charismatic leader Theobold Wolfe Tone actively sought the support of the French to wage war against the English—on Irish soil. They knew that the Americans could not have defeated the English but for the help of the French and it was to the French that the Irish now turned for help. The three nations believed that together they could usher in a new era of democratic government that would unify all of Europe, England, Ireland and the Americas and bring equality, peace and prosperity to a civilised world.

The English were not keen on that idea. The last thing they were interested in was democracy. The English lawmakers believed that only those with property deserved the right to the protection of parliament and civil law. It was quite simple. Only those with property needed the vote, as they were the

Memorial statue of Wolfe Tone, St Stephen's Green, Dublin

A charismatic figure, Tone is honoured with this larger-than-life bronze figure standing beside Dublin's famous central park.
(Author's photograph, 2005)

Opposite: Hand-coloured etching, published London, 4 October 1798
(National Library of Australia)

only ones needing the protection of the law. The ruling classes who had appropriated all of the land, made the laws that ensured their continued domination, and also enacted laws that stopped anyone else from attempting to, or even talking about, making any attempt to change.

The writings of Thomas Paine were therefore considered to be seditious, and many Irish, along with numerous other British subjects, were gaoled, even transported for simply possessing a copy of 'Common Sense'.

Having been expelled in 1795 for his political activities, Wolfe Tone sailed from America to France on behalf of the United Irishmen and convinced the new French administration, the Directory, to throw the weight of their forces against the weakest point of the English empire–Ireland.

A thirty-five-ship French fleet carrying 12,000 troops sailed for Ireland on 16 December 1796. Without any interference from the British navy the French reached Bantry Bay, ninety miles to the west of the largely undefended military and naval base at Cork. There the fleet delayed until the frigate carrying commander-in-chief General Lazare Hoche, who had become separated from the rest of the fleet, could catch up.

The decision to delay the landing was disastrous for the Irish rebels and caused the invasion to be aborted. The wind disappeared and the sea was becalmed; the fleet was unable to make progress until the wind blew up again over a week later. Still without General Hoche no landing was attempted. Two days later the wind gathered strength and blew into a storm. By 27 December the storm was severe enough to force the fleet to turn back to France. Wolfe Tone was on board the *Indomptable*, an eighty-gun battleship that had been so badly damaged that she was forced to abort any attempt at a landing and limped back to Brest. Tone remarked that 'England had not had such an escape since the Armada'.

It was three more years before Tone was able to gain an audience with Napoleon Bonaparte. Having once been obsessed with the idea of conquering England, the French emperor was soon to turn his attention elsewhere. Although it appeared to Tone that he had won the support of Bonaparte through the commitment of 50,000 veterans of the Italian campaign who were now ready for service elsewhere, this support never came. The French had marched on Russia instead. However, the swelling tide of Irish revolution could not be turned.

Acting on the intelligence of their spies the government operated a 'scorched earth policy', particularly in the north and the midlands, and instilled terror into the population. In retribution, the murder of magistrates was commonplace, and the aristocracy and loyalist gentry began to live their lives in constant fear of attack. Although they were able to pick off one by one the scores of rebel groups who were coming together to plan for a united Irish future, the desire for change would not be thwarted.

The English sought to 'pacify' the Irish by 'free-quartering' its army—billeting them—in the homes of the Irish people. The army flogged those caught with firearms and burned the homes of suspected supporters of the United Irish movement. It seemed that the English were intent on flogging the country into submission but all they did in the end was to light the spark of rebellion.

In February of 1798, no longer prepared to await the support of the French, the country erupted into open warfare. Largely armed with pikes and staves, the Irish took on the English army and battles raged across the length and breadth of the country. In many areas martial law was declared and Irish rebels were summarily executed, hanged, beheaded, drawn and quartered. The English pursued their objective with diligence; one Captain Swayne was made famous by his predilection for 'pitch-capping', placing a cap soaked in pitch onto the head of his prisoners and setting it alight. He was not alone in this practice—it was a form of torture widely used by the government forces. When the garrison at Prosperous was wiped out on 23 May, Swayne was shot and the rebels took their revenge; his body was burned in a barrel of tar.

Wherever they were to be found, the leaders were arrested, tried and executed. These were by and large men of education and breeding; few were from the labouring classes. England, hastily and very publicly, dispatched a large portion of the intellectual class

Queen's Own Royal Dublin militia going into action at Vinegar Hill,
the Light Company advancing and firing covering the band

Original pen sketch by Sadler
(National Library of Ireland)

of eighteenth-century Ireland, while the common Irish peasant set about with pike, blade and torch to rid their lands of the loyalists. Excesses by both loyalist and rebel were terrible in the extreme. Prisoners on both sides were simply lined up and shot. Four hundred unarmed rebels were slaughtered by one government force after having just surrendered their arms to another. After learning of the slaughter of more than 3000 rebels, sympathisers at New Ross rounded up a hundred loyalists, including women and children, forced them into a makeshift gaol and set it alight.

While it seemed for the better part of 1798 that the Irish were about to take control of the country, the undisciplined Irish peasant forces were to prove no match for the trained armies of the English.

It was the abortive battle of Vinegar Hill that remains the most devastating defeat suffered by the United Irishmen in the 1798 rebellion. The rebel forces had taken refuge on top of a hill just to the north of the Enniscorthy Bridge. From this vantage point they commanded a view over the entire district, but they were no match for English artillery and charging cavalry. The English forces under General Lake bombarded the trapped rebels who had held out for days; only a remnant force made their escape through a gap in the British lines. After the siege of Vinegar Hill was over, Lake took his retribution on those left alive on the hill. The rebel field hospital was set alight and fugitives were shot on sight as Lake's men exacted revenge in an orgy of death and destruction.

On 12 October Wolfe Tone was captured by an English fleet commanded by Rear Admiral Sir John Warren. Buoyed by Nelson's success over the French in the battle of the Nile, Warren captured all but two of a French fleet that had sailed from Brest into the mouth of Lough Swilly on the north coast of Ulster. It was almost a month later when Tone was brought back to Dublin to face trial. Fully aware of the fate that was before him, he admitted to all charges and asked only one concession–to be allowed a soldier's death before a firing squad. His request was denied.

Convicted of treason, Tone was sentenced to be hanged, but before he would swing from an English gallows he attempted to take his life, cutting his own throat while he lay in his prison cell. Like so many other patriotic sons of Ireland, the awful humiliation of a public execution for the pleasure of the vainglorious English was more than he could bear. Unfortunately Tone had not cut deeply enough, only damaging his windpipe, and he lay on his bed for a further five days until he bled slowly to death. A government official, annoyed at not being able to hang him, declared that he would rather 'have sewn up his neck and finished the business' properly. Tone's slow death was the cross he had chosen to bear for the salvation of his beloved homeland, and his painful demise ensured his place as a true martyr of the revolution.

Gentleman Joseph Holt

Protestant gentleman farmer 'General' Joseph Holt had only joined the rebellion to lead the Wicklow rebels, after his farmhouse was burned by loyalist forces. He surrendered to the English on the same day that Wolfe Tone was taken prisoner.

General Joseph Holt
Lithograph by George Peacock, 1846
(State Library of New South Wales)

Holt was offered an amnesty by Lord Cornwallis if he agreed to exile without trial. Rather than rot in an English gaol Holt accepted his punishment of transportation to New South Wales.

There were critics among the establishment who believed that such light sentences would only incite revenge. They insisted that terror was the answer. The English Parliament advised the undersecretary in Dublin that he should transport all prisoners held in Irish gaols and give full power to the generals, no doubt to punish them as they wished.

Unlike most of his wretched ship-mates Holt arrived in Port Jackson on board the *Minerva* on 11 January 1800, not to serve as a prisoner in chains, but as a free settler who was able to resume his life as a gentleman farmer and prosper in the warm climate of the colony. He did just that for some years until the rumoured 'rising of the croppies'.

Fear Stalks the Colony

Acting on information from his spies among the convicts, New South Wales Governor Hunter heard rumours of an uprising of the Irish transportees in his colony. His spies told of an expected rising that was to take place on 28 September 1800. Hunter took immediate action and questioned a large number of prisoners, most of whom were Irish convicts who had been transported to the colonies for sedition in Ireland.

Although he was unable to discover the truth, or the where-abouts, of the large number of pikes, it was rumoured that the convicts had hidden them at Toongabbie and Parramatta. None of the twenty-one prisoners he interrogated admitted any knowledge of the supposed hoard of arms, yet he sentenced five of them to 500 lashes and four more to 100 strokes across their backs. When that was done he then decided that a further twelve should be removed 'to some distant and remote place, where the baneful influence of their example cannot be experienced'. Presumably

Commemorative marker at the site of Joseph Holt's farm 'Mullinaveigh' near Avonmore, County Wicklow, Ireland
(Author's photograph, 2005)

Hunter intended that the troublesome convicts be transported to the notorious hellhole of Norfolk Island where they could no longer influence other similarly disaffected prisoners.

Hunter retired from his post and sailed from the colony on 27 September. He was replaced by the former commander of Norfolk Island, Philip Gidley King, a man well versed in cunning, convict ways—and well prepared to deal with them. The 'Flogging Parson' Reverend Samuel Marsden, so-called for his predilection for the use of the lash to elicit information from reluctant prisoners, was convinced that the hoard of pikes did exist so he determined to flog the information out of some poor wretched fellows. He demanded that the exiled leader of the 1798 Wicklow rebellion, gentleman 'General' Joseph Holt, be brought up from his farm at Toongabbie and witness the flogger at work. Marsden was convinced that Holt was involved, and sought to instil the fear of God into him, but all he did was instil disgust.

Holt wrote this account of the day at the flogging tree, which began with the punishment of middle-aged Maurice Fitzgerald, an exiled farmer from Cork:

> The place they flogged them their arms pulled around a large tree and their breasts squeezed around the trunk so the men had no power

to cringe … There were two floggers, Richard Rice and John Johnson the Hangman from Sydney. Rice was a left-handed man and Johnson was right-handed, so they stood at each side, and I never saw two threshers in a barn move their strokes more handier than those two man-killers did.

The moment they began I turned my face round towards the other side and one of the constables came and desir'd me to turn and look on. I put my right hand in my pocket and pulled out my pen-knife, and swore I would rip him from the navel to the chin …

I was to leeward of the floggers … I was two perches from them. The flesh and skin blew in my face as it shook from the cats. Fitzgerald received his 300 lashes. Doctor Mason—I will never forget him—he used to go and feel his pulse, and he smiled, and said: 'This man will tire you before he will fail—Go on.' During the time Fitzgerald was getting his punishment he never gave so much as a word—only one, and that was saying, 'Don't strike me on the neck, flog me fair'.

When he was let loose, two of the constables went and took hold of him by the arms to keep him in the cart. I was standing by. He said to them, 'Let me go'. He struck both of them in the pit of the stomach and knocked them both down, and then stepped in the cart. I heard Doctor Mason say that man had strength enough to bear 200 more.

Next up was Paddy Galvin, a young boy of about twenty years of age. He was ordered to get 300 lashes. He got 100 on the back, and you could see his backbone between the shoulder blades. Then the Doctor ordered him to get another hundred on his bottom. He got it, and then his haunches were in such a jelly that the Doctor ordered him to be flogged on the calves of his legs. He got 100 there and as much as a whimper he never gave. They asked him if he would tell where the pikes were hid. He said he did not know, and would not tell. 'You may as well hang me now,' he said, 'for you will never get any music from me'. They put him in the cart and sent him to the hospital.

Marsden reported to the governor that Galvin would die before he revealed anything, but he survived and lived long enough to be granted a free pardon by Governor Macquarie in 1810. Fitzgerald was pardoned two years later.

Riot at Castle Hill

Governor John Hunter had complained of the large number of Irish political prisoners in his colony. He was fearful of the influence these prisoners would have over the ordinary convicted criminals, and critical of the wisdom of putting so many disaffected Irish nationals in the same place at the same time. The population of United Irish in the colony, who had been trans-ported for their seditious activities in Ireland, had risen to number 600 and was bolstered by the 'most diabolical characters from Cork'. Hunter's replacement, Governor King, complained to Westminster that the 'turbulent and worthless characters called Irish defenders' were threatening to resist all orders given them by the English authorities. He feared that they were simply banding together 'ready and waiting an opportunity to put their diabolical plans into action.'[1]

The governor's fears were well founded.

It took until 1804 before the prisoners came together and seriously planned a break for freedom. They thought they could break out from Castle Hill, march over to enlist the prisoners at Hawkesbury, and together, numbering more than 1100 men, make a run on Parramatta, overthrow

Major George Johnston, 1764–1823

Lithograph, artist unknown
Johnston was the hero of the Castle Hill Rising of Irish convicts, but overstepped his authority just a short while after when he led an insurrection of officers and troops against Governor Bligh.
(State Library of New South Wales Collection)

the governor and establish a 'liberty pole'* outside Government House. The rebel army then planned to march down to the harbour, seize some ships and sail away to America—to freedom. Such an undertaking took a considerable amount of planning, involving scores of men, all sworn to secrecy. As usual, the English had their spies and the convicts' plans were well known to the authorities.

On Saturday 3 March 1804, the day before the planned rising, Governor King was informed that the Irish intended to challenge his authority the following day. He strengthened the guard at Castle Hill.

At around 8 p.m. 200 convicts assembled. The catch word 'St Peter' had brought them silently together. A bell was rung and the rebels broke out, swarming across the camp searching for weapons of any kind. Bursting into the hut of chief flogger Robert Duggan, the rebels dragged him from beneath his cot, giving him a severe taste of his own medicine.

The news of the outbreak did not reach Sydney until after midnight. Lieutenant-Colonel William Paterson immediately set off with 150 armed troops from HMS *Calcutta*. Major George Johnston, in command of a further fifty-six men, headed for Parramatta where they confronted 400 rebels amassed on Rouse Hill.

Father James Dixon, a Catholic priest who had been transported in 1800 for his political activities, failed to get the rebels to stand down, and rebel leader, former soldier Phillip Cunningham, stepped out to confront Johnston.

Joseph Holt, whose farm at Toongabbie had placed him well within range of the outbreak, wrote of that awful day when the Irish prisoners finally rose up in a disastrous attempt to gain their freedom:

About three hundred men had assembled on the Castle Hill, and chosen one Cunningham, from the county of Kerry, as their leader.

---

* *Liberty pole*—A pole or flagstaff bearing a rebel flag or other symbol. The custom of flag-flying in defiance of the authorities was first seen in Concord, Massachusetts in 1775 at the outbreak of the American War of Independence. The custom originated in Boston in 1765 when effigies of English taxation officers were burned from the branches of an old elm tree on Hanover Square.

Convict Uprising at Castle Hill, 1804
Watercolour by artist unknown
The rising of transported convicts against the government forces on 4 March 1804
was the first armed insurrection on Australian soil. It did not last long and
did not have the desired outcome the mainly Irish rebels had hoped for.
(National Library of Australia)

Captain George Johnstone [sic] went up towards them, and demanded of Cunningham what he wanted, and why they had assembled. If they had any real grievance, he would endeavour to get it redressed. Cunningham advanced, and took off his hat, and with it in one hand and a sword in the other, replied 'Death, or liberty!' Captain Johnstone [sic] made no attempt to molest him, but Laycock, who stood six feet six inches, a quarter-master in his corps, came up, and with one blow, killed Cunningham on the spot. On this the whole of the mob took to their heels, and many were shot in the pursuit. Cunningham's body, although he was dead, was brought to Hawkesbury, and hanged up as an example to the rest.

John Byrne, one of Holt's own assignees, related this eyewitness account of the short-lived insurgency. Holt added, 'What else could

Colonel William Paterson

Oil painting by artist unknown

Paterson was instrumental in
re-establishing order in the colony
after the dismissal of Governor Bligh.
(State Library of New South Wales)

have been expected from the conduct of a general who would condescend to take off his hat to the captain of an opposing force? If I had been in Cunningham's place, I would have taken off Captain Johnstone's [sic] head, instead of my own hat.'

Byrne's account to Holt continued:

The unfortunate wretches who escaped by flight, were arrested by a party of forty soldiers, the constables, and some loyal settlers; and being brought before a court martial, it was arranged that lots should be drawn from a hat, and that every third man whose name was drawn, should be hanged. Many fine young men were strung up like dogs, but the arrival of the Governor put an end to this extraordinary proceeding. Among those hanged, there was the nephew of the Surgeon-general, Mr Jamison, but this was kept, as far as it could be so, a profound secret.

Later accounts suggest that when Cunningham had demanded his liberty Johnston put his pistol to Cunningham's head and ordered him to surrender. Johnston then ordered his men to open fire on the rebel prisoners, who turned and belted for the bush as the troops advanced with bayonets fixed. Published reports go on to suggest that Cunningham was taken prisoner and hanged, without trial, in Sydney the following day.

Wherever the real story lies, an undisciplined, untrained rabble of pike-wielding, dissident Irishmen defending themselves on the crest of a hill once again proved no match for an advancing red-coat army.

Fifteen convicts died in the affray, nine more were hanged and an untold number flogged. Major Johnston enjoyed his reputation as the hero of 'Castle Hill' for only a few years until he disgraced himself in the insurrection of the 'Rum Corps' against Governor Bligh on 26 January 1808. He was sent to London one year later to face the charge of sedition for that unseemly rush of blood to his head.

Transported to Norfolk Island

The colonial government did not let the leader of the Wicklow rebels stray too far from their sights. After the failed rising of September 1800, it was assumed by the New South Wales government that Joseph Holt had to have been involved. After all, it was rumoured that the pikes had been hidden at Toongabbie, and this was the precise location of Holt's farm.

After the Castle Hill riot Holt was arrested along with others whom Governor King described as '[those] artful and designing wretches, above the common class of those deluded people, are deeply implicated'. On the evidence of one witness who swore he heard Holt say that Governor King and Judge Atkins should themselves be put to death because men had died following the floggings they had ordered, Holt was arrested and sent for transportation for two years on Norfolk Island.

Master Mariner Captain William Eastwick witnessed the arrival of General Holt and other Irish prisoners at Norfolk Island. He wrote:

> It was a sorry sight to see so gallant a gentleman submit himself to these vulgar people in authority, and with a silent dignity obey the order given him. For, after all, he and many other prisoners were gentlemen of birth … They were persons of refinement, whose only crime was love of native land, and a desire for its freedom. Had they been Englishmen this would have been highly esteemed …

General Holt was granted a free pardon on 6 June 1809. He had been arrested three times in relation to the Irish uprisings in the colony but always denied his involvement maintaining that he was more interested in his farm than in political conspiracy.

THE RESTLESS COLONY
Macarthur vs Bligh

The Australian colony at Port Jackson, settled on the shores of possibly the world's most beautiful harbour, was anything but a peaceful haven or bush idyll basking in the sun. It was an open prison, run by military order. Every life was lived at the pleasure of the governor. Food was scarce, few crops succeeded, even fewer of those transported knew anything about providing for themselves in any other way than by stealing, and there was precious little worth stealing in the antipodes except for food.

The first man to suffer the extreme power of the governor's displeasure was Exeter-born 'lifer', transportee Thomas Barrett, one of four men convicted in 1788 of stealing food. Three were sentenced to be hanged and a fourth received 300 lashes for stealing butter, peas and pork. At 5 p.m. on 27 February 1788 all of the convicts and marines were gathered at a tree halfway between the male and

Left: John Macarthur
Oil on canvas, artist unknown
In Bligh, Macarthur found the nemesis of the 'Rum Corps'. He tried to best the governor at every turn, eventually leading an insurrection of his fellow officers resulting in the arrest of Bligh and the declaration of martial law in the colony.
(Dixson Gallery, State Library of New South Wales)
Right: New South Wales Governor, William Bligh
(From Picturesque Atlas of Australasia,*1888. Private Collection)*

female camps. Just as the condemned men were about to be strung up, a reprieve for all but Barrett was announced.

Barrett was a particularly vile fellow and no-one was sorry to see him hanged. He put on a show of bravado until he climbed the ladder, then he turned very pale and appeared shocked. The hangman, who was a fellow convict, refused to do his duty until Major Ross, who was in charge, threatened to have him shot as well.

Just before the black hood was placed over his head Barrett confessed the justice of his sentence, agreeing that he had 'led a very wicked life' and that he deserved to die.

Beatings and floggings were common. Men were almost beaten to death, their backs ripped to the bone until they could take no more. There was no quarter given for unlawful behaviour to either convict or trooper, every man and woman in the colony was essentially in the 'same boat', cast away on the far side of the globe to survive or not, as the case may be.

There were among the military corps many who took their opportunities where they saw them and soon began to appropriate large tracts of land for themselves, where they built fortunes on the scarred backs of freely available convict labour. The Corps became all-powerful in the running of the colony; they controlled all commerce, all trade, imports and exports and held sway over all decisions made about the lives and labours of the convict transportees.

In the early days the New South Wales Corps were the superior beings in the penal settlement. Even free settlers were forced to trade on the terms dictated by the Corps; in the absence of hard currency, settlers were usually paid by promissory notes, or hard liquor, with rum the currency of popular choice. The colony was, in effect, a military dictatorship, with all the spoils going in one direction only, into the pockets of the officers of the New South Wales Corps.

In 1806 Captain William Bligh arrived in Sydney after Sir Philip Gidley King had all but given up trying to reign in the excesses of first fleeter Lieutenant John Macarthur and his fellow officers of the 'Rum Corps'. Even before he had stepped ashore Bligh was affronted by the sight of barrels of rum being unloaded from a schooner onto the wharf. Bligh was immediately convinced that Sydney was a 'sink

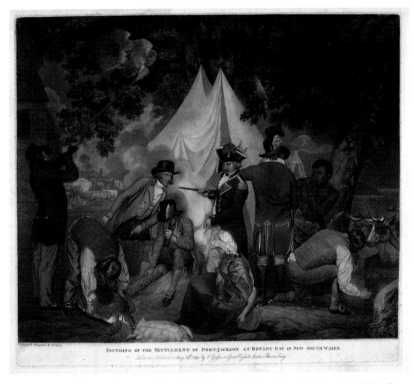

Founding of the settlement of Port Jackson at Botany Bay in New South Wales
Hand-coloured mezzotint by Thomas Gosse, 1799
(Rex Nan Kivell Collection NK11590, National Library of Australia)

of iniquity', and he determined to put this house in order. Bligh chose a course that would set him head-to-head against the Corps.

Attack of the Rum Rebels

On 28 June 1790 Lieutenant John Macarthur arrived in Port Jackson on board the *Neptune* accompanied by his wife Elizabeth. Elizabeth, the well-educated daughter of a country gentleman, was the first free woman in the colony.

Macarthur was an opinionated, feisty and quarrelsome young man who was never far from trouble. He had fought with his captain even before the ship had left the English port, and challenged him to a duel. He was not long in the colony before he argued with a fellow officer and they faced each other with pistols drawn; neither of the men was injured, but Macarthur continued to show his distaste for

Arrest of Governor Bligh, 26 January 1808
Watercolour and pencil by John Smart, 1808
Bligh was humiliated when he was discovered hiding under a bed
when the Rum Corps came calling; he claimed that he was
simply putting his private papers securely away.
(National Library of Australia)

those who sought to command him, and for those who soon rose to positions of influence in the affairs of the settlement.

The gentlemen officers of the Corps had the pick of the best farming land around the harbour and Macarthur had selected for himself a beautiful property along the Parramatta River, where he constructed the homestead he named Elizabeth Farm in honour of his wife. It was at Elizabeth Farm that together they bred a strain of Spanish merino sheep that became the foundation of an Australian wool industry that was soon to dominate the world. It was in fact Elizabeth who built the flocks; Macarthur was too busy fighting with a succession of governors and colonial magistrates to have much time for farming.

Macarthur and Bligh were determined to best one another from their first meeting, and Bligh was determined to clear his colony's decks of the corrupting influence of the New South Wales Corps. When Bligh dismissed Jamison, the surgeon, from his office of magistrate, Macarthur attacked the governor in defence of his old ally.

For this attack on the governor Macarthur was charged with sedition and sent for trial. Even before he stood before the courts Macarthur was contriving to test the governor's patience. He constructed a fence on Crown land in direct defiance of Bligh's orders. He challenged Bligh over the confiscation of two stills he had imported a month after Bligh had prohibited distilling. The straw that broke Bligh's back was the brouhaha that followed the virtual confiscation of the *Parramatta*, a ship jointly owned by Macarthur, on which an escaped prisoner had been found.

Macarthur simply handed the boat over to its master, claiming no further responsibility for its fate, its crew, or for the payment of £800 bond money. His cleverness infuriated Bligh, and his old enemies on the bench. Judge Atkins, an old adversary, claimed that Macarthur was defaming him from the dock and abandoned the trial for sedition, and Macarthur escaped into the 'custody' of his friends from the Corps.

On 26 January 1808 the order went out for Macarthur's re-arrest. The officers of the Corps, in response, arrested the Provost Marshall, who had issued the order. The Corps were now directly challenging the authority of the governor and Judge Atkins demanded that they be arrested for inciting rebellion—and it was rebellion that followed.

Major Johnston rode from his farm into Sydney where he called his men to arms. He released Macarthur and with fife and drum playing 'The British Grenadiers' they led a rum-soaked army up the steps of the governor's residence. In fear for his life Bligh hid under a cot in the servants' quarters, although he claimed later to be attempting to hide his private papers beneath a mattress for safekeeping. He was allowed to dress in his full uniform before he was brought out to face Johnston and Macarthur. Johnston arrested Bligh and placed himself in charge of the colony. Martial law was then declared in Sydney on the twentieth anniversary of the arrival of the First Fleet.

The Convict Knight

Another transportee to meet with the displeasure of the governor was Knight of the Realm, Sir Henry Browne Hayes, who, in 1803, was arrested in Sydney for holding a secret meeting of Freemasons.

Hayes had previously had his request to hold a meeting denied by Governor King but as a subterfuge Hayes organised a meeting in the house of Sergeant Thomas Whittle of the New South Wales Corps. Attended also by several Sydney residents and some ship's officers, most of them managed to escape when the authorities knocked on the door, but Hayes was taken into custody.

Hayes had once been the sheriff of the Irish city of Cork; at one time he acted as Crown Agent for Transportation, overseeing the exile of 150 Irish convicts to Botany Bay in 1791, no doubt not expecting to join them only a decade later after his conviction and transportation to Botany Bay for abducting a heiress near Cork in 1801.

Hayes had 'earned' his knighthood after hosting a lavish dinner for the Lord Lieutenant of Ireland, which cost the taxpayers of Cork the sum of £250.

Hayes had married Elizabeth Smyth in 1782. She had brought a considerable fortune to the marriage and the couple lived very well in a grand house named Mount Vernon in Cork, in which they raised their four children. However, Elizabeth died after only twelve years of marriage, leaving Henry with four young children to look after. Henry decided to take another bride—and that was precisely what he did.

He found Mary Pike, a likely young lady who had just come into her inheritance, living with her uncle and aunt just down the road. Henry couldn't get there quickly enough. What Henry did next was kidnap Miss Pike, the only daughter of Samuel Pike, owner of Pike's Bank in Cork. Henry rushed Mary back to his house where a man dressed as a priest was waiting and a marriage ceremony was performed. If it wasn't bad enough for Mary to be kidnapped by four great-coated coachmen and driven away at speed into a stormy night, this ceremony left her in no doubt of her groom's intentions. He quickly bundled her upstairs and threw himself upon her. She

claimed later that he had tried to rape her. Dismayed by the reluc-
tance of his 'wife' Henry demanded, 'Don't you know who I am?' Sir
Henry Hayes, sheriff of Cork, and prominent lieutenant in the local
militia, had probably expected that his position of power should have
been sufficient to convince Mary to be a compliant, even agreeable,
lover, but Mary demanded that she be allowed to contact her uncle.
By the time her uncle arrived at the door with the police, Hayes had
fled. He hid for two years, until he contacted Mary asking her to
withdraw a 500 guinea reward she had offered, then he would give
himself up to the police.

Narrowly escaping the noose for his crime, Hayes was sentenced
to fourteen years' transportation. Ever the opportunist, he bribed the
captain of the convict ship and was given a large cabin and allowed to
take his valet on board, along with a huge amount of luggage, including goods he intended to sell when they landed in Australia.

Hayes carried so much aboard and the ship lay so low in the
water that other poor convicts were forced to remain in chains for
the entire voyage, below decks with the air vents closed. Three died
before the ship even embarked, fifteen more before they reached
Rio de Janeiro, where Hayes brought more goods on board. Ship's
surgeon Thomas Jamison complained of the favourable treatment
given to Hayes and the subsequent poor treatment of the other
prisoners. After continued argument Jamison transferred to the
Hercules, the other ship sailing with them, which meant that the
captain 'sold' Jamison's cabin to Hayes for a further 300 guineas.

By this time a large number of the prisoners below decks had
contracted scurvy and by the time they landed in Sydney sixty-nine
had died. Jamison had landed well before them and had become
Acting Surgeon-General of New South Wales, and a local magistrate
as well. On arrival Hayes was imprisoned for six months, punished
for 'antagonising the surgeon Jamison,' and Governor King refused
to allow the captain of the ship to sell the spirits and wine he had
brought to the colony.

Although he was repeatedly in trouble with the governor, who
became his sworn enemy, Hayes was generally considered to be
a real charmer, although his physical appearance may have been

View of the Heads of Port Jackson, NSW, looking north
from a hill above Vaucluse bay, 1846
Oil on board by George Peacock, 1846
Vaucluse House, shown at lower left, was purchased in 1827 by WC Wentworth,
the first son of Australia, whose own father had been a transported convict.
(Dixson Library, State Library of New South Wales)

considered somewhat eccentric. He decided never again to cut the hair on his upper lip and thereafter sported the most magnificent moustaches, although they did give him a rather frightening appearance.

He is credited with bringing Freemasonry to Australia, but it was the act of defiance over the first meeting that saw him transported first to Van Diemen's Land and later to Norfolk Island, a prison from which few returned. However, Hayes did his time on the island, and by 1810 was back in New South Wales. He was almost free to come and go as he pleased, eventually establishing himself on a farm at Vaucluse on Sydney Harbour's south-eastern tip, overlooking Watson's Bay and the heads. At one stage he had also attempted to take possession of a house lived in by the Scottish exile Maurice Margarot.

Hayes did little with the Vaucluse farm; he had a private income and little head for farming, but he did manage to have seventy-five convicts dig a moat around the house into which was laid imported Irish turf–'to keep out the snakes'.

He contrived to get on the right side of a governor at least once in his time in Australia when he sided with William Bligh, in opposition to the mutinous push led by squatter John Macarthur and Colonel William Paterson in 1808. After Bligh was removed from office Hayes was dispatched to the Coal River penal settlement near Newcastle but was pardoned in November 1812 by the incoming Governor Lachlan Macquarie.

He left the colony for home in December. However, trouble was never far away from Henry Hayes. The overloaded ship *Isabella* ran aground off the Falkland Islands in February 1813, but Henry was one of four of the fifty-two on board who took the dinghy with the only oars available and rowed ashore. They were eventually rescued by an American ship and taken to Massachusetts.

Hayes returned to Cork, where he lived, apparently without further incident, until his death in 1832.

The Colonists at War

When Captain James Cook landed in 1770, he saw no evidence of civilisation of a European kind—no castles, fortified harbours, army, streets or shops, or anything at all that he could recognise. In declaring Australia 'Terra Nullius', a land belonging to no-one, he made one fundamental error: the land was already occupied. The people of Australia just happened to be black.

When Cook saw natives on the shore of Botany Bay shaking their spears at Cook and his group, one of his men fired to frighten them away, striking one man. This first encounter with the native Australians set a pattern of ignorance and antagonism that lasted for the first 150 years of white settlement in Australia. Modern-day Aboriginals refer to the landing as the invasion, and in the late nineteenth century among the tribes living around Parramatta there was one Aboriginal warrior who certainly saw it that way, and took it upon himself to try and send the pale-faced invaders packing. His name was Pemulwuy.

Pemulwuy, the Freedom Fighter

Pemulwuy was a native Bidjigal man of the Eora people who lived around the Castle Hill area to Sydney's north. The Eora-occupied land stretched from the Hawkesbury River to Botany Bay and the Georges River, the best and most beautiful land well suited to the needs of the white settlers. The settlers simply took the land as their own, and were surprised when someone fought to get it back.

Pemulwuy was a natural leader of his people; a tall man with a fine physique, athletic and clever, he outfoxed the British forces as he led attacks against settlers who had stolen the land of his people and built for themselves fine pastoral estates.

He saw the damage done to those among his people who had mixed with the white man, through disease, abuse and alcohol, and would not have anything to do with colonial society—as had others, such as Benelong, who was the first to accuse Pemulwuy of killing an escaped convict.

Pemulwuy did kill Governor Phillip's convict gamekeeper McIntyre in November 1790, but it does seem as if there was plenty of justification for the man's death. He was well known, by both black and white alike, for his violence against the Eora people. Captain David Collins described the death of the hated McIntyre with this disinterested and objective observation: 'Pemulwuy used his spear with a skill that was fatally unerring'.

In 1790 Governor Phillip effectively declared war on Pemulwuy and his clan. He blamed the Aboriginals for repeated attacks on British settlers and government forces, killing or wounding more than seventeen since the arrival of the First Fleet in 1788. Phillip's indiscriminate order was 'to bring in any six Bidjigal or their heads'. It obviously didn't matter whose heads they were as long as they were black. Phillip began a decade of attack and reprisal that resulted in many deaths, both black and white.

While the attack on Pemulwuy was contradictory to Governor Phillip's nature—he had made a lasting friendship with Benelong, another Port Jackson native—he simply would not tolerate a rebel in his midst, and Pemulwuy and his band of warriors would not be patronised as Benelong had allowed himself to be.

Pemulwuy gathered around him large gangs of Aboriginal war-riors that at times numbered more than 100; sometimes the gangs even included escaped white convicts who were also keen to take some revenge on the British.

In February 1797 Pemulwuy led an attack on the government settlement at Toongabbie. Armed settlers and soldiers chased the Aborigines through the night, then at sunrise the two bands of men confronted one another near Parramatta. The whites retreated to the settlement but 'were followed by a large body of natives, headed by Pe-mul-wy [sic], a notorious and troublesome savage', wrote David Collins. In anger Pemulwuy threw a spear at one soldier and a battle broke out. Pemulwuy was shot, taken prisoner and carted off to hos-pital in chains, but he soon managed to escape.

Pemulwuy had been wounded so many times that many believed him to be supernatural, that he could not be killed by British bullets. Governor Hunter wrote in 1798: 'A strange idea was found to prevail among the natives respecting the savage Pe-mul-way [sic], which is very likely to prove fatal to him in the end. Both he and they enter-tained an opinion, that, from his being frequently wounded, he could not be killed by our fire-arms.' In 1800 John Washington Price, surgeon from the transport *Minerva*, said: 'He [Pemulwuy] has now lodged in him, in shot, slugs and bullets, about ten ounces of lead, it is supposed he has killed over thirty of our people, but it is doubtful on which side the provocation was given.'

The indigenous gangs continued their harassment of the white settlers. With military-style planning they attacked farms and set fire to crops. When cattle herder Daniel Conroy was killed and another settler wounded, the new Governor Philip Gidley King ordered 'that the hordes of natives living around Parramatta, the George's River and Prospect Hill be driven back from the settlers' habitations by firing at them'. Governor King outlawed Pemulwuy in November 1801, offering a reward of twenty gallons of spirits to any settler, or a free pardon to any convict, who brought him in dead or alive. He also outlawed William Knight and Thomas Thrush, two escapees who had joined the Aborigines in their fight against the British.

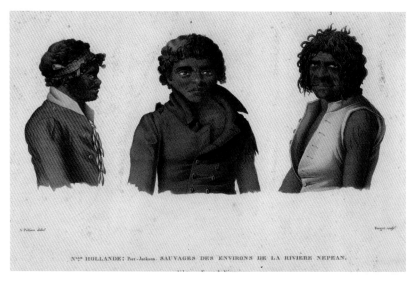

Port Jackson 'savages', from the Nepean River area
Coloured engraving from the *Atlas Historique* published by Louis de Freycinet, 1822
(Rex Nan Kivell Collection NK10983, National Library of Australia)

Almost one year later Pemulwuy was dead. King wrote to the Home Office in London advising Lord Hobart that 'two settlers, not having the means of securing the persons of Pemulwye [sic] and another native, shot them'. It was generally assumed that Knight and Thrush had done him in, but an account in the diary of seaman Samuel Smith, who had been with Matthew Flinders on the *Investigator*, has offered the name of Henry Hacking, game shooter for the *Nelson*, as responsible for the demise of Pemulwuy. Smith wrote on 20 July 1802 of an Aborigine named 'Bumbliway, a Severe Enemy to White people, as he had Kill'd several … at length, he was Shot by the Master of the Nelson Brig, that was Shooting in the Woods, his head being brought Tranquillity was again restor'd'.

The head of Pemulwuy was severed from his body, preserved in alcohol and sent to England as a gift to Sir Joseph Banks. Governor King wrote an accompanying letter, which read: 'altho' a terrible pest to the colony, he was a brave and independent character … an active and daring leader of his people'.

Just a shame he was Aboriginal and not British.

Musquito & the Oyster Bay Mob

While Pemulwuy may been seen as a 'freedom fighter' defending his country against white invasion, it is generally believed that the bandit known as Musquito and the Tasmanian Oyster Bay mob were simply hell-bent on revenge. However, his early years had seen Musquito transported to Norfolk Island for leading attacks on white settlers in the Lower Hawkesbury district up until 1805 in much the same manner as Pemulwuy, and it could be assumed for the same reasons. When he was captured, along with another fellow named Bulldog, Governor King found no British law that he could charge them with so he sent them away. When Norfolk was evacuated in 1813 Musquito was transferred to Port Dalrymple (Launceston), and even though he had been granted approval to return to New South Wales he did not take the passage.

Musquito was enlisted by the police to track the 'worst and last' of the Vandemonian bushrangers, Michael Howe. Howe, who styled himself as the 'Lieutenant-Governor of the Woods', had taken control of John Whitehead's gang after the brutal escapee gang-leader Whitehead was killed by soldiers in 1814. Howe was no friend to the Oyster Bay tribe, having attacked one encampment and stolen wives for his gang, shooting any Aborigine who resisted. Black tracker Musquito had led the police to the capture of many of the marauders of the bush, and quite a few had felt the hangman's knot because of him. After Howe was killed, the police had no longer any use for Musquito. Even though he was promised his freedom and a passage back to Sydney, the authorities let him down. He was dismissed without his reward. Musquito was then a man without status; the transportees hated him as he was held responsible for the capture of so many 'bolters'. Persecuted, he appealed to the police but they would offer him no protection.

He responded by becoming a bushranger himself.

He joined the Oyster Bay mob and led them on well-planned attacks on settler's homes and farms. Just as Pemulwuy had done before him, Musquito attacked with such cunning and discipline that the government was sure that a white man must have been leading the Aborigines. The Oyster Bay tribes were under terrible pressure from the expansion of British interests and it can be assumed that Musquito led them in acts of reprisal, fearing the same push for exclusion from their traditional lands as had happened around Parramatta.

He became such a nuisance that Governor George Arthur issued a reward for his capture. Musquito was eventually captured by a local Aborigine who found him alone, unarmed, by a campfire. He shot him three times. Although sorely wounded, Musquito fought back with sticks and rocks until, exhausted, he surrendered.

He was convicted for the killing of two stock-keepers, William Hollyoak and the Tahitian, Mammoa, at Grindstone Bay in 1823. Alongside him stood another Oyster Bay man, Black Jack, who was also convicted of murder. Although the only survivor of the attack at Grindstone Bay did not see who actually killed the two men, it was certain that Musquito had led the mob, and that was enough to secure his execution.

He was sentenced to be hanged in February 1825. When the sentence was passed he said, 'Hanging no bloody good for blackfellow … very good for white-fellow, he used to it.'

Arthur's 'Black Line Drive'

In response to the threat posed to white settlers from native attack it was now Governor Arthur's turn to declare war on the Tasmanian blacks. He could see no compatibility between the interests of white settlers and the Tasmanian indigenes and sought to drive them out of their land altogether:

> I regret that the natives led on by a Sydney black, and by two Aborigines of this island, men partially civilised (a circumstance which augurs ill for any endeavour to instruct these abject beings) have committed many murders [which] have so inflamed the passions of the settlers … that further forbearance would be totally indefensible.

Arthur began the 'Black Line Drive' in 1830, forcing all Aborigines from eastern Van Diemen's Land onto the Tasman Peninsula. The British had no qualms about this dispossession of a people from the land where they had lived since time immemorial; after all, over the years, the British had turned dispossession into an art form.

MARTYRS OF TOLPUDDLE
Transported for Attempting to Unionise the Farm

When the popular English novelist Charles Dickens wrote this opening line to his novel *A Tale of Two Cities* in 1857: 'It was the best of times, it was the worst of times ... it was the age of foolishness, it was the epoch of belief, it was the epoch of incredulity, it was the season of Light, it was the season of darkness ...', he accurately described the state of confusion in a world adjusting to the pace of social change that followed the shift from cottage-based industries to a highly mechanised capitalist-driven era of mass production.

The industrial revolution that began in England in the late eighteenth century and swept across Europe brought great wealth to the few who controlled the capital and widespread poverty to those without. The collapse of rural occupations saw a mass shift in the population away from the regions, as thousands of rural workers descended on the cities in search of work.

The bourgeois capitalists took advantage of this shift in social demographics; with the numbers of the under-employed swelling they suppressed wages, forcing the poor to live in the worst conditions while they built for themselves stately homes, surrounded by vast and manicured landscapes.

Martyr's Memorial, Tolpuddle, Dorset
(Author's photograph, 2005)

... it was the winter of despair, we had everything before us, we were all going direct to Heaven, we were all going direct the other way ...

Dickens expressed the polarisation of post-revolutionary society; there was so much that appeared to be righteous and good, yet for the majority of the population there was little hope for any improvement at all. For those who led lives of toil—the factory workers, underground miners, farm labourers and rural workers—it was the worst of times.

A Voice for Change

There were those who sought to halt the onward march of industrialisation. 'Captain' Ned Ludd came to notoriety after he smashed some large stocking-frames, introduced to produce cheap stockings, and undercutting the skilled stocking-knitters, putting them out of work. In protest, hundreds of weaving machines were wrecked by 'the Luddites', followers of Ludd, in the years 1811–13. The government responded by making such actions punishable by death. In 1813, seventeen men were executed in York, while scores of others were transported to Australia. For the unemployed textile workers it was probably not the best of times at all.

Along Came Captain Swing

Another, albeit fictional, character who gained notoriety was the ubiquitous 'Captain Swing'. He may not have actually existed, but it his was name that was signed to countless threats made to the ruling classes, the manufacturers and factory owners who seemed hell-bent on sending their workforce into poverty.

'Swing' letters turned up everywhere; farmhands sought to have thrashing machines removed, textile workers wanted the weaving and knitting machines stopped and a mobilised workforce attempted to make their voices heard, resorting to Swing-style direct action if necessary.

The Inclosures: 1770–1830

Privileged landholders took ownership of vast acreages of the land, building fences and hedgerows, effectively excluding ordinary peasant farmers from what had once been shared common ground. Farm workers no longer had plots where they had once grown their own vegetables, nor did they have access to the once-open commons where they had always grazed a single cow, a small flock of sheep or a few pigs.

The landholders just grew richer and fatter, producing great wealth on the backs of their labourers. Forced to work their vast and productive fields, the poor subsisted on a diet of bread and potatoes, with little hope of ever making a better life for themselves.

At the end of the war against the French in 1815 thousands of soldiers were repatriated to Britain, causing massive unemployment and social dislocation. The factory owners and the yeoman-farmers used this desperation for employment to depress wages and, in the interests of higher profits and wealth creation, take away whatever rights the workers had earned.

With increased mechanisation of the working environment there were movements right across Britain to bring a halt to the pace of change, or at least to protect the livelihood and wellbeing of the working man and his family. In effect the masters were being asked to be part of a reasonable social contract, to share some of the wealth created and contribute to the common good.

Few were interested. To most, the working classes were no more than slaves to the will of the wealthy. While every man was desperate enough to work for ever-decreasing wages, what could they do about it? It was the masters who made the rules, controlled the parliaments, made the law and administered it. Over centuries the English ruling elite had constructed an intricate web of rules and regulations that excluded the common peasant while always enriching themselves.

There would come a time when the common man had had enough, and they would stand together, side by side, against their masters and demand a fair share. While Tom Paine made 'Common Sense', his ideas echoed around the world, even into the cottages of the rural workers; the success of the American and the French revolutions, combined with agitation for reform that ranged from Europe to the industrial midlands in the north of England, soon became a critical mass of public opinion and expectation that would not be denied.

Someone had to make a stand.

The Peterloo Massacre

In the industrialised northern midland town of Manchester, government forces hacked their way into a peaceful crowd that had gathered to hear radical reformer Henry 'Orator' Hunt, among others. Hunt was a prominent Chartist whose ideals of universal suffrage, removal of property qualification for parliamentary representation, repeal of the Corn Laws and so on, brought him into conflict with the law.

Fearing that the meeting of more than 50,000 who had gathered on 16 August 1819 in St Peter's Field could end in riot, local magistrates had gathered together more than 1500 cavalrymen, Hussars, artillery forces, armed yeomen and local constables who were placed on standby. Once the military were given the order to arrest Hunt and the other radicals on the platform, they moved in; the riot they started became a massacre. Eleven lay dead on Manchester's St Peter's Field, 400 more lay wounded.

Hunt was accused of 'assembling with unlawful banners at an unlawful meeting for the purpose of exciting discontent', found guilty and sentenced to two and a half years' imprisonment.

'Peterloo' became one more touchstone for the radical movement, one more chink in the establishment armour. No-one would forget the unnecessary massacre of innocent people killed at St Peter's Field.

In reply, a group of dissenters in London gathered together in an attic to plot against the parliament. They formed a daring plan to attack and execute the entire cabinet as they were dining in Downing Street. The plot was exposed to the police by spies and the 'Cato Street Conspiracy' was brought to an end before they had even fired one shot. The leaders of the group ended their days on the chopping block, the rest transported to New South Wales.

Striking mill workers in Glasgow defended themselves against the police with pikes. The leaders of these men fighting for their rights were similarly beheaded, or hanged by the neck.

The British parliament would not tolerate working men taking a stand against the might of the ruling class, and the working class would not lie down and simply die for them. The war of the classes had begun and it was being fought out in the factories and on England's crowded streets.

In the country, farm workers were caught up in the same push for their rights. Almost a generation after 'Peterloo', George Loveless, a farm labourer from a tiny village in England's south-west county of Dorset, made a stand against his employer and attempted to establish a Friendly Society of Labourers, in the vain hope of being able to feed his family properly.

Loveless was a Methodist lay preacher and in a delicate balance between his loving God and the fearful 'Captain Swing', he stood his ground against his employer, the magistrate, the Anglican Church and eventually the Prime Minister of England.

When 'Swing' letters such as the following were nailed to farmers' doors all across the country, the local landholders became afraid, first for the value of their investments, then for the safety of their lives:

> This is to inform you what you have to undergo Gentlemen if providing you don't pull down your new schemes and rise the poor mens wages the married men give tow [sic] and six pence a day, the single tow shillings or we will burn down your barns and you in them—this is the last notis [sic].
> from WSR [Captain Swing]

The 'Seditious' John Wesley

Radical Christian evangelist John Wesley, the son of a Church of England vicar, was born in Epworth, England in 1703. A scholar at Oxford University where his brother Charles had established a religious study group called the Holy Club, John Wesley confirmed his faith through methodical study of the scriptures, devotion and the fellowship of like-minded fellows in the club.

Wesley turned his back on the grand buildings and social exclusivity of the established church and its oppressive elitism, and when parish churches closed their doors against him he preached in the open air to thousands of poor workers. He travelled on horseback all over England ready to preach wherever people would gather together. He took Christ to the people and celebrated him in song,

Site of the Martyr's Tree, Tolpuddle, Dorset
The original sycamore has long gone from the village green
in the village of Tolpuddle; only a stump remains.
(Author's photograph, 2005)

and some farm workers in the little village of Tolpuddle were soon to act upon the very tenet of his faith in them as men.

George Loveless took Wesley as his example and preached to whomever would listen beneath the sycamore tree on the village green in the heart of Tolpuddle, right beside the Anglican church.

The village of Tolpuddle sits among the lovely green rolling hills of Dorset. Its chequerboard fields, with high and broad-acres of golden corn, is Thomas Hardy country—the novelist's nostalgic world of buxom, rosy-cheeked milkmaids and lusty farm-boys, ruddy-necked and eager for sport among the 'ricks, while the threshing-machine puffs steam into the autumn air—Hardy obviously saw his Dorset through different eyes than 'Captain Swing'.

The radical preacher John Wesley had been a profound influence on Loveless and the Tolpuddle men, his belief in the worth of the individual saw each person as equal in the eyes of God. If humans could be equal in God, why not equal in the world of humankind? Where Wesley preached evangelistic Bible Christianity, the government saw sedition; where Thomas Hardy saw hay-ricks, haywains and harvest home, 'Swing' saw abject poverty and Loveless saw the

The Martyr's Memorial and St John's Parish Church stand
side by side in the village of Tolpuddle, Dorset.
(Author's photographs, 2005)

value of a person. Were the three incompatible? Loveless stood firm
and demanded his share.

A Secret Society

In the years 1831–32 there was a general movement throughout the
south-east for an increase in labourer's wages. The men of Tolpuddle
met and were given an assurance from their masters that they would
match the wages given to men in neighbouring districts. The men
went back to work, and as George Loveless recalled, 'no language of
intimidation or threatening was used on the occasion'.

One of the farmers assured Chief Magistrate James Frampton JP,
himself a prosperous landholder in the district whose own estates
earned him in excess of £7000 a year (approximately A$750,000
today), that although he had not promised any specific amount, if
the men 'went about their work quietly, they should have the same
pay as agreed to be given in other parishes'. Fearful of unrest, and
wishing to avoid damage to their property, some of the farmers
agreed to raise their workers' wages without any protest, which
caused a degree of concern among others who were not at all prepared to give in so eagerly.

In the winter of 1831 'Swing' rioters destroyed most of the thresh-
ing machines around Dorchester; some were even destroyed by the

farmers themselves rather than have a riotous mob on their lands. Fires were lit in haystacks and barns burned to the ground. The level of protest had risen to riot stage and the army was called in to quell the angry farm workers. A troop of lancers marched into Dorchester, taking men prisoner as they came; at any one time seventy men were confined in the Dorchester gaol. By the end of January 250 had been sentenced to death, but only nine were actually executed, while 500 were transported and another 600 sent to prison. Magistrate James Frampton had thirteen men transported for life.

The masters were still unwilling to listen to the demands of their workers and even looked to cut their wages. Wages in Tolpuddle were cut from nine to eight shillings a week, while men in neighbouring towns received ten. There was no surer way to cause discontent than for one man to be seen to be treated differently from another. All of the working men in Tolpuddle made application to see the local magistrate to seek his advice. He called in Chief Magistrate James Frampton for his opinion on the matter. Frampton told Loveless, who had been chosen to represent the men, that the employers were under no obligation to pay them any fixed sum at all. Loveless reminded him of the agreement that they had already made with their master. Reverend Warren, the local parson, was witness to that agreement, even commenting at the time: 'I am witness between you men and your masters, that if you go quietly to your work, you shall receive for your labour as much as any men in the district; and if your master should attempt to run from their word, I will undertake to see you righted, so help me God!'

When questioned by Frampton, Warren denied any knowledge of the agreement, and of his commitment to support the men. The local parson relied on the largesse of the parish for his living; he could not afford to support the dissenting Methodist in defiance of the Chief Magistrate, the wealthiest, most influential gentleman in his flock. The Tolpuddle men had their wages cut to seven shillings a week, and then to six. It was impossible for them to live honestly on such a small amount.

Loveless was aware of the trades societies that had been formed to protect the workers from the excesses of their masters in industrialised towns and enquired of his brother John, who was a member of the Flax Dressers Union, to send him some literature. Another brother, Robert, in London, put him in contact with the Grand National Consolidated Trades Union, founded by Robert Owen in 1833 and rapidly attracting more than half a million members.

Towards the end of October 1833 two union delegates were invited to Tolpuddle, where they addressed a gathering of forty men from across the district in an upstairs room in Thomas Standfield's cottage. A Friendly Society was formed at this meeting and the men went out to recruit members among the farm labourers.

The Friendly Society of Labourers developed a set of rules that prohibited violence, the use of bad language in either songs or toasts; and discussion of religion and politics during meetings. They demanded that the men should stick together; to strike if any one man was dismissed or treated unfairly, or had his wages reduced. They set a membership fee of one shilling, and one penny a week after that, to be paid into a common fund for the relief of workers who were ill or who had lost their jobs. They called the Society a 'Lodge' and created a password to be used by all members. Then they invented their own initiation ceremony. It was the secret oath-taking of this ceremony that swung the balance of justice against them.

James Frampton, 1833

Trade unions had been legal in England since 1824 and were guaranteed protection under the common law. The general principle of workers banding together to bargain collectively with their masters was protected after the Combinations Acts, which had prevented such associations, were repealed. It is interesting how, and why, Magistrate James Frampton manipulated the law to bring about the downfall of the union men gathering together on his patch.

Frampton moved to protect his class. Motivated by self-protection and greed, he needed to crush a movement that on the one hand was seeking to improve the lot of the working class at the expense of their masters, of which he certainly saw himself as one; and on the other, was being led by dissenters—the Methodists. For Loveless, acceptance of the example set by John Wesley set him against the

established Church. To stand against the Church meant
against the established order of English society, which must
fore constitute a stand against the authority of the Crown. In
Methodism equalled sedition!

Frampton moved to stop the seditious unionists of Tolpuddle,
first glance there was nothing they had done that was actually illegal.
In the time-honoured tradition of English law-makers everywhere,
Frampton enlisted the assistance of a couple of spies.

Five men from a nearby village, including Edward Legge and
John Lock, were initiated into the Friendly Society in Standfield's
cottage on 9 December 1833. The ceremony of initiation was a curious
mix of secret oaths and demonic symbolism, which must not have
sat comfortably with the Methodist men, and more than likely terrified the simple farm labourers from neighbouring Affpuddle. The
men were blindfolded and led to an upstairs room; there they were
met by the union men dressed in garments that resembled clergy-
men's surplices. The rules of the Society were read out and each man
repeated the secret oath before they kissed the Bible. They were told
to keep secret what had occurred that night.

Once they removed their blindfolds they were confronted by
two six-foot-high painted images, one depicting 'Death' with the
words 'Remember Thine End' painted above, the other a painting
of a skeleton. In the darkened, candlelit upper room of Thomas
Standfield's tiny cottage the effect must have been most dramatic.
Edward Legge's recollection of that terrible ceremony was the
evidence that Frampton needed to bring about the end of George
Loveless and the nuisance that was the Friendly Society. Frampton
wrote to Lord Melbourne:

> Owing to the formation of Trades Unions in all the large towns by
> which workmen were dictating to their Masters and refusing to work
> except on their own terms, a very great disorganisation of the whole
> labour orders has taken place.
>
> These Unions too, had also began to extend among the Agricultural
> labourers in this neighbourhood to a very alarming degree, partic-
> ularly in the villages of Tolpuddle, Bere Regis and the adjoining

parishes; in which places Lodges were formed and secret nightly meetings were held; when unlawful oaths attended by mysterious ceremonies were administered.

Fortunately after some time I was able to obtain sufficient information to cause some of the Leaders to be apprehended and committed to Gaol to take their trial at the Lent Assizes at Dorchester ...

Frampton had put Legge before a panel of magistrates in Dorchester where he swore that he had attended a ceremony and been initiated into the union, that he had taken an oath and was sworn to secrecy:

We went into a room ... and had our eyes blindfolded ... something was read to us, but I do not recollect any of the words ... we knelt down ... we had to kiss a book ... I repeated some words—something about our souls being plunged into eternity if we did not keep the secret. We were then unblinded ... I saw a picture in the room which represented death. The words 'society' and 'brothers' were used after we had been sworn ...

Chief Magistrate James Frampton ordered a 'Caution Notice' to be placed up throughout the district, warning anyone who would take a secret oath to become a member of an illegal Society would incur a mandatory punishment of seven years' transportation. The notice went up on 22 February 1834, two days before the Tolpuddle men were arrested for an action that was not considered a felony when it had taken place more than two months earlier.

Frampton had placed the Tolpuddle men in an invidious position. They could recant; the union would be finished, and they would simply go back to the way they had been before. Or they could rely on the law to see the justice in their actions and the deviousness of Frampton and his 'Caution'. For a common man the law was probably the last place to seek a fair outcome.

Six Tolpuddle farm labourers were arrested at dawn on the morning of Monday 24 February 1834. George Loveless, his brother James, James Brine, Thomas Standfield and his son John and loner James Hammett were forced to march with the local constable six miles to Dorchester to face Frampton and his magistrates.

Thomas Standfield's cottage in Tolpuddle
John Lock and Edward Legge were sworn into 'The Lodge'
in the upper room of Standfield's cottage.
(Author's photograph, 2005)

Edward Legge was there to speak against them, naming each man as having been at the initiation ceremony. Although it transpired that Hammett had never been at that meeting, he allowed himself to be committed in place of his younger brother John, whose wife was pregnant with their first child. Frampton believed that Legge's evidence was all he needed to send them to trial, but first he had to decide what he could charge them with.

Two Acts are Better than One

While the Tolpuddle men waited in the cells beneath the Dorchester Assize Court, stripped of their clothes and with heads shaven like common criminals, Frampton searched for a law that fitted the punishment he had devised. He was having difficulty; the act he was relying on, framed in 1817 for 'effectively preventing Seditious Meetings or Assemblies', would probably bring about a conviction, but the penalty was only three months' imprisonment or a £20 fine. Frampton had promised seven years' transportation. Lord Melbourne became increasingly concerned that the men might not be convicted at all. He instructed Frampton to dig a little deeper. He came upon the 1797 Mutiny Act, under whose provisions it was made a felony 'to administer an Oath binding a person to reveal an unlawful confederacy', and the maximum sentence allowable under this forty-year-old Act was seven years' transportation.

On 14 March 1834 a twenty-two-man grand jury was sworn in to hear the case brought against the Tolpuddle men. Its members comprised James Frampton, his step-brother Charles Wollaston, his son Henry and two others who had been signatory to the Caution Notice, and the foreman was William Ponsonby, local MP and Lord Melbourne's brother-in-law. The Petty Jury were all yeoman farmers who were most likely tenants of the gentlemen mentioned. The court was stacked against the Tolpuddle men, even if the evidence was not.

At that time the prisoners were not permitted to give evidence on their own behalf and the case went against them at every turn. George Loveless recalled the summing-up statement given by the judge to the jury, where among other things the judge told them that:

> If such Societies were allowed to exist it would ruin masters, cause a stagnation in trade, destroy property. And if they would find us not guilty, he was certain they would forfeit the opinion of the Grand Jury ... Under such a charge, from such a quarter, self-interest alone would induce them to say 'Guilty'.

The judge asked the prisoners if they had anything to say, and George Loveless handed over a paper on which he had written this statement:

> My Lord, if we have violated any law, it was not done intentionally. We have injured no man's reputation, character, person or property. We were uniting together to preserve ourselves, our wives and our children from utter degradation and starvation. We challenge any man or number of men to prove that we have acted, or intend to act, different from the above statement.

'The Dorchester Unionists Imploring Mercy!!! of their king'
Political drama, no. 32, published by G Drake, London
This satirical cartoon, clearly sympathetic to the Tolpuddle men,
shows the king turning his backside to his loyal subjects, while the
prime minister expresses his loyalty to the capitalists.
PM Lord Melbourne says: 'Guards turn the slaves out, they must be transported, my
duty to the Capitalists, landholders, the Tories and my nine hundred and ninety-nine
cousins demands it.' How little has changed over the following century-and-a-half.
(National Library of Tasmania)

After deliberating for two days Judge Baron Williams passed down
the only sentence anyone had expected. He sentenced each man to
seven years' transportation. As they were being taken back to the
cells, their hands manacled together to await their removal to the
hulks George Loveless passed a piece of paper to someone in the
watching crowd on which he had written the words to 'The Song
of Freedom':

> God is our guide, from field, from wave,
> From plough, from anvil, and from loom;
> We come, our country's right to save.
> And speak a tyrant fiction's doom:
> We raise the watchword, liberty
> We will, we will, we will be free!

God is our guide! No swords we draw.
We kindle not war's battle fires:
By reason, union, justice, law.
We claim the birth-right of our sires:
We raise the watchword, liberty
We will, we will, we will be free!

Uproar in the City

Two days later, when the news reached London of the harsh sentences passed on the Tolpuddle men, there was uproar led by the newspapers of all political stripes. The pro-Tory *Morning Herald* declared on 2 April 1834 that the court had brought down 'a verdict which shows rather the treachery than the energy of the law by throwing a noose of an Act of Parliament over the heads of sleeping men'. While the government falsely believed that they had put an end to unionism by punishing the poor men from Tolpuddle, they in fact rekindled the flame of freedom. Mass meetings were held across the country and 800,000 of the king's subjects signed their names to petition for the freedom of the farm labourers.

On Easter Monday, 21 April 1834, more than thirty unions brought greater than 35,000 members to march through London's streets, lined with a crowd that numbered thousands more. They had gathered in Copenhagen Fields and marched right through London to the seat of oppression, Whitehall, where a petition of 300,000 names was presented to Lord Melbourne, who refused to accept it until it was presented in the proper manner. The unionists were undeterred; they had the newspapers on their side and they kept the pressure for repeal on Melbourne. *The Pioneer* added its opinion to the cause: 'Last Monday was a day in Britain's history which will long be remembered; for labour put its hat on its head and walked towards the throne'. *The Weekly True Sun* added: 'This is not a common procession of petitioners but a nation in movement'.

Eventually Lord Melbourne accepted the petition but declined to act, stating that 'The King has not yet been pleased to issue any commands thereupon'. Supporter of the trade union cause *The Pioneer* on 29 March 1834 added to the clamour for justice: 'Will Britons see their honest labourers torn from home, and banished to a land of felony, the mark of infamy burned on their brows; and honest husbandmen imprisoned among thieves and pickpockets, to cure them of their patriotism?'

The government changed in November 1834 and changed back again the following April. As Prime Minister, Lord Melbourne was under renewed pressure from Home Secretary Lord John Russell and reformer and founder of the *The Lancet*, Thomas Wakley, to act on behalf of the Dorset labourers, but it was already too late for the transported men from Tolpuddle–they were in Australia, 12,000 miles away. However, by June 1835, Lord Russell was able to convince the king to grant conditional pardons for the Tolpuddle Martyrs. Four were to be freed from penal servitude and allowed to return to England after they had spent two years in the colonies. As ringleaders the Lovelesses were to serve three years and then remain in the colony as emancipists. Their freedom excused the king from an embarrassing situation that Lord Russell had used to good effect. The king's brother, the Duke of Cumberland, was Grand Master of the Orange Lodges, whose members were required to take an oath of secrecy. Writs were under preparation to bring the duke before the court and accuse him, just as the Tolpuddle men had been accused. The government quietly counselled the king and the Tolpuddle men were granted pardons. *The Radical* newspaper wrote:

> The indictment against His Royal Highness the Duke of Cumberland, for being head of an illegal Society, were all but prepared and would have been sent to the next Grand Inquest of Middlesex, had not Ministers, in a quiet way, interfered ... His Royal Highness would have been tried by Petty Jury.
>
> Ministers all bewigged as they are, were not radical enough to avoid a shudder at the thought of even the possibility of indicting a Prince of the blood royal, and as to transporting His Royal Highness, only imagine a Whig so much as thinking of such a thing. As it was an awkward affair, the labourers were pardoned to save the Prince.

It took several years before the Tolpuddle men were eventually able to leave the colonies. For one thing, they were no longer together. Having arrived in Sydney on 4 September 1834, they had waited in the prison barracks until they could be assigned, and then they went their separate ways.

Thomas Standfield was sent up the Hunter River, assigned to Timothy Nowland at Maitland. His son John Standfield was sent to Balwara, also near Maitland and only a few miles from his father. The oldest man among them all, Thomas had the worst of it, and was fortunate that his son was nearby. Richard Jones, to whom John was assigned, seemed to be a reasonable master and allowed John to visit and take care of his fifty-one-year-old father.

James Loveless had to walk 300 miles to Strathallan on the Victorian border to work for local Justice of the Peace McMillan.

James Brine travelled by steamboat up the Hunter River to Newcastle. He was forced to walk thirty miles to Glindon and, tired out by the journey, had everything he had been given for the journey stolen by bushrangers: clothing, blanket, bed, his shoes and a shilling, all stolen while he was asleep. When he arrived barefoot and penniless his new master Robert Scott did not believe his story and reprimanded him: 'You are one of the Dorset machine-breakers but you are caught at last. If you utter one word of complaint, I will put you in the lockup; and if you ask me for another article for six months to come I will send you up to the magistrate where no mercy will be shown you'. Brine had to go the next six months without shoes or a change of clothing, forced to sleep on the bare ground without any covering.

James Hammett walked 400 miles to Edward John Eyre's Woodland farm on the Molongo Plains, near the present capital of Canberra. Eyre was local Protector of Aborigines and had a deep concern for humanity. It is believed that Hammett was treated well by Eyre, but he must have got up to some mischief as his return was delayed for eighteen months while he served a sentence for assault.

George Loveless did not sail with the others on the *Surrey* to New South Wales on 11 April. His time in the cells beneath the Dorchester

| JAMES BRINE | THOMAS STANFIELD | JOHN STANFIELD | GEORGE LOVELESS | JAMES LOVELESS |
| Aged 25 | Aged 51 | aged 25 | Aged 41 | Aged 29 |

The Returned Convicts
Engraving published in *Cleave's Penny Gazette*, 12 May 1838

Assizes had been hard on him and he was declared unfit to travel. Although George had recovered sufficiently to go with them by the time the *Surrey* was ready to catch the wind there was no way for him to get from Dorchester to Plymouth in time. He had to wait another six weeks on board the prison hulk *York* before he caught the prison ship *William Metcalfe*, but it was bound for Van Diemen's Land, not Botany Bay.

He wrote to his wife on the eve of his departure:

> Be satisfied, my dear Betsy, on my account. Depend on it, it will work together for good and we shall yet rejoice together. I hope you will pay particular attention to the morals and spiritual interest of the children. Do not send me any money to distress yourself.
>
> I shall do well for He who is the Lord of the winds and waves will be support in life and death.

When George arrived in Van Diemen's Land he must have thought that his Lord had deserted him. He was first assigned to a chain gang working on the roads. He was singled out for more severe punishment than the others because he was a leader. But Governor George Arthur became convinced that Loveless and the Tolpuddle men had not been aware of the crime they were committing in 1833 and should be treated with leniency. He moved Loveless to easier work on the government farm. Loveless became a shepherd and stock-keeper. It was work he knew well, although he seemed to have a lot to do, with pasturing the sheep, lambing, herding the cows, milking and taking care of the calves. He was accused of neglect of duty after a year of this demanding work. Nine wild cattle escaped and he was brought before the magistrate. He pleaded that he had been attending to the lambing when the cattle got away, and that he had too much to do, and could not be expected to be in two places at the same time. He was discharged, narrowly escaping a flogging for his troubles.

While things were tough enough on the transported men, they were doubly difficult for the families they left behind. Without any income, they were thrown on the mercy of the parish. *The True Sun* newspaper reported on 31 March 1834:

> The prisoners' wives have repeatedly applied to the parish officers for relief, who have refused to help them any in any shape whatever, without a magistrate's order. They applied to Mr Frampton, the magistrate who committed the men, but he not only refuses to give an order, but commands the officers not give the families relief ... the poor women went to Mr Wollaston [Frampton's brother-in-law] for an order but he flatly refused, and wringing his fist in front of James Standfield's wife said, 'You shall suffer want. You shall have no mercy, because you ought to have known better than to have allowed such meetings to have been holden in your house.'

They were expected to starve to death for their husbands' seeking a fair day's pay.

George Loveless was the first of the Martyrs of Tolpuddle to arrive back in England. He stepped out onto the London wharf on 13 June 1837. While he was met by members of the London Dorchester Committee there was no fanfare; no newspaper expressed any interest in his arrival at all. He had arrived at a time when the biggest news was the imminent death of the king, who passed away a week later.

The remaining men, except James Hammett, arrived back in Plymouth on 17 March 1838, four years to the day after they had been transported to Australia. They had been welcomed at the Mechanic's Institute then went back to Tolpuddle. The London Dorchester Committee had been formed in August 1834 to provide support for the wives and children of the Tolpuddle men, ensuring that they were no longer needful of the parish charity and able to stay in their homes. The committee organised a grand celebratory dinner to honour the men and a great procession marched again through the streets of London, in reverse direction to the Copenhagen Fields march four years earlier. Thomas Wakley, principal guest at the dinner, sitting beside the five returned men, announced the 'Dorchester Labourers' Farm Tribute' after George Loveless had thanked the gathering of 1200 guests, who had paid two shillings and sixpence each to attend.

The Wesleyan Chapel at Tolpuddle showing the memorial arch to the transported men, erected 27 May 1912.
(Author's photograph, 2005)

In 1838 George Loveless published a small book with a very long title: *The Victims of Whiggery. A Statement of the Persecutions Experienced by the Dorchester Labourers; with a Report of their Trial; Also a Description of Van Diemen's Land and Reflections upon the System of Transportation.* Profits from the sale of this book went into the Tribute fund.

The Tribute collected enough money to be able to obtain the lease on two farms in Essex, which were presented to the men. While the families settled for a while it would appear that England no longer had charms to hold them. The Loveless and Standfield families emigrated to Canada, in two groups, in 1844 and 1846.

James Hammett was the only one to remain in Dorset. A bit of an enigma, he is the only one to be buried on English soil, yet set apart from the other graves in St John's churchyard because he was not a member of the Anglican Church—nor Methodist either.

A CHARTIST IN EXILE

Chartism grew from a meeting of the London Working Man's Association, which had been established in 1836. William Lovett stated that the intention of the organisation was 'to draw into one bond of Unity the intelligent and influential portion of the working classes in town and country. To seek by every legal means to place all classes of society in possession of the equal political and social rights'.

It seemed that they had chosen the very course that would bring them face to face against the authorities; and it seemed they had chosen a course that would bring many undone, and that was doomed to failure—in the immediate term, to say the very least.

Although enough pressure was being brought to bear against the British government to consider extending suffrage to every man of age—and some consideration was being given to the cause within the parliament. British privilege and position was far too entrenched to allow equal rights to be handed out to 'every man and his dog'.

The unassailable authority of the Crown lay a heavy blanket on the aspirations of every 'democrat', wherever he lived in the Empire. The English Crown was still smarting over the loss of the American colony, still fearful of the 'red republicans' of Europe and the insistent nuisance that was Ireland, when the declaration of The People's Charter was presented to parliament in February 1837.

The Charter, drawn up by a committee that included Dan O'Connell, outlined six demands, all requiring a radical change in thinking from within the British legislature. The petition began:

1. A VOTE for every man twenty-one years of age, of sound mind, and not undergoing punishment for crime.
2. THE BALLOT, to protect the elector in the exercise of his vote.
3. NO PROPERTY QUALIFICATION for members of Parliament—thus enabling the constituencies to return the man of their choice, be he rich or poor.
4. PAYMENT OF MEMBERS, thus enabling an honest tradesman, working man, or other person, to serve a

constituency, when taken from his business to attend to the interests of the country.

5. EQUAL CONSTITUENCIES, securing the same amount of representation for the same number of electors, instead of allowing small constituencies to swamp the votes of larger ones.

6. ANNUAL PARLIAMENTS, thus presenting the most effectual check to bribery and intimidation, since though a constituency might be bought once in seven years (even with the ballot), no purse could buy a constituency (under a system of universal suffrage) in each ensuing twelve months; and since members, when elected for a year only, would not be able to defy and betray their constituents as now.

It ended with the following demand: 'We demand universal suffrage. The suffrage to be exempt from the corruption of the wealthy and the violence of the powerful.' The Chartists also added that the voting system 'must be secret'. Apart from the demands for equality in political terms, the notion of the secret ballot would have been an anathema to the government. After all, men had been transported for the secrecy of their affiliations, and the government liked to be fully aware of who was thinking what.

Chartist, John Frost

John Frost was born in Newport, Wales on 25 May 1784. After his father died, he went to live with his grandparents, becoming apprenticed to his bootmaker grandfather after finishing school.

He left home aged sixteen years and started work as a tailor in Cardiff. Six years later he was back in Newport where he established his own business, and was made a freeman of the town.

An avid reader, Frost was greatly taken with the writings of Tom Paine and William Cobbett. In particular, Cobbett's approval of physical force to achieve political gain was to be Frost's undoing.

Frost accused a Newport solicitor, Prothero, of interfering in the content of his uncle's will, effectively excluding Frost from any inheritance. Prothero sued him for libel and the courts ordered Frost to pay him £1000 compensation. Unbowed by the court's adverse decision,

Frost continued to accuse the solicitor and was again found guilty of libel. This time he was sentenced to six months in prison. Aware that any further attack on Prothero would mean an even longer term in prison, he decided to attack the solicitor's closest friend, wealthy landowner Sir Charles Morgan. Frost wrote a pamphlet titled 'A Christmas Box for Sir Charles Morgan' in 1830, in which he accused Morgan of mistreating his tenants. He also included some thoughts on universal suffrage in the pamphlet, adding that suffrage and secret ballots were the only means by which the common man could curb the power of the upper classes.

Businessman Frost was not making too many friends among the class to which he had ascended. He was elected to the Municipal Council of Newport following the passing of Lord John Russell's bill, the Municipal Corporation Act, into legislature in 1835. He was also appointed magistrate in the same year, and Mayor of Newport the year following.

He attended the National Chartist Convention in 1836 where he became one of the leaders of the Physical Force movement. They promoted direct and violent action in support of their goals. His aggressive manner in pursuing the People's Charter brought him into conflict back in Newport. He was deposed as mayor in 1837. Home Secretary Lord Russell was so shocked that a magistrate was seen to be promoting violence that he had Frost's commission as magistrate revoked as well.

When prominent Chartist Henry Vincent was gaoled in 1838 for making inflammatory speeches, Frost led a march of 3000 protesters to demand his release. Arriving on 4 November 1839, the marchers discovered that more arrests had been made and the Chartists were being held prisoner in the Westgate Hotel. Frost led his march to the hotel, where they demanded the release of the Chartist prisoners. The soldiers in the hotel opened fire directly into the angry crowd assembled in the street. Twenty-six soldiers fired at will into the marchers, killing twenty men and wounding fifty others.

Frost, among other marchers, was arrested and charged with high treason. He was found guilty and sentenced to be hanged, drawn and quartered. His 'Physical Force' comrades were horrified

The Influential Ideas of William Cobbett

Cobbett was another champion of political reform, but unlike most he was a Luddite at heart, charged for seditious libel in 1830 for publishing his approval of the haystack burners and farm-machinery smashers who railed against the destruction of traditional English country life by the 'advances' of the industrial revolution. He wrote in 'Rural Wars' in *The Register* '... one thrashing machine takes wages from ten men; and they [the tenant farmers] also know that they should have none of this food; and that salt and potatoes do not burn'. On 17 February 1831, Cobbett was indicted for seditious libel.

Cobbett had fled to America in 1810 where, under the pseudonym of Peter Porcupine, he wrote with a pro-British pen. Having exhumed the remains of his political mentor Tom Paine from where he had been laid beneath American soil, Cobbett carried a bag containing Paine's bones with him back to England when he returned in 1819. Cobbett died in 1835.

at the severity of the sentence and called for an armed uprising but Chartist leader, Irishman Feargus O'Connor, a committed conservative O'Connellite, refused to raise an insurrection.

After a sustained public outcry, Prime Minister Lord Melbourne reviewed the sentences and Frost was sent for transportation to Van Diemen's Land for life. He spent his first years there working as a clerk and for the last eight years, before he was pardoned in 1854 on the condition that he not return to England, he was employed as a schoolteacher.

He emigrated to America with his daughter Caroline, who had joined him in Tasmania, before he was granted permission to return to England in 1856. Frost retired to Stapleton where he continued to write for newspapers and journals on his favourite topic of universal suffrage, to which he had added prison reform. He died on 27 July 1877, aged ninety-three years.

DESCRIPTION

OF THE

MANNER OF PUNISHMENT,

With the Instruments of Torture

INFLICTED ON THE PERSONS OF

JAMES SUDDS AND PATRICK THOMPSON,

SOLDIERS IN THE 57TH REGIMENT,

BY ORDER OF

GOVERNOR DARLING,

AT SYDNEY, NEW SOUTH WALES.

(Vide Parliamentary Papers, No. 56, July 1, 1830, and July 26, 1832.)

" The irons were made of round bolt iron formed into A COLLAR FOR THE NECK, with two pro
jections extending from a foot to eighteen inches from the collar, and weighing about fourteen or fift·en
pounds each."—Minute of the Executive Council of Sydney, May 28th, 1829.

London:

PUBLISHED BY BENJAMIN FRANKLIN,

No. 378, STRAND.

1833.

DARLING VS A FREE PRESS
The Terrible Case of Privates Sudds and Thompson

A free press is the most legitimate, and, at the same time, the most powerful weapon that can be employed to annihilate influence, frustrate the designs of tyranny, and restrain the arm of oppression
– Masthead of the Australian, *1824, published by William Charles Wentworth and Robert Wardell*

Hoping to be arrested, convicted and sentenced to a period of transportation, privates of the 57th Regiment stationed in Sydney, Joseph Sudds and Patrick Thompson, stole a bolt of calico cloth from a York Street store on 20 September 1826. It seems that transportation had lost its deterrent effect; most political prisoners were granted a 'ticket-of-leave' as soon as they arrived in the colony. Once off the government stores they were left to fend for themselves, and a lot did very well indeed, enjoying a better life than they would back home in Britain. The two soldiers believed that they too would be able to enjoy life in the colony away from the rigours of harsh military discipline.

They did not count on the ire of Governor Ralph Darling, who, dismayed at the frequency of such actions from among the lesser ranks, including one case of self-mutilation by a soldier who was seeking to be discharged and sent home, decided to make an example of the two foolish young men.

Even though a civil court sentenced them to transportation for five years, Darling ignored the bench. He overruled the court and directed that Sudds and Thompson spend that time on the roads, in irons, working in a government chain gang. After their sentence was up he ordered that they be sent back to serve out their time in the corps.

On Wednesday 22 September 1826 the two young soldiers were stripped naked in front of their former colleagues, outfitted in yellow and grey 'Canary' prison slops, and drummed out of the Regiment to the sound of 'The Rogues March'. They were then fitted with specially designed sets of manacles, leg and wrist irons, and iron collars with twelve-inch-long spikes that prevented them from even lying down. Unbeknown to Governor Darling, Sudds was already quite unwell and he could not survive the terrible privation that he was subjected to. He died five days later.

The newspapers attacked the governor and news of his tyranny soon spread to London. Darling could see his future prospects about to go up in flames, so he counterattacked. He was placed in an invidious position. He had already made enemies among the newspapers in the colony, insulting the publisher of the *Australian*, prominent emancipist William Charles Wentworth, describing him as a 'vulgar ill-bred fellow, utterly unconscious of the common civilities, due from one Gentleman to another'. Worse than that, he derided him for being an Australian. Darling had also run foul of Edward Smith Hall, publisher of the *Monitor*, who had come to Australia as a lay missionary and founded a local branch of the British and Foreign Bible Society in Sydney. Darling called him 'an apostate missionary … with a radical's faith in the perfectibility of Man, undiminished by the experience of the French Revolution'.

Darling levelled at Edward Hall seven charges of criminal libel. Hall was eventually caught out and imprisoned in 1829, but he continued to write his editorials from his prison cell.

Darling fought on. He proposed the introduction of a stamp duty of fourpence—a de facto licence fee—to be imposed on the newspapers. He was again challenged by Wentworth and Wardell. Chief Justice Forbes fought on behalf of the *Australian* on the grounds that the stamp duty was to be imposed for improper purpose, that the real reason was to price the papers out of existence rather than Darling's expressed intention of the creation of a fund to print public documents.

A technicality lost the case for Darling. The 4d Stamp Bill had not been properly certified and it could never pass into law. Darling was recalled to London in August 1831; Wentworth celebrated with a gala ball at Vaucluse House. The *Monitor* led with the headline 'He's off—The Reign of Terror is Ended!' The freedom of the press was ensured.

THE DEFEAT OF YOUNG IRELAND

After the Famine, Young Ireland in Exile

The Passion of Dan O'Connell

For all his life Dan O'Connell was a powerful influence on the lives of all who rose up against the British in the vain hope of achieving freedom for Ireland. For all those who followed in his footsteps and were transported to the colonies for their deeds–and a large number of them spent much of their youth in Van Diemen's Land–the passion of O'Connell for his homeland had been their seminal influence.

Also influenced by Thomas Paine, O'Connell was convinced of the need for religious tolerance, freedom of conscience, democratic reform and separation of Church and State. He sought to make his own contribution to the future of his own 'nation' –a free Ireland.

O'Connell's own history mirrors the history of revolutionary Ireland, his passion for his birthplace the spark that kept that flame alive. O'Connell had known both privilege and despair, immense popularity and imprisonment; he was Ireland's champion and yet his parliamentary manners seemed to belong to the past, and Young Ireland sought a direct influence on public affairs.

Dan O'Connell was born on 6 August 1775. He was adopted by childless uncle Maurice 'Hunting Cap' O'Connell and grew up in Derrynane on the Kerry peninsula. His childhood was a privileged one; although 'Hunting Cap' was involved in illicit importations with the French, and at times must have sailed pretty close to the wrong side of the law, the late eighteenth century was wonderful for adventurous men of property such as he.

Young Dan was sent to school in Europe, spending some time at Catholic schools in St Omer and Douai in France, this at a time when it was illegal to send young Irishmen to be educated abroad. He developed a distaste for violence as he witnessed the excesses of the French Revolution.

Dan O'Connell Memorial, St Patrick's Cathedral, Melbourne

Inspirational leader of a generation of Irish nationalists, at home in Ireland and abroad, parliamentarian Daniel O'Connell did not live to see his young supporters—'Young Ireland'—rise against the English and fail, exiled to the colonies.

For the sake of his failing health O'Connell travelled to Italy to seek restitution in the sun, but died soon after he arrived at Genoa, on 15 May 1847.

'My body to Ireland. My heart to Rome. My soul to God,' were O'Connell's last words, and in accordance with his wishes his heart was interred in Rome, his bodily remains carried back to the Emerald Isle.

(Author's photograph, 2005)

He returned to England where he studied law at London's Lincoln's Inn. He completed his studies in Dublin where he was called to the bar in the year of the great uprising of 1798. He saw his countrymen cut down in their prime, the forward march of Irish nationalism routed, faltering on the slopes of Vinegar Hill. The heroes of its revolution, Wolfe Tone and Emmett, were dead, and to O'Connell it must have felt as if the Irish heart had been broken.

O'Connell was a true Irish nationalist; he spoke the Irish language and took a passionate interest in Irish traditions and history. He became politically active, but the failed insurrection of 1798 forced O'Connell into hiding. He abhorred the use of violence and was against the use of revolution to achieve political gain, but still feared that the prominent role he had played in public affairs put his life at risk.

He decided to keep out of politics altogether and devoted his energies to developing his practice at the bar; before long O'Connell was the most successful barrister in Ireland. However, the reformist zeal would not let him be. In 1815, after he had been critical of the affairs of the Dublin Corporation, he was challenged to a duel by one of its members and to his dismay and eternal regret, O'Connell shot the man dead. O'Connell vowed never to take up arms again. His pacifist stance infuriated his supporters in later years and would cause a split between the moderates of his generation and the firebrands of the next.

O'Connell founded the Catholic Association in 1823 and through it sought emancipation for Irish Catholics. Parish priests were employed as recruiting agents, extracting a 'Catholic Rent' of one penny per month from their parishioners as they left mass. This provided the association with a fighting fund used to support O'Connell in his cause.

O'Connell was elected to parliament to represent the seat of Clare in 1828, displacing the entrenched Vesty-Fitzgeralds who had held the seat for generations. O'Connell had to wait until the Emancipation Act was passed through the parliament before he was eligible to take his seat. He became the first Catholic of his time to sit in the House of Commons.

In 1841 O'Connell was elected Lord Mayor of Dublin. With a slush fund of £48,000 collected from the penny-a-month parishioners he began to organise monster meetings across the country, with the aim of putting pressure on the government to repeal the Act of Union which had failed in its promise to guarantee equality for the Catholic Irish in a unified state with the English Crown. An estimated crowd of 750,000 turned out to hear the great 'Liberator' when he addressed a meeting on the Hill of Tara, a medieval hill fort that was the ancient seat of the High Kings of Ireland. The symbolism proved too much for Prime Minister Sir Robert Peel, who banned the next meeting, which was to be held at Clontarf. Although O'Connell pleaded with his supporters to observe Peel's ban he was arrested anyway, charged with conspiracy, sent to prison for twelve months and fined £2000.

On the day he was released, after serving only three months of his sentence, O'Connell was pulled through the streets of Dublin on an oversized carriage, seated on a large throne, the symbols of Irish nationalism—the harp, the wolfhound, the round tower painted on its sides—and scores of supporters battled to take their place in the shafts.

'Derrynane', O'Connell's house in Kerry
(Author's photograph)

Although his release was celebrated by his countrymen, the time for a new generation had come. At almost seventy years of age O'Connell's day had passed. Without him, Young Ireland, a group of educated middle-class young radicals ready for a fight, had reached their maturity. However, there was still much that O'Connell could achieve—without resorting to violence.

Still hurting from the loss of the American colonies to the republican forces of George Washington and conscious of the influence of American sympathies from across the seas, the English government did respond to the continued agitation from the Irish for political reform before they too rose in armed rebellion. After constant pressure from the parliamentary representative from County Kerry, Dan O'Connell pushed the Catholic Emancipation Act of 1829 through the English Parliament, removing the barriers that had precluded any Catholic from gaining public office in Ireland. The only offices still denied them were those of Lord Chancellor, Lord Lieutenant of Ireland, judicial appointments to any ecclesiastical court and, of course, monarch. While Catholics were then eligible to sit in parliament, the property qualification for eligibility of franchise was raised from 40 shillings to £10, which effectively excluded most peasant and rural voters. While the parliament had agreed to extending Irish representation, they had taken this measure, presumably, to ensure that only the 'right' class ever sat in the House.

O'Connell disappointed the peasant class by accepting these terms. The raising of the freehold qualification had cut the Irish apart from the political process. The majority of his supporters in the Catholic Association—who had tithed one penny per month to the coffers primarily to finance the relief of any fellow Catholics evicted by aggressive landlords or dismissed from their employment, but also to fund O'Connell in his fight for their rights—now regarded him as a traitor. It was to this class that the exponents of 'physical force' among Young Ireland looked for support. They believed it would be the peasants who would become their army of rebellion, when the time was right.

The Great Hunger

Other factors soon came into play, which caused great distress right across Ireland and forced the hand of the agitators desperate for reform.

In 1845 a fungal disease destroyed the Irish potato crop, causing widespread devastation. The failure of this staple crop, combined with poor grain harvests across England, gave British Prime Minister Peel the very opportunity he needed to bring about repeal to the Corn Laws. He was able to free up the market for the importation of foreign grain into England while also appearing to accede to demands made by O'Connell—and demands from the Chartists, the Anti-Poor League, the Ten-Hour Movement and the Anti–Corn Law League, all of whom had been demanding free trade for Ireland.

By the end of the decade more than 1.5 million Irish had starved to death. In 1845 Ireland's population had been eight million; by 1850 it had fallen to six and a half million. One million Irishmen, women and children had fled the country, most of them crammed on board so-called 'coffin ships' bound for the United States.

The English should never have allowed the Irish to starve during the great famine; Ireland was quite capable of producing enough grain to feed herself, enough wool to clothe herself, but her grain was bound for English mouths, her wool for English backs. The

Destitution in Ireland. Failure of the potato crop
Illustration published in *Pictorial Times*, August 1846
A family gathers outside their humble cottage around a pile of ruined potatoes.
The failure of the 1845 crop caused the deaths of thousands of poor country folk.
(National Library of Ireland)

Irish were left with the potatoes—or nothing at all. With the failure of the crop that is precisely what they had—nothing. Even though some attempts were made to assist the starving population, for every one ship that sailed into an Irish port with relief, six more carrying Irish grain sailed away.

To make matters even worse, a devastating storm known locally as 'The Great Wind' raged across the entire country, uprooting trees, flattening crops, unroofing cottages and blowing down walls, leaving destruction and desolation in its wake. No-one came to help the Irish; they were left to fend for themselves, to leave the country if they could afford a berth—or just simply left to die.

This situation was no longer acceptable to the radicalised members of the movement, and there were plenty of articulate, influential and energetic young men who were ready, and eager, to make yet another strike for liberty. For the next generation of Irish rebels their hour had come.

The Disaffection of Young Ireland

O'Connell had been a dominating influence on Irish affairs for more than half a century—he had been instrumental in arguing the Catholic Emancipation Act through the parliament, he had agitated for repeal of the Act of Union and put his name to the Chartist petition 'The People's Charter'—but the pace of reform through this eighteenth-century gentleman was evolutionary; the younger generation, those young men who were born of the nineteenth century, desperately longed for revolution. Whereas Young Ireland had once supported O'Connell, they soon abandoned his concept of 'moral force' in favour of 'physical force'. The devastation caused by the famine had forced their hand.

In his last speech to the House of Commons in January 1847, O'Connell pleaded for his homeland. He told the British Parliament that 'Ireland is in your hands—she cannot save herself', and was roundly ignored.

Four decades had passed since the defeat of the rebellion of 1798 and Young Ireland was ready to accept the same challenge. Impatient for the fruits of reform, Young Ireland determined to take the offensive against the English. Young Ireland proposed direct action; the time for moral persuasion had gone.

When England turned her back on Ireland and let her people starve, Young Ireland rose up against her.

The Radical John Mitchel

John Mitchel was born at Camnish in County Derry in 1815. He was educated at Trinity College and began his working life as a lawyer and journalist.

Disillusioned at the slow pace of reform, Mitchel broke away from Young Ireland and began to publish his own revolutionary paper, *The United Irishman*. Through its pages Mitchel advocated open rebellion against the English, and in direct contrast to the conciliatory arguments of O'Connell and his 'moral force' affiliates, through *The United Irishman* Mitchel promoted physical force—direct and violent action. He openly preached sedition to the 'numerous and respectable class of the community, the men without property'.

John Mitchel, the First Martyr of Ireland in Her Revolution of 1848
Engraving by N Currier, New York, 1848
(State Library of Tasmania)

It seemed as if Mitchel had no care for his own future, or that his desire to make his mark was so great that he was prepared to sacrifice himself for it. He must have been fully aware of the inflammatory nature of his ideas, and yet the English ignored him for quite some time.

Mitchel had lived all of his life in the cities. He had no real understanding of the lives of the rural people who he was hoping to influence, and on whom he pinned his hopes for a successful rebellion. His was an erratic personality: on the one hand he openly challenged the British, even addressing Lord Clarendon, the Lord Lieutenant of Ireland, as Her Majesty's Executioner General and General Butcher in Ireland, at one stage he offered to entertain any detective from Dublin Castle—the seat of government; in his office each day, providing he was sober and honest, and through him provide daily reports to the Government; on the other hand he expected that the time would come when all patriotic Irish would simply rise, as if by some unheard signal, that 'public wrath and indignation would suffice' to goad them into action. Even without any planning he believed that 'his Ireland' would rise as one and sweep the English from the land.

As political events unfolded across Europe the government began to take Mitchel seriously. On 21 March 1848, following an aborted uprising in Tipperary and Waterford, Mitchel, along with eight other leaders of the Young Ireland movement, were arrested and charged with sedition.

A conviction for sedition still demanded the death penalty, but that was not the worst of it; this meant hanging, then drawing and quartering. By the mid-nineteenth century even the English considered that to be a bit excessive. All were held on bail until the government could form new laws that could be used to convict them without subjecting them to such severe and improper punishment. The new Treason and Felony Act was passed into law in record time. The new Act had the statutory punishment of fourteen years' transportation. Mitchel was found guilty of 'compassing the intimidation of the Crown' and within the hour, not withstanding a rush on the dock to release him made by his friends, he was in chains and on his way to Dublin's Spike Island to await transportation to Van Diemen's Land.

After serving five years Mitchel contrived to escape from Van Diemen's Land. While he was on parole he took possession of a fast horse and prepared a dash for freedom. But before he made a run for the coast where some supporters had laid on a ship ready to ferry him away to the safety of the United States, Mitchel couldn't resist the temptation to flaunt himself before the authorities. He strolled as bold as brass into the office of the magistrate who had granted him bail and pronounced: 'I have come to tell you that I will no longer be a prisoner on parole, I take back my word.' He then turned around, walked back through the door, leapt into the saddle of his waiting mount and galloped off to meet the American ship.

Once safely ensconced in New York Mitchel wrote and published his famous work *Jail Journal; or Five Years in British Prisons* in 1854, which gave a first-hand account of the conditions of British prison life. He returned to his former career as a journalist and established a newspaper, which, for a man dedicated to the freedom of the Irish from British tyranny, took an unusual editorial stance in support of slavery. In his paper he even argued against the emancipation of the Jews. It seems as if Mitchel was not motivated so much by his love of liberty, but by his hatred of the English.

Mitchel volunteered for service in the Confederate Army during the American Civil War but was declared unfit for active service. He was posted to the Ambulance Corps but it is not known how much action he actually saw as he seemed to spend most of his time continuing in his position as a newspaper editor, where he showed no lack of his former zeal for upsetting his readers.

Mitchel was arrested after the Civil War ended and was imprisoned for aiding the Confederate rebellion. A deputation of Irishmen petitioned the president to release him from Fort Monroe, claiming that Mitchel was vital to the cause of Irish Freedom.

Upon his release the Fenian Movement sent him to Paris, where he acted as 'fiscal agent' responsible for transferring funds from the United States through France to assist the Irish revolutionaries.

By 1866 Mitchel was back in the United States where he planned to live out his remaining years; however, he was enticed back to Ireland to stand for parliament. After the initial success of his gaining office, he was disqualified from his seat. The contest was held again and he was elected for a second time. On his long-awaited arrival in Dublin the horses were removed from the shafts of his carriage and his supporters dragged it through the streets themselves.

Even then Mitchel was not without his usual drama. On 20 March 1866, he died before he had a chance to take his seat in the House.

William Smith O'Brien

The life of William Smith O'Brien runs almost parallel to that of John Mitchel, although it does appear that while Mitchel seemed determined to place himself in danger, Smith O'Brien sought change from within the system. Well, in the beginning, anyway.

Born in Dromoland Castle, County Clare on 17 October 1803, William O'Brien was the second son of Sir Edward O'Brien, Fourth Baronet of Dromoland. The O'Briens claimed to have been able to trace their ancestry back to the legendary warrior king of Ireland, Brian Boru.

William had enjoyed a privileged childhood, was fortunate to attend Harrow School in England and later studied law at Trinity College, Cambridge. Broadly educated, he was able to read and write in several languages including Latin, Greek, French and German, and in later life he also added Gaelic to this list. The only drawback for William O'Brien seemed to have been that he spoke with a pronounced English accent, which proved to distance him somewhat from his Irish contemporaries—although, when push came to shove, O'Brien was in the vanguard with the rest of them, and was duly arrested, tried, sentenced and transported along with all his mates.

After he had inherited the substantial country property, Cahirmoyle in Limerick, from his mother Charlotte he took her maiden name as well. Thereafter known as William Smith O'Brien he first entered parliament in 1828 as the Tory MP for Ennis, County Clare, a seat he held until 1831. He re-entered parliament when he was elected as the member for Limerick in 1835, holding this seat until his eventual arrest and transportation in 1848.

As Conservative member of the House, Smith O'Brien was at first opposed to O'Connell and his calls for repeal of the Parliamentary Act of Union between England and Ireland. Smith O'Brien believed that England would offer relief to Ireland while keeping her in the Empire. As the years of famine dragged on, and England simply looked away from the death, despair and devastation caused to his homeland, like so many others Smith O'Brien sought a better way. Although he was a Protestant he supported O'Connell in the call for Catholic emancipation, while at the same time he remained committed to the union of Britain with Ireland. In protest at the imprisonment of Dan O'Connell in 1843 Smith O'Brien joined with O'Connell's anti-union Repeal Association, becoming his strongest supporter in parliament.

However, disillusioned by the slow pace of reform, Smith O'Brien joined Young Ireland, and along with John Mitchel, Thomas Meagher and Charles Gavan Duffy, they abandoned O'Connell and sought a quicker path to Irish Nationalism—direct action.

Portrait of William Smith O'Brien, Irish nationalist

Lithograph by Henry O'Neil, 1848
Although imprisoned, the popularity and influence of the rebels such as William Smith O'Brien did not wane, and souvenirs such as this image continued to reach a wide audience of loyal supporters.
(National Library of Australia. NK6603)

To campaign for famine relief they formed the Irish Confederation in 1847, and as the pace of revolutionary fervour quickened, by March 1848 Smith O'Brien was calling for the establishment of a National Guard. Meagher believed, 'There [was] no solution save the edge of the sword,' and it seems as if Young Ireland was set to test the sharpness of their blade.

In July 1848 Smith O'Brien led an uprising at Ballingarry, County Tipperary, where he attacked the police barracks. In what became known as the 'battle of widow McCormack's cabbage patch', Smith O'Brien's rebel force was routed by a superior body of government police. They had risen against the government but their revolution was short-lived. The famine had left the Irish people in a dispirited state; years of defeat, rising after failed rising, with almost all of the national heroes hanged, drawn, quartered, disgraced or banished, the Irish people had little taste left for such adventure and little enough energy to even try.

Smith O'Brien was arrested, found guilty of high treason and sentenced to death. Immediately after the pronouncement of this sentence petitions for clemency were signed by more than 80,000 supporters from all across Ireland, Liverpool and Manchester, as well as from other parts of England. At the same time there were others who called for his immediate execution.

The sentence was commuted to five years' transportation to Van Diemen's Land. Although on arrival he had refused a ticket-of-leave and was exiled to a small cottage on Maria Island, Smith O'Brien lived comparatively well in the penal colony, separated from the common convict prisoners. After an aborted attempt at escape to America, he was transferred to Port Arthur where he lived in a cottage overlooking the main prison buildings. Smith O'Brien was released from imprisonment in 1854 on the understanding that he never return to his homeland. He lived for two years in Brussels where he published the book *Principles of Government, or, Meditations in Exile*, and in 1856 was granted an unconditional pardon and was able to return to Ireland. Although he continued to contribute to *The Nation* he took no further part in politics. At fifty-three years of age it appears that William Smith O'Brien was ready to settle into quiet obscurity.

William Smith O'Brien's House, Port Arthur
Political prisoners such as O'Brien lived independently of the
incarcerated criminals. Still subject to strict governance,
they were, however, expected to fend for themselves.
(Allport Library and Museum of Fine Arts, SLTAS)

He had fathered nine children, two born to Londoner Mary
Ann Wilton and seven more with Lucy Gabbet, the Irishwoman he
married in 1832. One of their sons was baptised in the Protestant
Chapel in Kilmainham Gaol while he was awaiting trial in 1848.

In seeking to improve his health William Smith O'Brien travelled to the United Kingdom but died at Bangor in Wales on
16 June 1864.

'Meagher of the Sword'

Thomas Francis Meagher managed to find himself in trouble on
both sides of the Atlantic. Born in Waterford on 3 August 1823,
Meagher was educated by the Jesuits, first in Kildare and later at
Stonyhurst College in Lancashire, England. He left college at the age
of twenty and was soon to find himself back in Ireland allied with
both Dan O'Connell and the Young Ireland movement.

The first time he came to public notice was at the age of twenty-
three, when he addressed a large crowd of O'Connell's supporters.
Meagher abandoned the great liberator's style of conciliation and

Thomas Meagher
After his first rousing speech to
a shocked audience in Dublin,
Thomas was known as 'Meagher
of the Sword'.
(State Library of New South Wales)

moral argument in favour of direct and violent action. Meagher railed at the crowd: 'Abhor the sword—stigmatise the sword? No my lord, for at its blow, a great nation was started from across the waters of the Atlantic—a crippled colony sprang into the attitude of a proud Republic—prosperous, limitless and invincible!' Meagher believed that Ireland too could emulate the victories of the great republics of France and America and take her place among these free nations in a new world.

After a visit to Paris in 1848 Meagher returned with a gift from the French, a tricolour flag of orange, white and green, which he presented to the Young Ireland movement—this the first fluttering of the Irish national flag held dear to the hearts of Republican Ireland to this day.

That same year he sought a delegation to Queen Victoria requesting an Irish Parliament be convened in the Irish capital, adding: 'If the claim be rejected, if the throne stand as a barrier between the Irish people and the supreme right—then loyalty will be a crime and obedience to the executive will be treason to the country ... If the Government of Ireland insists on being a government of dragoons and bombardiers, of detectives and light infantry, then, up with the barricades and invoke the God of Battles!'

In May 1849 Meagher stood before the courts charged with 'exciting the people to rise in rebellion', but luckily for him the trial was aborted. However, Young Ireland could not be swayed from its path to rebellion—and to certain defeat. The movement attempted an uprising against the English in July but it was easily crushed. In October Meagher was once again before the courts; this time a conviction of high treason was carried and he was sentenced to be hanged, drawn and quartered. When the sentence was passed the judge asked if he had anything to say. Meagher, fully aware of the fate that lay ahead of him, replied with candour:

> My Lord, this is our first offence but not our last. If you will be easy with us this once, we promise, on our word as gentlemen, to try better next time—sure we won't be fools, and get caught.

Representations were made on his behalf, and for all the other members of Young Ireland under the same sentence at that time, to Queen Victoria, who saw fit to commute the sentences to transportation.

Meagher joined William Smith O'Brien, Terence McManus and Patrick O'Donoghue, all bound for Van Diemen's Land. In 1852 Meagher managed to make his escape to America; landing first in San Francisco, he later studied law in New York and was admitted to the bar in 1855. He began a newspaper, the *Irish News*, the following year, in which he was assisted by members of the Lalor family of County Laois who had emigrated to the United States during the years of the famine.

When civil war broke out across America Meagher's first sympathies lay with the rebels of the south, but he switched sides after the battle at Fort Sumnter. Sensing which would be the winning side, he offered his support to the Union, claiming, 'It is not only our duty to America, but also to Ireland. We could not hope to succeed in our effort to make Ireland a Republic without the moral and material support of the liberty-loving citizens of the United States.'

Donning the navy-blue uniform Meagher fought with distinction at the battle of Bull Run. He was one of the few of the 69th New York Volunteers left standing after the dust settled on that bloodied ground. He organised the famous and feared Irish Brigade—The Wild Geese—and was commissioned Brigadier General, fighting with the Army of the Potomac. Meagher was ever in the thick of battle. He carried the Stars and Stripes along with the flag of Erin in the six famous charges of the battle of Fredericksburg in 1862, where the Union pitted themselves against the almost impregnable position of the rebel army. The determination of the Irishman caused a Confederate General to cry out above the din of battle: 'There are those damned green flags again'.

After the war Meagher served for a year as Territorial Secretary of Montana. He retired to live on the Missouri River.

He disappeared over the side of a steamer late one night in July 1867 and was never seen again. Meagher, who was suffering from a complaint of the bowel, had been drinking and needed to take a little walk in the dark onto the upper deck. It is assumed that he took one or two steps in the wrong direction, or tripped on a coil of rope, toppling into the water. No-one saw him go. A thorough search was made for his body but it was never recovered.

Terence McManus

Terence McManus was born in 1823 in Monaghan County. He became a wealthy gentleman after emigrating to Liverpool where he was a very successful shipping agent, earning himself, on average, £2000 per year. He was soon one of the leading figures in the Liverpool Irish community.

His downfall came after he returned to his homeland and became involved with Young Ireland. McManus was one of the rebel leaders arrested after the uprising of 1848, and faced execution alongside John Mitchel, William Smith O'Brien, Thomas Meagher, Patrick O'Donoghue, John Martin and Kevin O'Doherty. All sentences were commuted to transportation and the seven rebel leaders were exiled to Van Diemen's Land.

In 1851 McManus escaped to the California coast, stealing a passage on an American ship bound for San Francisco. However, he must have been one of the few emigrants to have failed in that bustling goldfields port.

Although he was considered to be one of the great 'rebel leaders of the 1848 rebellion' and, like all the others, was feted by the Americans, he died in poverty in San Francisco in 1861.

He had served with the Union Army, rising to the rank of Brigadier General. In his honour, his remains were carried in a military-style procession across America. Huge crowds followed the slow progress of his cortege as it made the long journey to New York.

His coffin was then carried across the Atlantic to Cork, and on to Dublin where a torchlight procession of more than 50,000 escorted him to his final resting place. It had been a long circuitous journey from humble beginnings to wealth and influence, exile, escape, glory, honour, humility again, then dust and ashes.

Patrick O'Donoghue

Born to hearty peasant stock in Carlow County, Patrick O'Donoghue was a self-made man. Self-educated, he gained a place in Dublin's Trinity College, which may have been at the root of his downfall. It seems that Trinity had produced more than its fair share of free thinkers, academic revolutionaries, radical journalists and red republicans. O'Donoghue fell under the spell of the Young Ireland movement. After the revolt of 1848 he too was sentenced to be hanged, but escaped the gallows to face exile in Van Diemen's Land.

O'Donoghue continued in his radical ways even in exile, editing the newspaper the *Irish Exile* while in the colony.

In 1852 he too escaped to San Francisco, after hiding himself on board the *Yarra Yarra* bound for the Californian coast. Like Terence McManus before him O'Donoghue had little luck in America and he died, impoverished, in New York two years later.

'Honest' John Martin

Protestant thirty-six-year-old John Martin was first imprisoned in October 1848, charged with treason for his opinions on the question of self-rule for Ireland published in the *Irish Felon*. The case did not go well for Martin; however, there were plenty who sympathised with him—even some within the court itself wanted to shake his hand:

> While I sat in Court there were several applications for me for my autograph and several acquaintances came to shake hands with me. Young Drinan of Cork whispered in my ear that 'it is not all over yet'—Well I hope not.
>
> On Friday O'Brien Meagher McManus and O'Donoghue reached Dublin and were brought to Queens Bench to assign their errors.

And on Saturday morning I had the privilege of seeing them all for we met at Mr Marques' office to be conveyed together in a very disagreeable jail van to Court.

Martin described the conditions under which the prisoners were kept, these same conditions that brought about the premature demise of Young Ireland's James Fintan Lalor:

> O'Brien looks but poorly—thin sallow and rather low spirited, or as if he were struggling to keep up his spirits. Meagher looks well, hearty, strong and in good spirits.
>
> McManus and O'Donoghue complain of suffering from the damp and uncomfortableness of their cell in Clonmel and say they were obligated to drink plenty of whiskey punch in contending against the rheumatic tendencies of their condition.
>
> Marques is disposed to be very civil with them all. O'B is lodged for the present in Marques' house. Meagher and the others have cells adjacent to O'Doherty [sic].

The following year Martin joined his fellow 'conspirators' on their way to Van Diemen's Land. He departed his homeland on 28 June 1849 on board the convict ship *Mountstuart Elphinstone*, bound for Botany Bay. As he sailed away, disappointed the steamer carrying Meagher and McManus had missed them, he wrote in his diary:

> Poor Ireland! What misery lies hid behind those dim headlands of thine! Will thy misery be still thy national characteristic when next I come in sight of these dear headlands? Am I ever to return to my country? Am I ever to enjoy the proud happiness of serving my wretched country?

Travelling as gentlemen prisoners, Martin, O'Doherty and Smith O'Brien enjoyed cabin accommodation. Martin even wrote in his diary that he was 'snug and comfortable', yet they were all still expected to pay for this privilege, even contributing funds to their own upkeep, a situation that caused them some concern after they arrived in Sydney.

The gentlemen prisoners were affronted when the medical authorities first demanded that they be inspected along with the common felons from below decks. Smith O'Brien proffered a letter he had from Sir John Grey, countersigned by his brother Sir Lucius Smith O'Brien, Thirteenth Baron of Inchiquin, Conservative MP for Clare, demanding that he not be subjected to any such physical interrogation. The other gentlemen insisted that the letter was meant to speak for them all, and as a result they were not expected to strip naked, as the lesser felons were forced to do, and the medical officer had to estimate their statistics at arm's length.

On arrival in Australia Martin was transferred to the *Emma*, a ship owned by an Irish merchant who had prospered in the colonies and had taken it upon himself to see that the 'fenian rebels' were offered an appropriately comfortable passage into exile.

Martin was pleased to note as they boarded the vessel that 'a conspicuous Irish Harp, surrounded by a wreath of Shamrocks, decorated her stern'.

All of the gentlemen were offered a ticket-of-leave when they disembarked in Van Diemen's Land, which meant that they were free to look after themselves, as long as they didn't try to escape. Smith O'Brien refused, and for his obstinance was exiled to Maria Island. Martin and Mitchel obtained a cottage at Fordell, where they lived until Martin was pardoned, Mitchel having already escaped.

Martin was granted an unconditional pardon in 1856. While waiting to leave from Melbourne he learned of a feud that had blown up between Mitchel and Charles Duffy, over Mitchel's attitude to slavery. Martin wrote:

> For a long time now I am subject to low spirits. I think the commencement of this state of mind was about the time of my quitting Australia in virtue of the 'conditional pardon'. While I was in Melbourne, waiting for the deputation of the ship in which I was to sail, came the news of the abominable quarrel between Mitchel and Duffy.
>
> About the same time or very shortly previous I had seen how Mitchel had excited the rage and grief of many thousands of his political friends against him by the course he took on the question

of Negro-slavery. Then was also the distressing subject of his escape from VD Land which was condemned as inconsistent with honour by some honest and friendly persons … I lost the confident hopes that I had rested on him.

I saw that his power for uniting and organising the Irish patriots was gone, and the haughty violence he was displaying and the wrong-headedness that I attributed to some of his acts made me despair of his ever regaining his power. Nobody else appeared to me to possess the qualities for a leader in our cause so eminently as Mitchel.

Living in self-imposed exile in France, Martin was frustrated with his inability to do anything to help his homeland from across the channel, and he returned to Ireland in 1858 on a mission of mercy. His sister-in-law, Millicent, had died after giving birth; his brother Robert, a gentleman farmer in Kilbroney, County Down, had succumbed to scarlet fever, dying while attempting to sign his name to a will that Martin had drawn for him. He was followed by their nanny, leaving Martin in charge of seven children who were all still under the age of fifteen.

John Martin died on 29 March 1875 and is buried in the family plot at Donaghmore Church in County Down. His tombstone carries the following epitaph: 'He lived for his country, suffered for her cause, pled for her wrongs, and died beloved and lamented by every true-hearted Irishman.'

Kevin O'Doherty

Dubliner Kevin Izard O'Doherty was born in 1812 and educated at Wall's School and studied medicine at the Catholic University. Like so many other young idealists who seemed determined to abandon any hope for a peaceful future, he was still at university when he joined Young Ireland.

Incensed at John Mitchel's arrest and imprisonment, O'Doherty established the *Irish Tribune*, which soon brought him to the attention of the authorities. Before long he too found himself in court, charged with high treason. Presiding at his trial, Justice Crompton snorted from the dock that he had 'never read any publication more

O'Doherty's cottage, Oatlands, Tasmania
(State Library of Tasmania)

dangerous, more wicked, more clearly designed to excite insurrection, rebellion and revolution'. O'Doherty was sentenced to ten years' penal servitude in the colonies.

He sailed for Australia on the same ship as Martin and the other rebels of the Young Ireland movement in June 1849.

Pardoned in 1854, he returned to Ireland via Paris where he married Mary Kelly, a popular Irish poet known as 'Eva of the Nation'.

O'Doherty finished his studies in Dublin, graduating as a fellow of the Royal College of Surgeons in 1857, and returned to Australia in 1860, settling in Brisbane, Queensland in 1865. He had a successful career as one

O'Doherty in Brisbane
(State Library of Tasmania)

of Queensland's leading physicians but before long he heard the call to the heady world of politics once again. He gained a seat in the Queensland Legislative Assembly and represented Brisbane from 1867 to 1873. He was responsible for the first Health Act in Queensland.

In 1885 he returned again to Ireland where he joined Charles Stewart Parnell's Irish Party and was elected to Parliament. Three years later he was back in Queensland where he lived until his death in impoverished circumstances in 1905.

James Fintan Lalor

> 'Who strikes the first blow for Ireland?
> Who draws the first blood for Ireland?
> Who wins a wreath that will be green for ever?'
> – *James Fintan Lalor*

The only confederate of the Dublin rebels who was not transported was James Fintan Lalor. He was the eldest son of Patrick Lalor and Anne Dillon, who had lived near Abbelyleix, County Laois, in Ireland's green and fertile heart. James Fintan was born on 10 March 1807. He was never a strong child, almost deaf and with poor eyesight; he also suffered from a congenital spinal deformity that had stunted his growth and left him almost crippled.

However, his physical shortcomings did not deter his strength of character, the clarity of his beliefs or the commitment of his political will. Like his father before him, James Fintan Lalor was a passionate advocate of land reform, claiming, 'The land of Ireland [was] for the people of Ireland'. He wrote openly in Duffy's radical journal *The Nation*, expressing views that may have been considered seditious. When Mitchel was arrested and transported to the Australian colonies in 1848, Lalor became co-editor and continued to write under the banner of *The Irish Felon*. Through the power of his pen Lalor was linked to the Young Ireland movement, although he was at times critical of the movement's disavowal of the great patriot Dan O'Connell's moderate constitutionalism, and their predilection towards direct and violent action.

A Punishment Fit for Traitors?

The statutory punishment 'to be hanged, drawn and quartered' was a terrible death for all convicted of high treason at the time that the sentence was passed on Meagher, Smith O'Brien, Mitchel, McManus and O'Donoghue.
The law demanded:

> That you be drawn on a hurdle to the place of execution where you shall be hanged by the neck and being alive cut down, your privy members shall be cut off and your bowels taken out and burned before you, your head severed from your body and your body divided into four quarters to be disposed of at the Queen's pleasure.

However, this sentence was rarely carried out by the middle of the nineteenth century. Most Englishmen had lost their taste for senseless barbarity; maybe they had looked over their shoulders at the revenge the French had taken on the aristocracy after their Revolution and sought a more civilised manner with which to deal with their own miscreants. The rise of republican activity and the popularity of its leaders may have meant that even the English were taking a more conciliatory line. For the rebels of the 1848 rebellion, their sentences were commuted to transportation.

When Queen Victoria learned of Charles Gavan Duffy's appointment as Premier of the Colony of Victoria in 1877 she requested that the records of all the seven exiles be examined, and she was shocked to learn of the success of the men who had once been sentenced to a terrible death in her name.

Patrick O'Donoghue: Brigadier General, United States Army.

Sir Charles Gavan Duffy: Premier of the Colony of Victoria.

Terence McManus: Brigadier General, United States Army.

Thomas Francis Meagher: Brigadier General, United States Army, and Governor of Montana.

John Mitchel: Prominent New York politician.

William Smith O'Brien: Pardoned and retired back in Ireland.

There did come the time, however, when James Lalor joined with his 'physical force' brothers in arms and faced the English army in battle. The devastation wrought by the famine, and the subsequent loss of more than one million lives to starvation, caused him to take direct action. He organised rent strikes by the impoverished and starving farmers, founded tenant-rights societies, and even devised plans for defensive stockades from which pike- and pitchfork-wielding farmhands could defend themselves against eviction by their English landlords.

He was arrested following an insurrection of Irish patriots at Clonakilty, County Tipperary, in June 1848, and although his poor health was almost shattered by a period of close confinement in Dublin's Nenagh Gaol, on his release he joined with the Fenian Movement and attempted yet another rising in Tipperary and Waterford in September 1849, where he led an attack on the Cappoquin Barracks. Due to a lack of support from the Irish peasantry, this rising was also doomed to fail, yet Lalor was satisfied that he had been able to fan the spark of revolution in Ireland one more time.

Three months later he was dead. The years of intrigue had taken their toll; imprisoned yet again, this time his confinement exacerbated his failing health and he died from chronic bronchitis on 27 December 1849. More than 25,000 people attended his funeral.

The translation of the Gaelic inscription on his headstone in Glasnevin cemetery in Dublin reads:

In loving memory of James Fintan Lalor.
Born 10th March 1809, and died 27 Dec. 1849.
A faithful (loyal) Irishman who gave his life seeking the freedom of our country and improving the state of the Irish people in their native land.
May his soul be at God's right hand.

WILD COLONIAL BOYS
Not Revolutionaries, Just Men Behaving Very Badly

Unofficial National Anthem

Transported convict John Donohoe was one of a very few cheeky fellows to have fallen from favour then have 'seditious' ballads written about him that commemorate his evil ways.

Dublin-born Donohoe epitomised the rebellious spirit of the disaffected Irish youth when he was transported to New South Wales in 1825, for life, convicted of the 'intent to commit a felony'. He was not in the colony long before the farm to which he had been assigned was attacked and robbed by a gang of escaped convicts known as 'Mr Jacob's Irish Brigade'.

Donohoe was no doubt influenced by the daring of his fellow countrymen and soon made his own escape into the freedom of the bush. With two other escapees Donohoe took to attacking wagon drays as they plodded their way along the Windsor road. Before long they too were arrested, and convicted of highway robbery. His two mates felt the noose around their necks, but Donohoe managed to escape before he was to face the hangman.

Once again Donohoe took to the roads, even robbing the flogging parson, Reverend Samuel Marsden, a man few dared to insult. Donohoe and his gang became 'Robin Hood' figures, robbing the

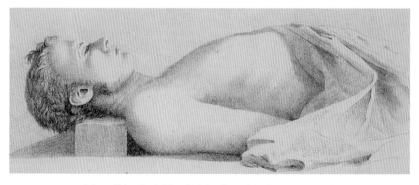

'The wild colonial boy', John Donohoe (post mortem)
Pencil drawing by Thomas Mitchell, 1830
(Mitchell Library Collection, State Library of New South Wales)

rich and 'giving' to the poor. They fenced their booty through a wide network of poor settlers and ex-cons who were glad to profit from their escapades.

'Bold Jack Donohoe' was a hero to the oppressed convicts; coming and going as he pleased, flaxen-haired and blue-eyed, he dressed in flashy clothes, smooching with any woman he fancied. 'Bold Jack' was the epitome of the Wild Colonial Boy. There were plenty among the free settlers and emancipated convicts who took great delight as he thumbed his nose at the authorities, and made the governor and his troopers look like fools. Few would have ever considered turning him in, even though the government had offered a 'pardon and passage' to anyone who brought about his demise.

It was one of his gang who turned Donohoe in to save his own neck. After a reward of £100 was offered for his capture he was betrayed by Jack Walmsley, who led the police to him in the bush near Campbelltown. Trapped, Donohoe cried out to trooper Muggleston as he levelled his carbine at him: 'Come on you effing buggers, we're ready, if there's a dozen of you …' and the trooper fired, one clean shot, straight through Donohoe's forehead.

'Bold Jack' Donohoe was so popular that within days it was possible to buy souvenir clay pipes in the streets of Sydney—with a tiny bullet hole in the forehead of the pipe from which smoke would arise. The ballad 'The Wild Colonial Boy' soon became Australia's unofficial national anthem. Sung to the tune of 'The Wearing of the Green', it was considered by the authorities to be equally seditious and just singing the tune could land the singer in gaol. However, the spirit of rebellion could not be stemmed; balladeers changed Donohoe to Doolan, or Donohoo or whatever pleased them, and they sang away, much to the displeasure of the governor.

Kings of the Road

Among the transportees were two classes of convict—the political and the criminal. The well-behaved politicals were treated quite differently from the common herd of street-walkers, pick-pockets, petty criminals, forgers and murderous thugs. Many were offered a ticket-of-leave on arrival, given preferential accommodation within

The Wild Colonial Boy (traditional)

There was a Wild Colonial Boy,
Jack Doolan was his name.
Of poor but honest parents
He was born in Castlemaine,
He was his father's only hope,
His mother's pride and joy
And dearly did his parents love
Their Wild Colonial Boy.

Chorus
So come away, me hearties,
We'll roam the mountains high,
Together we will plunder,
And together we will die.
We'll scour along the valleys,
And we'll gallop o'er the plains,
And scorn to live in slavery,
Bound down by iron chains.

At the age of sixteen years
He left his native home,
And to Australia's sunny shore
A bushranger did roam.
They put him in the iron gang
In the government employ,
But never an iron on earth could
  hold
The Wild Colonial Boy.

In sixty-one this daring youth
Commenced his wild career,
With a heart that knew no danger
and no foeman did he fear.

He stuck up the Beechworth mail
  coach,
And robbed Judge MacEvoy
Who, trembling cold, gave up his gold
To the Wild Colonial Boy.

One day as Jack was riding
The mountainside along,
A-listening to the little birds,
Their happy laughing song,
Three mounted troopers came along,
Kelly, Davis and Fitzroy,
With a warrant for the capture of
The Wild Colonial Boy.

'Surrender now! Jack Doolan,
For you see it's three to one;
Surrender in the Queen's own name,
You are a highwayman.'
Jack drew a pistol from his belt,
And waved it like a toy,
'I'll fight, but not surrender,' cried
The Wild Colonial Boy.

He fired at trooper Kelly,
And brought him to the ground,
And in return from Davis
Received a mortal wound,
All shattered through the jaws he lay
Still firing at Fitzroy,
And that's the way they
  captured him,
The Wild Colonial Boy.

the prison walls, allowed to move among their fellows after working hours and assigned to positions of responsibility, even to remote settlements, as long as they could be taken off the government stores and look after themselves.

The political prisoner rarely felt any guilt for his alleged crimes, which were usually against the Crown, usually of a seditious nature; however, if pushed, punished unfairly or mistreated by the

Bold Jack Donohoe (traditional)

In Dublin Town I was brought up,
  in that city of great fame.
My decent friends and parents
  they will tell you the same.
It was for the sake of five hundred
    pounds
  I was sent across the main,
For seven long years, in New South
    Wales,
  to wear a convict's chain.

I'd scarce been there twelve months
    or more
  upon the Australian shore,
When I took to the highway,
  as I'd oft-times done before.
There was me and Jacky Underwood,
  and Webber and Webster too,
These were the true associates of bold
  Jack Donohoe.

Now, Donahoe was taken, all for a
  notorious crime,
And sentenced to be hanged upon
  the gallows-tree so high.
But when they came to Sydney gaol,
  he left them in a stew,
And when they came to call the roll,
  they missed bold Donohoe.

As Donahoe made his escape,
  to the bush he went straight-away.
The squatters they were all afraid to
  travel night or day—

For every week in the newspapers
  there was published something new
Concerning this dauntless hero, the
  bold Jack Donohoe.

As Donohoe was cruising, one
    summer's afternoon,
Little was his notion his death was
  near so soon,
When a sergeant of the horse police
  discharged his car-a-bine,
And called aloud on Donohoe to fight
  or to resign.

'Resign to you—you cowardly dogs,
  a thing n'er will do,
For I'll fight this night with all my
    might,'
  cried bold Jack Donohoe,
'I'd rather roam these hills and dales
  like a wolf or kangaroo,
Than work one hour for Government,'
  cried bold Jack Donohoe.

He fought six rounds with the horse
  police until the fatal ball,
Which pierced his heart and made
    him start,
  caused Donohoe to fall.
And as he closed his mournful eyes,
  he bade this world *Adieu*,
Saying, 'Convicts all, both large and
    small,
  say prayers for Donohoe.'

Two versions of the same song.
In order to protect the liberty of the singer, the lyrics of 'The Wild Colonial Boy', page 107, are so changed that the original story (bottom) is barely recognisable. It is believed that 'The Wild Colonial Boy' was lustily sung in the bar of the Glenrowan Hotel on 27 June 1880, the night before Ned Kelly was captured.

authorities they were of a mind to take their leave of colonial society and bolt for the safety of the bush.

In the bush, bands of similarly disaffected, often brutalised, young men created their own society, a society with its own rules and with quite unlawful means of survival. They took to the roads, robbing the rich and giving to the poor—and looking after themselves, of course. They helped themselves to supplies from outlying homesteads, took the best and fastest horses and earned fanciful reputations among the poor and convict classes for their refusal to bend to the demands of their oppressors. The poor delighted to see the high and mighty brought down, humbled in the dust, their purses emptied of their gold. They revelled in the inability of the police and troopers to find, or capture, the dashing, daring 'Kings of the Road'.

There were also those who had genuine grievances against the law. Men who had suffered in a system that ignored the rights of the ordinary person in favour of the elite, denied any rights to the convict classes except the right to struggle and survive as best they could, just for as long as the elite were prepared to tolerate them.

Currency Lads at Large

Then there was a new generation of young Australians—'currency lads'—born beneath the Southern Cross and, unfortunately, drenched with a convict stain. These fit and tall, stringy, well-fed, muscular young men would never be considered the equal of a home-born Englishman—'sterling'—and the English did their best to keep the Australians in their place, at the very bottom of the social scale.

The authorities brutalised these young men. Ever on the lookout for any misbehaviour by the ticket-of-leave transportees, the ex-convicts, the Catholic Irish and their offspring were the first to be accused when anything went awry, and there was little love lost between the transported Irishman abroad, whether political prisoner or criminal, and the 'born-to-rule' Englishman swanning around in the colonies.

There was a time when the English, the squatters, having taken the best land, rarely bothered to fence the outlying edges of their properties. It placed the onus on other 'selectors', the poor dirt-

'Stuck up', a once common episode of Australian life
Hand-coloured wood engraving published in *Illustrated Sydney News*, 1870
(National Library of Australia)

farmers, to make sure that the squatters' cattle were not found in the wrong paddock. So many of the young men who fell foul of the squatter and the rule of English law were first incarcerated for livestock offenses. No doubt there were many who saw it as a bonus when the squatters' cow came calling, and many a good steak was cooked in a bark hut with the squatters' brand on its hide, but the Australian-born sons of ex-con transportees had little to argue with when they were bundled into court charged with cattle-stealing. Who would believe the story of a Catholic 'con' in the face of a gentleman with a fine English surname?

The first generation of native-born Australians had just reached its majority when the English came knocking at the humpy door, looking for trouble. John Piesley, 'Darkie' Gardiner, 'Bold' Ben Hall, 'Mad Dan' Morgan, Johnny Gilbert and Frederick Ward soon typified the scores of young currency lads who answered the Englishman's call with guns blazing.

Piesley was the First

John Piesley was probably the first of this second generation of Australian bushrangers. He was born in Abercrombie in New South Wales–a true-blue currency lad. He was first charged with cattle-stealing in 1834 when he was twenty years old. Piesley was sentenced to five years in Darlinghurst Gaol but managed to escape on the way down to Sydney. Free again, he stole some horses and was caught again, only this time he was sent to Cockatoo Island on Sydney Harbour. It was there that he met Frank Gardiner and when they were both released they joined together and took to the roads.

Piesley was not a violent man; he was tall, well fitted out with a grog-flushed complexion and never meant harm to any person, but was eventually caught out for killing a man in a drunken brawl. He was hanged in Bathurst on 23 March 1862. Piesley maintained to the last his innocence of most of the crimes laid against him; he said that he 'must certainly be the Invisible Prince to commit one-tenth of what is laid to my charge'.

'Bold' Ben Hall

Ben Hall was the son of transportees to Van Diemen's Land. His father had selected his mother from the 'Female Factory', a workhouse for female convicts. Ben Hall grew to manhood on the family farm at Breeza in north-central New South Wales and worked alongside his father in the Lachlan district. Ben grew up with horses and cattle and developed an astute eye for a quality beast–and a pretty girl. When his father went back to Murrurundi Ben stayed behind. He was smitten with Bridget Walsh, daughter of a local storekeeper in Wheogo. Ben took a job as stock-keeper for Bridget's father and within the year the young couple were married.

One year later Ben Hall leased a property at Sandy Creek where he soon built for himself a fine herd of cattle. Everyone in the district regarded young Ben Hall as a fine young man, a good stockman, good with cattle and horses; all traits highly esteemed in those days. No-one thought ill of him; even after the events of the ensuing years few ever changed their mind.

Ben Hall, 1863
Carte de visite photograph by
Freeman Brothers, Sydney
*(Mitchell Library, State Library of
New South Wales)*

While Ben was away mustering cattle Bridget ran off with former policeman John Taylor, taking their two young children with her.

Ben Hall was arrested by Sir Frederick Pottinger not long after. Pottinger had arrived from England to begin a long and moderately successful career hunting Australian bushrangers. In April 1862 Hall was charged with robbery under arms and thrown into Forbes lockup. He was released four weeks later due to lack of any evidence against him.

Ben Hall went back to his lonely farm and continued mustering horses but was arrested again, suspected of complicity in the robbery of a mail-coach at the Eugowra Rocks near Forbes. Pottinger was sceptical of the time Ben Hall had spent mustering and was convinced that he was part of Frank Gardiner's gang. No-one in the district believed Ben to have been guilty as they well knew of his dislike for the activities of Gardiner and his marauding gang.

Hall spent another five weeks in the Forbes lock-up and was again released due to lack of evidence against him. When he arrived back at his farm he was devastated to find his house had been burned down and his cattle and horses all lay dead, still in their yards, with no-one to feed or water them. Ben Hall had lost everything.

He took to the roads and threw in his lot with Frank Gardiner and his gang. Gardiner, Hall, John O'Meally, Johnny Gilbert and John Dunn moved with unbelievable speed around the Riverina. They ranged far and wide, from Yass to the Weddin Ranges. They displayed great horsemanship and knew where to find the best and fastest horses in the district—and take them.

The Australian Dick Turpin—Bushranger's Flight
Lithograph by JJ Blundell & Co., from a drawing by ST Gill, c. 1862
(Rex Nan Kivell Collection NK9841/7b, National Library of Australia)

Frank 'Darkie' Gardiner

'Darkie' was in fact a Scotsman. How he got his name is quite unclear, as he was of sallow complexion typical of the northern Celt. He came to Australia in 1834 when he was still a child and the family took up a farm near Goulburn in central New South Wales, right in the heart of bushranging country. Frank Gardiner grew up as an Australian lad, energetic, free to roam about the bush; lively lads such as he were soon to find mischief for themselves.

Gardiner was twenty years old when he was first arrested and imprisoned for having the wrong horse. Gardiner began his illustrious career on the diggings at Lambing Flat (Young) in the New South Wales Riverina district, where he set himself up as a butcher. His only drawback was that he never really bothered to own the beasts he was butchering. While this may have proved to be very profitable, it soon brought him into contact with the law. Before long Gardiner was patrolling the highways with a highly organised gang of young blokes just like himself. He became one of the notorious 'Kings of the Road'; a cattle-duffer, horse thief and highway robber, his were daring exploits as he led a gang of other likely lads and terrorised the roads of New South Wales.

On 15 June 1862, with blackened faces and scarves pulled over their heads, drawn back like nightcaps, the gang held up the Eugowra Gold escort on the Forbes to Orange road. They made off with a large haul of 2717 ounces of gold, £3700 in cash and several mailbags. The haul was worth £14,000 in total.

The police sergeant in charge of the escort was sure that he recognised the voice of the man who had given the orders during the attack on the coach. He was sure that it was the ex-butcher from Lambing Flat. He was sure that it was Frank 'Darkie' Gardiner.

Gardiner escaped from the district. He bolted for Apis Creek in Queensland, taking Ben Hall's sister-in-law Katherine with him. This was to prove his undoing. Kate wrote to her sister Bridget, who had left Ben Hall for ex-policeman John Taylor. She foolishly showed the letter to Taylor, who, one night, after a few drinks, boasted that he knew the whereabouts of 'Darkie' Gardiner, the 'King of the Road'.

Police followed Katherine's trail to Queensland and no doubt Gardiner was very surprised to see them. He was brought back to Sydney to stand trial, where he faced the next thirty-two years in prison.

'They'll Never Hang Ben Hall'

After the Eugowra robbery and the disappearance of Frank Gardiner, Ben Hall took over leadership of the old gang, and with Gilbert and Dunn attacked every coach and dray that came their way. Hall was regarded as a hero among the ordinary labouring classes. He made a mockery of the pompous baronet Sir Frederick Pottinger, who never even recognised the bushrangers at the Wowingragong races where he had entered in a gentlemen's race. Derided locally as 'Blind Freddy' because no matter how he tried he couldn't find the wanted men, the term 'even Blind Freddy couldn't find it' entered the vernacular in his dubious honour.

The government was so embarrassed by the inability of the police to apprehend Hall and his gang of highwaymen that they rushed the Felon's Apprehension Act through parliament and declared that Ben Hall, Johnny Gilbert and John Dunn were then outlawed, on 8 April 1865. One month later Hall was dead.

Ben Hall's statement to Inspector Norton:

I am not a criminal. I've been driven to this life, Pottinger arrested me on Forbes racecourse last year in April, and I was held for a month in the gaol, an innocent man.

While I was away me wife ran away—with a policeman. Well, a cove who used to be in the force. Then I was arrested for the mail-coach robbery and held another month before I was out on bail. When I came home, I found my house had been burned down and my cattle perished of thirst, left locked in the yards.

Pottinger has threatened and bullied everybody in this district just because he can't catch Gardiner. Next thing I know the troopers fired on me three weeks ago for robbing the Pinnacle police station, when I had nothing to do with that little joke.

Trooper Hollister has skited that he'll shoot me on sight. Can you wonder why I'm wild?

By Gawd, Mr Norton, it's your mob have driven me to it and, I tell you straight, you'll never catch me alive!

Betrayed by an old friend, blacktracker Billy Dargin, who had led the police to the bush camp where he had been hiding, Hall was gunned down in a volley of lead. He lay on the ground and cried out to Billy, 'I am dying! I am dying! Shoot me dead!' He had once vowed that the English would 'never hang Ben Hall'.

It was early in the morning, 5 May 1865, that the reluctant bush-ranger Ben Hall, a bright, smart, much-admired young man, who had never injured anybody, lay dead. Thirty English bullets had done their job.

A Pardon for Frank

A bitter argument consumed parliamentary debate in 1874 over the case of Frank Gardiner. The public had pressured the government to reconsider the harsh penalties handed out to a number of bushrangers during the years when public fear was at its height.

Many of the old bushrangers now appeared as likeable rogues, and there were plenty of bush ballads that celebrated them as bold, brash and daring folk heroes. In time the bushranger had passed from a hazardous nuisance into folk legend and the public were hungry for their notoriety.

Author Rolf Boldrewood added fuel to this fire of popular idolatry when he published his romantic fictional story of 'Captain Starlight' and the dashing 'Jack Marsden' when 'Robbery Under Arms' was first serialised in the *Sydney Mail* in 1871. The bushranger had at last become respectable, in the pot-boiling pages of the *Mail*, at least.

Henry Parkes, Premier of New South Wales, granted Gardiner a pardon in 1874. He was released on the provision that he be deported to China. He jumped ship in Hong Kong, where he boarded an American ship bound for San Francisco. Under the name of Frank Smith Gardiner established The Twilight Star, a saloon and restaurant on Kearney Street, which he ran until his death in 1904.

'Mad Dan' Morgan

Dan Morgan was arrested only once in his short but bloody bushranging career. In 1854 he was charged with sticking up a hawker at Barker's Creek, near Castlemaine, on the Mt Alexander diggings where he kept a butcher's shambles. He was brought before the nemesis of all unruly lads, Judge Redmond Barry, and sentenced to twelve years' hard labour.

Morgan insisted that he had been framed by a squatter who was not enamoured of the goldfields butcher but, like so many other 'innocent' young men, was sent to Pentridge prison to serve his term. Once inside, Morgan developed a pathological hatred of authority and reserved a special hatred for the Victorian police who had incarcerated him.

He did serve his time and was released on a ticket-of-leave into the Ovens-Yackandandah district in 1860. Little did the good folk of the Ovens know of the madness released unto them. Morgan began a bitter campaign of retribution against the society that had robbed him of his six years.

A large, brooding man with hawk-like nose and deep-set eyes, his hair falling in ringlets across his shoulders, Morgan looked the image of the pirate whose name he had taken for himself. His were senseless acts of violence, unnecessarily brutal, often murderous, yet he did enjoy some popularity among the settlers and old lags in the district as he set the authorities a pretty chase.

It was not too long before the law caught up with him, at Peechelba Station, twenty miles out from Wangaratta, where Morgan had bailed up the station and held the occupants hostage. Nursemaid Alice MacDonald pleaded with Morgan to allow her to attend to one of the children she heard crying in another room. He refused, so she slapped his face. Morgan was amused by the defiance of the feisty lass and let her go. She left the room and summoned a station hand who had evaded capture, who rode to a nearby station to alert the police.

MORGAN, THE BUSHRANGER. — SEE PAGE 10.

'Mad Dan' Morgan
(National Library of Australia Collection)

Morgan invited Mrs McPherson, the squatter's wife, to play the piano for him while he regaled his captive audience with tales of his life, how he was blamed for things he had never done, even speaking of his mother and father, who he said were still alive. He claimed that he hadn't slept for five days but remained awake all night with a cigar clamped between his teeth; he may have dozed but never let his revolver drop from his grasp.

At around daybreak Morgan stepped outside; by now a large number of armed men were waiting hidden around the farmyard. Sensing danger Morgan stepped back inside, drank a draught of whisky, then reappeared, pushing the squatter McPherson and three others ahead of him. McPherson turned to speak to Morgan and saw a gunman step out from behind a tree. The squatter stepped away from Morgan as a single shot ripped into the bushranger's back. Morgan fell to the ground asking, 'Why didn't you challenge me fair, and give me a chance?' Morgan lingered for six more hours until two in the afternoon when, pointing to his throat as if he were choking, he died.

A Spectacle in Death

Morgan's body was propped up on a wooden pallet so artists and photographers could record his corpse.

Then Morgan was mutilated. The coroner Dr Dobbyn requested that his head be cut off, as he wanted to study the skull. Locks of his beard and hair were souvenired. His facial skin was flayed from the skull so police superintendent Cobham could 'peg it out and dry it like a possum skin', and his testicles were cut off and made into a nice little money pouch. Morgan had hated the Victorian police, once stating that he would take 'the bloody flashness out of them' if they were to confront one another. They repaid him with as much disrespect as they could muster. Morgan was much feared in life and humiliated by the police in death.

Johnny Gilbert

John Gilbert was born in Canada of English parents and arrived in Australia at the height of the gold rush in October 1852. The family went first to the Mt Alexander diggings and John went to work as a stable boy in Kilmore in Victoria's north-east, on the road to Sydney.

The twelve-year-old lad, a long way from home, fell in with a group of con men who worked the diggings. Flashy young Gilbert did not escape the notice of the police. He was nabbed for horse stealing and sent to Cockatoo Island, where he met Frank Gardiner.

On his release Gilbert sought out his old mate from 'inside' and joined him on the roads. The pair were likable, cheeky young men; while they created a nuisance of themselves holding up the mails and robbing the well-to-do, they also created amusement for the settlers when they took over country inns and invited all the townsfolk in for celebrations, drinks on the house, displays of horsemanship and pistol shooting. They were admired for their larrikin spirit and derring-do, and for giving the authorities a hard time of it.

When Gilbert shot and killed Sergeant Parry in the Black Springs mail coach robbery the cocky young 'Canadian' crossed the line. Gardiner was back in prison and Hall was already dead; Gilbert and John Dunn were the only ones left of the old gang at large, and the government had also declared them outlaws.

He was cornered in the hut owned by John Dunn's grandfather, who had given them away to the police. Gilbert and Dunn escaped through a back window, but Gilbert decided to turn back and fight it out. Trying to cover Dunn as he made his escape, Gilbert raised his rifle to shoot at the police but his rifle jammed. He raised his pistol, but before he could get one shot away he was killed by a bullet to the chest.

Gilbert's body was taken into Binalong where it was exhibited at the police station for three days. Locks of his hair and shreds of his shirt were taken as souvenirs, before he was unceremoniously buried on a slight rise in the police station's horse paddock beside the Young to Yass road.

John Dunn

John Dunn was another one of the young Roman Catholic 'currency lads' who got caught up in all the excitement of a life lived free and easy on the roads. At the age of seventeen Dunn joined Ben Hall's gang and joined in the fun, mocking the police, giving them a merry chase and humiliating the author-ities. However, life on the run was to be short for young John Dunn.

Soon in the thick of trouble, Dunn was outlawed along with Hall and Gilbert after the murder of Sergeant Parry in the Black Springs mail coach hold-up.

Dunn had managed to escape from his grandfather's hut the day that Gilbert was killed by the police and headed north for Queensland. He was well away when two policemen were attracted to a campfire he was sharing on Christmas Eve 1865. Unable to account for his move-ments, Dunn sought to make a

Dunn, the Bushranger.
FROM A SKETCH TAKEN ON THE SPOT. — [SEE PAGE

Dunn the bushranger
Wood engraving published in *Illustrated Melbourne Post*, 23 February 1866
(La Trobe Picture Collection, State Library of Victoria)

run for it; he shot at the police, wounding one, and was shot in the foot in reply. Dunn was taken prisoner and brought back to Dubbo Gaol. He escaped from the gaol hospital; already quite weakened by his injuries, he collapsed in the bush before he had got very far at all. Dunn still managed to put up a good fight when the police came upon him at last, but he was overpowered and sent to await his fate in Darlinghurst Gaol.

He was convicted of the murder of Constable Nelson, killed the day Hall and Gilbert raided Kimberley's Inn in Collector. Dunn had shot Nelson in the stomach with his shotgun as the constable was running up the street to the inn. As the poor fellow lay writhing on the ground in pain Dunn coolly walked over to him and finished him off with two shots from his revolver in his face.

At only twenty years of age, John Dunn was set to hang on 19 March 1866. More than sixty people turned out to watch the last of his generation of 'currency lads', the last of 'Bold Ben' Hall's gang to take the drop into eternity. Dunn was left to swing for ten minutes before he was cut down and taken away to be buried.

Captain Thunderbolt

Born in Windsor, New South Wales in 1836, Frederick Ward was another of the Australian-born young men who fell foul of the law for his love of horseflesh.

Ward had been working as a groom, horsebreaker and stockman, enjoying quite a reputation as a jockey when he was first caught for horsestealing. He was sentenced to ten years on Cockatoo Island for the theft of seventy-five horses. Released after only serving four, Ward was sent back to the Mudgee district where he soon broke parole, stole a couple of horses and bolted. He was captured again after a reward of £25 was posted, and returned to Cockatoo with a further three years added to his original sentence. He got away again and simply vanished—until 'Captain Thunderbolt' appeared on the highways.

Like Dan Morgan before him, 'Thunderbolt' liked to work alone. Although several younger fellows were attracted to ride at his side, few lived to make old bones. Ward was at his best when he was alone astride a fast horse—and he knew where to find them. Ward stole the best and fastest steeds in New England; and some well-known racehorses were his animal of choice.

He had earned the nickname 'Thunderbolt' when he was a jockey—that was how he rode, 'like a bloody thunderbolt'—and he certainly made his mark on the New England landscape for his legendary horsemanship. He knew every road, every gully, every town and every escape route; the police just could not keep up with him. Thunderbolt was eventually caught near Uralla after a hawker rode into town boasting that he had just been stuck up by the infamous 'Thunderbolt', at Blanche's Inn just three miles out of town. Constables Walker and Mulhall leapt to the chase, galloping off as fast as they could, hoping to overtake him. Nearing the inn they noted two horses move away from the rear. One headed for the roadway, the other took to the bush. Mulhall went after the man on the road; Walker chased after Thunderbolt in the other direction. As Thunderbolt tried to clear a paddock at the rear of the inn Walker blocked his escape. Thunderbolt was forced into a swampy gully and rode his horse into the water.

Walker could see that Thunderbolt planned to swim his horse across and get away; Walker took aim and shot Thunderbolt's horse from under him. Walker then rode in after Thunderbolt; his horse slipped, tumbling him into the water as well. The two men fought hand-to-hand until Walker managed to raise his revolver. He pulled the trigger and a shot ripped through Thunderbolt's chest. Even though he was mortally wounded, Thunderbolt fought on until Walker swung his gun around and clubbed him. Thunderbolt fell back into the water, dead.

Thunderbolt was another one of these young men, these cocky bushrangers who—as bad as they were, as unlawful, cheeky and disrespectful of the authorities—were celebrated as folk heroes by the labouring classes whose lives were just like theirs, only without the excitement, derring-do or dramatic death.

NED KELLY, THE BUSHRANGER.

Wood engraving published in *Australasian Sketcher*, 31 July 1880
(Private Collection)

THE DAYS
~ *of* ~
GOLD

GOLD RUSH TO FEDERATION

THE RUSH TO DEMOCRACY
Old Enmities Foment Big Trouble on the Diggings

On the Australian diggings among the free settlers, runaway labourers, ex-convict vandemonians and patriotic English adventurers were also the citizens of the new republican democracies who had cast away the English crown, or cut off the heads of their own.

Colonial Governor Charles Joseph La Trobe feared the influence those who had no allegiance to the Crown were having in his newly separated colony of Victoria. He sought to find any means to prevent their enthusiasm for liberty, equality and fraternity being transplanted into his little corner of the queen's undemocratic Empire.

As soon as gold was discovered in Victoria in September 1851 the government joined the rush, only not to dig for gold, but to dig their

Swearing Allegiance to the 'Southern Cross'
Watercolour by Charles Doudiet, 1 December 1854
Canadian artist-digger, Charles Doudiet, was eyewitness to the Eureka story.
His primitive watercolours are the only images made on the spot and
provide the best record of the events as they unfolded day by day.
(Ballarat Fine Art Gallery Collection)

hands deep into the pockets of the miners in search of licence fees. Everyone on the diggings had to be in possession of a gold licence, whether or not they were actually engaged in digging. The government set the fee at the ridiculously high rate of £1.10 shillings per month. Few diggers could afford this fee and many took great pains to avoid paying. Armed troops, with bayonets fixed, roamed the diggings, seeking out these unlicensed fellows with manners that resembled the worst excesses of any military dictatorship.

The diggers protested at their treatment right from the very start. La Trobe responded to almost every attempt by the diggers to seek reform of the licensing system with a show of military might.

First Rush–First Protest

When Commissioner Armstrong rode onto the Ballarat diggings on 1 September 1851 the diggers showed their distaste for the licence fee by simply disappearing into the bush. This first, albeit silent protest was the beginning of three years of continued agitation against the government because of the fee.

When the commissioner announced to the diggers near Golden Point on the Yarrowee field two and a half weeks later that although the month was half over they were still expected to pay the fee, at half rates, he was met with a short but angry rebuke. One man jumped upon a stump and, waving his pistol in the air, declared that 'he would shoot someone, before he was satisfied'. The commissioner, unmoved by the angry mob, rallied his men and forced the diggers to take out the half-rate licence for the rest of the month. Herbert Swindells, the angry pistol-waving digger, was denied a licence by the commissioner and eventually had to leave the goldfields altogether as he was unable to buy the right to dig on any field.

La Trobe visited Ballarat and was shown a rich shaft by some over-zealous diggers who overplayed the good fortune they were having. La Trobe concluded that the Ballarat men were having so much success that on return to Melbourne he decided to double the fee.

The Great Meeting of Diggers

It had been only twelve weeks since the first rush to the diggings north of the Great Dividing Range when the first real protest against the rise was held in Chewton on the Forest Creek diggings. A notice went up across these diggings proclaiming:

> FELLOW DIGGERS!
> The intelligence has just arrived of the resolution of the Government to double the licence fee.
>
> Will you tamely submit to the imposition or assert your rights as men? You are called upon to pay a tax originated and concocted by heartless selfishness, a tax imposed by Legislators for the purpose of detaining you in their workshops, in their stable yards, and by their flocks and herds … Remember that union is strength, that though a single twig be bent or broken, a bundle of them tied together yields not nor breaks.

Meetings were held outside Captain Harrison's tent on the Bendigo diggings on 8 and 9 December, where the diggers resolved to 'stand by each other to the last'. After the *Argus* newspaper warned the government to prepare for a violent outbreak, La Trobe dispatched a squad of army pensioners of the 99th Regiment to reinforce the camp at Bendigo.

However, the old soldiers were no match for the 25,000 men now at Bendigo and La Trobe was forced to back down, leaving the licence fee unchanged.

More than 14,000 men gathered near the old shepherd's hut beside the track between Elphinstone and Forest Creek on 15 December 1851. Delegates were selected and travelled to Melbourne to petition the governor against raising the fee. La Trobe responded, as usual, by sending a further 130 troops to those diggings.

Journalist David Tulloch, who had witnessed 'The Great Meeting of Diggers', wrote:

> While jealous of their rights, and prepared to withstand opposition, [the diggers] were not desirous to evade any just claim of the Government, they were willing to submit to equitable taxation.

The Great Meeting of Diggers, 15 December 1851
Hand-coloured engraving by Thomas Ham, 1852
(State Library of Tasmania)

The resolve of the Great Meeting to simply refuse to comply with the new licence was to prove to the Government that although the resistance was unlawful, the Miners were not a demoralised and treasonable set of men.[2]

The police were undaunted by the protests; they continued to harass the diggers as they hunted for their licences, searching for sly grog, arresting diggers, destroying property and firing tents at their pleasure. The diggers, most of whom were honest, hard-working, decent men and among whom were quite a number of well-educated, professional gentlemen making a fresh start in the colony, resented the indolent young Englishmen strutting around dressed in their scarlet tunics trimmed with gold braid, their soft hands clad in delicate white gloves, so afraid were they of actually touching the dirt or a digger. It was the behaviour of these untrained young English 'popinjays' that infuriated the diggers the most.

While the licence was an irritant, the capricious, indiscriminate petulance of the military was unavoidable.

J Bonwick observed: 'Those were the dark days of the diggings, in which, under the supremacy of the squatting lords, [the diggers] were viewed as intruders in the wilds, tolerated because of their numbers, but not always treated with consideration ... That was the glorious era, when men were chained to logs for trivial offenses ... troopers have been known to follow diggers up, even on a Sunday, and compel them to show their licences.'

The Bendigo Petition

An Anti–Gold Licence Association was formed in Bendigo at a meeting held on the Camp Reserve in June 1853. Leaders George Thomson, Dr Jones and the Irish-American 'Captain' Edward Brown set out immediately afterwards to gather a total of 23,000 signatures on a petition to the governor, demanding reform. While they were at it they also added almost a complete copy of the Chartists' demands outlined in the People's Charter of 1839, a document that had been rejected time and again by the British parliament.

Unfortunately only a fraction of the petition was able to be sent to the governor; the largest collection of signatures gathered on the McIvor diggings is believed to have disappeared in the gold escort robbery near Kyneton in July, where two-thirds were lost. Only 7000 remained; these were mounted on a thirty-metre length of material edged with silken handkerchiefs and sent to Melbourne—but to no avail.

The Digger's Banner

Early in August 1853 a monster procession of diggers marched up to the Bendigo Camp behind the 'Digger's Banner', a new flag painted by Mr Dexter, a china painter from Devon whose time in revolutionary France had obviously filled him with a democratic zeal. The Digger's Banner led a long parade followed by the black, red and gold flag of the German revolution; a long, green Irish banner on which the Harp of Erin was painted; a French tri-colour; and the stars and stripes of Republican America. Mixed in among these flags

Commissioner's Camp, Bendigo, 1853
Watercolour by Ludwig Becker
Commissioner Panton is seen with two diggers in
the camp overlooking the Bendigo flat.
(Mitchell Library, State Library of New South Wales)

of revolution was the good old Union Jack, its dominant cross of St George reminding the diggers of the superior status of the English above all others within its Empire.

They had gathered at the camp to hear the result of their petition to La Trobe. When they were told that in response La Trobe was sending a further 154 police troopers to Bendigo they jeered; when they were told that the governor had objected to the number of German names on the petition they sent up 'three groans for old Joe' (a nickname given to Charles Joseph La Trobe). George Thomson reminded the crowd that although they had been disappointed by La Trobe's reply, he was there for 'reform not revolution'. When some hotheads among the crowd began to deride the Crown and mock the Union Jack, Thomson called for three cheers for the ensign. He in no way wanted to be seen to represent a seditious mob; he wanted to show the defiant patriotism of the British in the face of the 'red republicans', and not allow them to dictate terms in what he believed to be a tussle among loyal Britons.

129

La Trobe dismissed these diggers as 'agitators', 'people of no account', 'would-be Yankees' or, worst of all, 'foreigners'. He was to become convinced that the Germans, the French and the Americans on the diggings were at the root cause of his trouble, spreading their own brand of 'red republicanism' and advocating democracy among the loyal subjects of the Crown.

After another meeting of 10,000 men held in Bendigo on 21 August 1853, the diggers resolved to fly scraps of red ribbon from their hats as a symbol of their defiance of the government and its failure to respond appropriately to their petition. This became known as the 'Red Ribbon Agitation', or more commonly as the 'Red Ribbon Rebellion'. Diggers from across all the diggings from Ballarat to Beechworth soon adopted the red ribbon in sympathy with the Bendigo men, who resolved to pay no more than ten shillings when licence fees again fell due on the first of the month.

On 27 August George Thomson, Captain Brown and Henry Holyoake, a prominent Chartist who with his brother George had a profound influence on the Eureka affair a year later, led hundreds of diggers rushing forward to volunteer to be the first to challenge the government by making the ten shilling offer. Their plan worked. The following day La Trobe backed down again. In a fit of panic he considered abandoning the fee altogether but was persuaded to reduce it instead, creating a sliding scale beginning at £1 per month, rising to £8 for a full year.

The squatters who dominated the Legislative Assembly were unimpressed; they would have preferred to see a return to rule by squattocracy rather than this notion of democracy—where government had to take into account the wishes of the people.

The *London Illustrated News* reported: 'The Government of Victoria is humbled before a lawless mob.' When the squatters became aware of this report they determined to have their revenge on the digger rebels.

The diggers thought that they had won. Signs went up that read, 'Old Licence. You Dead', and they looked forward to a future without harassment. How wrong they were. La Trobe had not fully informed all of his commissioners in the field of the changes and

The Digger's Banner

Journalist William Howitt witnessed the march of diggers up to the Government Camp in Bendigo on 13 August 1853. He described Mr Dexter's hand-painted flag as showing 'the pick, the shovel and the cradle—that represented labour. There were the scales—that meant justice. There was the Roman bundle of sticks—that meant union: "altogether, all up at once". There were the kangaroo and emu—that meant Australia ... '

Oddly enough the authorities did not object to the diggers marching under this banner, which rather resembled the style of trade union banners commonly seen in industrial centres in England. It was to be a different story on the Eureka field a year later when armed diggers trained, marching back and forth beneath the simple, symbolic flag of the Southern Cross.

The contemporary rendering of the flag, shown above, is based upon William Howitt's description in his book *Land, Labour and Gold*, published in 1855.

Commissioner Wright went out placarding the diggings, stating that although repeal of the licence fee was under consideration by the government that the fees were still in place—and must be paid, in full.

The Victorian colonists had endured enough of the vacillating Governor La Trobe. The *Argus* ran a daily headline that read 'WANTED! A Governor. Apply to the people of Victoria.' In the heat of all this fuss La Trobe was recalled to London. He resigned his post and left for England on 1 June 1854. Naval officer Sir Charles Hotham was his replacement. A career officer, Hotham had requested a posting to the Crimea where he had hoped for fame and fortune. He was set for disaster in Ballarat instead.

'New-Chum Charlie'

At first the diggers were most pleased with the new governor—
'New-Chum Charlie'—and Hotham seemed pleased with them as
well. The diggings did not appear to be the troublesome place they
had been made out to be. Wherever he and Lady Hotham went they
were treated with great respect and enjoyed the hospitality of the
goldfields from Ballarat to Bendigo—and beyond. Even though the
digger leaders presented him with petitions for repeal wherever
they went, the vice-regal couple were still welcomed with open
hearts and feted at lavish banquets. Diggers even removed the
horses from their carriage as it crested the Big Hill, pulling it all the
way into Bendigo with themselves in the shafts. What fun was had
by all.

Just as La Trobe had made the mistake of thinking that the
diggers were all making easy money, Hotham mistook their enthusiasm for unswerving allegiance to the office of the Crown. He soon
set about to disappoint them all.

La Trobe had left the colony with a massive one million pound
deficit in the treasury accounts. In a bold attempt to balance the
books Hotham introduced twice-weekly licence hunts. 'New-Chum
Charlie' had set the traps against the diggers with a vengeance and
he was soon to see them rise up against him.

Rise of the Ballarat Miners

The Ballarat diggings were unique among all the Victorian goldfields.
Unlike the nearby alluvial fields where lucky diggers could simply
pick up nuggets from the creeks, the seams on the Ballarat field
lay deep below the surface, tracing the old gravelled river beds. It
required sustained effort, and considerable capital investment, to
be a Ballarat gold miner. The constant demands by an avaricious
government for the payment of the £1 monthly licence fee was at
times more than a Ballarat man could afford, but the government
remained persistent in its demands for the monthly fee.

Diggers avoided the troops as they swept across the fields on their
licence hunts. The unlucky digger who was caught unawares without
a licence was sent to the log lockup to await rough justice—sometimes

a wait of a week or two chained to a fallen log in all weathers, until a magistrate could preside over his 'kangaroo court'; sometimes a £5 fine, which few could pay. If not, it was then off to work on the roads in the government chain gang.

For men such as Irishman Peter Lalor, the treatment of the ordinary working digger at the hands of the capricious English military troopers, the rough justice meted out by the unruly goldfields police and the determined execution of the governor's decrees by corrupt magistrates soon brought to mind something that he had seen all too often before, and something he had travelled halfway across the globe to escape.

In the wide-open vista of the Australian bushland, under bright blue skies the likes of which the diggers had never seen in their homeland, freedom was in their grasp, but the English legislated to deny them their rights as men—again and again.

The Californians in Ballarat, and there were many veterans of the Sacramento rush, had no love for the English Queen; neither did the French among them. There were also Scottish Chartists; Bolshevik Jews; Republican Austrians, who had escaped the bloodletting of their own fractured Empire; the firebrand Italian Raffaello, who later joined with Garibaldi in the fight for a unified Italian Republic. And then there were the Irish, boatloads of them, unable to throw off generations of resentment for the English Crown—or reverence for the Crown Prince of Rome. In Ballarat, on the Eureka field, the Catholics were in the majority and they soon came together in opposition to their old foe. Ballarat was to become a melting pot of sedition, and Peter Lalor was drawn into its fire.

The Death of Scobie

Three events, one after the other, lit the spark that engulfed Eureka.

The first occurred on the night of 7 October 1854. Peter Martin and James Scobie, two Scottish diggers, had spent the night celebrating their reunion on the diggings. Hoping to continue their drunken revelry, they rapped at the door of James Bentley's Eureka Hotel, a notorious rough-house close to the Eureka field.

Bentley refused them entry and, having shouted some indelicate opinions of Bentley's wife, the Scotsmen staggered off into the dark. Angered by the uncalled-for insult, Bentley and a few of his henchmen crept after them and belted Scobie over the head with a shovel, while kicking Peter Martin to the ground. Martin managed to scramble away but Scobie was already dead.

Bentley was arrested, but an open verdict was returned and he was set free. Everyone knew that he had been in league with the commissioners of the camp, having managed to secure his licence for the hotel through the help of Police Magistrate John D'Ewes, and D'Ewes was not going to see Bentley blamed for Scobie's murder. The ex-convict publican had been profitably protecting the magistrate's investment in his Eureka Hotel.

The second event occurred on 10 October 1854 when troopers arrested Johann Gregorious, the crippled servant of Father Patrick Smyth, the popular priest whose canvas tent church St Alipius was at the centre of the Eureka field, and at the centre of the predominately Irish community on the Ballarat diggings. Gregorious was arrested for being without a licence, when everyone knew that as servant of the priest he had never needed one. He was fined £5; then the charge was withdrawn; then he was fined again for attacking the trooper, a charge that was quite ridiculous. Father Smyth was forced to pay this £5 fine. The Irishmen were incensed; they saw this insult to their priest through the injustice to his servant as an attack on them all, an attack on the Church—and more importantly an attack on the Irish nation.

The Fire at Bentley's Hotel

The third incident occurred one week later, on 17 October. Diggers gathered outside the hotel where they demanded Bentley's arrest. Tempers were raised and a fight broke out; a young lad picked up a stone and smashed the lamp above Bentley's front door.

The shattering of the glass was the catalyst that set the crowd ablaze. Before long the hotel itself was in flames. Three diggers were arrested and sent to Melbourne to stand trial. Bentley was re-arrested, re-tried for Scobie's murder and ultimately sent to prison,

Eureka Riot (Burning of Bentley's Eureka Hotel)
Watercolour by Charles Doudiet, 17 October 1854
(Ballarat Fine Art Gallery Collection)

convicted of manslaughter. But it was too late; the fire in the rebel heart had been ignited, at last, in Ballarat.

On 16 November Hotham established a royal commission to examine the unrest on the diggings. Although he was informed that there was widespread corruption, particularly on the Ballarat goldfield, he responded by sending a further 450 foot soldiers to Ballarat. Colonial Secretary Foster recommended that the troops of the 12th Regiment be placed on immediate stand-by just in case they were needed to quell an insurrection.

'Moral force' advocates John Basson Humffray, editor of the *Digger's Advocate*, George Black, and the impatient Scottish Chartist Thomas Kennedy were sent to Melbourne to demand the release of the three diggers arrested for the fire at the Eureka Hotel. While Hotham may have been prepared to listen to their grievances he baulked at the word 'demand' and sent them away empty-handed. Before they had even set off on their return journey to Ballarat,

Governor Hotham had dispatched the 40th Regiment who, on 28 November, marched onto the diggings with their swords drawn, along with the 12th Regiment, who were attacked as they marched through the Eureka field by diggers lining the roadway.

Chairman of the Ballarat Reform League Timothy Hayes called for a 'Monster Meeting' on 29 November, where more than 10,000 diggers were addressed for the first time by Peter Lalor. At this meeting the diggers agreed not to show their licenses when asked, forcing the government to arrest them all, and by sheer weight of numbers hoping to force the government to reconsider the licence fee. At the end of the meeting the 'red republican' German Frederick Vern, on consigning his own licence to the flames of a bonfire declared:

> That this meeting, being convinced that the obnoxious fee is an imposition and an unjustifiable tax on free labour, pledges itself to take immediate steps to abolish the same by at once burning all their licences; that in the event of any party being arrested for having no licence, that the united people will, under all circumstances, defend and protect them.

The diggers were openly challenging the government to confront them and to give them an excuse to fight for their rights as free men in an English colony. Not everyone was happy with the way things were heading. The 'physical force' element was now in the ascendancy; the 'moral force' advocates were rapidly losing their influence. In what seemed to be a reprise of the decline of the influence of O'Connell in the face of an anxious Young Ireland, the Ballarat Catholics were now running towards rebellion.

Swearing Allegiance

Just before noon on 29 November the troopers swept out of the camp and hit the Gravel Pits at Eureka with a vengeance. Unbeknownst to them at the time, this was to be the last big digger hunt. It was a filthy, hot and dusty summer's day; scorching winds swirled around the digger's camp. Diggers who refused to show their licences were arrested and driven away to 'the logs'. When Commissioner Robert

Flag of the Southern Cross

The flag of the Southern Cross flew over the Eureka goldfield for the first time on 30 November 1854.

Only three days later it was torn from its crude staff, trampled and bayonetted into the ground. Trooper John King grabbed the tattered blue rag and stuffed it down the front of his tunic. It stayed in his family for years until it was given over to the Ballarat Fine Art Gallery for safekeeping in the 1930s.

The flag is believed to have been designed by Canadian stockader Captain Charles Ross, who was mortally wounded in the battle. Some suggest that the inspiration for the flag came from John Wilson, Inspector of Works for the Police, a 'government' man sympathetic to the diggers who had been responsible for cutting the twenty-four-metre flagpole from a nearby swamp. Wilson had stepped outside the tent where a meeting was being held planning the following day's 'Monster Meeting'; looking up into the sky he exclaimed, 'I've got it ... There, the Southern Cross, five white stars on a blue field.'

The flag was sewn together using a 'petticoat' length of fine blue wool; variations in the stitching suggest that it was constructed by three different women. Two of them, Anastasia Withers and Anne Duke, were the wives of diggers who were in the stockade on that ill-fated Sunday morning.

Today, this iconic flag still hangs in the Ballarat Fine Art Gallery. It is ironic that the gallery stands on the very spot in Ballarat where the police were stationed in 1854, and from where they crept as silent as the grave towards the Eureka field in the still hours before the dawn on 3 December 1854.

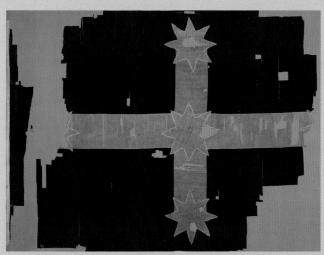

The flag is displayed in the Ballarat Art Gallery.
(Ballarat Fine Art Gallery Collection)

Rede saw the Eureka mob running towards him he quickly read the Riot Act, his voice trailing off into the wind as he called for reinforcements. When he spied John Basson Humffray he shouted out, 'See now the consequences of your agitation.' Humffray replied, 'See now the consequences of impolitic coercion.' The diggings were at tinder point and neither side seemed prepared to back away from the conflagration.

Another 'Monster Meeting' was called for 30 November at Bakery Hill, halfway between the Camp and the Eureka diggings. In the absence of any other leaders on that day Peter Lalor stepped up to take charge of the diggers, who were gathering as if by some unseen command.

He mounted a stump in the centre of a clearing where the blue standard of the Southern Cross was set flying in the hot wind twenty-four metres in the air. He placed his hand over his heart and proclaimed the digger's oath: 'We swear by the Southern Cross to stand by each other, and defend our rights and our liberties.' The men knelt before him, and with hands over their hearts, they swore allegiance to the bright blue flag.

For the next few days the diggers constructed a crude stockade on the highest ridge of the Eureka field, which was flanked by the track to Melbourne. Carts were upturned, fallen trees and logs levered into position and pit slabs piled in a disorderly fashion to create a barrier difficult to attack and easy to defend. They fashioned pikes on longstaffs, prepared ammunition and paraded back and forth in quasi-military style. There were about 1000 men training inside the stockade while others scoured the district seizing weapons, leaving promissory notes signed on behalf of the 'Comtee'.

Rede reported to Hotham that 'the most determined man and the greatest scoundrels in the colony were in the stockade'; that Hotham should move quickly to crush them where they stood, for the 'future welfare of the colony depends on the crushing of this movement in such a manner that it may act as a warning.'

Men from neighbouring goldfields marched over to Ballarat but few joined in the stockade. The Creswick men who had marched over the ranges turned back when they discovered there was little

The Storming of the Eureka Stockade, 3 December 1854
Watercolour by JB Henderson
(Dixson Galleries, State Library of New South Wales)

food to be had and no grog at all in the stockade. It was rumoured that an army of men from Bendigo were on their way but they didn't even have time to depart before it was all over.

Everything was going to plan until Peter Lalor made the mistake of issuing the password 'Vinegar Hill'. The majority of the Englishmen inside the stockade walked away, convinced that Lalor had made it an Irish fight, and they did not want to be involved in any battle fought on those sectarian grounds.

The Attack

Foolishly believing that no English army would attack on the Sabbath, the diggers within the stockade spent the night of Saturday 2 December around the campfire; nobblers were drunk and quite a number retired to their tents outside the barricade. Only about 250 men were left sleeping inside when Captain Thomas and the army of the 12th and 40th Regiments attacked just before dawn on Sunday morning.

1.Hayes.   2. Campbell.   3. Raphele.   4. Sorenson.   5. Manning.   6. Phelan.   7. Dignum.   8. Joseph.   9. Beattie.   10. Molloy.   11. Jan Vannick.   12. Tuhey.   13. Read.

'Rebels' in the dock

Wood engraving by Samuel Calvert, published in *The Age*, 10 March 1855
The Eureka 'rebels' are all arraigned in the dock during the treason trials that
caused Governor Hotham so much heartburn. They are seated from the left:
Timothy Hayes, James McFie Campbell; Raffaello Carboni; Jacob Sorenson;
John Manning; John Phelan; Thomas Dignum; John Joseph; James Beattie;
William Molloy; Jan Vannick; Michael Tuhey and Henry Read.
(La Trobe Picture Collection, State Library of Victoria)

A shot rang out in the darkness when the army had got to within
about 100 metres of the barricade. Captain Thomas cried out to
the bugler to sound the call to skirmishing order as he yelled, 'The
Queen's troops have been fired upon. Fire!' Then the troopers scrambled up the rise to breach the stockade. The short but bloody battle
lasted only twenty minutes. Fourteen diggers lay dead; many more
wounded lay among them. Only one trooper was killed during the
battle. Twenty-one-year-old Belfast-born Private Michael Roney
was killed by a shot to the head.

Ten more men died later that day. Captain Wise, who led the 40th
Regiment, had been shot in the legs in the first rush to the barricade;
he died several days later from his wounds. Canadian 'rebel' Captain
Charles Ross, who was felled by a shot to the groin, died later that
day in the Star Hotel. Lalor had been standing on top of some logs
with his pistol in his hand when his arm was shattered by a musket
ball. He dropped to the ground where he was secreted beneath
a pile of slabs until the smoke had cleared from the battleground.

He was taken to Father Smyth's presbytery later in the day, where his mutilated arm was amputated. Anastasia Hayes assisted the doctor on that fateful day.

The troopers scoured the field, arresting more than 100 men and throwing them into the log lockup at the camp. Only thirteen of these men were brought to trial in Melbourne, charged with treason, including English digger James Beattie; Jamaican-born James McFie; red-bearded Italian revolutionary Raffaello Carboni, who had hid up the chimney of his hut outside the barricade during the battle; pikeman Thomas Dignum, from Sydney; Timothy Hayes, chairman of the Ballarat Reform League, who was not even in the stockade at the time of the battle; African American New Yorker John Joseph; Irish digger, journalist John Manning; William Molloy; Irish digger John Phelan, who had been a neighbour of the Lalors in Ireland; Henry Reid; Jacob Sorenson; and Irish digger Michael Touhey from County Clare.

The trials began on 22 February 1855. Justice Sir Redmond Barry, a loyalist, Protestant Orangeman from Dublin who had little time for the poorly behaved Catholic Irishman abroad, supervised the trials and sat as judge on Timothy Hayes. One by one the Eureka 'rebels' stood before the bench; each man was acquitted until the court advised Hotham that it would be sensible to abandon the treason trials altogether in the face of a humiliating defeat for the government. Hotham expostulated that just because the jury would not do their duty, he could see no reason why he should not do his. The trials began again on 27 March, when all remaining prisoners were acquitted. No jury in the colony would have sent any of their fellow colonists to suffer the punishment still on the statutes for the crime of treason. If Hotham had sought a lesser charge, with less exacting punishment, he may have reached a more satisfactory outcome—for him anyway.

Lalor remained in hiding in Geelong until a general amnesty was announced and he could show his face in the open again without fear of capture. He was in an invidious position; a reward of £500 for his arrest was still on offer for some months after the rest of the rebels had been set free.

Hotham only lived another year. He suffered an attack of diarrhoea on 22 December, had several epileptic fits, then collapsed into a coma and died just after noon on 31 December 1855. The prospect of Lalor and Humffray in the House, both were elected to parliament in 1855, must have proven too much for him to bear.

The Lalors of County Laois

Patriarch Patrick 'Honest Pat' Lalor was a gentleman farmer at Tenakill, near Abbeyleix in Laois (Leix) County, sixty miles from Dublin. Following the passing of the Catholic Emancipation Act of 1827 Lalor was elected to Parliament in 1833, the first Catholic MP for Leix since the reign of James II, and was instrumental in the abolition of the Tithe system, which had impoverished thousands of poor Irish farmers. 'Honest Pat' and Anne Dillon married in 1806 and produced twelve children; ten boys and two girls. Their eldest son James Fintan Lalor, born in 1807, was to write his name in the history of Ireland's disastrous uprising of 1848–49; the youngest, Peter Fintan, in the history of the Australian colonies' second rebellion of united Irishmen, at the battle of the Eureka Stockade in 1854.

Both men were to make a profound mark on revolutionary politics on both sides of the world—James, whose demands for land reform as an influential journalist were promoted in the radical journal *The Nation*; and Peter, as committee member of the Ballarat Reform League, and after the battle of Eureka and the subsequent acquittal of the charge of treason laid against the stockaders, as representative of the Ballarat miners in the Victorian Legislative Assembly.

Peter's elder brother Richard, who had sailed with him on board the *Scindian* in 1852 to join the Australian gold rush, returned to Ireland at his ailing father's request. Richard also served as the representative for Queen's County in the parliament from 1880 to 1892.

Peter had trained as a civil engineer at Trinity College in Dublin once, it seems, a breeding ground of radicals, democrats, agitating politicians and Irish nationalists.

Most of the rest of the family had emigrated to America during the famine, a time when England had deserted them all and mother Ireland could no longer sustain them. For the youngest of the Lalors it must have seemed that on the Ballarat goldfields the same old story was beginning all over again. For Peter Lalor his was a personal history from which he could not escape.

Peter Lalor

Peter Lalor was an enigma. While he is mostly remembered for the prominent role he had played in the battle of the Eureka Stockade, it could be assumed that he was a dyed-in-the-wool 'red' revolutionary. However, the stance he often took in both political and public life after the years of struggle showed him to be anything but a rebel.

Fellow emigrant William Craig, who had also been a passenger on the *Scindian*, recalled of Lalor, 'He appeared to have made up his mind before he left

PETER LALOR

Peter Lalor

It is a strange world where once these men all stood together against the government, when in government themselves Eureka leader Peter Lalor distanced himself from his former allies. A digger turned capitalist, Lalor sought to deny that he was ever a rebel. He insisted that his fight had been for justice, not for reform, and often stood alone in the House, an enigma without a cause.
(National Library of Australia)

to engage in politics in the land of his adoption.' When they were once discussing Irish affairs Lalor said that, once in Victoria, 'I intend to have a voice in government before two years are over. The Lalors have always had a weakness for politics. My father sat in the British Parliament for Queen's County, and I intend to sit in the Victorian Parliament after I find out where improvements are needed.' Craig said that Lalor 'never tired of descanting upon the wrongs of Ireland' and that he believed in 'the use of physical force for redressing the wrongs of his native country'.[3]

On his arrival in Port Phillip Lalor put his energies to the task of railway engineer on the construction of the new Melbourne to Geelong railway, but he soon answered the call to the Ballarat diggings.

Yet he kept away from the constant argument over government taxation and the treatment of the diggers by the goldfields police, until his hand was forced by the clash of circumstance. Lalor was an Irish Catholic digger working among other Irish Catholic diggers who dominated the population on the Eureka goldfield. At the centre of the Catholic community stood the large tent church St Alipius. Father Patrick Smyth carefully nurtured his flock and they were faithful to him and to the church. When Smyth was insulted over the arrest of his servant, Johann Gregorious, the Catholic community felt insulted along with him. When Scottish digger James Scobie, who had his tent beside Lalor on the Eureka field, was brutally murdered by the liquor-licensing commissioner's mate James Bentley, Lalor had lost a friend. When he stood in front of thousands of his fellow diggers who had gathered at Bakery Hill on 30 November, in the absence of any other leaders of the Ballarat Reform League, Lalor heard the call, stepped forward, and stepped into history. Lalor recalled:

I looked around me; I saw brave and honest men, who had come thousands of miles to labour for independence. I knew that hundreds were in great poverty, who would possess wealth and happiness if allowed to cultivate the wilderness that surrounded us. The grievance under which we had long suffered, and the brutal attack of the day, flashed across my mind; and with the burning feelings of an injured man, I mounted the stump and proclaimed 'Liberty'.

Peter Lalor had written his name in the pages of the family history; at that moment he echoed James Fintan's aspirations and became a 'revolutionary'. He too had stood against the Crown. Lalor continued:

I called for volunteers to come forward and enrol themselves in companies. Hundreds responded to the call; I then called to the volunteers to kneel down. They did so, and with their heads uncovered, and hands raised to Heaven, they solemnly swore at all hazards to defend their rights and their liberties.

In years to come Lalor would deny that he ever intended to be a revolutionary; he insisted that his was a stand for independence—not a 'republican democratic' style of Independence, as HR Nicholls put it, 'Independence with a capital "I"'; but 'independence from arbitrary rule, from encroachments by the Crown on British Liberty'. Lalor claimed he had stood against a corrupt administration and 'tyrannical government'. Not long before, such an admission would have easily described the very spirit of the 'red revolutionary'.

Lalor in parliament had become a capitalist. He was a director of the Lothiar mine in Clunes, which turned against its own men after a dispute over working conditions. The mine owners in Clunes wanted to change the pattern of working hours and introduce shifts on Saturday afternoon and Sunday night; the miners demanded Saturday afternoon off and were refused.

The miners downed tools and refused to work. After fourteen weeks the directors of the mine sought to bring in Chinese from Ballarat to break the strike, resulting in a violent confrontation between the angry men, the Chinese and the police.

On 9 December 1873 five coachloads of Chinese miners were halted by a barricade of upturned carts, timbers taken from a nearby building site and fallen trees across the road from Creswick. More than 1000 miners, their wives and children waited all night until the first coach came into sight. They pelted it with rocks, and bricks rained down on the roof of the coach as the miners and their wives charged forward to assault the poor Chinese on board. One policeman, Sergeant Larner, was hit on the head by a rock in the first barrage and knocked from his horse; with blood streaming from his wounds he was still able to leap onto the barricade and thrust his pistol into the breast of one of the striking miners. The man did not flinch. He stood his ground against the sergeant. In the face of such defiance the police guard was forced to withdraw and the coaches turned back to Ballarat. This scene must have put Lalor in mind of one similar on the Eureka field two decades earlier, only this time the diggers tasted victory over their masters.

In parliament Lalor was not attached to any faction, his vote was 'independent', he listened to his conscience and trusted his own

Butler Cole Aspinall—Defending the Indefensible

In the aftermath of the Eureka affray all kinds of characters were thrown into the political limelight. English born London barrister Butler Cole Aspinall was one of the new chums in the colony whose spirited defence of the Eureka rebels let all the colony see what he was capable of.

Aspinall had emigrated in 1854 on the great iron-clad steamship SS *Great Britain*, and began to work as law reporter for the *Argus*. Following the events of the morning of 3 December he offered his services free of charge in the defence of the hapless African American John Joseph, who had been abandoned by his countrymen, and the Italian firebrand Raffaello.

It was not long before the handsome, young and erudite Aspinall established a reputation for his sharpness of wit and engaging good humour. Even half a century after his early death in 1875, tales of his quick-witted repartee in the courts of the Crown were still the stuff of legend. One story that has stood the test of the years, retold over and over again, reads: 'On one occasion a presiding judge questioned Aspinall's behaviour in his court: "Mr Aspinall, are you trying to show your contempt of this Court?" Aspinall replied "No, Your Honour, I was merely trying to conceal it."'

In 1868 Aspinall defended the disgruntled, ex-Ballarat mining investor Henry James O'Farrell after he failed in his attempt to assassinate the Duke of Edinburgh at a picnic in Sydney on 12 March.

Aspinall had been elected to the Victorian Legislative Assembly in 1856, serving as member for the mining district of Talbot. He had joined a large number of digger rebels and Chartists who had also taken their place in the House. Aspinall rose to the position of Solicitor-General, but he was only able to serve in this capacity for a short while between January and April 1870. He left Parliament towards the end of the year.

The rising star that was this brilliant young advocate had burned just too brightly. Aspinall suffered a mental breakdown soon after he left the House and was forced into confinement. He made a partial recovery and retired back to England at the age of forty-one where he died four years later on 4 April 1875. He had left his wife behind in Melbourne and she died six days later.

judgement; and he had a lifetime of experience from which to draw. Lalor's had been a rich personal experience in the works and world of man, of political intrigue and the destructive influence of corruption at the highest levels. He had seen good men die for many noble causes, and corrupt men brought to bear the responsibility of their actions—and Lalor had played a critical role in effecting change in the Colony of Victoria. His actions on 30 November 1854 had rallied the men to his cause, on 3 December he had suffered in their name, was accused of treason and survived to take his place in the parliament as the representative of the men he had once led. Yet Lalor disappointed many of those same men.

In supporting plural voting on property ownership and a six-month residency qualification for the franchise, while opposing the payment of members of the Legislature, Lalor had effectively turned away from the spirit of Eureka, for which he was soundly criticised. In response to attacks from Charles Gavan Duffy and the Irish Catholics in the House, Lalor responded:

> It is assumed by my editorial friends that previous to my election I was an ultra-democrat, but that now I take the opposite course from selfish moves, and consequently that I am degraded, and unworthy of being trusted.
>
> I would ask these gentleman what they mean by the term 'democracy'? Do they mean Chartism, or Communism or Republicanism? If so, I never was, I am not now, nor do I ever intend to be a democrat. But if democracy means opposition to tyrannical press, or a tyrannical government, then I have ever been, I am still, and I ever will remain a democrat.[4]

Peter Lalor held a number of appointments in his thirty years in parliament. He was Minister for Railways, Commissioner for Customs and, lastly, Speaker of the House from 1880 until his retirement in 1887.

He died in his son John's home on 9 February 1889.

THE NEW NATIONALISTS

'We'll plant a tree of liberty, In the centre of the land,
And round it ranged as guardians we, A vowed and trusty
    band
And woe unto the traitor, who would break one branch away'
  – *Charles Harpur*

Scrubbing Away at the Convict Stain

From among the first generation of native-born Australians came any number of young men and women who had little desire to emulate an English Empire abroad. Mostly born of convict transportees they had little regard for Imperial manners and were not invited to enjoy the fruits of 'Colonial Society'.

The push for independence began with the 'currency' generation who scrubbed away at the convict stain. Men such as Charles Harpur, the son of transported convicts whose father had once been assigned to John and Elizabeth Macarthur, had seen both sides of colonial life. Harpur had witnessed the privilege and excess conferred on the few who had arrived in uniform and how different life had been for those who had arrived in chains.

Harpur was dedicated to achieving an end to transportation, the destruction of the power of the landed elite, and the opening up of public lands for the labouring classes. He was not alone. He soon found himself in the company of other nationalists, republicans such as Daniel Deniehy, the native-born son of Irish convict transportees, and Henry Parkes. Although Parkes was born an Englishman, he had little love for the trappings of the Empire and sought an Australia for Australians; Parkes had certainly remade himself since he had arrived in the colony almost penniless in 1839.

Harpur was born in 1813 at Windsor on the Hawkesbury River in New South Wales. Like most young men born of the convict labouring class he grew up and took any kind of job available to him. He was a sheep herder, timber cutter and labourer before he travelled down to Sydney, where he took a job as a clerk in the post office. He had received an education, better than most, as his father had become

The Poetic Patriotism of Charles Harpur

This Southern Land of Ours

With alien hearts to frame our laws
  And cheat us as of old,
In vain our soil is rich, in vain
  'Tis seamed with virgin gold:
But the present only yields us nought,
  The future only lours
Till we dare to be a people
  In this Southern Land of Ours.
What would pygmean statesmen but
  Our new-world prospects blast,
By chaining native enterprise
  To Europe's pauper past,
With all its misery for the mass,
  And fraud-upholden powers;
But we'll yet have men, like Cromwell,
  In this Southern Land of Ours.
And lo, the unploughed future, boys,
  May yet be all our own,
If hearts that love their Native Land
  Determine this alone:
To sow its years with crops of truth,
  And border these with flowers,
Till we have a birth of heroes
  In this Southern Land of Ours.
Where worth is trampled on by vulgar
  pride!
And where all beauty of the mind,
  decried,
Hangs dying o'er a Mammon-delved
  grave.

Forward Ho!

Forward ho! Forward ho! Soldiers of
  liberty,
Hope on; fight on; till man's whole race
  shall be
Free of all good under heaven's wide
  dome.
And doubt not, the earth that has
  grown old in sorrow
Shall grow young again in the light of
  that morrow
Predestined to make her fraternity's
  home.
Forward ho! Forward ho! Lovers of
  truth and good!
Think on; write on; till earth's whole
  herohood
Stand in one faith under heaven's wide
  dome;
And shout to behold all the hilltops
  adorning
With sunflowers of glory the glow of
  that morning
Predestined to mark her fraternity's
  home.

By the equalising glory
Of the cause with which we start!
By the blood of honour thrilling
Through each patriotic heart!
By the majesty of manhood
Righteously and nobly free,
We will pause not till Australia
All our own—our own shall be.

— Charles Harpur, 11 March 1854

a schoolmaster and parish clerk in Windsor, and counted Reverend Samuel Marsden among his friends.

Harpur submitted his poems to Henry Parkes' newspaper *Empire* and it was through this that the two became friends. Harpur was an ardent nationalist and republican; much of his verse reflects his love of the country and heartfelt desire for it to throw off the shackles of Empire, to reach for its destiny as one nation.

Harpur is widely regarded as the first poet of Australia, although he had his detractors as well as his supporters; Harpur's views on a political future for Australia put him in direct opposition to the ruling elite, who no doubt saw him as seditious with lines such as: '... we'll yet have men, like Cromwell, In this Southern Land of Ours', taken from the poem, *This Southern Land of Ours*.

He was never sure of the value of his life's work, and his humility shines through in the following statement:

> In short, my name and fame up to this moment, except as bye words in the mean mouths of such defamers and detractors, are utterly blanks in their day and generation; and I conclude, therefore, that either I am unworthy of my country and countrymen, or my countrymen are unworthy of it and me. Time will ratify this conclusion one way or the other—and to Time I refer it accordingly.

Pride and Prejudice

A growing sense of nationalism wrought changes in the political life of the colonies. By the middle of the nineteenth century there were enough native-born Australians, who cared little for old Europe, to call for direct rule for Australia by those who considered themselves to be Australians first.

To administer the interests of the English abroad the British parliament had established local colonial governments, but they rarely represented the aspirations of the majority of the people who were to make Australia permanently their home.

The opposite was more often the case. Parliaments tended to represent the aspirations of a select few, who used the Crown as the excuse for their domination over public and financial affairs. The colonies were effectively Imperial outposts, with all the trappings of Westminster but none of the power; those sterling fellows who sat in government seemed perfectly happy with the status quo—England Rules!—for the English, wherever they lived.

The Bunyip Aristocrat

Requests to Westminster to enable the colonies to establish truly local administrations had been made by the Australians for some years. However, when British Prime Minister Lord John Russell asked the governor of New South Wales and the lieutenant governors of South Australia, Victoria and Tasmania to draft new parliamentary constitutions in December 1852, it came as quite a surprise. Britain had at last recognised that the great wealth that had been won on the gold-fields had changed the Australian colonies and, in many ways to stem the continued agitation at home

Parliamentarian William Charles Wentworth
(Government Printing Office Collection, State Library of New South Wales)

and abroad for reform, the British government moved to grant 'full powers of self-government [to] the hands of a people so advanced in wealth and prosperity'. If they hadn't moved when they did, full-scale insurrection was on the cards. As it was, the Australian goldfields could not wait and ignited with the flames of sedition before the bills for responsible government could be enacted.

William Wentworth was selected to draft a constitution for New South Wales. Although he considered himself to be the 'first son of Australia'–he had been born in 1790 on a convict ship in sight of Sydney Heads–he had become a conservative, a wealthy news-paperman and pastoralist who despised the 'democratic rabble' who lusted after his kind of power. When the common people were able to seriously consider political influence over their own governance, divisions between Conservatives and true Liberals emerged quite clearly.

While Wentworth, who had once fought with despotic gover-nors, had championed the cause of emancipation for the convict

151

class—after all, his father D'Arcy, and mother, had both been transported—it was this convict stain that he had desperately tried to
wash away. In rebuttal of his critics who were pushing for a constitution that reflected their republican aspirations, Wentworth said,
'I became a Whig [conservative] in middle age, and … I shall die a
Conservative … at all events, I shall die with Conservative principles; but however I may die, I deny emphatically that I ever was a
democrat or a republican.'

Curiously, Wentworth's draft constitution reflected the same
ideals that were the catalyst for the republican Americans' action
against the British in Boston Harbour in 1773: freedom on the part
of the colony from taxation by the British government; and control
of the customs department and investment of all colonial patronage
in the Governor and the Executive Council—until such time as the
right kind of Australians could assume their place in power.

In Wentworth's new world he envisaged an Australian upper
class, an aristocracy of graziers and pastoralists and men of means
who would rule the independent colonies as they wished, on behalf
of the Crown of course, but without need to consult Westminster
at all.

Wentworth decried the notion of hereditary titles for the colonies. He noted that 'the most brilliant fathers have the most stupid
sons', so he looked for a class he felt embodied the spirit of his new
Australia worthy of 'hereditary rights' and he found the 'Shepherd
Kings'. Wentworth offered as his reasoning: 'I believe that, as they are
a body peculiar to this colony, so are they, as a general proposition,
the body most fitted of all in the colonies—to receive these hereditary
distinctions.'

Not everyone agreed; in fact, very few did.

As a newspaperman Wentworth was not really a squatter any
longer so he felt able to recommend this class, but he was howled
down in a chorus of dissent. Native-born Sydney solicitor of Irish-
convict parentage Daniel Deniehy railed against Wentworth in a
speech reported in the *Sydney Morning Herald* on 16 August 1853,
when he attacked those who would aspire to the heights of an
Australian aristocracy:

The first Australian Ministry under responsible Government
Seated from the left: Squatter and landowner Thomas Holt; barrister and
pastoralist Sir William Manning; merchant and pastoralist Sir Stuart Donaldson
(Premier); barrister John Darvall; and barrister George Nichols.
These were just the sort of men that Wentworth was thinking
about when he considered the 'Shepherd Kings'.
(Mitchell Library, State Library of New South Wales)

…these Botany Bay magnificos, these Australian mandarins. Let them walk across the stage in all the pomp and circumstance of hereditary titles; first, then, in the procession stalks the hoary Wentworth … Next came the native aristocrat Mr James Macarthur, he would he supposed aspire to the coronet of an earl, he would call him the earl of Cambden, and he suggests for his coat of arms a field of green—and emblazoned on this field should be a rum keg of a New South Wales order of chivalry.[5]

Deniehy coined the term 'bunyip aristocracy' when he went on: 'They would bring contempt on a country whose interest he was sure they all had at heart, even until the poor Irishman in the streets of Dublin would fling his jibe at the Botany Bay aristocrats.' Deniehy spoke of the northern hemisphere's water mole's transformation in the antipodes into the duck-billed platypus, and wondered whether the aristocrat abroad had undergone a similar metamorphosis and become the 'bunyip aristocrat'.

In the end, New South Wales was given a new parliament and the men who sat in the House were selected from the English free-settling squatting class, including English barrister Sir John Darvall; Devon-born barrister and pastoralist Sir William Manning; Londoner, merchant, pastoralist and first premier of New South Wales Sir Stuart Donaldson; and Thomas Holt, a Yorkshireman, wool merchant and squatter who had arrived in the colony already a wealthy man. Holt acquired vast tracts of Crown land, which he sold after the gold rush, making himself a fortune.

Only one man, George Nicholls, could be considered to be Australian and even he was the grandson of 'first fleeter' Esther Abrahams, a London-Jewish convict lass who had formed a relationship with Captain George Johnston on board a convict ship. Even though she had given birth to a child while awaiting transport in Newgate gaol, they lived as husband and wife once they settled in the colony and had several more children. Against this background Nicholls was also used to a life lived comfortably on the land, as his grandfather had also been granted some attractive property in the days of the 'Rum Corps'.

The Ire of Daniel Deniehy

Noted solicitor and orator Daniel Deniehy, the son of convict transportees, was born in Sydney in 1828. A true native son of Australia, Deniehy, like Harpur, was committed to an Australian republic. He wrote: 'Our cause—the cause of Australian Republicanism ... my eye is fixed on one point—doing my duty in establishing Republican Institutions and advancing in every genuine method, my native land'.

Deniehy was opposed to Wentworth's constitution and his proposal to grant hereditary status to the 'Shepherd Kings'. In opposition, he helped to form the New South Wales Electoral Reform League, which was successful in gaining electoral representation by population rather than by landowner.

He was a democrat, a description not many would gladly accept in those days, and committed to unlocking the lands for the ordinary settler. This issue rankled as one of the reasons why the Eureka rebels went to the barricades in Victoria in 1854. Deniehy stood with John Dunmore Lang in opposition to the British war in the Crimea, and together they stood in opposition to the great influx of Chinese immigration to Australia. He even came out of retirement to address a large meeting in Sydney after the Lambing Flat riot in June 1861. While Deniehy deplored the use of violence against the Chinese, he was bitterly opposed to the 'Asianisation of Australia'.

No Honour in the Chinese Question

There was one issue that bridged the divide between the sectarian camps, and that was 'The Chinese Question'. The colonials may have disagreed on most things—Catholic disagreed with Protestant, Presbyterian with almost everybody else—but they all agreed to be disagreeable on the subject of Chinese immigration.

There was always trouble on the goldfields between the European diggers and the Chinese. Everything about the Chinese rankled with both the sons of Empire and white Australian nationals. While the Chinese worked hard, worked cooperatively, and made the most out of the ground that the Europeans had abandoned, the Europeans simply disliked and distrusted them. While the European was perfectly happy to 'see the other side of the world' in the Chinese camp, they would not tolerate them for any other purpose.

Scottish chartist WDC Denovan had railed against the Chinese on the Bendigo diggings so often that he soon became afraid for his life. Believing that a bounty had been offered for his murder, he soon changed his tune and called off a mass rally of expulsion he had planned for 4 July 1853. On 29 August he wrote to the *Bendigo Advertiser* confirming his opposition to any further immigration but stating: 'when they were here they should be treated as men, whatever the colour of their skin'. With that he no doubt hoped that he had saved his own. The Chinese accepted this as an offer of conciliation and asked Denovan to take their own protest against taxation to the government. While he refused at first, he soon lived up to his Chartist principles and worked for many years on their behalf.

The nineteenth-century colonists saw no inconsistency with their having on the one hand a fervent desire for equality, democracy and personal freedom, while on the other pursuing positive discrimination simply on the basis of race. After all, that was exactly the policy pursued for centuries by the Crown against its subjects in all of its dominions, whether or not their skin was a different colour. It more often than not just came down to which particular part of the island one came from.

In a totally racist broadside Deniehy said that the rush to gold in Australia had attracted an 'overwhelming influx of barbarians'; that if the Chinese were allowed to continue to emigrate, Australia would descend to a 'decidedly inferior caste'. It seems there was nothing unusual, among Europeans, in these views.

Deniehy blamed a corrupt colonial administration for the immigration of the Chinese. He blamed the squatting class for throwing the 'Australians' out of their jobs and importing coolies, bringing about the eventual demise of his white-faced, Anglo-Saxon Australia:

> The unscrupulous efforts of its leaders to fasten upon this colony the disgraceful badge of penalism; hence their endeavours to import amongst us coolies, Chinamen, and cannibals; hence their opposition to an extension of the franchise, and a reduction of the qualification for members of the legislature; and hence their support of the present most abominable and arbitrary land regulations, which ... are now driving the industrious and most useful portion of our rural population from the face of the land.
>
> It is therefore necessary that you, the industrious men of New South Wales, should direct your attention to the study of political matters ... with you it rests whether the colony of New South Wales shall be a mere insignificant sheep walk peopled by serfs, for the benefit of a few rapacious tyrants, or whether it shall possess a free, independent, and enlightened community.

The Attack on Lambing Flat

On 30 June 1861, just one week after troops had been pulled out of the New South Wales gold-mining district around Young, a procession of diggers, fired up with liquor, marched through the Chinese camp at Lambing Flat and destroyed everything that stood before them.

Marching behind a banner bearing the words 'No Chinese–Roll Up, Roll Up', to the strains of a 'military' band, the diggers wrecked the Chinese camp.

Governor Sir Hercules Robinson ordered the troops back to bring order to the diggings, yet only three men were arrested for inciting a riot. The diggers rushed the police lockup and demanded that their mates be freed. They fired at police horses and the police fired back, shooting one man through the forehead–he dropped down dead. Only one digger was gaoled for this vicious and angry race-inspired spree.

Among the Europeans that raged that day against the Chinese at Lambing Flat were Ben Hall, 'Darkie' Gardiner, Johnny Gilbert and John Dunn, just the right type of likely lads to sort out the 'Chinese Question'.

The government acted immediately and created a new Chinese Immigration Act and Goldfields Act in November 1861, which restricted the movements of the Chinese, excluding them from certain goldfields and charging a tax on entry to the colony of £10 per head. The same restrictions applied to both Victoria and South Australia. The Chinese responded by sailing to Guichen Bay, near Robe, south of Adelaide, and walking overland to the diggings, thus avoiding the tax.

'A Good Hater' – J D Lang

While Reverend John Dunmore Lang, the first Presbyterian clergyman in New South Wales, actively promoted emigration of white Anglo-Saxon Protestants, he too railed against the Chinese with even more vehemence than he usually reserved for the Catholics. While he despised the thought of Australia becoming an outpost of Rome, declaring: 'The church of Rome is an apostate church and her faith a system of delusion,' he did expect the state to offer Catholics the same protection, privileges and amenities granted to all other citizens–except the Chinese.

Lang insisted that emigration should be controlled to ensure equal numbers of both men and women in the colony. He actively encouraged the emigration of families–as long as they were Protestant. Lang sought to balance the number of poor Catholics of the criminal classes that he had often accused Caroline Chisholm of importing into Australia, by travelling to England where he promised land grants on arrival to Protestant families, encouraging them to emigrate. He filled six shiploads in 1857 but had forgotten to make arrangements for the land before he left. The poor emigrants arrived to be sorely disappointed with Mr Lang's emigration schemes. In contrast to this position of family migration and reunification, Lang did not consider the emigration of Chinese women, to balance the number of men on the goldfields, with anything but distaste.

While he was a true Christian believer, his was a Christianity of extreme prejudice. The good Reverend Lang was described as a bitter and unrelenting religious prosecutor–a good hater–and he used his bile to play to the crowd at a meeting in Brisbane with his unflattering remarks on the desirability of Chinese women:

> I confess I am not sorry at this insurmountable repugnance to emigration on the part of Chinese ladies. The fact is, we don't want them. We don't want the flat faces, the pug noses, the yellow complexions, the small feet, and the long tails multiplied a thousand-fold among us, as they would very soon be if the Chinese ladies came to us as well as the gentlemen.
>
> Considering there are upwards of 400,000,000 people in China, it would require only a few years of uninhibited Chinese immigration to swamp the whole European population of these colonies–to obliterate every trace of British progress and civilisation.

Even so, he was far less complimentary to the inhabitants of Ireland's south-west: 'According to every ... person of experience and observation, they are the most ignorant, the most superstitious, and the very lowest in the scale of European civilisation.'

Lang's Declaration of Independence for New South Wales

John Dunmore Lang was committed to the concept of an Australian Republic. He entered this fanciful yet unquestionably seditious 'Declaration of Independence' in a private notebook on 7 July 1845—never to be published:

FELLOW Countrymen! Fellow citizens!
The galling and degrading yoke under which we have so long groaned as a British colony governed by absolute Secretaries of State and tyrannical Governors, is broken at last. The Government of George Gipps and his satellites is at an end. Their persons are in safe-keeping and will be held sacred from violence, but their power is now forever subverted in this territory, and we are now free to govern ourselves cheaply, wisely and well, as an independent republic. Be true to the sacred cause of freedom and we have nothing to fear, either from our late tyrant or his masters. Let no violence be done to any person. Let no man's property or rights be injured or invaded in any way. Above all let there be no rioting or bloodshed. Let peace be our watchword that the enemy of freedom may have no handle against its friends. Peace! Freedom! and a Republic of New South Wales! In the name and on behalf of the League of Liberators of New South Wales.
Sydney, AD 1845, First Year of the Republic.[6]

Reverend John Dunmore Lang

Watercolour portrait by William Nicholas, 1841

(Mitchell Library, State Library of New South Wales)

Yet, in later years, Lang was surprised that the mass influx of Chinese had not come to pass. Few women travelled to the colonies, and the majority of Chinese gold diggers went back home. He found that they were not as numerous, nor as barbarous as had been believed; most lived peaceably, and were industrious and law-abiding. He was also surprised at the number of Chinese who had taken European wives, and that the marriages were usually successful. He was even more surprised to find that when it came to signing their marriage certificates, the Chinese were quite able to sign, in their own writing, and were proficient in English as well, while few of the white girls they were marrying could do little more than add a cross. He no doubt wondered which was the barbarian, after all?

This wrought a change of heart, and Lang sought to amend the laws that discriminated so heavily against the Chinese. By 1867 he had managed to move amendments to the Act of 1861 and freed the Chinese from heavy restrictions. The Chinese never forgot that it was 'the hater', John Dunmore Lang, who had won them relative freedom in colonial Australia, although, always in the back of his mind, Lang kept the notion that the barriers could be easily erected again if the hordes did flow down from China after all.

A Tight, White Labour Market

Towards the latter half of the century, after the gold boom lost its shine, when jobs were scarce and labour plentiful, pressure was again brought to bear on the government from the labour unions. Once again, the Chinese question was uppermost in the mind of the working man, while men of capital had few qualms about choosing cheaper Chinese labour to the exclusion of the white man.

In 1878, amid a wave of anti-Chinese hysteria, Henry Parkes introduced another Bill to restrict Chinese immigration. Parkes argued that the Chinese had incompatible interests with the country, that they unfairly competed with the working class and that they would swamp the British population of the Colonies. He also argued that a continued presence of the Chinese would be a permanent blight on the country, it would 'continue to engender disturbances, inimical to the country's wellbeing, peace, harmony, stability and prosperity'.

Kicking the Chinese can has always been one sure means of attracting public support in Australian politics, and the colonists knew that as much as leaders of any other time. It had always been so easy to make a scapegoat of the community that did not share a common heritage, religion, or even a history of enmity with the white-faced Englishman, and the Chinese bore the brunt of it.

The Trades Union Congress led the fight in favour of restricted immigration. Having been successful with the introduction of the eight-hour day, the unions were fearful that unscrupulous employers would take revenge on them, take advantage of cheap 'foreign' labour and cast the white man on to the unemployment scrap heap. At the first intercolonial conference in Sydney in October 1879, delegates denounced the Chinese, yet again, as having immoral habits, running dens of iniquity and behaving in ways that 'frequently led to riot', that they 'supplanted white labour, and would leave no work or hope for the rising generation, who would fill the jails in consequence'.

Attending the first International Trades Union Congress held in Sydney in 1879, delegate W Edmonds wondered: 'What is the use of the country being a British dependency, if Chinamen are brought here in unmeasured numbers?'

Parkes, who had championed the cause of the down-trodden, having arrived in the colony with only three shillings in his pocket, had no time for the Chinese. At one large meeting held in Sydney, which he attended to denounce them, he once again described them as 'racially inferior, carriers of vice, and competitors for the means by which Europeans derived a livelihood'.

Following Victoria's lead, the New South Wales government finally adopted legislation to restrict the Chinese presence. There was a provision of a £10 poll tax for every Chinese entering the colonies by land or sea and their numbers restricted in the ratio of one Chinese to every 100 tons of a ship's cargo. Chinese leaving the colonies were to be granted certificates of exemption for their return journeys.

The Bill did not pass unchecked; a proposal to deny the Chinese the right to buy property was removed, as was the imposition of a mandatory twenty-one-day quarantine on any ship carrying Chinese persons into Australia. It seems that interests of trade, real estate and commerce overrode the fear of loss of national identity and public morality. It was not until June 1888 that the Chinese Exclusion Bill was passed through the New South Wales parliament—in a single sitting.

'White Australia'

Writing in his journal *Boomerang* in 1888, radical unionist William Lane coined the phrase, 'The White Australia Policy', and three

Cartoon by Phil May, published in the *Bulletin*, 11 April 1888
A dishevelled Henry Parkes, patches on his trousers and wearing a
battered top-hat, is seen erecting a barrier at the docks to protect
'white Australia' from the invading hordes of cheap Chinese labour.

years later, writing in the *Worker*, he still had little to say in favour
of the Chinese:

> We must be white in order to keep our white civilisation. Our children
> must be white in order that they may take the lamp of progress from
> us and be able to keep it burning for the generations to come. No
> matter what the mongolian vices are, or what their virtues, the two
> races cannot mingle without ours going down, just as they cannot
> meet in competition without ours being swept away.[7]

The fear of unemployment caused by bosses taking on cheap Asian
labour was the root cause of most discontent, and the politicians did
little to dispel this fear. They used the Chinese as a scapegoat for
all society's ills. It was so easy to blame the 'yellow peril' and turn
disgruntled white people away from action or retribution against
the administration or their employers.

The attack on the Chinese heaped no great honour on the
Australian republicans. They had freely abandoned their republican
principles of 'equality, fraternity, liberty' in the face of blind prejudice. They abandoned their Christian principles in the face of blind
hatred. None took the time to look beyond the colour of a person's
skin and into their heart; they may have seen what the person was
worth but rarely saw the worth of the person.

THE HIBERNIAN BROTHERHOOD

Sir Charles Gavan Duffy

In many ways Charles Gavan Duffy had been a very fortunate Irish gentleman. He was fortunate to have grown up in what was quite unusual at the time of his birth in 1816, a prosperous Catholic family. Duffy first attended a 'poor school' in his home district but was later fortunate enough to have been sponsored by his local priest to attend a proper school, the classical academy, in Monaghan.

This school was run by a Presbyterian Minister for the education of good young Protestants, sons of minor gentry and professional men; Duffy was the first papist to ever walk through the doors of the school and the other students never let him forget it. Yet Duffy was soon able to use his considerable intellect and enthusiasm to overcome the taunts and jibes of the young Orangemen. He applied his mind to the boys' parliament, brigade and newspaper, which he helped to initiate; the majority of students voted in favour of his 'emancipation' in opposition to some who declared that only Protestants should be allowed to participate. As a result Duffy declared himself to be the first truly emancipated Catholic in Ireland, yet he was never allowed to forget that his was the side that was thrashed at the Boyne.

Charles Gavan Duffy
Duffy rose from the ranks of the rebels who stood against Queen Victoria's dominance of Ireland to Premier of the Colony honoured with her name. When the Queen heard of his success in the Colony she demanded to be told the fate of all those Young Irelanders who had been transported in her name. She was shocked to discover that most had risen to positions of respect and influence in the former British colony of America as well as her dominions.
(National Library of Australia)

He recalled that his earliest exposure to ideas of political discontent was listening in on discussions held around his father's table when he was a boy. He recalled his father reading aloud the letters of Wellington and Peel, who had both refused to serve in parliament with reformer George Canning because he sympathised with the Catholic emancipists. Young Charles learned very early of the difficulties he would face as a Catholic seeking a fair go in a Protestant-dominated Ireland.

Duffy began working as a journalist on the Dublin *Morning Register* and later as editor of the Belfast *Vindicator*. In 1842 he founded the radical literary journal *The Nation*, and invited John Mitchel to join him one year later.

In the first issue of *The Nation*, published on 15 October 1842, Duffy wrote: 'With all the nicknames that serve to delude and divide us—with all their Orange-men and Ribbonmen, Torymen and Whigmen, Ultras and Moderados, and Heaven knows what rubbish besides—there are in truth, but two parties in Ireland—those who suffer through her national degradation and those who profit by it. To a country like ours, all other nations are unimportant.'

The Nation was a hotbed of seditious ideas and it is no surprise that Duffy constantly ran foul of the authorities. James Fintan Lalor became co-editor of the paper after Mitchel's arrest and transportation in 1848.

Arrested for advocating rebellion, Duffy also had the good fortune to have already been in prison at the time of the failed insurrection of 1848. As a result he did not share the misfortune of his fellow 'rebels' Smith O'Brien, Mitchel and others who were transported.

After the Famine

Duffy was fortunate that he survived the awful years of famine that had caused so much devastation to his homeland. Although he was sent to trial five times for his seditious activities, it was also fortunate that he was a forceful orator, well educated and articulate as he challenged the authority of the bench and argued his way to freedom each time.

Duffy eventually took a seat in the British parliament where he continued to press for reform, establishing the Independent Irish Party in 1852. In sympathy with Dan O'Connell, Duffy agitated for repeal of the union between England and Ireland, but also became impatient with the slow pace of reform. He had joined with the Young Ireland movement in seeking to bring Catholic and Protestant Irishmen together in the push for land reform but the dream of a unified, free Irish state continued to elude him.

After the years of famine and the great diaspora of the Irish across the seas, the discovery of gold in the Australian colonies saw another wave of Irish emigration. This time, men of good will packed all their worldly goods into sailing ships and set off to find their fortune and, for many, a taste of real freedom, for the first time.

Duffy also sought a fresh start in the Colonies. He claimed to have been exhausted by the years of fighting, to no apparent worthwhile end, for justice for Ireland through the parliament. He had also worked long and hard in seeing the new constitution for the separate Colony of Victoria through the British parliament and was no doubt convinced that he should see for himself what life could be like for him in the new world.

When he wrote to Smith O'Brien seeking his advice on life in the Colonies, he told O'Brien: 'I have laboured till my health broke down. I have neglected my family and lived only for the Irish cause, and at every point I have been thwarted by men who thought themselves justified in distrusting me for my share in the affairs of '48 ... or for resisting O'Connell.'

Duffy went on, wondering whether there were any good men of intellect and culture among whom he could live a contented life. He also corresponded with Governor La Trobe, journalist William Howitt and even Thomas Woolner, Australia's first sculptor and former member of the London Pre-Raphaelite group; their replies must have been sufficiently convincing. Duffy joined the exodus to the Australian colonies in 1855. Duffy was so well connected to the greatest men of his day that the radical John Stuart Mill was chairman of his farewelling committee.

When he arrived in Australia in early 1856 Duffy was welcomed with great fanfare. Thousands gathered to celebrate his arrival. He was only twelve months in Victoria before he was assisted by prominent 'emancipists' from all over the country, who subscribed the sum of £5,000, enabling him to purchase property in the Melbourne suburb of Hawthorn, qualifying him to stand for parliament. He travelled to Sydney where he was welcomed by Henry Parkes, who tried to convince him to make his contribution in New South Wales; although he was impressed by Sydney society, believing it to be 'a hundred years in advance of Melbourne', he was keen to work with O'Shanassy in Victoria, where he felt the prospects for radical politics were going to be much more interesting.

He would never recant his activities in Ireland, which no doubt offended many of the conservatives in Australian society, but took pains to remind them that he was no longer in Ireland but had made his home in Australia. In a speech given at a welcoming banquet held in his honour Duffy said: '… this [is] not Ireland but Australia–Australia, where no nationality need stand on the defensive, for there was fair play for all. In such a land,' he said, 'I could be a man who lent a willing and cheerful obedience to the laws … who desired no more than to be permitted to live in peace under their protection.' Not to disappoint the faithful Fenians among his audience, Duffy continued: 'Let me not be misunderstood, I am not here to repudiate or apologise for any part of my past life. I am still an Irish rebel to the backbone and spinal marrow.' [8]

Duffy took a seat in the Victoria's first Legislative Assembly, which was opened by General Edward Macarthur, eldest son of John Macarthur, the so-called 'father of the Australian wool industry'.

Duffy became Minister of Land and Works in 1857 and was responsible for the introduction of the Land Act that checked the dominance of squatters and assisted immigrant farmers to establish a fair foothold in the new world–although pushing this Act through the squatter-dominated Victorian Assembly was no easy task. He fought in the parliament for the abolition of property qualification, even introducing a private bill when it seemed that the assembly had lost its heart for reform.

Duffy was once again called upon to argue his way to success. There was a move towards the abolishment of property qualification in almost all imperial legislature; the British abandoned it in 1858, yet Victoria was holding on to its idea of privilege. Duffy argued that 'Victoria, instead of standing at the head of the countries for free institutions and popular progress, was to retain shackles and restrictions which the others had thrown away in contempt'.

Virtual suffrage had been won in 1855 after the debacle at the Eureka Stockade, when anyone with the £1 to pay for a miner's licence also earned the right to a vote. Victoria eventually gained manhood suffrage, although it did allow for plural voting, which meant that men of property did still have more than one vote; in fact, they could vote in any constituency where property to the value of £50 was held.

One restriction was that six months' residency was required to be able to vote; this disqualified the tens of thousands of diggers and itinerant workers who had been so vocal in their demands for suffrage only a few years earlier.

For the first time the settled working classes, who had been in the vanguard of parliamentary reform, felt they had a government that truly represented them. The old agitators from across the diggings were coming together in parliament in a show of unity–Aspinall, Cathie, Denovan the Scottish Chartist from Bendigo, Gillies and Humffray from Ballarat, Grant and Owens, who had been a driving force on the Ovens diggings and then at the beginning of the Red Ribbon Movement in Bendigo. These inspirational men, who had led the opinions of the diggers from Buckland to Ballarat, stood together in the House; curiously though, Peter Lalor often stood opposed to them.

There were plenty of others who opposed the rise of the working men. The 'father of Melbourne' John Pascoe Faulkner jibed that 'the low-class Ministry now ruled the country!' yet the Catholic Premier O'Shanassy was pleased to reflect that 'for the first time, politicians will be divided into two parties', and for him that made the fight a fair one.

A Push to Federation

Duffy was one of the most passionate of all colonial politicians in his desire for the creation of a Federation of Australian governments. In 1857 he threw his support behind William C Wentworth when he presented a draft bill for federation to the Colonial Office in 1857. Duffy was to apply all the energy he had once reserved for the cause of Catholic emancipation to this notion of a new nation of Australia. He believed that 'neighbouring states … inevitably become confederates or enemies'; but he had to wait almost half a century before he saw his dream of confederation come to fruition.

Duffy was the only member of the Victorian House who had also been a member of the British parliament and as a result he became an arbiter of parliamentary procedure, rising to the position of Speaker of the House on two occasions in 1877 and 1880, a position he did not enjoy as it was too removed from active participation in the affairs of state.

Duffy was able to achieve those aims in the Australian colonies that had evaded him at home. Although he maintained that he was an Irish rebel at heart, like so many others dispossessed of their homeland he had found a new freedom in an Australia that, following the aftermath of the battle at the Eureka Stockade, had pioneered democratic change within the reluctant British Empire. 'If a man can find a second home on this earth, I have found it here,' wrote Charles Gavan Duffy to his family back home in Ireland.

Charles Gavan Duffy published several accounts of his life– the troubled years in Ireland and of his achievements in Australia including: *Young Ireland* (Dublin, 1884); *Four Years of Irish History* (London, 1883); *The League of North and South* (London, 1886) and *My Life in Two Hemispheres* (London, 1903).

John Boyle O'Reilly and the Flight of the Wild Geese

The English Crown seemed determined to exile from Britain all of the energetic young men who were to remake themselves as heroes in foreign nations hostile to the Empire.

The Crown seemed more likely to promote the sycophants, the fawning spies and corrupt beaurocrats whose obsequience bore no threat to the authority of the establishment. Britain would not listen to its people; she turned her back on their aspirations; ignored their plight in adversity; continually rejected their petitions for justice; had starved, exiled and martyred them—consequentially casting aside the brightest and bravest of all them all.

All she did was strengthen the resolve of her disaffected, and gave to her enemies generations of fighters who battled, and won, the same causes on foreign soils.

John Boyle O'Reilly
(Collection: Fremantle Gaol, Western Australia)

While no memorial will ever stand on England's soil for convicted Fenian John Boyle O'Reilly, the citizens of Boston, Massachusetts honour him as a great hero of their battle for freedom and justice for all.

A Model Soldier

John Boyle O'Reilly was born in Dowth Castle, County Meath on 28 June 1844. Dowth is not far from Drogheda, nestled in the gently rolling hills of the picturesque Boyne Valley, halfway between Dublin and Ulster. It was on 1 July 1760 that the pretty Boyne Valley once ran with the blood of Irish nationalists, when the Jacobite army of James II was cut down in his quest to wrench the Crown from his Protestant son-in-law, William III of Orange, and reinstate himself, a Catholic king, back on the English throne.

This devastating defeat of Irish hopes on the battlefield flanking the River Boyne has never been forgotten. Even in the twenty-first century, Orangemen celebrate this victory by marching through the Catholic areas of British-occupied Belfast, reminding the Papists of their defeat three centuries before.

John Boyle O'Reilly, the second son of scholar William David O'Reilly and Eliza Boyle, grew up tutored in the memory of this loss. He left school at the age of eleven and was apprenticed to the Drogheda *Argus* as a typesetter. He later worked on the *Guardian* in Lancashire where he became a reporter.

It was while he was in Lancashire that he enlisted in the English army, joining the Eleventh Lancashire Rifle Company. On his return to Ireland, still only aged nineteen, John Boyle O'Reilly joined the Prince of Wales' own regiment, the Tenth Hussars. It was while on service with the Hussars that he witnessed first-hand the brutal treatment of his countrymen by the English authorities.

O'Reilly began to develop a hatred for the way the army treated the Irish, and soon sought others who felt the same way. In 1865 he was recruited into the Irish Republican Brotherhood by John Devoy, for whom O'Reilly–the popular, well-respected model soldier–was the perfect man to enlist other discontented Irishmen to the cause. Planning to be able to support an uprising of Irishmen led by James Stephens from within the armed forces, they enlisted more than 8000 regular troops into the Brotherhood circle–but the call to arms never came. James Stephens hesitated at the last and the moment was lost. The authorities came to hear rumours of the rebellion that never was; through a network of spies O'Reilly and the Irish Republican Brotherhood were exposed.

Spies had posed as committed Catholics, or Fenians, infiltrated the Brotherhood and earned its trust, but simply served to offer the rebels up to the English authorities. Just as they had done a generation earlier, the government suspended *habeas corpus* in Ireland and hundreds of Irish soldiers serving in the British Army were arrested and imprisoned without trial.

O'Reilly was betrayed by one of his fellow officers and was thrown into Arbor Hill Military Prison on 6 March 1866. He was sentenced to be executed by firing squad for the crime of high treason. First he was ceremoniously drummed out of the army; stripped of his uniform and dressed in rough, woollen prison garb, he was sent to await his fate in Mountjoy Prison.

Hundreds had been arrested for this insurrection that never happened. While the civilians among them were treated as political prisoners, those from the armed forces were treated as ordinary criminals.

O'Reilly's sentence was commuted to twenty years' penal servitude and for the next twelve months he was kept in a number of English prisons. In 1867 John Boyle O'Reilly was finally transported to Australia for the crime of gathering up and burying the scattered bones of French and American prisoners that had died at the hands of the English in the war of 1814.

Years later John Devoy wrote of O'Reilly: 'The signal never came, all of his and other men's risks and sacrifices were thrown away through incompetence and nerveless leadership.'

Transportation into Exile

The struggling colony of Western Australia had sent a request to the British government for a shipload of much-needed convict labour. Although the practice of transportation had ceased twenty years earlier, the government agreed to send one more ship to the west in 1867. John Boyle O'Reilly was one of the sixty-two Fenians among 280 convicts who were sent to Fremantle on board the *Hougoumont*, the last prison ship of all. Seventeen of the Fenians on board were former soldiers from the Irish Regiments of the British Army.

On transit to Australia the captain of the ship allowed O'Reilly and his compatriots to write and publish a weekly journal they called the *Wild Goose*, named in memory of Jacobite Captain Patrick Sarsfield who had led the flight of patriotic Irish troops, 'The Wild Geese of Ireland', to join the French in their battle with the English in the war of 1814.

It had been eighty years since the first ships had arrived at Botany Bay. In that time 160,500 convicts had been transported to Australia. Pressure on the government from free settlers, and a second generation of 'free-born' Australians, finally convinced Westminster to put an end to the practice of transportation in 1868—after the *Hougoumont* and her cargo of convict 'labourers' was sent in Fremantle.

Orangemen and Catholics Battle it Out in Melbourne

Melbourne, 28 November 1867: One man was killed and several others severely wounded following an affray between loyalists and Papists.

A large crowd had gathered outside the Protestant hall, which had been prepared for a visit from Prince Alfred, Duke of Edinburgh, second son of Queen Victoria, who was making his way around the Colonies.

In fact, the colonial loyalists had gone overboard trying to outdo one another in their preparations for the prince's visit. In Adelaide the German population turned out in strength and the prince, who was by birth half-German, was able to converse with them in their own language. Patriotic German songs had been sung before they even got to the British national anthem.

In the Protestant hall a large portrait of William the Duke of Orange had been placed on display. How a painting of the Dutch-born King of England was meant to impress the half-German prince is a moot point, but the image of the Protestant hero was too much for the Victorian Catholics. No matter the royal lineage, the symbolism was enough to bring them to the boil. A large crowd gathered outside the hall as the Orangemen held a meeting inside. The Catholics rattled the windows and banged on the doors, all the while lustily rendering patriotic Irish songs, of which there are many, including the seditious 'The Wearing of the Green'. This prompted one of the Orangemen inside to fling open an upstairs window and fire into the crowd.

Twenty-seven-year-old John Kean was mortally wounded as several others also dropped to the ground. Several arrests were made—one man while attempting to flee from the rear of the building, quite a few others from among the crowd in the street.

Australian author Marcus Clarke wrote in the *Australasian* of the excesses of the prince's visit:

> I have been poisoned by bad brandy, drunk to the health of the Prince. I have had my clothes burnt with crackers, my hat crushed by excitable youths, my eyes, limbs and body in general, anathemised by enraged cab drivers. I have got bunting on the brain . . .

A few months later an Irishman from Ballarat took his revenge on the English Crown when he shot the prince as he enjoyed a picnic at Sydney's Clontarf Naval Base. Saved by his braces the prince lived. His assailant, Henry James O'Farrell, was hanged.

Escape from the West

In 1869 the British government proclaimed an amnesty for all of the political prisoners who had been convicted in 1866, but the Fenians in exile in Western Australia were excluded.

O'Reilly had been put to labour in Bunbury where he had formed a friendship with the local Catholic priest, Father Patrick McCabe. He confided in McCabe about his intention to escape and, in time, the priest introduced him to Jim Maguire, an Irish settler working on clearing the ground for the new Bunbury racecourse. Maguire arranged for O'Reilly to stow away on an American whaling ship that was taking on supplies in Fremantle Harbour. O'Reilly was again transported across the seas, although this time when he stepped ashore in Philadelphia on 23 November 1869, he was a free man.

O'Reilly was feted in America—lecturing, writing for journals, even following the Fenian raid into Canada, which he reported for the Boston press, eventually becoming editor and part-owner of the Boston *Pilot*, but he did not forget his companions back in the West.

In 1875 with the financial help of Clan na Gael, the American arm of the Irish Republican Brotherhood, O'Reilly mounted a daring plan to rescue his Fenian brothers. They purchased the *Catalpa*, a cargo ship from New Bedford, Massachusetts for $US5250, and converted it to resemble a whaler for a further $15,000. Only the captain, George Anthony, knew the secret of their mission when he sailed out of New Bedford harbour on 29 April 1875, bound, supposedly, for the Atlantic whaling grounds.

Most of the crew of Africans, Indians and Chinese jumped ship when they stopped in the Azores for supplies. However, Anthony was able to take on a completely unregistered crew, men stranded without passports, who didn't really care where they were going.

In March 1876 the *Catalpa* finally made it into Bunbury where Captain Anthony boarded a coastal steamer, the *Georgette*, bound for Fremantle, accompanied by the Fenian agent John Breslin, who had already ingratiated himself with the authorities. They were able to get a message to the prisoners who were working on gangs outside the prison, to let them know that their freedom was imminent; all they had to do was make a run for it at the right time.

A coded message was sent via telegraph from Bunbury to Fremantle, announcing the date of the rescue. When the day came the men made their break, racing two horse-drawn buggies to the coast at Rockingham on Easter Monday, 17 April 1876.

They then leapt into a longboat and rowed out to meet the *Catalpa* at sea, abandoning the horses on the beach. A timber worker, having seen them arrive, rode to Fremantle to announce their escape.

The water police sent their fastest cutter to Rockingham but arrived just in time to see the *Catalpa* head for the horizon. They rushed back to Fremantle, where they commandeered *Georgette* and steamed after the whaler. Meanwhile, the weather was closing in on the men in the longboat and they were unable to catch the *Catalpa*, forcing them to spend a stormy night at sea in the open boat. At around 2 p.m. the following day the escapees scrambled on board *Catalpa* just as *Georgette* spied its quarry in the distance.

It took until the following day before *Georgette* finally caught up to the American ship. Firing several shots from a twelve-pound howitzer across *Catalpa*'s bow, the police superintendent in charge demanded he be allowed on board to search for the escaped Fenians. Captain Anthony refused. Pointing to the Stars and Stripes flying from his stern he challenged the policeman to arrest him, as *Catalpa* was then in international waters. Fearing a repeat of a recent international incident where the British government had lost £3,000,000 in a similar case with the Americans, the police backed off and let *Catalpa* sail away. She reached New York four months later on 19 August 1876.

The rescue of the prisoners was a humiliation for the British government and the freed men were feted as heroes across the United States. O'Reilly became one of America's favourite sons, regarded as the greatest Irishman in America at the time of his death in 1890. He had continued to write, published two volumes of poems, written several novels—among other works—and spent his years dedicated to the integration of the Catholic-Irish community into Protestant Boston.

James Stephens, the Fenians, the Irish Republican Brotherhood, Clan na Gael and the IRA

James Stephens had been a Young Irelander who was wounded in the 1848 uprising; he avoided arrest by escaping to France. On his return to Ireland he became one of the founders of the Irish Republican Brotherhood. Stephens was arrested in 1865, charged with conspiracy and imprisoned in Dublin's Richmond Prison. Once again he escaped to France, then travelled to America where the Fenians denounced him for having failed to call for a rebellion in '65, the failure of which had brought about the arrest and exile of many of their supporters.

The Fenians—or Clan na Gael—was an organisation formed by Irish Republicans who had fled or emigrated to the United States of America. After the diaspora the Irish made up a large proportion of the population in the eastern states, centred on New York, New England and Massachusetts. Even though they had enjoyed prosperity and freedom in the 'New World', they never forgot those they had left behind in the old. The Fenians raised funds, and at times supplied arms to their 'brothers' fighting for the freedom of Ireland.

The Irish Republican Brotherhood was the homeland counterpart of the Fenians. There is a direct line from the Fenians and the Brotherhood to the Irish Republican Army (IRA) and on to Sinn Fein, the twentieth century's political wing of the IRA. Right throughout the latter half of the nineteenth century, the twentieth, and even into the twenty-first, the Americans have supported their brothers at home.

In July 2005, after almost a century of fighting against the British in Ulster (the British province of Northern Ireland), the IRA ordered its secret army to lay down its weapons. The Republic in the south had matured to enjoy a glorious era of peace and prosperity, and it seems that the Orangemen and the Catholics in Northern Ireland were, at last, prepared to step together into the future.

Almost 250 years since their defeat at the battle of the Boyne, John Boyle O'Reilly was about to be vindicated as the military checkpoints on the border between Ulster and the Republic, just a few miles to the north of Drogheda, were being dismantled, and the Irish and the English made ready to forgive the past—for a cooperative future.

Attempt on the life of the Duke of Edinburgh, arrest of O'Farrell
Wood engraving, printed in Melbourne, 1868
(National Library of Australia)

A Shot at the Crown

Disaffected, dissolute and desperate Dubliner Henry James O'Farrell left the Ballarat goldfields where he had once been a shrewd investor, seen daily on 'The Corner', buying stock cheap and selling dear. Afflicted with the 'Irish virus', O'Farrell spent his afternoons in Craig's Hotel and soon saw his fortunes slip into decline. His investments in Ballarat mining companies collapsed and he left the colony.

O'Farrell was next heard of when he turned up in Sydney on 12 March 1868 at the picnic given to honour the visit of Prince Alfred, Duke of Edinburgh. Just as the crowds gathered after luncheon to enjoy the afternoon in the company of the royal personage, O'Farrell stepped forward and took a potshot, shooting the prince in the back.

Prince Alfred fell to the ground as he cried out, 'Good God, I'm shot. My back is broken.' One man, Mr Viall, a coach builder from Sydney, rushed from among the crowd and grappled with O'Farrell. Another man, George Thorne, was struck by a second shot. The mob thought that Thorne was the would-be assassin and turned upon him, but soon realised their mistake. O'Farrell was attacked by the angry mob hell-bent on revenge for the life of the popular prince. But for the quick thinking of some police who dragged him clear, O'Farrell may have breathed his last there and then, dangling from a sailor's rope thrown over a handy tree.

The prince was carried to his tent where doctors from HMS *Challenger* and *Galatea* treated him. He made a miraculous recovery. The bullet had hit his thick rubber braces and been deflected from its evil path, missing all vital organs. Prince Alfred was in no danger of any lasting effect from his ordeal.

Thorne's daughter Emily wrote in her diary later that day of her great pleasure of seeing the prince, even taking her seat at a table so close that she could hear his conversation, not unhappy that the table had been covered with dirty plates and food left over by the party who had sat there before them. She wrote:

> We went in at a door close to the Prince's table, and we had a long look at HRH. He was just asking the Countess what she would take. In a short time we managed to find places which had just been left by some other people … we were about ten minutes eating our lunch and then we walked up to the Prince's table again. Where we were stopped again by the crush of people. (Lord Newry gave us a good stare) …

The Thornes went outside after the prince took his leave and were just about to go and speak with him:

> … when we heard a sharp noise like a chinese cracker and looking towards the place from where the sound came I just saw the Prince fall. Then the whole flashed across our minds in a moment and we all exclaimed, 'The Prince is shot.' I covered my face with my hands … all I can remember is someone falling down beside me. [her sister Annie had fainted] someone falling down beside the Prince … when Annie and I were alone we saw Papa limping out of the crowd. I almost screamed out, 'Oh papa what is the matter', and he said, 'I'm shot. I'm Shot' I then caught hold of his arm … Papa kept asking, 'Is the Prince alive', 'How is the Prince', and when someone said, 'The Prince is alive,' [Papa] seemed better.[9]

As O'Farrell was being taken away he shouted: 'I don't care for death … I am sorry I missed my aim—I made a bloody mess of it … God save Ireland.'

O'Farrell was tried and sentenced to be hanged for his attack on the prince. There is no doubt that the court, at that time, would have considered his insult to the Crown a hanging offence, and the humiliation he had caused worthy of drawing and quartering as well.

Publisher of the *Empire*, Henry Parkes, seized upon O'Farrell's declaration. He visited O'Farrell in his cell in Darlinghurst Gaol, and went to his lodgings where he discovered the tools of revolution among O'Farrell's possessions—gunpowder, shotgun and an Irish bible. He was convinced that the Fenian had brought American-styled revolution to Australia. Vehemently anti-Catholic, English-born, but an Australian patriot, Parkes wanted to build a case against O'Farrell to prove the dangers of accommodating the secret Fenian Brotherhood and Irish-Catholic influence in a post-gold-rush colonial society headed for the modern era of Australian nationhood and federation. Parkes had long fought against giving state aid to church schools and used O'Farrell to justify his distrust of Catholics.

Four weeks after the shooting at Clontarf Sailor's Home O'Farrell joined the large number of his fellow countrymen who were dropped through a gallows floor, hanged for the vain hope of extracting some revenge on the English for generations of wrongs perpetrated against their native Ireland.

The Pride of Erin—Forged in a Rebel Mould

While the founding fathers of Australian Federation were busy holding committee meetings and drafting lengthy documents for one another, looking forward to Australia's future, others in the community were still inextricably linked to the past. One was a young lad from north-eastern Victoria who could not keep himself out of trouble.

Edward 'Ned' Kelly was born in 1854, the year of the Eureka Stockade, at Beveridge in Victoria. He was the son of transported Irish Catholics and grew up in the north-east surrounded by an extended family who all bore the same convict stain. The Quinns, the Lloyds and the Kellys were well known to be horse thieves and cattle duffers, and like the 'currency lads' of an earlier generation Ned was to find trouble in exactly the same way—in misappropriated horse flesh. He first found trouble for 'sticking up a Chinaman' when he was still a child; next he held up a hawker and was charged with 'robbery under arms' but was let off. He was not yet fourteen.

His real bushranging career began when Police Constable Fitzpatrick, who was enamoured with Ned's sister Kate, came calling unexpectedly on the pretext of looking for his brother Dan, who was wanted for horse stealing. The constable was drunk and Kate did not appreciate his unwanted attentions; a scuffle ensued and he was shot with his own gun. No-one knew who pulled the trigger, but when Fitzpatrick got back to the police station he blamed both Ned and Dan, and that was to be the end of freedom for the Kellys.

In a cruel act of injustice Judge Redmond Barry sentenced Ned's mother to three years' imprisonment for the attempted murder of Constable Fitzpatrick. When he passed sentence Barry said: 'If your son Ned was here I would make an example of him. I would give him a sentence of five years.' The fact that Ned had been 400 miles away at the time of Fitzpatrick's shooting escaped the notice of the court.

Ned and Dan took to the hills to avoid the law, but the family was continually harassed. The Kelly boys formed a gang with a few mates, and took the law into their own hands. When Ned was outlawed in November 1878 there was no turning back. He was either free or dead, and his freedom could not last for long. The government had enacted the same Felon's Apprehension Act that had brought about the demise of Ned Kelly's boyhood hero, Ben Hall. Ned wrote in December: 'I was outlawed without any cause and cannot be no worse and have but once to die. If the public do not see justice done I will seek revenge for the name and character which has been given to me and my relations while God gives me strength to pull a trigger,' and signed the note 'Edward Kelly, *a forced outlaw*'.

It seems that Ned Kelly was caught between two worlds. Although Australian born, he was deeply connected to his Irish past, a past filled with the likes of Wolfe Tone, Dan O'Connell, Smith O'Brien,

Meagher and the Lalors, and he could not fully embrace the promise of the future. In reality, Ned and his kind were yesterday's men, excluded from the destiny of the new nation; they were dirt-poor, mired in convict ways, with a bad experience of authority. They had little prospect of climbing out of their class, so they tried to fight their way out. Why he thought he could be victorious over the majesty of English law when so many great men had failed before him is anybody's guess.

There is no doubt that Ned came to believe in himself as some sort of avenging leader of a private republican army. He took on the might of the Queen's lawmakers and they, in turn, threw their full weight against him.

Death in the Wombat Ranges

A party of policemen had found their way into the Wombat Ranges near Wangaratta, hot on Ned's trail. Ned and the boys surprised them in the bush where they were shooting at parrots; an exchange of fire took place and three policemen, constables Scanlan, Lonigan and Kennedy, all Irishmen, were killed. At first, Michael Kennedy was badly wounded and tried to make his escape, but Ned chased him for half a mile and cut him down. As he lay mortally wounded on the forest floor, Ned walked over to him and finished him off with a shot to the head. Ned claimed later that this was an act of mercy, not one of brutal murder. Kennedy could not live and Ned believed it callous to leave him to suffer a slow death. Before he left Ned took his own greatcoat from his back and laid it over the dead man. He felt no malice, just pity that the police had started a fight that had ended so badly for them.

In an attempt to explain his actions Ned dictated a long letter to Joe Byrne, which he tried to have printed by the Jerilderie newspaper editor Samuel Gill. Gill was hiding in the bush, having recently published an unsympathetic article about Kelly and his gang, so Ned gave a copy of the letter to the accountant of the Jerilderie branch of the Bank of New South Wales—which they were holding up at the time—and asked him to give the letter to Gill for printing. Mr Living, the accountant, managed to slip away from the bank and rushed by train to Melbourne where he handed Ned's letter to the police. Living saw his account of the bank raid published in the morning edition of the *Herald*; Ned's letter was not published until it appeared in the *Melbourne Herald* fifty years later, too late to do him any good at all.

The Jerilderie Letter

Ned's fifty-six-page letter was a rambling narrative in which he shared his thoughts on a range of topics, from his first brushes with the law to his dislike for the police and Irish nationalism. He then turned his mind to the concept of an Australian republic. Not that Ned expressed his thoughts in exactly that way, but he did echo the sentiments of the true patriots of the Emerald Isle who fought against English domination, at home and abroad.

The following excerpts from the Jerilderie letter express his anti-English sentiments quite clearly, and with some vehemence (the original has little punctuation; amendments have been made for ease of reading):

> (Pages 44–46) What would people say if they saw a strapping big lump of an Irishman shepherding sheep for fifteen bob a week or tailing turkeys in Tallarook ranges for a smile from Julia, or even begging his tucker, they would say he ought to be ashamed of himself and tar and feather him.
>
> But he would be a king to a policeman who for a lazy loafing cowardly bilit left the ash corner, deserted the shamrock, the emblem of true wit and beauty, to serve under a flag and nation that has destroyed, massacred, and murdered their forefathers by the greatest of torture as rolling them downhill in spiked barrels, pulling their toe and finger nails, and on the wheel, and every torture imaginable—was transported to Van Diemen's Land to pine their young lives away in starvation and misery, among tyrants worse than the promised hell itself, all of true blood, bone and beauty, that was not murdered on their own soil, or had fled to America, or other countries to bloom again another day; were doomed to Port McQuarie, Toweringabbie, Norfolk Island and Emu Plains, and in those places of tyranny and

condemnation many a blooming Irishman, rather than subdue to the saxon yoke, were flogged to death, and bravely died in servile chains, but true to the shamrock and a credit to Paddy's land.

Here Ned was referring to the Young Irelanders and other transportees. He also refers to Toweringabbie [Toongabbie], the government farm where Captain Joseph Holt had lived before he was transported to Norfolk Island following the Castle Hill riot.

(Page 48) What would England do if America declared war and hoisted a green flag, as its all Irishmen that has got command of her armies, forts and batteries; even her very life guards and beef tasters are Irish, would they not slew around and fight her with their own arms for the sake of the colour they dare not wear for years; and to reinstate it and rise old Erin's isle once more, from the pressure and tyrannism of the English yoke, which has kept it in poverty and starvation, and caused them to wear the enemy's coats.

Ned refers to the large number of Fenians who had been important to the success of the American Republican Army of the north in the Civil War. He also refers to the Irishmen who serve in the British Army.

Ned reserved his most florid prose for the Victorian police, a large number of whom were Irishmen in the uniform of the Crown; even ex-convicts wore the policeman's tunic. Ned thought they should have known better:

(Page 44) I have been wronged, and my mother and four or five men lagged innocent and is my brothers and sisters and my mother not to be pitied also who has no alternative only to put with the brutal and cowardly conduct of a parcel of big, ugly, fat-necked, wombat-headed, big-bellied, magpie-legged, narrow-hipped, splay-footed sons of Irish Bailiffs or English landlords, which is better known as Officers of Justice or Victorian Police, who some calls honest gentlemen, but I would like to know what business an honest man would have in the Police as it is an old saying—It takes a rogue to catch a rogue.

Left: **Ned Kelly at Bay**
(La Trobe Picture Collection, State Library of Victoria)
Right: **Ned Kelly, photographed in Pentridge Gaol**
(Courtesy: Ian Jones Collection)

Ned and the gang were caught in a shoot-out at the Glenrowan Hotel on Monday morning, 28 June 1880. They had been in the hotel since early Sunday evening with a large number of locals, among whom were many sympathisers, and had spent the night dancing and drinking in a genuine party atmosphere. Ned gave several orations during the night, claiming that he was not a common criminal, that he had been driven to the life by the discrimination of the police. But there was no going back. The die had been cast and Ned had to see the game to its bitter end.

The police, who had come up from Melbourne by train, had waited armed and ready all night. Nothing was happening so at about 3 p.m. the police decided to set fire to the hotel to flush the Kelly gang into the open.

The ploy worked. The gang—Ned and Dan, Steve Hart and Joe Byrne—stepped out from the front of the hotel and fired into the police lines, wounding Superintendent Hare. They turned back inside the hotel. The police allowed Ned's 'guests' to leave one at a time, before they poured a barrage of lead into the front. Dan and

Steve were killed; Joe fell next, struck in the throat as he stood at the bar to take a drink. Ned made his way out the rear and around the side of the hotel in an attempt to get behind the police lines. Already wounded, he collapsed under the weight of his armour but recovered and advanced towards the police.

Ned was clad in a suit of heavy steel, a helmet like a large pail on his head. He was like the knights of old, marching into battle. The police could not penetrate his metal suit, but his legs were exposed. Police Sergeant Steele, who had come to Glenrowan dressed in a hunting suit as if out for a day's sport, shot Ned in the legs and he fell, exhausted. Ned was captured where he lay behind a fallen log and taken to Melbourne by train to stand trial for the murder of the police.

The trial was presided over by Judge Sir Redmond Barry. A Protestant, Redmond Barry could not tolerate the poorly behaved Irish Catholics abroad and Ned had no chance of staying the cruel hand of English justice when Barry determined to wreak its vengeance. Although Ned had gained a huge following among the general population, and there were many who petitioned for mercy from the courts, he was convicted and sentenced to be hanged for the murder of Lonigan.

When Sir Redmond Barry placed the black cap on his head and pronounced the sentence of death, he asked Ned if he had anything to say. Ned answered: 'I don't care one straw about my life, nor for the result of the trial; and I know very well from the stories I've been told, of how I am spoken of—that the public at large execrate my name ... let the hand of the law strike me down if it will; but I ask that my story be heard and considered.'

The reckless spirit of 1798 that had flowed from the Emerald Isle, through the convict transportees to Botany Bay and Van Diemen's Land, had flourished on Australian soil but was crushed again on the gallows at Pentridge gaol when Ned was hanged at 10 o'clock on the morning of 11 November 1880.

As the hood was pulled down over his head, he looked around and said: 'Ah well, I suppose it has come to this ... such is life!'

EIGHT HOURS A DAY
The Time Had Come for the Working Man

The Rise of the Union

The gold rush had brought great wealth to the colonies, and cities such as Melbourne and Sydney were booming. Melbourne in particular was growing so grand that it earned the sobriquet 'Marvellous Melbourne'. The city was equal to any of the great cities of the world, ranked with Paris, New York and Chicago for the elegance of its Victorian architecture, broad avenues and generous boulevards. Melbourne was constructing itself virtually from scratch and could borrow the best and most stylish from the world and make it its own.

At the heart of this boom was labour, and the goldfields competed with the cities for the labour of the working man. Labour was short and the workers soon exercised their muscle.

For almost half a century the concept of a day divided equally into three parts–eight hours for work, eight hours for recreation

The float of the Watchmen, Caretakers and Cleaners Union of New South Wales prepare for the Eight Hour Day Demonstration, 1915
(Mitchell Library, State Library of New South Wales)

and eight hours for rest—had been a dream that seemed impossible to entertain, but for the stonemasons working on the construction of Victoria's new Parliament House, dreams could become reality. All they needed was to pick the right fight at the right time.

Stonemasons in New South Wales began a campaign for reduced working hours in August 1855 when their Society issued employers with an ultimatum: in six months they would work an eight-hour day—or down tools. Some of the stonemasons working on the Holy Trinity Church in Argyle Cut, and Mariner's Church in Lower George Street, jumped the gun, went on strike and won. Six months later stonemasons all over Sydney followed through on their ultimatum and demanded the eight-hour day. Employers resisted again, but were soon brought into line following a two-week-long strike on the construction of the new Parramatta Road Tooth's Brewery building. The workers won the reduced hours but had to accept a wage reduction in compensation.

It had been only four months since Victoria had celebrated its separation from New South Wales. The newly formed Colony was in a frenzy of self-determination and the new parliament was keen that its new home be completed by November 1856.

James Galloway, a young Scottish-born stonemason, met Welsh Chartist James Stephens in a room at Thomas McVae's 'Mac's' Hotel in Collingwood. They planned a concerted push for a reduction in the working hours for members of the Operative Stonemason's Society.

Fully aware of the expectations of parliament, the Society requested a reduction in the working hours for the stonemasons working on the construction of the new building—from ten hours a day to eight. The Society offered the following argument in justification of their request: '... that Australian conditions do not allow the Anglo-Saxon to work such long hours as in England and ... that long hours discourage the pursuit of self-improving activities'.

One mechanic wrote: 'Fifty or sixty weeks of unremitting exertion of the most laborious kind in a warm climate exhausts the system in a way scarcely to be conceived from the experience of a cold climate. An invincible lassitude takes possession of the whole frame; and without anything like illness one feels destitute of all alacrity that is usually associated with health.'

The stonemasons won with relative ease. Most employers had been masons themselves and sympathised with their workers. A few held out; WC Cornish, who had won the contract for the parliament building, held out for so long the government was forced to allow him an extra £1700 to cover his additional wage costs. George Caldwell, who was engaged in the construction of Melbourne Grammar, and George Holmes, who was building the Western Market, were brought to the nego-

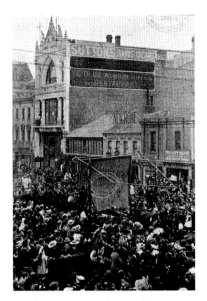

Celebrating the eight-hour day, the crowd at the corner of Bourke Street, Melbourne, 1 May 1896
(La Trobe Picture Collection, State Library of Victoria)

tiating table after a rally led by James Stephens marched through the city on 21 April 1856. All of the men working on those big projects downed tools and joined the first great march of the Eight-Hours Movement.

Their success was celebrated on 12 May when 700 workers, representing nineteen trades, marched again through Melbourne, beginning more than a century of 'May Day' marches around the country. The unions made the first of May a public holiday and celebrated victory over their employers in realisation of Welsh reformer Robert Owens' dream, first proposed in 1817, of eight hours' work, eight hours' recreation, eight hours' rest.

Not all employers were ready to give in so easily. Most were fearful of a working class with time on its hands, fearful that men at leisure could get up to all sorts of mischief; if they were not exhausted by the labour of the day they may take to drink or, worse still, education.

In New South Wales Henry Parkes had long promoted education as the saviour of the working classes, and the *Empire* emphasised the

Trade Union Banner of Federated
Mining Employees Association of
Australia, New South Wales Branch
(National Library of Australia)

benefits of a reduction in working hours and of time spent profitably: '… they [the workers] might improve their minds, and thereby elevate their social position'.

Following the gold rush, most communities had built their own free lending libraries and mechanic's, or working men's, institutes. It was there that the working man could improve himself through self-education; it was there that the capitalist class was most afraid that the men may be 'thinking, improving themselves with reading, education, socialising, enjoying life and maybe organising and challenging the status quo'.[10]

One mason wrote anonymously to the *Sydney Morning Herald* on 11 February 1856: 'Masons are men of different stamp, and if they had time, many, I doubt not, would have their names enrolled as members of that valuable Institution—the Mechanics School of Arts; and their desire for mental improvement is another and a strong reason which urges them on to obtain a reduction in their present hours of labour.'

Others argued against shorter hours, fearing that men would spent their free time drinking—just like the ruling classes.

By 1860 the eight-hour working day was commonly accepted as the norm in Victoria, but across the border, New South Wales was almost a decade behind. Union delegates in New South Wales met on 21 August 1869 and formed The Eight Hours Extension Committee, which was dedicated solely to winning the shorter day for all workers in that colony.

At that time some were still working fourteen hours a day, while most were on ten, with a shorter, eight-hour day on Saturday. Shop assistants could be working twelve to fourteen hours a day and children under the age of thirteen were still working in mines for more than fifty hours a week up until 1876.

Mason inside the House

Scottish-born Chartist, Owenite, Unitarian, Socialist stonemason Charles Don was working on the construction of the new Parliament House when he was elected as representative of the Political and Social Labour League of Victoria, for the Legislative Assembly seat of Collingwood. When asked who was backing him he replied that he was backing himself. The new shorter working day had enabled him to finish earlier, giving him time to be in the House in the evenings. Charles Don's campaign had been run from the Belvedere Hotel in Fitzroy, where radicals such as Galloway and Stephens congregated.

In his campaign speech Don warned that 'labour never would be represented until its voice should be heard in the councils of the nation, where, perhaps, it would not be listened to from being adorned with the graces of what was called a classical education, but solely for the stern heart of honesty which inspired its utterances'. He promised to drive out the capitalists who kept labourers 'in want on the very edge of the richest abundance' and destroy the very seat of oppression, the squatting class.

Scottish-born Chartist Charles Don MP

Don was a stonemason working on the construction of Parliament House during the day, who took his seat in Parliament at night. The eight-hour day made this possible.

(La Trobe Picture Collection, State Library of Victoria)

Progress was slow but union movements were gradually having success across the country. Queensland accepted the eight-hour day in 1858; South Australia in 1873; Tasmania 1874 and the West in 1896.

The first May Day celebrations were held in New South Wales in 1871 when the first of May was declared a public holiday, as it also had been in Victoria since 1879. However, it was almost another eighty years before the forty-hour, five-day working week was finally approved for all workers by the Commonwealth Arbitration Court, effective from 1 January 1948.

A NEW AUSTRALIA
Dissent in the Working Man's Paradise

There were several publications that pushed for an Australian Republic. One of the more prominent was the *Bulletin*, a pro-republican weekly paper that was first published in Sydney in January 1880. Twenty-four-year-old JF Archibald and his partner John Haynes printed their first edition of 3000 copies on old borrowed machinery and it sold out within hours of hitting the Sydney streets. Within eighteen months they were printing 15,000 copies a week and the paper was read by thousands more.

The editorial style of the *Bulletin* reflected the opinion of its publishers, in particular JF Archibald, who was irreverent, anti-English, anti-monarchist, pro-republican and fiercely Australian nationalist. In an article titled 'Australia for the Australians', the *Bulletin* published this definition of an Australian on 2 July 1887:

> By the term Australian we mean not those who have merely been born in Australia. All white men who come to these shores—with a clean record—and who leave behind them the memory of the class-distinctions and the religious differences of the old world; all men who place happiness, the prosperity, the advancement of their adopted country before the interests of Imperialism, are Australian.
>
> In this regard all men who leave the tyrant-ridden lands of Europe for freedom of speech and right of personal liberty are Australians before they set foot on the ship which brings them hither.
>
> Those who fly from an odious military conscription; those who leave their fatherland because they cannot swallow the worm-eaten lie

Publisher of the radical paper *Boomerang*, trade unionist, 'dictatorial' communist William Lane, and his wife Annie
(State Library of Queensland)

of the divine right of kings to murder peasants, are Australians by instinct–Australian and Republican are synonymous.

The *Bulletin* had little time for the coloured person, denying those who sold their labour cheap, at the expense of the working white man, the name Australian:

No nigger, no Chinaman, no lascar, no kanaka, no purveyor of cheap coloured labour, the Chinaman in Australia is a toady and a 'loyalist' ...

Louisa Lawson, mother of Henry, publisher of the *Republic*, and the feminist journal *The Dawn*
(State Library of New South Wales)

Looking back to the years of transportation, the success of Australians in all manner of enterprise, from the goldfields to the sheep's back, the *Bulletin* continued:

Once the name Australian was a 'red-hot burning brand of shame', the scarlet letters flaming on the breast of every colonist. In those days it was title written with a lash, and the 'i' was dotted and the 't' was crossed with the gyes and the gallows. England did not want our company–then.

The Australian native looks upon England not as a mother–we have too much experience of her bumptious children. We are wooed and wedded by her hectoring offspring, and even if we do tolerate them as husbands we object to the introduction of

Poet, socialist, Mary Gilmore (nee Cameron) travelled to Paraguay in 1893 with Lane's New Australia Association
(State Library of New South Wales)

Freedom on the Wallaby

Australia's a big country
An' Freedom's humping bluey,
An' Freedom's on the wallaby
Oh! don't you hear 'er cooey?

She's just begun to boomerang,
She'll knock the tyrants silly,
She's goin' to light another fire
And boil another billy.

Our fathers toiled for bitter bread
While loafers thrived beside 'em,
But food to eat and clothes to wear,
Their native land denied 'em.

An' so they left their native land
In spite of their devotion,
An' so they came, or if they stole,
Were sent across the ocean.

Then Freedom couldn't stand the glare
O' Royalty's regalia,
She left the loafers where they were,
An' came out to Australia.

But now across the mighty main
The chains have come ter bind her
She little thought to see again
The wrongs she left behind her.

Our parents toil'd to make a home
Hard grubbin 'twas an' clearin'
They wasn't crowded much with lords
When they was pioneering.

But now that we have made the land
A garden full of promise,
Old Greed must crook 'is dirty hand
And come ter take it from us.

So we must fly a rebel flag,
As others did before us,
And we must sing a rebel song
And join in rebel chorus.

We'll make the tyrants feel the sting
O' those that they would throttle;
They needn't say the fault is ours
If blood should stain the wattle!

— Henry Lawson, 1891

Written during the Shearer's Strike of 1891.

In May 1891 3000 striking shearers gathered at the 'tree of knowledge' in Barcaldine, Northern Queensland, marching behind the Eureka Flag, to protest against poor working conditions and falling wages. Thirteen of the shearers' leaders were gaoled for their agitation against the powers of capital—the 'squatting classes'.

The great strike led to the formation of the Australian Labor Party. The party held its first meetings under the lofty branches of the tall ghost gum which was thereafter known as 'the tree of knowledge'.

our mother-in-law in our homes—we cannot live peaceably in the same political house with England ... The cause of Democracy in Australia is gaining strength, and every fresh act of repression serves simply to call to the surface the hidden forces that have hitherto been unsuspected. Republicanism in the colonies is as sure, though possibly slower in its consummation, as are intercolonial Freetrade and Protection against the world ...

The Star of Australasia
(first verse)

We boast no more of our bloodless flag that rose from nation's slime;
  Better a shred of a deep-dyed rag from the storms of a golden time.
From grander clouds in our peaceful skies than ever were before
  I tell you the Star of the South shall rise in the lurid clouds of war.
It ever must be while blood is warm and the sons of men increase;
  For ever the nations rose in storm, to rot in a deadly peace.
There comes a point that we will not yield, no matter if right or wrong,
  And man will fight on the battle-field while passion and pride are strong—
So long as he will not kiss the rod, and his stubborn spirit sours,
  And the scorn of Nature and curse of God are heavy on peace like ours.

— Henry Lawson, 1895

Although primarily republican, the *Bulletin* was also seen as the first working man's paper, a title later assumed by William Lane's *Boomerang*, which he first published in 1887. Archibald drew to his paper the brightest young Australians he could find–Lawson, Paterson, Gilmore, Barfold Boake and John Manly Hopkins; and artists such as Norman and Lionel Lindsay, Phil May, the American Livingstone 'Hop' Hopkins, Dyson, Low and Leason. Archibald told them what to write; his was a benevolent dictatorship with one goal in mind, a change to the established order in Australia.

The *Bulletin* openly mocked the monarchy and derided Britain's transplanted colonial aristocracy, the clergy of all denominations and colonial politicians who sailed too close to the British wind. It was critical of imperial honours that Queen Victoria handed out with reckless abandon to keep her colonials compliant in her Jubilee year. The *Bulletin* accused the monarch of bribery, and accused Henry Parkes of turning his back on his republican colleagues by accepting a knighthood, then promoting the idea of 'Federation under the Crown' while espousing the superiority of the English race.

Lawson's mother Louisa had established her own paper, the *Republican*, printed on an old press she set up in her own home in Sydney. Although it ran for only a year, it declared itself, calling for Australians to unite under the 'Flag of a Federated Australia, the Great Republic of the Southern Seas'. After the *Republican* came the

Nationalist, which lasted only two issues; then in 1888 she launched her feminist monthly journal *The Dawn*, which was much less radical politically, but over the seventeen years of its publication promoted controversial women's issues to an eager readership.

Lawson had his work published first by his mother, then by the *Bulletin* and also by William Lane. Lawson was strongly committed to an Australian republic, and wrote powerfully on nationalism and the struggle of the worker to rise up against their oppressors. Lawson was deeply moved by the struggle at the Eureka Stockade—he maintained the belief that the flag of the Southern Cross should have been accepted as the right standard for a new Australian nation—and concluded his moving poem 'Eureka—a Fragment', published in the *Bulletin* in March 1889, with the lines:

'Twas of such stuff the men were made who saw our nation born,
And such as Lalor were the men who led their footsteps on;
And of such men there'll many be, and of such leaders some,
In the roll-up of Australians on some dark day yet to come.

'New Australia'

The charismatic messiah of nineteenth-century socialism in Australia was an unprepossessing club-footed Englishman with a droopy moustache and round, wire-rimmed spectacles.

Born in Bristol, England in 1861, sixteen-year-old William Lane left his home, bound for Canada, two years after his mother died. He worked at any job he could find, eventually finding his calling as a newspaper reporter. After his marriage to Annie Macquire in 1882, the couple migrated to Australia to settle in Brisbane, arriving in 1885.

Lane arrived in Queensland at a time of great upheaval. The rush to gold had subsided, leaving a large number of men underemployed. The squatting classes saw their opportunity and sought to lower the wages paid to the workers; in particular, a large army of itinerant shearers were soon to come under attack, and they were to fight back in one of the longest strikes in the early colony's history.

Lane's 'New Australia Association' ready to sail
Photograph by Walter Scott-Barry, 1893
The first group of new settlers line up on the Adelaide
wharf before setting sail for Paraguay.
(State Library of South Australia. SLSA B12158)

Lane was just the right sort of man to arrive at the right time. He began working for the *Brisbane Courier*, then for the more radical evening newspaper the *Observer*. He canvassed his philosophy of social reform, and used his columns to promote his concept of rural settlement as a remedy for social ills. Lane's 'Rural Notes' were widely read; his influence saw the formation of the Brisbane Trades and Labour Council several years ahead of the formation of any political party that would grow out of the labour movement.

In 1887 Lane began his own journal, *Boomerang*, and through its pages advocated land reform. Lane persisted in his belief that all of society deserved a fairer distribution of the proceeds of enterprise, that great wealth was accumulated at the expense of, and because of, the efforts of the worker. He believed that it was 'the duty of the state to undertake the task of insisting upon a fair division of the products of labour'.

The barque *Royal Tar* in Adelaide
Photograph by Ernest Gall, 1893
(Photograph Courtesy of the State Library of South Australia. SLSA B6432)

Lane was promoting the concept of state regulation of capital for the benefit of all who engage in the creation of that capital. He was promoting the concept of socialism.

Lane began to assist in the organisation of trade unions; his influence was pivotal during the shearers' strike of 1894, which heralded the beginnings of the Australian Labor Party in Barcaldine, Queensland. He was committed to an international brotherhood of the worker and again used his influence to raise £30,000 for the relief of striking London dock workers in 1890.

He soon sold *Boomerang* and began another more radical, left-leaning paper, *The Worker*, whose motto read 'Socialism in our time'. *The Worker* published the radical writers of its day–Henry Lawson and Mary Cameron (later Gilmore) among them. Using the pen-name 'John Miller', Lane published his novel *Working Man's Paradise* in 1892, in which he explored themes of a socialist utopia in conversation with Christian dogma. Lane envisaged the end of class-ridden European civilisation and rebirth in an egalitarian idyll where everyone was truly equal and free to pursue their own happiness.

Writing in the *Boomerang* on 4 February 1888, Lane expressed his view of Australian nationalism:

> We are for Australia, for the nationality that is creeping to the verge of being, for the progressive people that is just plucking aside the curtain that veils its fate. Behind us lies the Past with its crashing empires, its falling thrones, its dotard races; before us lies the Future into which Australia is plunging, this Australia of ours that burns with the feverish energy of youth, and that is wise with the wisdom for which ten thousand generations have suffered and toiled.
>
> We are for Australia, for that which will work her weal, against which will work her woe. We yield no other allegiance, profess no other loyalty; we recognise no duty as owing to others, we set above all other claims the claims of our land.

Lane was convinced that ordinary people 'with high ideals could, in the right place, and away from corrupting influences, create a perfectly equal society'. He developed the idea to create that new society—a 'new Australia'—and began his New Australia Cooperative Settlement Association, which soon had a membership of more than 1000.

Bound for Paraguay

Lane decided to leave Australia and begin again, this time in South America. The Association purchased a barque, the *Royal Tar* (fellow socialist Jack Lang wryly observed that it was a strange name for the first ship in a communist navy), and she was made ready for the first journey of 'utopians' to re-settle in South America. Everyone had put in a minimum of £60; some gave more, while Lane invested £1000 in the venture.

Lane had always been an absolute idealist; he had explained his dream in an article published in the Wagga newspaper the previous year:

> This to me is what new Australia means, to the landless, the homeless, the wifeless, the childless, to those whose hearts are sick and sore, to

those who long to be manly, to be true, to be what men should be ...
come out of this hateful life, the life that is full of unspoken misery,
of heart-sickening longing, of evil habits growing with the years, of
sin and slavery that lead to nothing but death. Come altogether in all
unselfishness and trust each other and be free!

Lane had friends and supporters in all levels of society; the future
Premier of New South Wales Jack Lang was still a young man filled
with the fervour of socialist ideals when he was asked to make the
journey to Paraguay, as was Henry Lawson; both declined. Lang said
he didn't have the necessary £10 deposit, and anyway he could see no
good reason to leave Australia just to start again somewhere else.

Both Lawson and Lang met William Lane at MacNamara's radical
bookstore in Castlereagh Street, Sydney, a meeting place for politi-
cally active young minds, all of whom featured prominently in the
Labor movement in later years—men such as the *Bulletin* editor
George Black, unionist WG Spence and parliamentarian Billy
Hughes.

The young poet Mary Cameron, who exercised a profound influence on Lawson when they first met at Louisa Lawson's home in
Sydney, agreed to make the trip to Lane's 'utopia'. Lawson asked
Cameron to marry him a few years before she departed for South
America, but she said she was not yet ready. Louisa Lawson sent
her son Henry away to save some money before the two young poets
were wed; although Mary wrote to him constantly, Louisa never for-
warded the letters to her son. Mary Cameron joined William Lane's
socialist adventure and sailed to Paraguay in 1893. There she met and
married shearer William Gilmore from Casterton in Victoria. Mary
put her literary skills to work when she arrived in the colony, taking
over as schoolmistress and editing the weekly *Cosme Journal*.

Lang and Lawson were later to marry the Bredt sisters, step-
daughters of bookshop proprietor MacNamara.

Before the ship sailed tensions were mounting as the new settlers
were forced to wait for longer than anticipated in tent accommodation at Balmain. A Quaker by birth, Lane was opposed to strong
drink and violence. He soon found that those he was preparing to

create his new society with did not all share his views. He tried to ban alcohol, requiring each new settler to sign a pledge of abstinence, and was also affronted by the behaviour of the bohemian element among his members. Where they promoted free love, Lane was rather more prudish. It was not an auspicious beginning for his new nation, where his new settlers were expecting absolute freedom; as far as their personal behaviour was concerned Lane became increasingly dictatorial.

The first group of new settlers sailed from Sydney on 18 July 1893 and arrived at Montevideo on 13 September. They still had to journey 1200 miles up the La Plata River before they finally arrived at their destination—the 'new Australian' nation on 400,000 acres of land granted by the South American republican government of Paraguay.

Before they sailed Lane said 'that the world will be changed' if they succeeded: 'If this is a wild dream, an impossible hope, what hope is there for humanity? Is it so extravagant to expect this, even in a new settlement where our ranks are steadily drawing in the stoutest and strongest arms in Australia? How can we fail?'

Just in case the 'stoutest and strongest' were to become difficult to control and the community about to fail, Lane had been granted the authority of a local magistrate by the Paraguayan government and the promise of troops if necessary.

In his socialist experiment settlers were to build their own homes, grow their own food, make their own clothing and furniture; women would be equal to men and all property would be shared. When they got to Paraguay they discovered that even under communism they still needed leadership; by secret ballot overseers were elected who, once they had a little power, behaved just like capitalists, ordering their 'workers' around. Even though tensions between the settlers were apparent right from the start there was so much work to do that, at first, the experiment went according to plan.

They had just twelve weeks before the first crack in the facade of utopian happiness appeared. Just prior to their first Christmas three of the men had got drunk on a visit to a neighbouring village, and as they staggered back into the settlement they began to fight.

The Wide-ranging Ideas of William Lane

Lane had little time for the Chinese; he may have been a democrat but he reserved his democracy for whites only. His discriminatory attitude may have stemmed from 'scab labour' used in the shearers' strike, where he saw Chinese employed in preference to white men. In defence of the European working class he was afraid that the Chinese would simply lower living standards in Australia. Lane exposed himself as a 'wowser' when comparing the behaviour of the 'vile Chinaman' with the boisterous drunken European:

> Vile as these fellows are in many ways, in others they are simply sublime. Their very vices, crawling and unspeakable sins, commend them to those who are irritated by the white man's more boisterous evils. Opium smoking is more deadly than liquor drinking, but it isn't quarrelsome. It is only when they insult unprotected women that many realise how unrestrained sensuality elbows the domestic virtues in the Chinaman's heart.

Lane was first and last a socialist, bound up in notions of nationalism and republicanism:

> Our principles are easily declared. They are Australian. Whatever will benefit Australia, that we are for; whatever will harm Australia that we are against.
>
> As a natural result of common school education, the common man is beginning to have opinions and to criticise institutions. In every country where common thought is thus started its first encounter is with the customs which give one man authority over other men regardless of the consent of those others.
>
> If there is an absolute dictator men ask by what right John dictates to Tom.
>
> If there is a despotic emperor men ask who William is that Peter should be born to stand up or lie down as William directs. And if there is so-called representative government through which a quarter of the community puts a ring through the noses of the other three-quarters, the common men whose noses are ringed enquire energetically why this is . . .
>
> . . . if we suppose that it is right to do unto others as we would have others do to us, there can be no two answers about one-man-one-vote. Free states are manifestly those in which government is by the will and with the consent of the governed, in which every man stands equal before the law.
>
> One-man-one-vote is an attempt to reach a more equitable method of governance; it is a protest against the usurpation of governance which reached its climax under kingcraft and has been passed along from autocrat to aristocrat to plutocrat, until it nearly confronts the democrat whom it has so long wronged.

The Worker 13 June 1891

Lane was furious with these men for breaking their commitment to abstinence. They had broken his immutable laws. He ordered them from the colony.

Lane's dictatorial stance drove the wedge deeper. Friends of the offending men rallied behind them; others sided with Lane. After a period of bickering between themselves Lane invited the local military to restore order and expel the three men. The rift in the settlement never healed. While some thought Lane had overstepped his authority, others simply drifted away.

A new group arrived in the colony in March 1894, led by Englishman Gilbert Casey, who soon became leader of the insurgents among Lane's first settlers. Unable to reconcile himself with Casey and his growing band of dissenting supporters, Lane left to begin again. With forty-five adults, twelve children, a few cattle and a share of the tools, he established a second colony near a river crossing called Paso Cosme, twenty miles from the first.

Unable to negotiate a second grant from the Paraguayan government, they were forced to purchase this land. With only £400 left they began the business of land clearing, building and planting all over again. By January the following year they had almost run out of supplies; almost beaten by the forces of nature, with the constant effort to hold back the bush, they resorted to eating the seeds they had left for planting.

Lane sailed to England and returned with fifty new settlers, hoping to inject some new blood into his failing commune. However, the new English settlers were totally unsuited to the climate and the conditions. They complained that it was too hot, the weather was intolerable and the food too basic and monotonous. Most of these new arrivals also drifted away.

Still at only thirty eight years of age, William Lane was ready to give up. Never a robust man, this experiment had proved too much for him, and his health deteriorated; constant stress caused Annie to fall ill. They decided to abandon the commune at Cosme. At the fifth annual meeting of the colony he resigned from office and left in August 1899; he did, however, remain an honourary member of the community and was committed to repaying the settlement's debts.

For the rest of his life Lane worked to repay investments lost by the original settlers in 'his working man's paradise'.

William Lane and his family returned to England, then headed south again, this time to New Zealand. He later accepted an appointment in Sydney, as editor of the *Australian Worker*, but soon returned to New Zealand to his wife and family. After a few weeks with the *Wellington Post* he took the position of leader-writer for the conservative *New Zealand Herald*. In a curious reversal of ideology, he began to express imperial values. He became an influential advocate of compulsory military training in New Zealand and backed Britain to the hilt when war broke out in 1914.

Although he was small in stature and crippled with a club foot, Lane never lost his ability to inspire others. A charismatic character with a great mind, his legacy remains in the improvement made to the lives of the ordinary working men and women of Australia gained by the organisation of trade unions, which he had helped create in the 1890s.

The failure of Cosme was largely beyond his control. He had placed too much faith in the good nature of his fellow man, and refused to acknowledge the flaws in his own personality. He had not recognised the dictator he was to become when his colony did not fulfil his expectations. He discovered that even in 'utopia' mankind still needed leadership; while few enjoy dictatorship, Cosme had shown that it takes generations to breed benevolence in authority, and it was that born-to-rule sense of 'noblesse oblige' they had sailed to Paraguay to escape.

Jack Lang wrote:

> As an experiment in Communism, New Australia was a great disillusionment. They searched for the equality of mankind and could not find it. The theory did not work out in practice. Even Lane found himself drifting into dictatorship. The weak went to the wall while the strong survived. Human nature could not be changed even under conditions which should have been ideal. Still Australia had given the world its first experiment in Communism. It ended in disaster. Was it to be a premonition of things to come?

INDEPENDENCE IN MIND
The Push to Federate and 'Free' Australia

Until federation in 1901 each of the Australian colonies were quite separate from one another. Each had its own parliament, its own legislature, its own laws, customs and port officials, import and export tariffs—each colony even raised its own militia, each with its own colonial uniform. Each colony had its own flag and governor, and believed in its own special place in the pantheon of a global imperial power.

Before the invention of the electric telegraph, communication between continents took weeks—even months. It was sensible to allow governance of each and every corner of the Empire at a truly local level; but Westminster still made the rules, and each colonial administration still needed to take advice from London on almost every decision that had imperial or constitutional importance.

To wait for anything up to six months for any decision from Westminster was just too long. Even in the age of the great steam leviathans, when the travelling time between England and the Australian colonies was almost cut by half, it still made the cogs of government turn very slowly indeed. Every memorandum, every request, every command and every communication between the various government Houses in Australia and the Colonial Office in London took months. It was not until 1871, when the electric telegraphic was finally connected between Australia and England, that communication became a relatively fast, almost two-way conversation. Long before then a desire to act alone without need to consult with London was coming to the fore.

Portrait of Henry Parkes, c.1880
(National Library of Australia Collection)

Eureka to Federation

Colonial parliaments bore little resemblance to the parliaments of the twenty-first century. For one, there were no political parties as such, no formal opposition; the House was comprised of a collection of loosely affiliated sectional interests. The capitalists, pastoralists, Orangemen and men of means gathered together in self-interest on one side and the Chartists, republicans, Catholics and 'red' rebels on the other.

In an assembly of individual members there were always loose cannons, and the affiliations of various members resembled at times the shuffling of a deck of cards, as one man crossed the floor to vote on one issue with one group, and crossed again to vote with another bloc on any other issue.

Cabinets were rarely created on party lines; that had only occurred after the election of trade union representatives to the parliament, then the 'war of the classes' divided the House—labour stood against capital, and the two rarely saw eye to eye again.

After Eureka the cards were really placed on the table. A new deck had been shuffled and the House was never to play the same game again. Workers stood in parliament—common people, miners, masons and mechanics; people who had known hard labour and the worth of a person—which was a lot different from knowing what someone is worth by the hour.

The world of colonial politics was a volatile world of currents and cross-currents, the ebb and flow of ideals, with torrents of passion and floods of self-interest; yet the candidates just kept on diving right in.

In Victoria, Catholic revolutionaries lined up opposite Protestant squatters and set in place a pattern of antagonism that would last for more than a century as sweated labour confronted indolent capital. Chartists from the goldfields; 'physical force' men stood alongside 'moral force' men, together, against the establishment.

The *Examiner* newspaper expressed the following view on 29 September 1855, in an editorial that once would have seen the author charged with sedition and transported to the Colonies in chains. The *Examiner* questioned the ability of the British Parliament

The first Parliamentary Election, Bendigo 1855
Oil by Theodore King, 1855
Chartist, diggers' leader Dr John Downes Owens was elected as the first member
for the goldfields twelve months after the battle at the Eureka Stockade.
(Bendigo Art Gallery)

to rule over a legislature so far away from London. The *Examiner*,
writing about Victoria in particular, considered the Colony was no
longer:

> … an infant state, but full of age, and replete in intelligence … [but]
> so bound about and trammelled by the swaddling bonds of infancy
> that she is unable to right herself … she may be crippled, before her
> negligent mother can release her.

The article suggested that all those rights enjoyed by the English
at home were being denied abroad in a colony ruled as a military
state, and presided over by self-serving landholders, land-grabbing
squatters and a handful of freeman graziers:

> All those rights, and privileges besides, are theirs, and must be
> conceded to them, which were conceded to their ancestors in the reign
> of John, by Magna Carta, and established by William III, in the Bill of

Rights, by his confirmation of all those statutes, charters and customs which make up what has been called the English Constitution. Their powers must be similar to those enjoyed by the English people at home, and besides a full and complete representation in the house of assembly, that house of assembly must have as free and unfettered control over the affairs of this colony as the Irish parliament had before the Union over the affairs of Ireland. Victoria must be as independent of the English Parliament as it is of Van Diemen's Land, or New South Wales, or of Jersey or of the Isle of Man.

The *Examiner* questioned the relationship of the far-flung colonies with the English Parliament; how could 'Australians' be represented without sitting members in the House of Commons? The editorial suggested that this was impossible:

> But since we are not so represented, and cannot be, it is as much usurpation of authority on their side to give us laws as it is vile and slavish submission on our part to obey them.

The Tenterfield Oration

After the rise of the working man in the 1850s, the granting of universal male suffrage and the popular election of parliamentary representatives, a succession of freely elected colonial administrators disavowed the heavy hand of Westminster in Australian affairs. Government ministers and colonial premiers were of a class that had fought long and hard against domination by the English ruling classes and were determined to stand on their own two feet, in their own 'states', even forging their own nation. The first thing the 'founding fathers of Australian Federation' had to do was to bring all the colonies together and forge that 'nation' into being.

There was considerable jealousy between the colonies; while some had been established as penal colonies, others had never known the convict stain, and all remained proudly independent of one another. In just over 100 years each colony had even developed its own characteristics—settlement by various emigrant groups had endowed each colony with its own personality; where New South Wales promoted free trade, Victoria protected its borders, and South

THE HAPPY FEDERAL FAMILY—CLEARING AWAY THE BARRIERS.

The Happy Federal Family Clearing Away the Barriers
Published in *Review of Reviews*, 1901
State premiers working together to make Australia truly one nation.
(La Trobe Library, State Library of Victoria)

Australia led the march to international trade by harnessing the riverboat trade on the Murray River, and capturing agricultural export markets.

There was little cooperation between the colonies. As Victoria and New South Wales rushed to build rail links to the Murray to counter South Australia's lead, they even failed to cooperate over a common rail gauge, ensuring that travel and carriage of freight between the two most populated colonies would remain complicated for more than a century to follow.

Even though the colonies continued to compete with one another, the concept of an inter-colonial body that could work on behalf of the entire continent had been considered even before the gold rush of the 1850s. Victoria led the way in 1857 when it proposed the establishment of a 'federal council', with Tasmania's support, but New South Wales refused to have anything to do with a Victorian idea.

Henry Parkes announced in 1867: 'I think the time has arrived when these colonies should be united by some federal bond of connection', but twenty years later he was still pursuing the goal of a Federated Australian Nation. However, when both Russia and Germany began casting a wide net in the Pacific, the Australian colonies, facing the possibility of invasion, seriously considered coming together in their own defence.

A conference was held in Tenterfield in 1889, at which Parkes discussed a report from the British Army's Major General Edwards into the state of the colonial armed forces. The Edwards report recommended that all colonial forces be united into one. Parkes told the conference that there was not one body who could command such an army, and further, that no Australian colony should accept imperial parliamentary command over their own forces.

Parkes continued: 'The time has come for the creation on this Australian continent of an Australian government.' Where New South Wales had been dragging its heels–they could see no reason why they, the biggest, most prosperous colony, should share with the smaller–this 'call to the nation' by the old warhorse of New South Wales politics finally brought them to the table.

Parkes returned to this theme in 1891; when speaking at the Gaiety Theatre in Sydney he said:

> There is no other way for true federation of this Australia than to unite under one government. It will be a fatal mistake to curtail the power of the government we shall create when we are one as an Australian nation, as brave and as powerful as any nation on the face of the earth, when we shall have become 'one people, with one destiny' and when we shall be bound together by the crimson thread of kinship that can never perish.

A speech such as this, even forty years earlier, would have seen Parkes clapped in irons. Parkes continued: 'Surely what the Americans have done by war, the Australians could bring about in peace without breaking the ties that held them to the mother country.'

Parkes was honoured by Queen Victoria in her Jubilee year (1887), much to the dismay of many of his nationalist supporters who believed that by accepting imperial honours he had turned his back on the Australian republic. There were others who had also spurned the Crown yet knelt graciously before it to receive the ceremonial tap on the shoulder, making the excuse that it was their wives who desired the honour, more than they.

Sir Henry Parkes did not live to see a federated Australian nation; he died in April 1896. Even though New South Wales Premier George Reid had a lot of trouble making up his mind whether he was in, or whether he was out, the Australian colonies did come together and the new nation was born on 1 January 1901.

A New Flag for a New Nation?

The Federation Flag was created by the Australian Federation League and was to be unfurled for the first time at a banquet to be held in Melbourne in honour of the first royal visitor to Australia, Prince Alfred, in 1867. Fearing for his safety, the prince changed his itinerary and cancelled his appearance. The flag was raised anyway, even without his royal assent. A design similar to this, known then as the 'National Flag of Australia' and bearing a red cross of St George rather than a blue cross, was used by New South Wales and for merchant shipping as early as 1832. When the time came to consider a new flag for a new nation, the Federation Flag was too closely linked to New South Wales for any of the other colonies to readily agree to this design.

When Australia became a federated commonwealth in 1901, the fanfare saw the Union Jack flying from every post, but there was not a blue ensign to be seen anywhere. It had not seemed compelling enough to those massaging in the era of Federation to worry about a new flag. They were after all not seditionists; they were loyal to the Crown, loyal to the Empire, therefore the imperial standard, the Union Jack, would still do the job as a flag for the Australian nation.

There were others in the new nation who sought a symbolic representation of this spirit of a new nationalism as well. The journal *Review of Reviews*, in concert with the Havelock Tobacco Co., offered a prize for the design of a new flag for Australia. More than 30,000 entries were submitted and the winners were announced at a display held at the Exhibition Buildings in Melbourne on 3 September 1901,

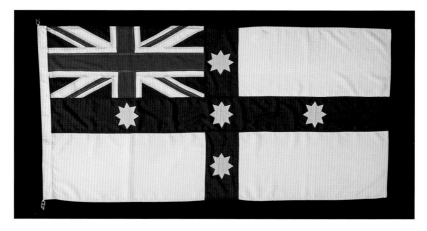

Federation Flag
The design of the Federation flag dates back to 1832.
Most Australians expected this to become the new flag, but it was too close to the
colonial flag of New South Wales for the rest of the colonies to agree.

however the flag was not endorsed by the King until 20 February 1903 almost two years after the nation had come into being. Following the decision by the Flag Committee to award the prize to five entries, who all submitted an almost identical design—a variation on the British Ensign with the stars of the Southern Cross and one large six-pointed star directly beneath the cross of St George—The *Bulletin* offered this opinion on 28 September 1901:

> Naturally, in the present condition of things the flag proposed as the future emblem of the Commonwealth is vulgar and ill-fitting—a staled reshuffle of the British flag, with no artistic virtue, no national significance … One could not expect otherwise. Minds move slowly; and Australia is still Britain's little boy. What more natural than he should accept his father's cut-down garments—lacking the power to protest, and only dimly realising his will, that bastard flag is a true symbol of the bastard state of Australian opinion, still in large part biased by British tradition, British customs, still lacking many years to the sufficiency of manhood which will determine a path of its own.

The *Bulletin* observed that Australians really couldn't care less; they felt no resentment, no indignation at a foreign symbol usurping

The Flag Act 1953

The Flag Act of 1953 states that the Australian national flag will be a blue flag, and the Australian Ensign will be a red flag.

Prior to this date the national flag was in fact red and the ensign blue. However, few Australians, private or public, cared much anyway and flew whichever flag they liked—or the Union Jack instead if it suited them.

Prime Minister Robert Menzies, unable to outlaw the Communist Party in the 1950s, made a decision that was at least a symbolic gesture. Without reference to the parliament, or the people, he decided to reverse the colours of the flag to make the national flag blue. The Flag Act enshrined this in legislation.

Menzies had been born into an era when most of the nations of the Empire were coloured red on his atlas; as Menzies said: 'At a time when red was a respectable colour.' By the 1950s red had come to represent for him a most reprehensible state, the Soviet state. It would appear that Menzies would tolerate a red flag no longer.

Australia's own national identity, for most it was simply confirming the accepted, and quite comforting, status quo.

The *Bulletin* continued:

> The flag represents the old generation, the old leaven. But the new generations are growing; the new leaven is working. The New Spirit is beginning to be felt in Literature and in Art; even in Politics ...

The *Bulletin* ended hopefully: 'With the New Leaders will come a new Flag.'

Australians have examined the prospect of designs for a new flag for the better part of the last century, and as with the matter of a republic, a majority of Australians really still couldn't care less. They have forged their identity without the usual trappings, created a new nation without an armed struggle and, in defiance of those who would dare try and mould them, Australians continue to define themselves—'Australians all let us rejoice, for we are young and free'.

POETS OF THE BUSH
The Birth of 'The Banjo'

Andrew Barton Paterson was born in 1864 on a New South Wales farming property at Narrambla. His was a family of hard-working Scottish graziers and horse breeders, who had emigrated at the height of the gold rush.

Paterson had studied law and practised as a Sydney solicitor before he became a writer. After the death of his father he decided to devote himself to full-time writing. In October 1899 he sailed for the South African War with the New South Wales Volunteers. Although he had gone off to be a war correspondent, reporting from the frontline for Sir James Fairfax's *Sydney Morning Herald*, he was soon in the thick of things.

Born into the saddle, when among the volunteer horsemen Paterson mixed comfortably with men of his own kind. He was the first to gallop into Bloemfontein the day the town surrendered to the English commander Lord Roberts.

While in South Africa Paterson developed a lifelong friendship with English writer Rudyard Kipling, and was thrilled by the great men of the Empire who also made their names in the Boer War. Men such as Robert Baden Powell, Winston Churchill and Arthur Conan Doyle, the man who gave to the world the immortal, infallible detective Sherlock Holmes, all cut their teeth on the bushveldt, and so did 'The Banjo'.

Death at Dagworth Station

'The Banjo', who had his first verse published in the *Bulletin* in 1886, was spending the Christmas of 1894 at Dagworth Station on the Diamantina with his fiancée Sarah Riley, a friend of Christina Macpherson, the squatter's daughter. Dagworth was caught up in the shearers' strike and Paterson observed at first hand the bitter struggle between the two classes of men.

The shearers' strike of 1894 caused a long and bitter struggle between the squatters, the police and the itinerant shearers. The strike represented a real 'war of the classes' reminiscent of the struggle of the farm labourers in southern England almost a century earlier. At the end of the nineteenth century—and well into the twentieth—the union movement was well aware of the power of a well-aimed strike and was not afraid to use industrial muscle to achieve their aims when it came to improving the lot of the worker at the expense of the bosses.

The shearers had taken direct action against the squatter and burned down a woolshed at Dagworth. One man was killed and found the following morning inside the burnt-out shed.

Andrew 'Banjo' Paterson

In response Paterson wrote the words to a song that expressed something of the attitude of the free-wheeling bushman, who, comfortable on the road, lived his life in opposition to the restrictions of the ruling classes.

Waltzing Matilda

'The Banjo' called his song 'Waltzing Matilda', which he set to the tune of 'The Craigalee March', an old Scottish folk tune that he first heard Miss Macpherson play on her zither. This song eventually became Australia's unofficial national anthem, displacing 'The Wild Colonial Boy' from its position as number one. 'Waltzing Matilda' is a curious tale of the ubiquitous Australian bushman—the swaggie— who chooses death rather than be nabbed by the squatter's police for the crime of taking a sheep.

The 'war of the classes' is central to Paterson's theme; here a poor but happy fellow, camped out in the bush by the riverside, helps himself to a wandering sheep. What harm can there be in that? He takes what he needs to survive and puts the rest in his tuckerbag for later. On to the scene rides the squatter, the big man of the district, seated on his fine, thoroughbred horse; he is accompanied by not

WITHOUT

FREEDOM

DISHONOR

UNIONIST PRISONERS

Sentenced at Rockhampton, Q, May 1891, for causes arising out of Bush Strike.

H.C. SMITH-BARRY   W FOTHERGILL   A FORRESTER   J A S STUART

G. TAYLOR   P F GRIFFIN   E H MURPHY   H O BLACKWELL

A J BROWN   R PRINCE   W J BENNETT   D MURPHY

WILLIAM HAMILTON

one, not two, but three policemen, all eager to apprehend the poor swaggie.

Rather than give in to the law and spend his time staring at the walls of a dank prison cell, the swaggie prefers death to the loss of his liberty, and his humiliation at the hands of the police. He jumps into the billabong and drowns himself.

In the last verse the ghost of this free spirit of the Australian bush haunts the billabong as a reminder to all who would deny the poor man his liberty.

This theme is well recognised in the history of any nation struggling for freedom from oppression. The cry 'Death or Liberty' has been a catchcry from the rebel heart for as long as one person has been oppressed by another.

As a song 'Waltzing Matilda' was first heard publicly on 6 April 1895 when it was performed in the North Gregory Hotel in Winton, Central Queensland. Although it had been written several years before the Boer War it was not until 1903 that the tea importer James Inglis & Co. published the words as a song sheet, on which they placed an advertisement for the 'Billy Tea' on the back page. The song was an instant success.

The appeal of 'Waltzing Matilda' has endured for more than a century, making it possibly the most popular song in Australian history. It is recognised all around the world and is occasionally played, by mistake, instead of the real anthem of Australia.

The film version of Neville Shute's 1957 apocalyptic novel *On the Beach* sets Australia in the aftermath of a nuclear war. Towards the end of his story doomed Melbournians head for the hills in the Dandenongs for one last picnic before they face certain death by radiation poisoning. As they party on the banks of the Yarra River, draining bottles of Foster's beer, someone breaks into song.

'Unionist Prisoners' after the shearers' strike, Barcaldine, Queensland, 1893
Photograph taken after their release from prison.
Back row: HC Smith-Barry, W Fothergal, A Forrester, JAS Stuart
Second row: G Taylor, PF Griffin, EH Murphy, HD Blackwell
Front row: AJ Brown, R Prince, WJ Bennett, D Murphy
Reclining: W Hamilton
(John Oxley Library, State Library of Queensland)

It is 'Waltzing Matilda'. From the massed voices of these reluctant heroes, drawn together in the bonds of common humanity, ready to face certain death together–'Waltzing Matilda' had never sounded so poignant, so hauntingly beautiful.

'The Breaker', Poet of the Veldt

Edwin Henry Murrant was born an Englishman but soon came to typify the popular image of the hard-riding, hard-playing, wise-cracking, romantic, knockabout character of the late nineteenth-century Australian bush larrikin.

He was a natural in the saddle, an excellent shot (a skill that would later prove to be his downfall), had a fine voice, wrote charming poetry and rollicking bush ballads in the 'back-block bard' style–and was generally considered an all-round good bloke. Except by his wife. He had married Tipperary lass Daisy May O'Dwyer, the governess of Fanning Downs Station, in March 1884, just one year after he had arrived in the Colony of Queensland. Later known throughout the Empire as Daisy Bates, a woman who suffered no fool gladly, she booted him out after he had been caught stealing a few pigs and passing dud cheques.

Murrant re-invented himself as Harry 'The Breaker' Morant, and soon penned his way into the heart of rural Australia. 'The Breaker', so-called for his skill with horse flesh, began submitting his poems and ballads to the *Bulletin*, and Australia saw his first words in print.

'The Breaker' was a larger-than-life character. His good looks, easy charm, jovial good humour and fine singing voice made him a favourite around the campfire, popular with the ladies and a good mate among men.

When the war against the rebel South African Dutch colonists began towards the end of 1899, 'The Breaker' joined with more than 16,000 other young Australians, keen for adventure. He enlisted in the South Australian Mounted Rifles and left to fight the Boers for 'Queen and Country' on 26 January 1900.

As usual, politicians claimed that the 'war would be over by Christmas', but when the South Australian men arrived there was still plenty of fighting for them all to enjoy. The Boers had laid siege to the British garrison towns of Ladysmith, Mafeking and Kimberley and for the next four months it looked as if an English defeat was certain, but the hot winds of change blew across the veldt and the Boers were eventually routed—a cry went up all around the British colonies that 'Mafeking had been relieved' when the Royal Canadian Field Artillery arrived on 17 May 1900. That simple sentence entered the imperial lexicon on that day.

By June the English were convinced that the war was over; however, the Boers were not prepared to relinquish governance of their diamond and gold-rich republics of Transvaal and Orange Free State so readily. For two more years the Boer commando units harassed the British, blowing up trains, ambushing troop movements, attacking garrisons. The British retaliated with the same terrible tactics. They burned farms, destroyed crops, stopped food supplies and herded more than 25,000 white women and children into 'concentration camps' and virtually starved them to death.

For the Boers it was a new type of fighting—guerrilla warfare; for the English it was a return to form—they had done it all before, they simply decided to starve the enemy into submission. The colonial forces, caught in the middle, played follow the leader. The tail end of this war degenerated into a desperate struggle between opposing forces that ignored any of the proud traditions of noble warfare and became a bitter, cruel, drawn-out, bloody brawl.

The Bushveldt Carbineers

Lord Kitchener, Chief of Staff to the Commander of the British forces, was forced to spread his army across a wide area. He formed a number of irregular units, including the Bushveldt Carbineers, a regiment of 350 men commanded by the Australian Major Lenehan, almost half of whom were Australian volunteers.

This largely colonial regiment was in the thick of the action against the guerrilla Boer. Brave, fearful and fast, they had performed outstanding service and Morant had been responsible for the capture of a large number of the enemy. It was what they did with the captive Boers that brought the Bushveldt Carbineers into

Edwin Henry Murrant, better known as Harry Harboard 'The Breaker' Morant, in the uniform of the South Australian Mounted Rifles
(Australian War Memorial)

disrepute. Although Kitchener had given the order to take no prisoners, what was implied in his command was to make sure that the Boers did not surrender first. Countless numbers of the enemy were executed in the field, but it was the shooting of eight men who had surrendered to Lieutenant Morant's patrol on 3 August 1900, and the murder of the only witness, Reverend Hesse, by Lieutenant Handcock that brought them undone.

Anxious to bring an end to disquiet over the excesses on both sides in this seemingly endless reign of terror, and fearful of a public backlash if it became known that Boer prisoners were being summarily executed on the orders of the moustachioed hero of the Jubilee Queen's Imperial Army, Lord Kitchener instigated a show trial of the Australian light-horsemen.

'Shoot Straight You Bastards'

Both Morant and Handcock were found guilty of murder and sentenced to execution by firing squad at 6 a.m. on 27 February 1902. A third officer, George Whitton from Drouin, was sentenced to life imprisonment. Standing beside an open grave, the two Australians faced a line of British soldiers. As the firing squad raised their carbines to take aim, Morant, a larrikin to the last, shouted out, 'Shoot straight you bastards, don't make a mess of it.' Morant and Handcock were buried, one on top of the other, in a single, narrow grave in Pretoria.

Australians had just celebrated their becoming a new nation in 1901, and as Australians, were rightly incensed at the execution of two of their own at the hands of the English. After the executions the

Butchered to Make a Dutchman's Holiday
or *The Last Rhyme and Testament of Tony Lumpkin*

In prison cell I sadly sit,
A damned crest-fallen chappie!
And own to you I feel a bit—
A little bit—unhappy!

It really ain't the place nor time
To reel off rhyming diction—
But yet we'll write a final rhyme
Whilst waiting cru-ci-fixion!

No matter what 'end' they decide—
Quick-lime or 'b'iling ile', sir?
We'll do our best when crucified
To finish off in style, sir!

But we bequeath a parting tip
For sound advice of such men.

Who come across in transport ship
To polish off the Dutchmen!

If you encounter any Boers
You really must not loot 'em!
And if you wish to leave these shores,
For pity's sake, DON'T SHOOT 'EM!!

And if you'd earn a DSO,
Why every British sinner
Should know the proper way to go
Is: 'ASK THE BOER TO DINNER!'

Let's toss a bumper down our throat,
Before we pass to Heaven,
And toast: 'The trim-set petticoat
We leave behind in Devon.'

'The Breaker' Morant's last poem written from the doomed cell
First published in the *Bulletin*, 19 April 1902

English suffered such a backlash that no Australian has ever faced the prospect of execution by an English court martial since.

The deaths of Morant and Handcock proved the growing difficulty of the relationship between an independent Australian nation and an old colonial power. This fractured relationship between the Imperial and Colonial military remained for decades, causing the English to complain about the lack of respect shown to its officers by Australian troops on the battlefields of World War I.

It took more than 100 years for the name of Lieutenant Peter Joseph Handcock to be finally added to the list of Australians who served in the Boer War on the memorial in his home town of Bathurst in central New South Wales.

Recruiting Poster WWI, 1915
This poster shows a likeness of Albert Jacka, the first Australian
to be awarded the Victoria Cross at Gallipoli.
(La Trobe Picture Collection, State Library of Victoria)

A TIME
~ for ~
WAR

ONE PEOPLE, ONE NATION, ONE 'GLORIOUS' DESTINY

A CENTURY OF BLOOD

There Will be War, and Rumours of War, and More War

The twentieth century began where the nineteenth finished– awash with blood. The old queen died and the Victorian age, with its dark melancholy and repressed morality, died with her. For Australia a new age beckoned–a new nation was formed and Australians looked forward to an era of prosperity, an era of new technologies, the motor car, the electric telegraph, fast travel to all corners of the earth and a spirit of international cooperation between workers of all nations. This new age cast aside the enmity of the old century, signalled the end of the Empire and heralded in an age of the brotherhood of all humankind.

However, the world reckoned without the stupidity of the imperial family. The century was just into the second decade and the world was at war again. The last war against the Boers was a war fought for the Empire; this 'Great War' was to be fought for pride, revenge and capital over territory, and the new Australian nation could not wait for its first taste of blood. Where Britain was at war, so too Australia was at war.

The new nation of Australia saw the battlefields of France as a great opportunity to strut its stuff on the biggest stage of all, the theatre of war. However, Australia's defining moment

Recruiting Poster WWI, New South Wales 1915

This poster is signed by General Sir Ian Hamilton, the Oxford scholar whose command at Gallipoli was nothing short of disastrous for the Anzac troops. Hamilton was thrilled to have been sent to Gallipoli; for him it was an expedition to Troy, his opportunity to re-enact the classical battles of Homer.

(National Library of Australia)

would be its greatest defeat on the craggy cliff tops and narrow beaches of the Turkish peninsula at Gallipoli.

This defeat became the legend of Anzac. Australia had blooded itself on the world stage and showed the stuff it was made of. The spirit of Anzac was created on that beachhead and has become indelibly engraved on the nation's heart. The Anzac is epitomised in the good-humoured Aussie larrikin; the irreverent, dismissive of authority, hard working, fast shooting, reliable, trustworthy, charming, guileless and ultimately expendable Australian 'good bloke'.

The devil-may-care, free-wheeling egalitarianism of the Australians at war did create the Anzac legend; English author James Morris described the Anzacs in *Farewell to Arms*:

> Nobody had seen such soldiers before. They were truly like men from another world, or survivors from an old one. Tall, lean, powerful, cocky, their beauty was not merely physical, but sprang from their easy air of freedom. Their discipline was lax by British standards; they made terrible fun of the British officers, and regarded the British other ranks with a mixture of pity and affectionate condescension; but they brought to [the army] a loose-limbed authority all their own, as though they were not the subjects of events, but their sardonic masters.

To the British the colonials were a constant source of annoyance. They were insubordinate, and refused to take any notice of British army protocol. They displayed an independence of spirit that could not be tolerated among their own troops, and the Australian command could not allow any Australian be disciplined by an Englishman. Walter Guiness, British Staff Officer at Gallipoli, remarked: 'They all seem to address their officers as Bill or Dick and though wonderfully brave have absolutely no discipline.' One British general complained of the Australians in Egypt: 'Not only do your men fail to salute me, but they laugh at my orderlies.' English war correspondent Henry Nevinson wrote in 1915:

> A finer set of men ... could not be found in any country ... They walked the ground with careless and dare-devil self-confidence.

Rally Round the Flag
Published by the Central London Recruiting Depot, c.1915
(Australian War Memorial—ARTV05143)

Gifted with the intelligence that comes from freedom and healthy physique ... they could be counted on to face death, but hardly to salute an officer. Except in action, the control of such men was inevitably difficult.

Even Prime Minister Asquith wrote on 27 January 1915 of the Australians from Mena Camp after a Christmas raid on Cairo: 'The Australians have given a lot of trouble from their want of discipline and their strange habits ... but they are improving ... they are splendid raw material.'

The push to war did have its opponents. A large number among the Australian population who saw the war for what it was, a blue among old Europe's cousins, who for reasons of national pride were prepared to sacrifice the lives of hundreds of thousands of their loyal subjects to prove which branch of the family was the strongest; like old bulls bashing their heads together, the imperial crowned heads of Europe allowed themselves to be dragged back to war.

Conscription, Yes or No?

In Australia the large Irish Catholic community was not as eager to rush into uniform to support the English king as were the rest of the Australian population; the country almost divided into two opposing camps. In Ireland itself, the Irish nationalists actively sought support from the Germans during the war, hoping to be able to finally rid Ireland of the British. The British Army brutally crushed a rising in April 1916 and executed the Irish nationalist leaders by firing squad. Irish Catholics around the world, sympathetic to the cause of Irish independence, were horrified by the terrible vengeance of the British over the Easter Rebellion, and the hearts of most Irish Catholics in Australia were hardened against support for the English fighting in Flanders or on the Gallipoli Peninsula.

As a consequence of the English reprisals against the Irish nationalists the biggest issue for Australians at home was the question of conscription, and the Australian wartime prime minister, a fiery little Welshman named Billy Hughes, took on a bitter struggle he could not win.

Anglo-Protestants were anxious to arrest the decline in volunteer enrolments and urged the government to introduce conscription, as had Britain and New Zealand at the beginning of the war, but the Catholic Church in Australia would not hear of it. The Church denounced Hughes' plans and demanded that the issue of conscription be put to a referendum. The government defied the church with a pre-emptive strike; using the Defence Act, Hughes called up 200,000 for military training in Australia.

Hughes took on the nation. He railed against the Catholics championed by the Archbishop of Melbourne, Irish-born Daniel Mannix, a powerhouse of a man who led Melbourne Catholics for more than half a century with his example of humility, faithfulness, a strong belief in Irish family and community, and a good nose for politics; and influential Labor premier of Queensland Tom Ryan, the native-born son of illiterate Irish migrants.

The Labor Party was divided by its loyalty to Hughes and the seat of government and loyalty to the Catholic Church and the Irish state of mind. Hughes became increasingly imperialistic, which served to drive a wedge deeper into the heart of the Labor Party.

When the trade unions declared a national strike in protest, Hughes declared strikes illegal. The future prime minister of Australia, Victorian Labor official John Curtin, spent three days in gaol as one of 9000 men who refused to sign up for Hughes' national service. When members of International Workers of the World were charged for planning sabotage, Hughes had stacked up against his conscription appeal the unions, the Catholics and the socialists.

The referendum held on 28 October 1916 was soundly defeated by more than 75,000 votes. On 14 November when the party passed a vote of no confidence in Hughes, he stood up and said: 'Enough of this. Those who are prepared to stand by the British Empire and see the war to the end, please come with me.' As he left the room twenty-three others followed him, effectively destroying the Labor Party as they left. In February the following year Billy Hughes' National Labor Party joined with the Liberals to form the Nationalist Party.

A second referendum was held in December 1917 and this time Hughes was defeated by 94,000 votes. Even the Australians on the battle lines overseas voted against conscription; they believed that only those who wanted to fight for the Empire should enlist, and they didn't want to fight alongside any man whose heart was not in it. The division in the community created by Hughes' push for conscription to support the imperial power would never be completely healed.

An ambulance driver with the Australian Motor Transport Service in France wrote to his family in Ballarat: 'So Australia votes NO for conscription, to tell you the truth I didn't think they would get it by votes. You see the boys who have the stuff in them to go to a war have left and found what the word means, while those at home do not want to come and have voted accordingly.'

The Australians had rejected their prime minister's call to give their all for the Empire. While the majority of Australians may have supported the battle against the Germans, the safety of France and relief of poor Belgium, Australians were divided between loyalty to Empire and loyalty to a new Australian nation, and half of that nation remembered what Britain had done to its people in its past.

'BLUE STOCKINGS' AT WAR

"The ideal woman according to accepted ideas is the one who has spent her years in the seclusion of her home, bringing up her children in the precepts of religion and social behaviour, and refining by gentle demeanour, the rough edges of domestic life,' said TA Fitzgerald in *Australian Catholic Record* in 1903.

In the midst of pressure for women's rights in Australia by the suffragette movement, led by Vida Goldstein and Adele Pankhurst, daughter of Britain's Emily Pankhurst, Fitzgerald was describing an idealised view of middle-class gentility where a gentlewoman's touch smoothed the furrowed brow of her middle-class husband after a hard day making decisions on her behalf.

A large number of middle-class women were, however, demanding their right to participate in the decision making that determined the status, health and happiness of more than half of the Australian population.

When the 'blue stockings' of the women's movement in Australia began to agitate for reform to electoral laws and demand equal rights for Australian women, they were up against centuries of

'Vote No', anti-conscription poster produced by the Australian Labor Party
(Australian War Memorial)

Great suffragette demonstration in London, 1911

Vida Goldstein can be seen to the right of this group marching before a banner bearing the Australian coat of arms. While in London Vida met with Adele Pankhurst, estranged daughter of prominent British suffragette Emily Pankhurst, and encouraged her to join the fight in Australia.

Adele was a fiery personality, who introduced suffragette-style direct action to Australia. Often arrested, often gaoled, the *Argus* called her a 'notoriety hunter'. Prime Minister Hughes wrote: 'Adele Pankhurst is making herself a damned nuisance and I really don't know what to do with the little devil . . . I fear I shall have to deport her'.[11]

(National Library of Australia)

conservative male domination at all levels of society. Fitzgerald continued:

> It cannot be expected that the embedded prejudices of thousands of years will be easily removed, for there are legions of women of all grades of education who refuse to be reconciled to the iconoclastic doctrines of the new era, and prefer their womanly dignity and their domestic and social potentialities to any participation in the turmoil of political life.

Fitzgerald was not considering the determination of women such as Catherine Spence, Vida Goldstein, Rose Scott, Cecilia John and Adele Pankhurst.

Few men in power were prepared to accept that a woman in parliament would prove any worth at all. Moreover, most men were not prepared to allow women to see how it was they ran things.

Men's business was secret business, and most men wanted it
to stay that way. Business was
transacted in smoke-filled rooms
and sealed with a clink of a glass
and the wink of an eye. Men knew
that women could not fit into
that world; what men in power
failed to realise was that women
did not want to fit that world,
they wanted to change it to fit
themselves.

Across the globe there were
women who persistently led the
charge against prejudice and
power to demand their equal
rights. The international suffragette movement had thrown
up charismatic and determined

Portrait of Vida Goldstein used for
publicity in her election campaign
*(La Trobe Picture Collection, State Library of
Victoria)*

leaders and the women of the Australian movement were inspired
by, and integrated with, them.

The international women's movement was passionate about
reforms to all levels of social life (ignored by men) with a profound
impact on their lives, social cohesion—education, maternity allowances, children's courts, divorce laws, inheritance laws, contraception,
birth control, establishment of women's hospitals, conscription—and
the struggle against war.

The women's suffrage movement had been active in Australia
since the 1880s, when the determined South Australian political
activist Catherine Spence took on the world of men. Spence published her book *Plea for Pure Democracy* in 1880 and her persistence
led to South Australian women being the first in any Australian
colony to gain the right to vote. No records were kept of how many
women actually did vote when they went to the polls in 1896;
although for the first time women were also eligible to stand for
election, none did.

Catherine Spence was the first female political candidate in Australia when she nominated for election to the 1897 Federal Convention. The only woman on the ballot, one group put her name on their ticket, which bore the heading '10 Best Men' and Spence was considered the 'best man of the lot'. However, she was not successful.

Spence continued to campaign for the welfare of working women; she was committed to social, educational and political reform, and was instrumental in the establishment of the world's first Children's Court, which was established in South Australia. Where Spence carried the campaign in South Australia, Rose Scott led the Womanhood Suffrage League in New South Wales and Vida Goldstein in Victoria.

Although Catherine Spence was forty years older than Vida Goldstein they became close friends and in many ways Goldstein took over where Spence left off after she died in 1910. Four years later the Empire was at war again and the new Australian nation rushed to join in the fray. The women's movement swung its considerable energies into opposition to the war effort.

The Peace Army

Vida Goldstein's response to the declaration of war on Germany was reported in the *Herald* on 11 August 1914:

> I think that it is a fearful reflection on 2000 years of Christianity that men have rushed into war before using every combined effort to prevent this appalling conflict. It is my earnest hope that women in all parts of the world will stand together, demanding a more reasonable and civilised way of dealing with international disputes.
>
> The time has come for women to show that they, as givers of life, refuse to give their sons as material for slaughter, and that they recognise that human life must be the first consideration of nations.

An ardent pacifist, Goldstein used the pages of her journal *The Woman Voter* to pursue her agitation against the war and her fight against conscription. She risked a split from her supporters in the Women's Political Alliance over her establishment of the Women's Peace Army in 1915.

Pro-conscription poster
(National Library of Australia)

There were many, both men and women, who had supported her in her fight for the rights of women, who turned away from her anti-conscription stance. An organisation called the One Woman, One Recruit League emerged; its patriotic members used all their feminine charms to urge young men to enlist. Whenever Goldstein and members of WPA spoke in public, the meetings were attended by gangs of men, returned and wounded soldiers who heckled and jostled the speakers as they took the stand. They became so concerned for their safety when they spoke in the open air on the Yarra Bank that they even undid their shoelaces before they rose to speak in case they were picked up and thrown in the river. The police moved against them whenever they spoke out; they didn't want to see a repeat of the events that had taken place in England when buildings were destroyed during the struggle of the suffragettes.

The fight against conscription was a bitter struggle. The WPA was just one group who took the argument right up to the government. In the end, a referendum failed to deliver to the government a majority 'Yes' vote. Even soldiers at the front voted overwhelmingly against conscription, but their agitation could not stop the war. Goldstein was convinced that the armaments manufacturers, who made huge profits from the war, should be stopped: 'The policy of huge armaments which made war inevitable, and rendered it so dreadful when it came, was dictated by an international ring of armament firms under the direction of prominent and all-powerful statesmen and financiers who control parliaments, government and the press.' (There were armaments used by the Turks on Gallipoli, made from Australian raw materials, which were thrown back against Australian soldiers.)

However, the influence of the Women's Peace Army was at its greatest when tugging at the nation's heartstrings. The appeal to the mothers of the nation did not go unheard; even the government pushed hard to counter the emotional appeal made by the female activists. Singing the anti-war song 'I Didn't Raise My Son to be a Soldier' was banned by the authorities but that did not stop activist Cecilia John from raising her voice in song at the closure of their many public meetings:

> I didn't raise my son to be a soldier
> I raised him up to be my pride and joy
> Who dares to put a musket to his shoulder
> To kill some other mother's darling boy
> Why should he fight in someone else's quarrels
> It's time to put the sword and gun away
> There would be no war today
> If the nations all would say:
> No I didn't raise my son to be a soldier.

Pro-war supporters changed this song's lyrics:

> I didn't raise my son to be a soldier
> But as a soldier he's my pride and joy
> I'd have him bear a musket to his shoulder
> Like every patriot mother's darling boy
> God grant Australia never will have mothers
> Like Pankhurst, Goldstein, John and all their crew;
> Our boys must fight today
> And never will I say
> I didn't raise my son to be a soldier.[12]

THE SPIRIT OF ANZAC
Larrikin Pommie Becomes an Anzac Legend

There is one man who epitomises *the* true spirit of Anzac and he was neither Australian nor New Zealander. He was Jack Simpson Kirkpatrick of South Shields, a Geordie from Tyneside in the north of England.

Born in 1892 to Scottish parents, Jack spent his youth around the Tyneside docks, watching the merchant ships go in and out, marvelling at the strangely garbed sailors from all the world over tumbling down the gangplanks and onto the streets around the docks; to Jack this was a world apart and he could not wait to join it.

His father was crippled in an accident on board ship and it was a time when there was no compensation or pension, so Jack was forced to leave school at the age of ten and become the family breadwinner.

He took a job as a milk boy, pushing a hand cart through the streets and lanes of the Tyne Dock area crying out 'Milko', ladling out the pints and collecting the copper coins in payment.

Left: 'Simpson' and his donkey, Gallipoli, 1915
(National Library of Australia)

Right: Privates AJ Currie (left) and John Simpson Kirkpatrick, both of the 3rd Field Ambulance, in Blackboy Camp WA
(Australian War Memorial—A03116)

In 1909, Jack left home two days after his father died. He had signed on as a storeman/steward on board a ship bound for the Mediterranean. This meant a steady wage, and he would always send money home to his mother; his empty room meant Mum could take in a boarder as well, to supplement what little he could give.

A year later he signed on as stoker on board a merchant ship bound, this time, for South America and Australia. To the young Tyneside lad this was to be a great adventure to the other side of the world, but it was to be no Mediterranean cruise this time. The conditions were so hard that Jack and thirteen others jumped ship—a serious offense in the merchant navy—when they docked in Newcastle in New South Wales.

Jack headed for the bush. He went up to Queensland to try his hand at cane cutting, but it was far too hot for him and the pay was way too low. He threw a swag over his shoulder and, with a mate, took to the 'wallaby track'. He found work as a jackeroo and a coal miner, and was even charged with the assault of a drunken landlord before he found his way back to the sea. He signed on again as stoker on board the *Yakalilla* out of Fremantle in Western Australia.

They were at sea when war broke out between Britain and Germany. Jack heard the news as soon as they arrived back in Fremantle, so he jumped ship again and headed for Perth to enlist with the Australian Army. He was a little fearful of the army checking his past; a runaway merchantman was probably not the best of pedigrees, so he signed on as simply John Simpson.

The years shovelling coal had made Jack a fine figure of British manhood so he was selected to join C Bearer Section, 3rd Field Ambulance. Only the strongest were suitable for this heavy work as they could be expected to carry the wounded day after day.

He wrote to his mother, expecting to be sent to England to train before they joined the Allied Forces on the battlefields of France and hoping that he may have time to make a flying visit to South Shields, but the 3rd Field Ambulance was sent to Egypt instead to prepare for the British invasion of Turkey on the Gallipoli Peninsula.

The war in France was at a stalemate. The troops, on both sides, were literally bogged down in the mud on the Western Front.

The Russian Army facing the Germans on the Eastern Front were in danger of collapse. They were fast running out of supplies, and the heavy machinery needed for this new kind of modern warfare was all but destroyed. The British decided to help re-arm the Russians, turn them back against the Germans and force the enemy to fight on two fronts at once, but first they needed to re-open the supply route to the Black Sea, and that route, through the Dardanelles and the Sea of Marmora, was guarded by heavy Turkish armaments on the shores of the Gallipoli Peninsula. The British needed to push the Turkish out of the way, disarm their guns and allow the allied fleet to pass unhindered through to Russia. The British were confident they would meet with little resistance, sure that they could simply drive the Turks from the peninsula, anchor in the shadow of Constantinople and force Turkey to surrender. The allied fleet steamed in through the Dardanelles on 18 March 1915, and at around 9 a.m. began to bombard the Turkish defences. The fleet was quite surprised when the Turks fired back with alarming accuracy.

Minesweepers—old fishing trawlers fitted with cable-cutters—were sent in to clear the mines that blocked the sea lanes, but they were hit by such withering fire from the Turkish guns the merchant crewmen turned and fled. The bombardment from both sides lasted until around five in the afternoon and then it stopped. The British, having done a day's work, closed up shop and turned for home. Little did they know at the time that the Turks had almost exhausted their ammunition and could have been easily overrun if only the fleet had kept the bombardment up for just a little longer.

Three allied ships had been either sunk or disabled, 750 allied troops killed, and they had achieved nothing. Not one of the Turkish guns or mines had been destroyed. Probably the only thing the fleet had done was to warn the Turks that they were keen on taking Gallipoli. Where the great British navy had once ruled the waves they were defeated for the first time since Nelson by the Turkish soldiers on the cliff tops defending their homeland.

The Landing at Anzac Cove, 8 a.m., 25 April 1915
Photograph published in the *Argus* newspaper, 1915
An Australian engineer was the first man to fall at Gallipoli on 25 April 1915;
he can be seen here in the foreground of this photograph, still lying where
he fell dead on the beach. Soldiers from the 4th Battalion are seen landing,
as are mules for the 26th Indian Mountain Battery.
(National Archives of Australia)

The Invasion of Anzac Cove

The allied invasion of the Gallipoli Peninsula was set for dawn on
25 April 1915. Having failed to knock out the Turkish from the sea
the British thought they could be successful by attacking overland,
driving the Turks out and disabling the seaward defences in three
days. Fifty thousand men were landed on the Aegean shores on that
fateful morning. The British landed at Helles Point and met little
resistance; a strong current pushed the Australians one mile north
of their proposed landing point to what is now known as Anzac Cove.
When the small craft motored towards the beach in the grey light
of dawn, all hell broke loose. The Turks rained everything they had
down upon the Australians; the sea was virtually whipped into a
frenzy of spray, so much lead was pounding into it.

The troops were packed in so tightly that two men on either
side of Simpson were both killed where they stood together in the

landing craft, the third member of his stretcher crew was also killed. Infantrymen who fell overboard were drowned, dragged down by the weight of their kit before any sailors could haul them back to the surface. When Simpson scrambled onto the beach at Anzac Cove he was the only one of his team still alive.

Once ashore and out of danger, Simpson began to carry wounded men back to an aid station that had been set up on a beachhead secured below an outcrop known as the Sphinx. With other bearers he went to clear the beach of wounded below an old fisherman's hut when they discovered a terrible sight: two boats, slapping against the shore were still filled with Australian soldiers. Men sat upright staring at the beach, so tightly packed into the small craft they looked as if they would leap out and dash ashore, but every single man was dead. Simpson began to carry wounded back along the beach until the sand between the cliff face and the sea was covered in bloodied men. Gallipoli had taken a terrible toll on both sides, each losing an estimated 2000 men on that first day.

The following day, 26 April, John Simpson found himself alone. He had lost the three men who were to be his squad and did not want to join with any others. At that time hundreds of horses, and other pack animals had been landed so Simpson commandeered a stray donkey, naming him Duffy, and began to ferry wounded men from the front line to the aid station on the shore on his own.

He only carried men who could sit upright, men with leg or sometimes head wounds, and made hundreds of trips every day through some of the most dangerous parts of the Gallipoli terrain. He seemed oblivious to the danger around him; so long as he could help another man to safety, he did not take care for his own.

He remained a singular figure, refusing to return to his own unit at the end of a day's shift, even after he had been ordered to do so. He chose to spend the night with the Indian artillery troops, tying his donkey alongside their mules to feed and water them. Once again Simpson was playing outside the rules. He could have been considered a deserter after he refused the order to return to his unit given him by Sergeant Oscar Hookaway. Simpson told another bearer: 'To hell with them, the old donk and I can do as much as four men.'

The officers knew what he was doing did not fit any part of army regulations, but while he did it so well they left him to get on with it, as long as he reported back to his unit at least once a day.

Simpson kept at it day after day. He saw a number of his donkeys killed, and lost some wounded men, shot by Turkish snipers as he ferried them across the battlefield, but he kept at his self-appointed task. Everybody knew John Simpson, even the Turks were aware of the daring bravery of the 'man with the donkey'. He saved the lives of countless men, including one fellow Geordie who he had known as a child, but the two men did not even recognise each other on the hot and dusty battlefield.

The Turks mounted an all-out attack on 19 May 1915. Turkish commander Mustafa Kemal threw more than 40,000 men against the Anzac force of only 17,000 men. The Turks lost 3000 men in a failed attempt to push the Anzacs back into the sea. They were caught in the open and wave after wave of Turkish soldiers were cut to ribbons. The Anzacs lost only 168. One of those was Jack Simpson Kirkpatrick.

A Turkish machine-gunner strafing the Anzac lines along Monash Valley finally hit his mark, and a bullet struck Simpson in the back, killing him instantly. After twenty-four days on the Gallipoli battlefield Simpson lay dead, sprawled face down in the dust, his faithful donkey standing over his lifeless body.

When the news went out that night that the man with the 'donk' had copped a bullet, the Anzac lines fell into silence as they buried his body in the sand at Hell Spit. Private John Simpson had passed from larrikin to legend.

Both John Monash and Lieutenant Colonel Sutton sought to have him awarded the Victoria Cross, but the request was made incorrectly, under the category of heroism, and was denied. Sutton wrote: 'It is difficult to get evidence of any one act to justify the VC; the fact is he did so many.' Half a century later the Australian prime minister petitioned the British War Office again but the request was again denied, this time on the grounds that it would set a dangerous precedent, to award someone a medal after such a long time. Yet a precedent had already been set by the English themselves when they awarded VCs to two British Officers in 1907, for service in South Africa twenty-eight years earlier. Trouble is, Simpson had not killed anyone in the name of 'King or country', he had just died in battle after saving hundreds from a senseless death in their name.

Simpson was not the ideal soldier; he was cheeky and irreverent, he disobeyed orders and displayed no real love for 'King', or even 'country' for that matter, but was dedicated to the service of his fellow man, no matter what his station. For that he became an Anzac legend.

Despite his rough and often larrikin behaviour Simpson was genuinely concerned for the welfare of other people—and not only that of his family and friends, but of total strangers—to the point that he was willing to jeopardise his life to help them. He was not only a hero, he was a human being.

The End of the Campaign

Although he had failed to gain an appointment as an official war correspondent—a ballot had gone in favour of Charles W Bean instead—Keith Murdoch, journalist and confidante of Australian Labor Prime Minister Andrew Fisher, gained permission to visit the Gallipoli battlefield. On his arrival Murdoch was shocked at the waste of life and lack of success at Gallipoli and was disturbed by the misuse of power by the English commander General Ian Hamilton. Renowned English correspondent Ellis Ashmead-Bartlett gave Murdoch a letter he had written to British Prime Minister Asquith. He asked Murdoch to present his account of the debacle at Gallipoli, bring an end to Hamilton's command and evacuate the peninsula before winter, before too many more lives were wasted. Ashmead-Bartlett was convinced that the peninsula could not be won by the allied forces unless there was a massive build-up of troops and change of command.

There were plenty of dissenting voices in the military command who believed that the Gallipoli campaign had been an unmitigated disaster. They wanted to take the allies out of Turkey and onto the fields of Flanders, where the war had stalled, for a concerted push

Recruiting Poster WWI

Printed in Melbourne by Troedel & Cooper, November 1915

Sporting identity John Wren had set the prize of £500 and a gold watch to the first Anzac to win a VC—Albert Jacka.

In Frank Hardy's book *Power Without Glory* 'John West' volunteered to join the Sportsman's Thousand, touring Australia in the company of his VC winner in a successful recruiting drive. However, West declined the invitation to join the boys in battle.

(National Library of Australia)

against the Bosch. Ashmead-Bartlett's letter would play right into the hands of the Dardanelles Committee, and bring Hamilton into disrepute.

Murdoch was on his way back to London when Hamilton became aware of the letter. Murdoch was arrested en route, in Marseilles, by French military police and the letter taken from him.

When Murdoch arrived back in London he dictated a copy of Ashmead-Bartlett's letter from memory, and addressed it to Australian Prime Minister Fisher. When Asquith received a copy of Murdoch's letter he made it public before Secretary of War Lord Kitchener had a chance to read it. Asquith effectively sidelined the leader of the expeditionary forces and sought an end to the disastrous Gallipoli campaign.

The Murdoch Letter

Before the campaign had started British Prime Minister Asquith asked Field Marshall Kitchener if the Australian and New Zealand forces would be good enough to invade at Gallipoli. Kitchener grunted in reply: 'Good enough, if a cruise on the Sea of Marmora is all that is contemplated.'

The British officers had little time for the undisciplined colonial troops; General Ian Hamilton had seen the Australians training at Lilydale in 1914, and thought they drilled poorly in comparison to New Zealanders he had seen. How things were changed by the events of 1915. At the end of the war British poet John Masefield described them as 'the finest army that served in the Great War', and it wasn't attention to military discipline or the correctness of a salute that made them so fine. Charles Bean agreed: 'It was the devil of the Australian, the wild pastoral independent life of Australia, if it makes rather wild men, makes superb soldiers.'

Murdoch wrote to Fisher of his impressions of the British troops he had seen at Suvla Bay:

> The spirit of Suvla is simply deplorable. You would refuse to believe that these are really British soldiers … They show an atrophy of mind and body that is appaling …
>
> I fear that the British physique is very much below that of the Turks. Our men have found it impossible to form a high opinion of the British K men and territorials …
>
> They are merely a lot of childlike youths without strength to endure or brains to improve their conditions. I do not like to dictate this sentence, even for your eyes, but the fact is that after the first day at Suvla an order had to be issued to officers to shoot without mercy any soldiers who lagged behind or loitered in advance. The Kitchener army showed perfection in manoeuvre training—but that is not the kind of training required at the Dardanelles … every Australian officer and man agree with what I say.
>
> At Anzac the morale is good. The men are thoroughly dispirited, except the new arrivals. They are weakened sadly by dysentery and illness. They have been overworked, through lack of reinforcements. And as an army of offence they are done … the one way to cheer them up is to pass the word that the Turks are going to attack, or that an assault by our forces is being planned. The great fighting spirit of our race is still burning in these men; but it does not burn among the toy soldiers of Suvla.
>
> You could imagine nothing finer than the spirit of some Australian boys—all of good parentage—who were stowed away on a troopship I was on in the Aegean, having deserted their posts in Alexandria out of mere shame of the thought of returning to Australia without having taken part in the fighting on Anzac's sacred soil. These fine country lads, magnificent men, knew that the desertion would cost

them their stripes, but that and the loss of pay did not worry them. How wonderfully generous is the Australian soldier's view of life! These lads discussed quite fearlessly the prospects of their deaths, and their view was, 'It is no disgrace for an Australian to die beside good pals in Anzac, where his best pals are under the dust.'

…I could pour into your ears so much truth about the grandeur of our Australian army, and the wonderful affection of these fine young soldiers for each other and their homeland, that your Australianism would become a more powerful sentiment than before. It is stirring to see them, magnificent manhood, swinging their fine limbs as they walk about Anzac. They have the noble faces of men who have endured. Oh, if you could picture Anzac as I have seen it, you would find that to be an Australian is the greatest privilege the world has to offer.

For the general staff, and I fear for Hamilton, officers and men have nothing but contempt. Sedition is talked around every tin of bully beef on the peninsula, and it is only loyalty that holds the forces together.

Colonel John Monash, a brilliant soldier who earned the admiration of every Australian who fought with him and later became the finest commander of Anzac forces on the Somme, wrote from Gallipoli:

If possible have the Colonial troops taken off the Peninsula altogether because they are miserably depressed since the last failure and with their active minds, and positions they occupy in civil life, a dreary winter in the trenches will have a deplorable effect on what is left of this once magnificent body of men, the finest any Empire has ever produced. If we are obliged to keep this army locked up in Gallipoli this winter large reserves will be necessary to make good its losses in sickness.

Yet Kitchener believed that he still could win against the Turks, and was prepared to sacrifice as many Anzacs as it would take to win. He visited Gallipoli in November and although the Dardanelles Committee had recommended evacuation, he gained assurance from the navy for their support for one last push. But it never came.

The Anzac troops were pulled out in a silent evacuation that began on the night of 11 December 1915.

Rifles had been rigged up to fire indiscriminantly during the night, and as the last few troops ranged back and forth along the trenches they fired into the Turkish lines, convincing them that the Anzac army was still in their dugouts. At 7.15 a.m. the Turks launched an attack on the Anzac lines, only to find them deserted.

After eight gruelling months of death, destruction and eventual defeat the Australian Expeditionary Forces had slipped away under the cloak of darkness, leaving 10,000 men dead on Turkish soil. As the small boats rowed silently from the shore, one departing soldier casting his eye back over the fading coastline murmured to his mate: 'I hope they don't hear us leave.' The last of the Anzacs were safely out of Gallipoli by 19 December, having lost only two men during the entire evacuation.

The British stayed at Capes Helles until they too abandoned their position, a day after a brutal Turkish offensive on 7 January 1916.

Eight months after what had been intended to be a quick four-week push to Constantinople, 46,000 allied troops lay dead—10,000 of these were Anzacs—220,000 men wounded, and more than 250,000 Turks killed.

The words of Colonel Mustafa Kemal, commander of the Turkish Forces on Gallipoli, have honoured the Australians on a memorial erected at Gallipoli:

> Those heroes that shed their blood and lost their lives ... you are now lying in the soil of a friendly country, therefore rest in peace. There is no difference between the Johnnies and the Mehmets to us where they lie side by side here in this country of ours ... You, the mothers, who sent their sons from far away countries wipe away your tears. Your sons are now lying in our bosom and are in peace. After having lost their lives on this land they have become our sons as well.

Artists on the Front Line

Artist Will Dyson had worked on the *Bulletin* and like his brother-in-law, another *Bulletin* artist, Norman Lindsay, he also had an acute

Postscript to Battle

It is believed that the sword carried by Peter Lalor at the battle of the Eureka Stockade in Ballarat, on 3 December 1854, was carried by his grandson Captain Joseph Peter Lalor at the invasion of Gallipoli. Captain Lalor was killed at around 3.30 p.m. on the first day of the landing; when he stood up to motion his men forward he cried out, 'Now then, 12th Battalion . . .' and was struck down by a Turkish bullet. The sword was picked up later by Lance Corporal Freame but lost again during heavy fighting at dusk.

Britain executed 346 of its own men for offences committed in the face of battle; 266 of these were for desertion. Not one Australian soldier was executed.

Twenty years after the war, the British Parliament considered abolishing the death penalty for desertion, arguing: 'If it can be demonstrated that the Australians could fight as gallantly as they did without the penalty, then it is a libel on the courage of other British troops to say they can't fight without it.'

eye for character and detail. Both viewed the world with a degree of cynicism—tinged with good humour—and both wielded their pens against the Hun. Dyson was an exceptional draughtsman, an accomplished engraver, cartoonist, writer and poet. Whereas Lindsay fought his war from behind the easel, Dyson chose to observe the campaign from the front line.

Will Dyson was one of seven children, born near Ballarat in 1880, the son of a mining engineer who was also an active socialist. He was first encouraged to draw by his older brothers, Ted and Ambrose, who were both working artists, both contributing drawings to the socialist paper the *Champion*.

Dyson began to have drawings published in the *Bulletin* and by 1904 took a position as a staff artist on the *Adelaide Critic*.

Dyson travelled to London in 1909 where he found ready employment, contributing to the *Weekly Despatch* and later as cartoonist for the radical *Daily Herald*, where he was given a full page to draw whatever he wished. The power and passion he exhibited on these pages caused him to be regarded as one of the finest cartoonists of his age. Then the world fell inexorably into war.

Although he abhorred the idea of war Dyson volunteered for the army, believing that he had a duty to join the defence of Belgium and

Fatalist
Charcoal and wash drawing by Will Dyson, 1917
This drawing bore the following caption '. . . the fatalist is born not made.
The growing strain of the game is not producing more fatalists if ducking
under shell fire is proof of an absence of fatalism.
For many who have never ducked are now ducking, whether from wisdom
or war strain they are taking this instinctive precaution . . . he can't prevent
the 'whiz-bangs' and the 'five-nines' but can defy them . . . as though he were to
say "If you are going to hit me, you swine, you will hit me, but you can't
stop me calling you bastard while you are doing it".'
(Australian War Memorial Collection—ART02224)

France against the onslaught of the Germans. He arrived in France
in December 1916 and for the first six months remained unpaid as
he sought an appointment not as a combatant, but as an official war
artist, a rank that did not exist at that time. Eventually Will Dyson
became both the first 'official' war artist of World War I and the
first artist at the front. At the front he formed a friendship with the
military historian WC Bean, who wrote of Dyson's artworks, some
which were published in Dyson's book *Australia at War*, that 'very
little that is equal to them exists in Australian literature'.

Dyson did not care too much to keep himself safely out of the
firing line, but preferred to be in the thick of the action where he
could accurately observe the tragedy, and the humour, of war in

the trenches. He was twice wounded in action. His drawings of front-line soldiers show a great empathy for the ordinary man in uniform, but he depicted 'the Brass' in much the same manner as he had drawn 'Big Business' in pre-war London, with derision. His socialist upbringing had made him champion the tommy—the worker, the bloke; and he had little time for those who pulled the strings sending decent working men to their deaths. His mocking depiction of Kaiser Bill, published regularly in the British press, had a profound influence on how the British regarded the German nation and served as influential propaganda in maintaining support for the war.

When a book of Dyson's anti-German cartoons was published in 1915, in which he regularly lampooned the figure of the Kaiser as an overweight, strutting, proud and jingoistic buffoon, the drawings were accompanied by the following foreword: 'Mr Dyson responds to all the fearful pressure of this war in cartoons. He perceives a militaristic monarchy and national pride a threat to the world, to civilisation, and all that he holds dear, and straightaway he sets about to slay it with his pencil … he turns his passionate gift against Berlin.'

Dyson's wife Ruby died in the influenza pandemic that followed the end of the war. He was devastated by her death and fell into deep depression, suffering a mental breakdown. On recovery he began to draw again and in May 1919 created his most famous cartoon, *Peace and Future Cannon Fodder*, which predicted that the onerous terms of the Treaty of Versailles would ultimately be the cause of a second war. He even suggested that twenty years—one generation—later, crowned heads and vainglorious politicians of Europe would once again be sending their sons into battle, slaughtering one another in the defence of their national pride.

Norman Lindsay–Patriot who Scandalised the 'Wowsers'

When it came to upsetting the applecart of conservative morality, there was none better at it than Victorian artist Norman Lindsay. Lindsay was a prolific artist, whose skills as an engraver remain

Left: Portrait of Norman Lindsay, c.1921
Photograph by Harold Cazneaux
(National Library of Australia)

Right: The Last Call
World War I recruiting poster by Norman Lindsay, published by WE Smith Ltd,
Sydney, for the Government of the Commonwealth of Australia, 1918
(National Library of Australia)

unparalleled even to the present day, and he used the power of this graphic medium to prod and poke at the hypocritical 'waspish' social conservatism of the society into which he was born in the latter decades of the nineteenth century.

Lindsay was born in 1879 in Creswick in the gold mining region of central Victoria, near Ballarat. His father was a doctor, his mother the daughter of a missionary, who both encouraged their children to engage in the arts and to use their talents to enjoy all that a civilised and modern world had to offer them.

Norman was not a healthy child and during one bout of illness he was forced to stay indoors over a long period of inactivity; it was during this time that he developed his love of drawing, and by age eleven was proving himself to be accomplished well beyond his years.

Norman Lindsay was the fifth of ten children. His elder brothers, Percy, Daryl and Lionel, were also accomplished artists who enjoyed their own popularity and built strong reputations, although in later years they were also often affronted by the scandal that the ribald works of their younger brother Norman brought to the family name.

Norman moved to Melbourne in 1895 to work with his brother Lionel on a local magazine. Six years later both artists moved to Sydney where they joined the staff of the *Bulletin*, the defiantly nationalistic Australian weekly newspaper published by JF Archibald. There the brothers produced scores of illustrations and cartoons on demand. They drew in almost identical styles, which were at times indistinguishable from one another. Norman's relationship with the *Bulletin* would last for more than the next fifty years. In that time he produced thousands of drawings that characterise the true nature of a nascent Australian national identity, and astute observations of the Australian character and Australian society, both town and country.

However, it was Norman's preoccupation with the curvature of the well-endowed female form, coupled with a curious, satirical and mocking view of the church, that put him at loggerheads with the influential 'wowsers' in turn-of-the-century Australian society.

Melbourne had barely recovered from the shock of *Chloe*, a large, oddly depilated nude by French artist Jules Lefebvre when, in 1904, Norman Lindsay produced the scandalous drawing titled 'Pollice Verso' (Thumbs Down). Once again the wowsers were outraged. His detailed drawing of Christ on the cross being given the 'thumbs down' by a large party of naked pagans sent Victorian society into uproar. It seems that Norman Lindsay was hell bent on scandalising all of Victorian society.

The uproar over 'Pollice Verso' and the constant attack by the moralising conservatives in society didn't stop Lindsay from making his mark. Throughout all of his life he did whatever it was that he wanted to do, and with every picture held up a mirror to society. Just as the wowsers abhorred the libertine, Lindsay abhorred hypocrisy. When John Norton, the hard-drinking, scandal-mongering

'Never since Man saw the face of the Devil have been such creations of absolute evil.'

—comment made by a clergyman when this drawing 'Pollice Verso' was purchased by the Art Gallery of Victoria in 1904 for the princely sum of £150.

The newspapers had a field day with Norman Lindsay, who was undeterred by the barrage of criticism he received over this work. He didn't stop there. When he published the engraving 'The Crucified Venus' in 1912 he was lucky to escape crucifixion himself.

(Reproduced by Permission. Collection, National Gallery of Victoria)

editor of the *Truth* newspaper who claimed to have invented the word 'wowser' in 1899 and railed against their influence year after year, wrote in the *Truth* in 1904, 'Watery wowsers who wouldn't be seen sipping a nobbler in a public house, but who swig good stif [sic] inches from the big black bottle on the bedroom shelf,' he was putting into words the same ideas that Lindsay was putting into his drawings. Both had enormous impact, but it is the description of Lindsay's erotic, voluptuous forms that leave nothing to the imagination. When a wowser looked at a Lindsay all he saw was the blatant sexuality of the ordinary human being in a natural state, coupled with a rejection of an established social order based on blind dogma and spirit-crippling 'calvanism'. The conservatives hated both men for their freedom to express themselves without fear or favour.

Fighting the Hun with his Pen

Throughout the years of the Great War, 1914–18, Lindsay put the power of his pen to work for the war effort. He produced scores of drawings that expressed the nation's attitude to the war and prepared designs for posters used to encourage fresh volunteers to join up and fight against 'the Hun'.

Lindsay's method of communicating was the epitome of brevity with a powerful and direct message. His graphic description of the

'Hun' leaves no doubt how he saw the enemy, the dauntless 'Aussie' more often than not depicted with his back to the wall. Lindsay knew how to tug at the heartstrings of the nation.

Shock of the Nude

Norman Lindsay was not alone in his ability to shock the staid citizens of 'marvellous Melbourne'. A work by Parisian artist Jules Lefebvre, having won gold medals in the Paris Salon in 1875, the Sydney International Exhibition in 1879 and the Melbourne International Exhibition the following year, scandalised Melbourne society when it was exhibited at the National Gallery of Victoria. Coincidentally, two prominent hangings were creating a furore at the same time in 1880–*Chloe* in the gallery and Ned Kelly in Pentridge–both dominated the news.

Chloe, an almost life-size oil painting of a strangely asexual yet pert young lass was purchased in 1882 by Melbourne surgeon Dr Thomas Fitzgerald for the not inconsiderable sum of £850. He loaned the work to the National Gallery of Victoria for a term of three years as he was planning a trip back to Ireland. Thereafter hangs the scandal.

Poster by Norman Lindsay, 1918
In direct contrast to his engravings, which were intended to shock the conservative, over-moralistic 'wowsers', Lindsay's posters were unashamedly patriotic, even at times bellicose.
(National Archives of Australia Collection)

The good citizens of Melbourne were mortified; apart from the fact that such an image could be hung for all and sundry to see, the gallery was open on Sunday. The 'wowsers' of Melbourne, the Sunday Observance League and the Presbyterian Church were outraged and forced the gallery to withdraw *Chloe* from public exhibition.

Years later Fitzgerald caused further indignation when he hung

250

'The Wowser':

*An ineffably pious person who mistakes this world for a penitentiary and himself for a warder—*CJ Dennis

Just as there have always been Australians who have bucked the system, there has always been another group that preferred to take the moral high ground. They earned for themselves the sobriquet 'wowsers'.

Rebels of all colours, from the opinion leaders among the politicians, music-hall performers, artists, poets, writers and journalists to the working man fond of his grog at the end of the day, a shilling on the ponies and a good ribald joke, have been the target of the prying eye of the conservative, moralising 'wowsers'.

Born of the white Anglo-Saxon Protestant temperance movement, the wowsers looked with disdain at almost every attempt of the ordinary Australians to enjoy themselves. They abhorred strong drink, were disdainful of gambling, were shocked by artworks and refused any attempt to allow any activity on the Sabbath other than bible-thumping, hellfire and damnation sermonising and hymn singing.

Is it any wonder that the Australians, a national character born of the cast-offs of British society, rejected the interference of the wowsers? Yet this class maintained an enormous influence on the conservative capitalists at the big end of town. Lindsay took his pen to them and mercilessly satirised them in print.

the painting in his front parlour in Lonsdale Street; passers-by could sometimes catch a glimpse of the painting and complaints were made. Fitzgerald was forced to move her to the back of his house.

After Fitzgerald's death *Chloe* was purchased for £800 by Irish gold digger Henry Figsby Young, co-owner with fellow Irishman Thomas Jackson of the Young & Jackson Hotel on the corner of Swanston and Flinders Streets in Melbourne. It is believed that Henry took *Chloe* back to his home above the hotel, and although he hid the painting from his wife she discovered it while spring cleaning when he was away. Henry's wife did not want the naked young

Chloe

Oil on canvas by Jules Lefebvre, 1875
The real 'Chloe' was a nineteen-year-old studio model named Marie who fell in love with the artist. Devastated after he married her sister, it is believed she committed suicide by drinking a concoction she had made by boiling up phosphorous taken from match-heads. She died aged twenty-one.
(Courtesy: Young & Jackson Hotel)

woman in her home and banished her to the public bar, where she soon became a great favourite.

Situated opposite Flinders Street Station and handy to the Melbourne docks, Y&J's became a popular watering hole with servicemen during World War II. Thousands of young Aussie diggers and American GIs in Melbourne on leave would have sunk a few pots standing beneath *Chloe's* pure, almost virginal, charms. She became a symbol of feminine beauty, without any of the eroticism that is often suggested in paintings of the naked female form; it is this rare quality in Lefebvre's work that earned him his reputation and gave to Melbourne an enduring but rather 'cheeky' cultural icon.

At the end of the war one group of returned servicemen were drinking in the bar when an American sailor, a little worse for wear, leapt up, smashed his pint glass over *Chloe's* shoulder and cried out, 'If I can't have her, no-one will.' A fight broke out that battled all the way down Flinders and Swanston Streets as Aussie diggers took their revenge on the Yanks. Naturally, the Aussies won. *Chloe* was covered in glass after repairs to torn canvas were made by the National Gallery of Victoria.

Chloe is rarely out of the news. In 2004 a drinker in the bar, taking a rest before the AFL grand final, sat back onto the lower edge of the frame around the painting and smashed the glass. He bolted from the scene.

RAAF airmen enjoy a beer, and *Chloe*'s charms, c. 1945
(Australian War Memorial, VIC1723)

As a result *Chloe* was back in the gallery again for the first time in more than fifty years. This time she lodged at the Ian Potter Gallery while repairs to a slight scratch were undertaken. Y&J's staff told anxious drinkers, who missed her hanging on the wall, that she was having a rest in a 'day spa'.

THE TROUBLE WITH LABOR
Keeping Out the Old Guard

Between the wars was a time of great conflict in Australia. Although peace had been declared between nations the country itself was dividing between the 'haves' and the 'have-nots'. Organised labour sought its inspiration from the success of the socialist experiment in Russia; the top end of town took its call from the laissez-faire economists running the United States.

The cooperative brotherhood of working men of all nations had not eventuated and 'big capital' in the manufacturing nations turned their war machine into peace-time reconstruction and fought, nation against nation, for supremacy in international markets.

Australia was still closely tied to Britain's 'dark satanic mills' and it seemed as if the prosperity that grew on the sheep's back could go on forever. By the beginning of the 1930s Australia was selling more wool to Japan than to Britain and a shift in Australian allegiances would soon emerge.

There were many among Australia's financial elite who openly patronised the Japanese, even up until the outbreak of war. Australia's major bankers, manufacturers and influential graziers believed they could accept a Japanese conquest of Australia as long as they were able to continue to build their wealth as they had always been able to—at the expense of the worker.

Following a rush on Wall Street that saw a record sixteen million shares traded, the American economy collapsed on 29 October 1929. Thirty billion dollars was wiped off the value of American manufacturing. Britain and France had defaulted on the repayment of war loans and America had been caught overexposed.

Intricately woven into international banking and borrowing, Australian monetary policy, in the hands of private banks, relied on foreign funds that were no longer available. Australia followed America and also descended into financial depression. Loss of exports, loss of confidence, depression in the housing construction industry and a drying up of available capital for investment

Crowds rally under Jack Lang banner 'Our leader', Labor Party
election rally, Moore Park, Sydney, NSW
Despite the huge crowds that gathered in support of 'The Big Fella',
they turned against Lang at the ballot box in 1932, once the governor
had dismissed him from office.
(Hood Collection, State Library of New South Wales)

saw Australia's economy collapse in ruins. When unemployment reached record levels of thirty per cent many Australians also lost confidence in the government's ability to find any solution to this great depression.

In this volatile and unstable environment all manner of radical political groups emerged—socialists, communists, workers' unions and welfare groups blossomed, all of them philosophically pitted against the new nationalists and extreme right groups such as the conservative paramilitary Old Guard, and the more extreme quasi-fascist New Guard led by World War I veteran Captain Eric Campbell.

The Coal-miners' Strike

Australian-born Irish Catholic Labor Prime Minister James Scullin had come to power one week before the Wall Street crash. His government was instantly dished up a crisis of unmeasurable dimensions. Scullin responded by allocating £1,000,000 to the states for unemployment relief, to be spent on road works; one year later a further £1,000,000 would be allocated to public works. A true socialist, Scullin pursued traditional Labor policies of deficit budgets to finance social infrastructure; he believed in the redistribution of wealth through government borrowing from the private sector to finance the public good. This may have seemed philosophically attractive but it was financially disastrous; eventually all borrowings had to be repaid.

Possibly the most difficult crisis Scullin had to face was the fifteen-month lockout of New South Wales' coal miners. The miners had gone on strike to protest at the owners' decision to cut pay by twelve and a half per cent. In defiance the mine owners agreed among themselves to shut down all the collieries.

Neither governments, capitalists nor unions could bring an end to this dispute. After talks with the mine owners broke down the government decided to re-open and run the mines itself, using non-union labour if necessary. The mine at Rothbury in the Hunter Valley was re-opened. Although no coal was actually being taken out, the government knew the workers would refuse to go back to the pit, and then they could legitimately deny the miners access to sustenance payments (dole) and starve them into submission,

A mass protest of 8000 miners camped outside the Rothbury mine in the Hunter Valley to protest at the use of 'scab' labour in the mines. When almost half of the miners rushed the gates the police counterattacked, firing into the crowd. A group at the mine-head refused to disperse; the police fired again and one man, Norman Brown, was shot dead. Dozens of others, both workers and police, were injured in the riot that had caused Brown's death. With the death of Norman Brown the unions were given a martyr to their cause, yet the government held firm. In May the following year, crushed by near starvation and deprived of the dole, the unions gave in and went back to the mines—having gained no concessions at all.

The *Sydney Morning Herald* reported on 20 December 1929: 'The penalty for refusal to perform duty was to be the withholding of the sustenance allowances distributed by the federation.' The *Herald* continued criticising the intentions of the government and the lack of common sense from the unions: 'Men were obliged to do this lawful thing on pain of starvation if they defaulted. Theirs may have been a difficult case, it is true, but the difficulties sprang from union tyranny and lawlessness and not from any consideration of civil obligation.'

On 21 December 1929 *Smith's Weekly* criticised union leadership for its obvious absence from the Rothbury frontline:

Portrait of Jack Lang
Oil painting by Fred Leist, 1930
Lang was a powerhouse of a man; a committed socialist with private wealth made from real estate, his was a curious mix of labor dogma, defiance and grass-roots humility.
(National Library of Australia)

While the poor pawns of the movement ... are gasping with lead in their throats ... While men look death in the eyes at Rothbury, while the gum leaves are whipped by bullets, while blood flows on the peaceful earth of our fathers ... the dead may lie with blank, accusing faces under their bloody shrouds, the bush may echo with the crackle and blaze of gunpowder, but Mr Garden [the union leader] ... is busy thinking out 'fighting policies' in his limousine in Sydney.

Labor Government Cabinet Minister Joseph Lyons resigned from the party in protest over Scullin's adherence to traditional Labor dogmatic, socialist economic direction. Lyons joined the All For Australia League. The League soon was transformed and emerged as the United Australia Party.

Pressure from Lyons forced Scullin into resignation and Lyons became prime minister in 1932. He was soon to find himself head to head with 'the Big Fella' Jack Lang, a powerhouse of a man who dominated Labor in New South Wales.

The Premier's Plan

To get the country back to a sound economic position private bankers proposed that the government should rein in spending, reducing public consumption by the repression of workers' wages. Sir Otto Niemeyer, Director of the Bank of England, the bank that held most of the state's debts, visited Australia and urged the states to reduce Australia's high standard of living by tightening the national belt. To achieve the agreed outcome of the scheme he forced each state premier to agree—every state had to plan for a balanced budget over the next few years.

Addressing a mass meeting in Paddington, Lang railed at the English demands made in 'the Premier's plan', declaring: 'The same people who conscripted our sons and laid them in Flanders' fields … now demand more blood, the interest on their lives …'

The Big Fella saw things differently. Like Scullin, Lang was 'old Labor', a socialist who saw that capital was for spending, and it didn't seem to matter where the capital came from. He dismissed the Niemeyer plan and the Bank of England, blaming the English for 'ruthlessly dragging [Australia] down'. He turned his back on the 'Premier's plan'.

Lang had some original ideas on the management of the state's finances, which he believed would help dig New South Wales out of the depression—he decided to withhold interest payments on loans advanced by Britain. Prime Minister Lyons could not allow this to happen; the federal government stepped in and made the payments for New South Wales, then Lyons tried to recover the money from the state treasury. Lang devised an innovative scheme to avoid the federal government getting its hands on state's money: rather than putting the money gathered from fees and taxes into the bank, he hoarded the cash in a locked room in the basement of the treasury, with members of the Timberworker's Union standing guard.

New South Wales Labor had decided not to meet its financial obligations. Lang had turned his back on the new federal ministry, committed to fiscal responsibility and a balanced budget, led by the turncoat Joseph Lyons. The government of New South Wales was at an impasse with the rest of the nation; even the districts of the

Riverina and New England were ready to declare their independence from Lang's rogue state. It seemed as if the federal government would soon have to take direct action against a recalcitrant New South Wales.

The top end of town became very nervous when Lang defaulted on the overseas debt repayment. Lang said it was a matter of whether the unemployed would be left to starve or whether the bond holders would be repaid. Fearing a run on the banks, Lang ordered the doors of the State Savings Bank be shut.

The currency was devalued in the hope that exports would be more competitive. Naturally this also had a serious impact on repayment of national debt.

The Rise of the Old Guard

In the period immediately following the end of World War I, ex-servicemen, comprising directors of major Australian corporations, wealthy investors from influential families and private bank owners, sought to keep the flame of Anzac alive and resist the rise of socialist influence of the trades union movement. This 'Old Guard' gathered together a large body of conservative men who supported traditional values. They supported the White Australia Policy, were in favour of conscription—for 'turning boys into men'—and remained loyal to the English Crown. They detested the 'Red Menace', epitomised by the socialist Labor leaders whom 'the Guard' believed were ineffective in grappling with a failed economy, and 'the Guard' were fearful of the rising militancy of an aggrieved and unionised labour force. So determined were they to arrest the perceived decline in social standards that at one stage the prominent Sydney financier, Hon. Sir Henry Braddon, approached war hero Sir John Monash and asked if he would act as dictator of Australia when the time came to overthrow the 'socialists'. Monash declined the offer.

As the financial crisis deepened in New South Wales, and Lang continued in his defiance of the federal government and the bankers, a group of more radical 'Guardsmen' were emerging to relegate the gentlemen of the Old Guard to the sidelines. Sympathetic to European fascism, the strong leadership of Mussolini and Adolf Hitler and

Members of the Nationalist Socialist Workers Party,
Adelaide Branch, Tanunda, 1934

This photograph shows German nationals in South Australia before the outbreak
of World War II. Some of these members of NSWP spent their war years in
internment camps; others had already returned to the fatherland.
(Australian War Memorial)

the example of England's Edward Mosley, this 'New Guard', led
by ex-serviceman, Sydney solicitor Colonel Eric Campbell, DSO,
was committed to unswerving loyalty to the throne and the British
Empire; to sane and honourable government in Australia; to suppression of disloyal and immoral elements in government, industrial
and social circles; and to the abolition of machine politics.

Demands of the New Guard

Campbell outlined the expectations the New Guard had for the
government of Australia in a speech given to a meeting of supporters
in Sydney Town Hall, reported by the *Sydney Morning Herald* on
23 July 1931:

> ... the New Guard demanded of every Government of this State and
> the Commonwealth—
>> Firstly, to be honest, strong and sincere;
>> Secondly, to restrict the functions of the Government to the barest

needs of the community, and consequently reduce taxation to the barest minimum;

Thirdly, that it will, by superannuation of the elder and by dismissal of the younger, and the elimination of the inefficient, reduce the Civil servants and employees down to nothing. We are sorry indeed for the precarious position of these men and women, but we think it only fair that the rigours of present conditions should fall on them rather than on the producer, who, to date, has suffered. As a class Civil servants are absolutely necessary, their function in a civilised country is essential, their standing should be above reproach, and the only reason that they are so unpopular with us is because there are ten where there should be one.

Fourthly, that all state-owned institutions and services, such as railways and Post Offices, must be made self-supporting and run as business concerns;

Fifthly, that public expenditure be limited to a fixed proportion of the previous year's national income;

Sixthly, that the fundamental economic principle be recognised that unemployment can only be solved by the stimulation of industry, and not by levies on production, to be distributed in doles which sap the moral fibre of the recipients;

Seventhly; that an era of plain honesty and economy be entered upon, and the people be allowed to save the State;

Eighthly, that Communism be declared illegal and that proper legislative authorities be obtained for the deportation of all Communists, imported or indigenous, and all other unworthy and disruptive individuals.

The New Guard soon had more than 50,000 members across New South Wales, with most centred in Sydney. In Victoria a group known as the League of National Security filled the same role. Members of the New Guard saw themselves as protectors of the nation's values; they were white supremacists, intolerantly Protestant, loyalist and monarchist.

The New Guard disrupted meetings of left-wing organisations in New South Wales and Victoria. They harassed those they were determined to crush; mobs of 1000 men from the New Guard would descend on a meeting of 'Reds' and take direct and violent action against their sworn enemy; bashings, setting fire to books and communist literature, and attacking delegates were stock in trade for these loyal sons of the Empire.

The New Guard had no time at all for dissenting Irish Catholic socialists who were in the majority in the New South Wales Labor Party. As far as the New Guard were concerned, while Lang remained in power New South Wales was heading for a fascist revolution. Eric Campbell wrote in 1932:

> Democracy cannot cure the existing state of affairs. Only discipline, patriotic and spiritual belief can do this. Discipline that is right and good for the country, respect for the things that count.
>
> The New Guard is the vanguard of a crusade for moral regeneration ... we will bring all classes to work for the common good, convince the people that objective morality is the only guide to human conduct and prove that the British race does not deteriorate under Southern Skies. Inspired by the example of Italy the new guard will create in Australia a new spirit in the people.

The Guard had became increasingly paranoid, even anticipating a ring of fire to be lit by the socialists across rural New South Wales that would put the country people out of action. Some had seen Lang's pronouncement at the Sydney Eight-Hour Dinner in October 1931 that 'the revolution has come' to mean 'that private property, enterprise, and freedom of thought and action would soon be abolished'.

However, things do change. The nation went to the polls in December and federal Labor was soundly defeated by United Australia, a party led by Joseph Lyons. Lyons won by a landslide, reducing Labor representation to only nineteen seats. Lang was left isolated as the only radical socialist left in power in the country.

De Groot at the Bridge
Furious that Lang had appointed himself to officially open the just completed Sydney Harbour Bridge the conservatives resolved to eject him from office. Some favoured kidnapping Lang and holding

Left: Jack Lang speaking from the dais at the opening ceremony of the Sydney Harbour Bridge, 19 March 1932

Photograph by Sam Hood, 1932

(Hood Collection, State Library of New South Wales)

Right: Captain Francis de Groot cuts the ribbon

Photograph by Sam Hood, 1932

Captain de Groot followed the official mounted guard onto the bridge. He waited until Premier Lang was about to cut the ribbon before he dashed forward.

(Mitchell Library, State Library of New South Wales)

him in the Berrima Gaol. World War I veteran Captain Francis de Groot suggested a much less dramatic move to thwart the Labor leader and embarrass him in front of the watching eyes of the nation. He proposed to steal the limelight from Lang at the opening ceremony.

Sydney was bathed in brilliant sunshine on the morning of Saturday 19 March 1932 as thousands gathered at the Sydney Harbour Bridge for the opening ceremony. De Groot, who had ridden onto the bridge behind the military escort mounted for Governor-General Sir Isaac Isaacs, was wearing the uniform of the British hussars, although slightly tatty in appearance. He waited, sword in hand, at the rear of the guard in full sight of policemen who had been checking the tickets of guests. When Premier Lang, golden scissors in hand, brought his official opening speech to a close with the words: 'in a few moments I shall complete the opening ceremony by severing the ribbon stretched across the highway', de Groot trotted out from behind the official honour guard then charged forward.

Eric Campbell (left) and Captain
de Groot arrive at court
Photograph by Sam Hood, 1932
(Mitchell Library, State Library of New South Wales)

He slashed at the ribbon with a military sword and shouted above the shocked crowd: 'I declare this bridge open in the name of the decent and respectable citizens of New South Wales.'

De Groot's horse shied at first, rearing back on its haunches as a swarm of policemen rushed from a nearby guard-room. He then sawed at the ribbon but could not cut it, then after waving the sword around above his head a few times he sliced down and cut the ribbon in half. The two severed ends of the silken barrier fluttered silently to the tarmac. The police swarmed over de Groot. As he was dragged from the saddle by New South Wales Police Commissioner Bill MacKay, de Groot said, 'You can't touch me. I am an officer of the Commonwealth.' Mackay replied, 'So am I.'

Lang had previously appointed MacKay, the toughest man in the New South Wales police force, to infiltrate the New Guard. The Guard was making attacks on meetings of unionists and other socialist organisations, and it is highly likely that MacKay had some inclination the New Guard would try to disrupt the opening ceremony.

De Groot was shunted away to a nearby building set aside for the official reception. The ribbon was tied back together and Lang cut it, for the second time.

De Groot was not taken to the police headquarters but held in the reception area until he was assessed by a psychiatrist. The government was sure that he must have been insane but the three doctors required to examine him dismissed the idea. These examinations took seven days to conclude. MacKay's detention of de Groot in the reception house had kept him out the limelight and away from the media. Even the governor had banned any public viewing of a film taken at the time. De Groot's story did not receive the attention that Campbell and the New Guard had expected, and they weren't keen to be part of any state enquiry that was bound to follow. Having done their work, the New Guard saw its members disappear into the woodwork.

When he was eventually brought to court to stand trial for his act of defiance, de Groot was charged with 'having maliciously injured a ribbon valued at £2' and fined £5. After his release he returned to Ireland.

The following February Eric Campbell also faced the courts, charged with using insulting language in describing the premier of New South Wales. Campbell had called Lang 'a nasty tyrant, a scoundrel, a buffoon and a hated old man of the sea'. Campbell was fined £2, although the judge added that he thought any man was entitled to his own opinion.

Lyons Would Not Let Go

In a bold attempt to put an end to Lang's supremacy in New South Wales, Prime Minister Joseph Lyons tried to take control of the assets of the state. Lang beat him to it by withdrawing all available cash from the banks. He installed a ten per cent levy on all mortgages to raise the revenue necessary for government. While this brought howls of protest from home-owners all around the state, it was the top end of town who were hardest hit. An additional levy on all their borrowings was more than they would tolerate.

Lyons counterattacked with the introduction of the Financial Emergency Bill, which was rushed through the federal parliament just one day before Governor-General Sir Phillip Game called Lang to Government House and demanded his resignation.

Lang was dismissed from office on 13 May 1932. Game had overstepped his constitutional authority. Lang's dismissal was undemocratic and thousands gathered to march in the streets of Sydney to make their protest felt. Although a large number of voters turned out to show their support for Lang and the New South Wales

Labor government, his defeat at the ensuing election told a different story. Lang never forgave the bankers, the federal government, the newspapers or the New Guard for his premature departure from New South Wales politics.

DH Conjures 'Kangaroo'

In 1922 renowned English author David Herbert Lawrence and his German-born wife Frieda made a short three-month visit to Australia. They took a house named 'Wyewurk' on the New South Wales south coast at Thirroul, sixty-nine kilometres from Sydney. It was on the kitchen table at Wyewurk that Lawrence wrote his 'Australian' novel *Kangaroo*. While not considered his best work, although the descriptions of Australian nature are thought by some critics to be sublime, the theme of the novel is Lawrence's 'supposedly' imagined depiction of conservative, right-wing politics at play in post-World War I Sydney.

DH Lawrence was born in Nottinghamshire in 1885. The son of a hard-drinking coalminer who was mismatched in marriage to a former schoolteacher, David grew up in a household filled with bitterness and disappointment amid poverty. His father had neither the time, nor the money, for the finer things in life that his educated mother longed for.

For Lawrence education was to be his way out of the paucity of life in the midlands. He won a scholarship to Nottingham High School and later matriculated from Nottingham University. He started work as a clerk in a surgical appliance factory and taught school for a short while himself. Lawrence was attracted to the arts; he drew and painted, and had some success with his expressionist painting later in his life, although they were often considered too racy for public viewing. Lawrence had his first poems published in 1909, and his first novel *The White Peacock* was published in 1911.

The following year he met the woman who was to become his wife. He fell in love with Frieda von Ricthofen, cousin of the Red Baron and wife of University of Nottingham Professor of Modern Languages Ernest Weekley. She left her husband and their three children and eloped to Bavaria with Lawrence where they married

Lawrence at 'Thirroul', 1922
David and Frieda Lawrence pose with friends in the front yard
of 'Wyewurk', the house they rented in Thirroul on the New South Wales
coast sixty-nine kilometres south of Sydney.
From the left: DH Lawrence, Laura Forrester, Frieda Lawrence,
Mrs Marchbanks and Denis Forrester.
(From the Collections of the Wollongong City Library and the Illawarra Historical Society)

in 1914. This marriage was to prove troublesome for them both over the ensuing war years. They were unable to obtain passports, kept under constant surveillance and harassed by the authorities, and eventually expelled from their home in Cornwall in 1917, accused of spying.

Lawrence's mother had been a profound influence on his life. She invested all her being in David, her cleverest son, and encouraged him to make something of himself away from the brutality of Nottingham pit life. Lawrence hated his father, for his commonness, his hard drinking and the way he treated his mother. While it seems that Lawrence wanted little more than to please her, all the time the young twentieth-century man was desperate to explore his own sexuality. The themes of filial love, oedipal love, unspoken sexual tension and illicitly savoured, consummated love were returned to again and again in Lawrence's work.

Kangaroo-in Allegory

After Sydney-born artist Garry Shead came across some of Lawrence's letters in the 1960s he was inspired to create, over the following three decades, a series of paintings based on *Kangaroo*.

The painting shown opposite is titled *The Guards*. In this work Shead portrays DH Lawrence (Richard Lovat Somers in the book) meeting with the overweight Jewish secret army leader, the Monash*-like Ben Cooley, shown at left with a cockatoo on his head, and a group of 'Monash's (Cooley's) heroes'—returned men—at attention beneath the Australian blue ensign.

Even though critics may argue that Lawrence's depiction of the 'facts' in *Kangaroo* are little more than a happy coincidence, after eighty years the relationship of his fiction to the known facts—just as Frank Hardy, *Power Without Glory* and John Wren are inextricably linked in the public mind—so too, Lawrence, *Kangaroo*, Jack Scott's Old Guard and now the artist Garry Shead are linked forever.

---

*　The 'Guards' had approached the highly-regarded hero of the Somme, Sir John Monash, offering him the position of benevolent dictator of an Australia freed from communism. Even though he loved his returned men, and never failed to honour their sacrifice in serving their country, Monash wisely declined.

Lawrence was influenced by the German writer Nietzche. *Kangaroo* shows this influence as Lawrence gives the reader a Nietzche-inspired vision of the leader of a secret army in Australia, World War I veteran and lawyer Ben Cooley, known as Kangaroo, a Nietzchian 'Superman'. It has been questioned whether Lawrence based the characters in the novel on any living persons, whether he was describing events that had actually occurred, or whether he had created an elaborate fiction that just coincidentally paralleled the political atmosphere of Sydney in the 1920s.

In *Kangaroo* Lawrence writes of his alter ego Somers meeting with Cooley, leader of a pro-fascist paramilitary organisation known as the Diggers. Through Somers Lawrence described the love he felt for Cooley and imagined the reciprocal love Cooley felt for him. This was not expressed as any kind of sexual longing but of the greater, spiritual love that can exist between individuals who share a common desire, bonded to each other in the search for fulfilment of that desire. In *Kangaroo* Somers continued to flirt with Cooley's political mantra and desired to be drawn into its physically violent

The Guards
Oil on board by Garry Shead, 1992 91.5 × 122cm
(Reproduced Courtesy of the Artist)

milieu. Lawrence himself appeared to desire a role in shaping the ideas for a modern society where the old strictures were abandoned in favour of spiritual emancipation, yet a society where democratic principles were replaced by benevolent dictatorship:

> The labour people, the reds, are always talking about a revolution, and the Conservatives are always talking about a disaster, Well, we keep ourselves fit and ready for as soon as the revolution comes—or the disaster. Then we step in, you see, and we are the revolution. We've got most of the trained fighting men behind us, and we can *make* the will of the people ... we shall have 'Australia': for the word. We stand for Australia, not for any of your parties. [13]

It would appear through the voices of the paramilitary leader, a left-leaning union official and other protagonists that Lawrence was fleshing out a personal argument about the future of radical political activism.

I don't want to be bullied by any damned Red International labour. I don't want to be kissing and hugging a lot of foreign labour tripe: niggers and what the hell. I'd rather have the British Empire ten thousand times over, and that bed's a bit too wide and too many in it, for me. I don't like sleeping with a lot of neighbours … That's why I like Kangaroo. We shall be just cosy and Australian with a boss like a father who gets up first in the morning, and locks up at night before you go to bed.' [14]

I hate the thought of being bossed and messed about by the Old Country, or by a Jew, capitalists and bankers, or by a lot of labour bullies, or a Soviet … And I don't altogether want the mills of the British Empire to go grinding slowly on, and yourself compelled to do nothing but grind slowly with 'em … Leave us Australians to ourselves, we shall manage.

Fascinated by the charismatic power that emanated from Cooley, Somers observed:

Kangaroo had become beautiful: huge and beautiful like some god that always seems clumsy, then flashes suddenly with all the agility of thunder and lightning. Huge and beautiful as he sat hulked in his chair. Somers did wish he could get up again, and carry him quite away … if Kangaroo had got up at that moment Somers would have given him heart and soul and body, for the asking, and damn all consequences …

Mateship

Lawrence wrote of the Australian concept of mateship, a bonding of one man to another often believed to have been forged on the slopes of Gallipoli or in the mud of the Somme. He described the yearning of one man for another's unwavering friendship as 'the latent power that is in man today, to love his near mate with a passionate, absolutely trusting love'. Lawrence described the phenomenon as 'the mate love … the depth of unfathomed, unrealized love … the new tie between men, in the new democracy … the new passional bond in the new society … the trusting love of a man for his mate'.[15]

After Lawrence's death in 1930, Frieda was asked whether there was any truth in *Kangaroo*, which she denied. She said that the only political information Lawrence had gathered while in Australia was from the pages of the *Bulletin*.

It seems that the *Bulletin* must have given some pretty convincing information about Jack Scott's Old Guard and the secret army training in empty building lots in Sydney ready for a determined push against left-wing politicians, socialist sympathisers and communists.

Was Cooley's secret army—'Diggers' and 'Maggies'—a substitute for the Old Guard or just a figment of Lawrence's imagination, or did he write of a slice of life acutely observed? Lawrence seemed to have imagined a scenario that was so accurate in his depiction of a quasi-fascist, right-wing army of anti-socialists that it would seem that he had been in conversation with the Old Guard himself, which many believe is highly likely.

Lawrence was fascinated by the exercise of power: a mother's, an employer's, the power of sexuality, the power one's sexuality has over another, the power of beauty, the powerful love of one man for another, the power of love between women, the power of political ideals. *Kangaroo* observed the play of power in an environment unused to such intrigue—in the raw beauty of Australia, like a virgin bride awaiting the moment of her metaphorical deflowering by the power of man.

Lawrence posed no threat to Australia; he challenged no orthodoxy. He was an inveterate traveller; he observed life and commented on it. He had observed an Australia at a political crossroads and created a convincing fiction as its record.

The Japanese Connection

There were some wealthy Australians who could not support a war effort with a Labor government in office. They were afraid that in the event of an Australian victory they would face a socialist revolution, losing their positions of power and privilege. They believed that in a defeated Australia, the Japanese would still need the established social elite to run the country.

United Australia Party leaders had close associations with the Japanese. Old Guard members were also prepared to accept a Japanese conquest of Australia and play their part in a 'Vichy-style' government. Both Lyons and Menzies played the role of appeasers to Japanese posturing in the Pacific, while their political sponsors at home continued to do business; as a result, little was done to prepare Australia for the coming war.

The Japanese were showing signs of aggression in the Pacific, and they had invaded the eastern Chinese province of Manchuria in 1931, yet the Australian government continued to pursue its economic objectives to the exclusion of all other concerns. The unions were not quite so sanguine about Japanese aggression. The waterside workers at Port Kembla refused to load a ship with pig-iron bound for the steel mills of Japan. Although Australia was not at war with Japan, the unions would not support a nation that may use Australian raw materials in her fight against the Chinese. There was also the fear that Japan would in the near future use these same munitions against Australian troops, as did prove to be the case. Menzies threatened the unions with invocation of the Transport Workers Act if they did not comply with his orders.

In August 1940 the Menzies government appointed New Guard member Sir John Latham, Chief Justice of the High Court, as its first ambassador to Japan, and Menzies hoped to welcome Japan's reciprocal appointment in Australia. Australia may have done nothing to halt the advance of the Japanese had not Britain's interest in the Far East been threatened or the bombing of Pearl Harbour brought the Americans into the war. Only one year after the cosy swapping of ambassadorial appointments Japan attacked the American fleet, then on 19 February 1942 Japan bombed Darwin.

Aubrey Abbott, Administrator of the Northern Territory and organiser of the Old Guard military wing, had done little to prepare for the defence of Darwin. Jack Scott, a man closely linked to Eric Campbell and Latham, had been a strong supporter of the Japanese since the early thirties; he had even travelled to Manchuria at the invitation of the Japanese in 1935. Scott was given command of the Australian force in Ambon in 1942, and he was well known for handing over individual Australians to the Japanese for punishment. Scott was detested by the survivors of his command after the war.

AP Elkin, member of the Committee on National Morale in the Curtin government, wrote in February 1942 that there was a growing concern among the general population 'that our leading business and financial folk would sell us out to Japan and make peace in the hope of preserving their businesses and profits—we cannot prevent Japan landing if it wants and therefore should not waste blood and money over it, but come to terms!'

During the election campaign in October 1942 Eddie Ward, soon to be Minister for Labour and National Services in the Curtin Labor government, accused the former Menzies government of devising a plan to abandon northern Australia to the Japanese. Menzies denied the existence of such a plan. A royal commission held later found no convincing evidence, yet the commander of American forces in the Pacific, General Douglas MacArthur, seemed to have been aware of the existence of the so-called 'Brisbane Line'—a line in the sand across northern Australia along the Darling River from Brisbane to Adelaide. MacArthur dismissed the idea as a 'defeatist strategy', and the Australian Labor Party accused the conservatives of cowardice, deceit and manipulation—the Liberals had promoted a xenophobic fear of the Japanese and milked Australian patriotism in an attempt to defend the party against its critics. Labor won the election.

Fred Paterson, the only communist to be elected to parliament in Australia, produced a pamphlet in 1942 titled 'The Truth About the Brisbane Line', in which he detailed Menzies' duplicity over the sale of raw materials such as pig-iron to Japan shortly before the war, his praise for Hitler, support for the Munich agreement, refusal to intervene in the Spanish Civil War and denial of the existence of the Brisbane Line.

It would seem that Menzies led a Liberal Party that took its charter straight from Eric Campbell and Menzies saw no reason to question his actions at all, even after the fact of the war with Japan. Menzies told the parliament on 22 June 1943: 'The government of which I had the honour to be the leader has no apology to make to history.'

AUSTRALIA FOR ALL AUSTRALIANS
'For Liberty and Freedom'

White Australia seemed unable to reconcile European development of colonial Australia, its professed Christian ethic, the White Australia Policy and a liberal democracy—each of these appeared to be mutually exclusive as governments simply ignored the aspirations of the Aboriginal people, a people dispossessed and cast to the fringes of the new Federation of Australian States.

Since the beginning of colonisation white Australia had sought to assimilate Aboriginal Australia into colonial life, rarely with equality of opportunity in mind, but to gradually smudge the colour out of existence. The first office of Protector of Aborigines was established in Tasmania in the 1830s, as it was in other colonies, and a century of civilising and Christianising followed, accompanied by a century of mass murder, disease and dispossession as the white settlers took whatever land they desired, while herding Aborigines into reserves.

The first Aborigines Protection Board was established in New South Wales in 1883; by 1895 114 Aboriginal reserves had been settled, mainly by individual family groups who had, by and large, made a successful transition into the European world, becoming self-sufficient farmers, graziers and business people.

Pressure for good coastal property for the re-settlement of returned servicemen from World War I once again saw Aborigines dispossessed of their lands. Once they were pushed aside the government could revoke the reserve status and the Aborigines lost their land for a second time.

In 1902 the Universal Franchise Act gave voting rights to all residents who had been in Australia for more than six months—excluding Aborigines, Asians and Africans. The White Australia Policy, once enacted to stop the influx of Chinese onto the goldfields, was now turned against Australia's own first people.

A group known as the Coloured Progressive Association, comprising mostly African American, West Indian and South African

Aboriginal Day of Mourning, 26 January 1938
A blackboard is displayed outside the Australia Hall in
Sydney urging Aborigines (only) to attend a conference of protest
against the loss of rights in a Federated Australia.
(Mitchell Library, State Library of New South Wales)

seamen, had formed in Sydney in 1903, promoting the cause of international black politics in demanding equality and civil rights.

In 1908 the CPA entertained African American boxer Jack
Johnson with a farewell dinner in Sydney after he had successfully
claimed the World Heavyweight Title from the white Canadian
Tommy Burns at the new Sydney Stadium. Johnson had been denied
a crack at the title for many years because he was 'a coloured man'. He
was given the opportunity in Australia and claimed the title when
the police stepped in and stopped the fight in the fourteenth round.
Burns had not landed a glove on the huge Texan at any time during
the one-sided fight.

The news of this battle between black and white was telegraphed
around the globe. American writer Jack London, who witnessed
the fight, wrote the following day that the white community had to
find 'someone to get rid of this ape'. Just before the fight London had
written that it would be dreadful if Johnson won because it would
show that white men were weaker than black men.

The *Sydney Morning Herald* reported: 'On the American side,
there would be the 'colour' consideration—a consideration of

tremendous import to many millions of Americans, both black and white. In England, the 'colour' question would not appeal in the same intense way … with us [Australians] the bias would be on the side of the white man, although … we can be just and even generous to a black man.'

Waterside worker Fred Maynard had been influenced by the large number of coloured seamen he had met on the docks who were members of the CPA and he became interested in 'Garveyism', the philosophy of Marcus Garvey, the American leader of the Universal Negro Improvement Association. Fred Maynard and fellow political activist Tom Lacy formed a similar organisation called The Australian Aborigines Progressive Association in 1924, which saw the first expression of an Australia-wide push for Aboriginal political mobilisation. They adopted the same credo as the American organisation for the AAPA–'One God, One Aim, One Destiny'.

Conferences featuring Aboriginal activists were held in Sydney in April 1925–at some only Aboriginal languages were spoken– where Fred Maynard spoke of the need for Aboriginal people to stand together, to create their own destiny in their own land. The AAPA demanded land for every Aboriginal family, citizenship for all Aborigines, protection of indigenous culture and an end to the removal of children by state-run Aboriginal Protection Boards.

They believed that the Aboriginal apprenticeship scheme that saw young Aboriginals taken from their families, and adolescent Aboriginal boys separated from girls and placed into virtual slavery with Europeans, was an attempt to exterminate the race.

The AAPA also sought a royal commission into Aboriginal affairs and an end to state-run Protection Boards, to be replaced with the creation of a federal administration. The *Daily Guardian* ran with the headlines on 7 May 1925: 'First Australians to Help Themselves–Self Determination. Aborigines in Conference–Self Determination is the Aim.' This should have sent shockwaves through to the government but it appears as if no-one was looking.

Maynard wrote to New South Wales Premier Jack Lang, disappointed at the failure of an AAPA petition concerning reform of the Protection Board:

I wish to make it perfectly clear on behalf of our people, that we accept no condition of inferiority as compared with European people. Two distinct civilisations are represented by the respective races ... That the European people by the arts of war destroyed our more ancient civilisation is freely admitted, and that by their vices and diseases our people have been decimated is also patent. But neither of these facts are evidence of superiority. Quite the contrary is the case. The members of the Board [AAPA] have also noticed the strenuous efforts of the trade union leaders to attain the conditions which existed in our country at the time of the invasion by Europeans—the men only worked when necessary, we called no man 'master' and we had no king.

The 'First' Day of Mourning

Aborigines remained stuck on the outskirts of white society. They had no rights, no status, were not permitted to move freely between states, were not included in the national census, had no vote, could not join the armed services (although several hundred did serve in World War I), could not marry into white society and had little protection from the law.

The only thing they could do was be exploited, raped, shot at or abused and work as virtual slaves for white people and see their children stolen to begin the cycle of despair all over again.

In any distressed community there are always those who manage to scramble up from the bottom and fight for others to have the right to stand tall. Yorta Yorta man William Cooper began the Australian Aborigines League in Melbourne in 1932. He was convinced that his people could live with dignity and make a valuable contribution to society, if only they could enjoy the same rights and protection of the law that all other Australians took for granted.

Cooper petitioned the king of England, but was warned that it was unconstitutional for him to do so; after all, Cooper was not even classed as a person under the Australian constitution. The passing of the Commonwealth of Australia Constitution Act of 1900 and the Franchise Act of 1902 had excluded Aboriginals from citizenship in a federated Australia. It was not until the 1967 referendum on

Aboriginal citizenship that the first Australians were granted equal rights in their own country; they were then granted the right to vote. The Commonwealth then had the legal status to create laws governing Aboriginal issues that stood for the whole nation, not just state laws, and Aborigines were at last included in the national census.

In 1935 Cooper suggested to the Federal Minister of the Interior that Aboriginal people should be represented in federal parliament with a Department of Native Affairs; he received no response. In 1937 he tried again, requesting that the Commonwealth government carry his petition to King George V on behalf of the Aboriginal people. Once again he received no response.

Disappointed at the lack of response from the Commonwealth government, Cooper persuaded leaders of the Aborigines Progressive Association, John Patten and William Ferguson, to organise a day of protest. The invitation to the first national Day of Mourning and Protest Conference read:

ABORIGINES AND PERSONS OF ABORIGINAL BLOOD
ONLY ARE INVITED TO ATTEND
The following resolutions will be moved:
We representing the Aborigines of Australia assembled in Conference at the Australian Hall, Sydney, on the 26th day of January, 1938, this being the 150th Anniversary of the whiteman's seizure of our country, hereby make protest against the callous treatment of our people by the whiteman during the past 150 years, and we appeal to the Australian Nation of today to make new laws for the education and care of Aborigines, and we ask for a new policy which will raise our people to full Citizenship status and equality within the community.

Risking police harassment and public outrage at their provocative action, members of the Australian Aborigines League and the Aborigines Progressive Association marched to Australia Hall in Elizabeth Street Sydney and conducted the first Aboriginal Day of Mourning in Sydney on Australia Day, 26 January 1938.

REDS UNDER THE BEDS
Menzies Milks the Threat of Communism

The threat of communism was the one bogeyman that demonstrated the ability of Australian politicians to manipulate public opinion to satisfy their own ends.

Robert Menzies was a master at kicking the communist can; he had banned the party in 1940 only to see the ban lifted under a Chifley government, by the federal Attorney-General Dr Evatt. At the time Evatt had said: 'I make it clear that this decision evidences no sympathy by the government with any communist views. As is well known, the doctrines of communism are opposed to those of the Labor movement of Australia, the rules of which absolutely forbid the admission of any communist.'

At the height of the Cold War, a period of great enmity and distrust, western democratic nations fighting for their style of freedom turned against their former ally in the European war against the fascists, Soviet Russia, and made Soviet collectivism their sworn enemy.

Communism once again became the big threat to western nations and the right-wing Christian-nationalist, laissez-faire capitalists revisited the position they had held before the war—anti-union, anti-communist, anti-Catholic. The philosophy of the New Guard had changed little over the period of international hostility and remained the bedrock for conservative policy for the immediate future.

Where Chifley had steered the Australian nation successfully through the war, had forged a new relationship with the United States of America at the expense of Australia's traditional ties to Britain, the conservatives soon wrested power from Labor.

The world was changing rapidly. The Soviets and their 'godless' expansion into eastern Europe, their influence in a war-ravaged east Asia, and entry into southern American politics frightened the capitalist countries who expected to be able to pick up after the war where they had left off. In the old colonies there was a fervour for home-grown leadership and the old colonial masters fought

Propaganda poster, c.1925
Prime Minister Stanley Bruce paints all Labor 'red', where
the opposition sees the future in the worker.
(Australian War Memorial)

a losing battle, unable to hold on against an unstoppable tide of
resentful nationalism. The communists were to be the bogeymen
for the second half of the twentieth century and conservatives
around the globe looked under everybody's 'bed for the reds'.
Freedoms fought long and hard for were thrown out of the
window, as right-wing politics labelled left-wing ideals unpatriotic.
Workers' unions became ideal targets for attack, and artists, writers,
academics were soon declared seditionists. Anyone who did not toe
the conservative line was branded 'un-Australian' as the conservatives sought to return Australian society to a long-established pattern
of power and privilege. The ideals of the New Guard appeared to
be winning.

Once again the Communist Party was banned. The Liberal
government led by Prime Minister Menzies officially banned membership of or affiliation with the Australian Communist Party in
October 1950. Under the new Act property and assets of anyone
believed to belong to the party could be seized; party members or
officials would be labelled 'declared' persons and excluded from

employment in Commonwealth public authorities or any official position in trade unions.

Affiliations such as the Eureka League were also banned. The government had given themselves the right to seize property and documents of suspected communists as they wished.

For Queen and Country

King George V died in 1953 and his eldest daughter Elizabeth ascended to the English throne. Elizabeth was crowned in May 1953 and in the following summer, for the first time in almost two hundred years, the reigning monarch of the British Empire made a visit to Australia's shores.

The visit was a triumph. The beautiful young queen, accompanied by her dashing young husband Phillip Mountbatten, toured around the country visiting hundreds of regional centres and country towns to a tumultuous welcome. Wherever the handsome young couple went they were met by huge flag-waving crowds; school children turned out in their thousands, eager to catch a glimpse of the young woman who would set her seal on Australia's imperial future.

Prime Minister Menzies was besotted with his royal guests. 'For Queen and Country' became his mantra, obedience and subservience to 'mother England' his credo. Australia, who had turned towards the United States at her time of crisis during World War II, was steered back towards England.

As Menzies sought to focus the attention of Australia back to its roots in 'mother England', the radicals who were seeking another path needed to be brought into line. In banning the Communist Party Menzies knew that any attempt to ban a political party in an Australian democracy would bring the country to turmoil, that left-wing organisations, the Catholic Church and the union movement would mount an attack on the right wing, but that was precisely what he desired—to watch the myriad of leftist groups battle for coherence against his determined push against them.

Menzies may have lost the referendum on the communist ban when it was put the people in 1954, but in the meantime he had managed to force the left to disintegrate.

Petrovs Stirred into the Mix

Convinced that 'red spies' were to be found among Australian civil servants, agent Ron Richards, Director of Operations with the Australian Security Intelligence Organisation (ASIO), befriended Russian embassy staffer Vladimir Petrov, whom he had met at the Russian Club in Sydney.

Richards had been introduced by double agent, Polish refugee, classically trained violinist and medical practitioner Dr Michael Bialoguski. Bialoguski and Petrov had become drinking buddies and together occasionally sampled the delights offered by Sydney's red-light district of Kings Cross.

Although Petrov and his wife had taken their appointment to the Russian embassy ostensibly as general staff, Vladimir was a colonel in the Russian Secret Service (KGB) and his wife Evdokia a captain, with a speciality in codes. Vladimir was charged with the responsibility of establishing a network of Australian spies, surveillance of Soviet citizens living in Australia and continuance of the post-war infiltration of political parties and government departments.

Vladimir Petrov was singularly unsuccessful at all of these tasks. About the only thing he managed was the re-awakening of one former Latvian agent and the subsequent surveillance of Latvian emigrants. After the death of Stalin in 1953 the Petrovs were enmeshed in internal squabbling within the Russian embassy; they were accused of forming a 'Beria Cell', in support of Lawrence Beria, head of Soviet Secret Police, until his arrest in mid-1953. The Petrovs were recalled to Russia.

Bialoguski had been putting pressure on his drinking buddy to defect and Richards had offered him £5000. Petrov defected on the day his successor arrived in Australia, just nine days before the parliament was to rise for a federal election.

Menzies announced the defection of the Russian spy to the world. Unfortunately Petrov had neglected to tell his wife. She was immediately picked up from her home at Griffith and placed under house arrest at the Soviet embassy. The KGB told her that Vladimir was dead.

Left: Evdokia Petrov being escorted to a waiting plane
Mrs Petrov lost one shoe when crowds grappled at her to try and release her from
the grip of her two Russian 'escorts'.
(National Archives of Australia)
Right: Vladimir Petrov playing chess
Petrov kills time inside an ASIO safe house immediately after his defection.
(National Archives of Australia)

Two KGB couriers arrived in Sydney to escort her home to
Russia. A huge crowd of anti-communists gathered at Mascot airport
to protest at what looked to them to be her forced removal from
Australia. The photographs taken at the time show a distraught and
frightened woman clasped between two burly 'goons' being hustled
to a waiting plane. She said later that it was the anger of the crowd
that had frightened her and as they ran towards her tugging at her
clothes, trying to pull her free, she lost one of her shoes. This 'false'
image of the shoeless, terrified KGB operative being dragged away
to her certain demise would become a most powerful propaganda
tool and was not left unused.

Menzies had planned to offer Evdokia Petrov asylum when
she had reached Singapore but, aware that the federal opposition
would accuse him of abandoning her to the Soviets, he instructed
ASIO Brigadier Spry to intercept her en route when the plane
landed to refuel in Darwin. The two couriers were confronted and

disarmed and Evdokia hustled away to take a phone call from her husband. Although he convinced her to stay in Australia she was not entirely comfortable with the decision; she had family in Russia and was terrified of what may happen to them after the defection was known.

Menzies had engineered a triumphant victory over the forces of evil–the communists–just days ahead of the election campaign. Menzies placed a gag on public discussion by Liberal Party members of the Petrov affair until a royal commission was held a week out from polling day; then Menzies milked it for all it was worth. The Liberal Party defeated Labor at the polls, winning seventy-five seats to Labor's forty-seven, although Labor had gained more votes.

The findings of the royal commission were that the KGB did have spies operating within the Department of External Affairs. When Labor leader, the brilliant but unstable Doc Evatt, dismissed the findings of the commission he played right into Menzies' hands. When he told the parliament that he had written to Soviet Foreign Minister Molotov who in reply had denied the existence of any Soviet spies in Australia, even his own party was shocked.

Menzies offered Evatt's denial as proof of left-wing duplicity and collaboration with the fearsome Soviet state. At the height of the Cold War, while Australian troops were still engaged in active combat against the communists in Korea, this admission indicated a far too cosy relationship between Australian Labor and the Soviet enemy. Evatt had thrown Labor to the political wolves.

The Big Split

Evatt, denied his chance to become the prime minister of Australia, became increasingly paranoid. He was convinced that all around him, from Menzies to ASIO and even the Victorian Branch of the ALP, led by right-wing, Catholic and anti-communist BA Santamaria, had conspired against him. When documents provided to ASIO by the Petrovs pointed to two of his staffers he was convinced that they were forged.

In Victoria Santamaria led a group known as The Movement; he believed that Evatt's conspiracy theories amounted to a defence

A Test for Egon Kisch

Alleged communist Egon Kisch arrived in Australia to attend the Anti-War Congress held in Melbourne in 1934. He was not allowed to disembark in Perth, so he sailed on to Melbourne where entry was also refused. Acting on information from England, the government had declared Kisch to be an 'undesirable visitor' and barred him under the Immigration Act of 1901.

He took immigration matters into his own hands and leapt from the deck of the ship, landing heavily on the wharf. Although he had broken his leg, he claimed to be on Australian soil and could not be deported without good reason. He was taken back on board the ship where he remained until he could disembark in Sydney. This incident was also retold in Frank Hardy's *Power Without Glory* (see page 287).

A brilliant scholar, able to speak several European languages fluently, Kisch was given a dictation test—in Scots Gaelic. The dictation test had been devised at the turn of the century in an attempt to stop the influx of Asian immigration. Unable to pass this unusual test he was promptly arrested and sentenced to six months' imprisonment.

Kisch was finally released by order of the High Court, who ruled that Scots Gaelic was not a European language; in fact, only one in 600 Scots could speak it themselves.

Kisch visited Ballarat in 1935. He thought the Battle at the Eureka Stockade had put 'the heroes and minions of the law, fighters and executioners on the same level', and that the flag of the Southern Cross had become a great republican symbol.

Egon Kisch appears before a crowd in the Domain.
The government tried to stop the prominent communist intellectual from entering the country. Kisch leapt from his ship onto the wharf and claimed refugee status.
(Hood Collection, State Library of New South Wales)

Dr Evatt appears before the royal commission, Darlinghurst, 16 August 1954

Photograph by Ern McQuillan
(Australian Photographic Agency Collection, State Library of New South Wales)

of communism. The left, led by Evatt, and the right, led by The Movement, tore federal Labor apart. The ALP Federal Executive sacked the Victorian State Executive and appointed a new one; when both turned up at a conference in Hobart, only the new one was allowed to attend.

Santamaria took his party and went home, splitting federal Labor in two. He formed the Democratic Labor Party and took the Catholic vote with him.

With the Labor Party in disarray Menzies called a snap election and, with preferences from the Democratic Labor Party, sent Labor into the political wilderness for the next seventeen years.

The voice of protest in Australia almost died with the split. It would not be until the rise of an urbane, civilised Sydney gentleman with a mellifluous voice equal to Menzies in stature, that Labor would enjoy a reverse in its fortunes. The rise of Whitlam would coincide with another attack by the Liberals on the communist 'force of evil', which would raise the heat of public debate in Australia yet again.

POWER WITHOUT GLORY
The Art of Political Influence

> The communists disdain to conceal their views and aims. They openly declare that their ends can be attained only by the forcible overthrow of all existing social conditions. Let the ruling classes tremble at a communistic revolution. The Proletarians have nothing to lose but their chains. They have a world to win. 'Working men of all countries, Unite!'
>
> – *Communist Manifesto*, International Socialist, *Sydney, 2 October 1920*

When the Australian-born son of Catholic Sicilian immigrants, the devout Bartholomew Augustine (Bob) Santamaria, led the fight against the communists in the federal Labor Party, one young Melbourne communist party member, author Frank Hardy, counterattacked with a 'novel' purportedly based on the life of the close associate of Archbishop Daniel Mannix, sporting entrepreneur John Wren.

Hardy's anger over the attacks on the left by the Melbourne-based Catholic push led by Santamaria, known as The Movement, may have urged him to take his revenge in the only way he knew, an attack in print; but Hardy needed clever subterfuge. In his so-called novel, *Power Without Glory*, published in 1950, Hardy alluded to corruption surrounding one of the most pervasive, self-protecting and powerful organisations on the face of the earth—the community of the Catholic Church.

It is hard to believe there could be any other explanation for Hardy's thinly veiled attack on the tightly interwoven power base of the Catholic Church, Mannix and local poor boy made good, John Wren. Even Hardy's setting of Carringbush, read Collingwood, during the depression of the 1930s was too close to be an accident.

In *Power* Hardy painted with a very broad brush; he demonised his character John West, made him appear as a thug, a corrupt fixer, even a murderer. However, it was his description of an adulterous affair between Nellie West, the wife of his leading character, and a married man, and the subsequent birth of an illegitimate

Left: Frank Hardy
Portrait by a *Sydney Morning Herald* staff photographer, 1951
(National Library of Australia)

Right: *Power Without Glory*, first edition
Unable to find a publisher for his dangerously close observation of a slice of
Collingwood life, Hardy published the book himself. It soon landed him in court, and
became a bestseller.
(Author's Private Collection)

child, that was more than seventy-five-year-old Mrs Ellen Wren
could bear. She was convinced, as were most who read the novel,
that Hardy was describing her, and she was sorely affronted to say
the very least.

In the pages of *Power* Ellen Wren recognised a shoddy attempt to
get at the pro-clergy anti-communists in Melbourne by defiling her
reputation; to throw mud at her husband and embarrass the church
and Mannix by association. In denial of Hardy's portrayal of Nellie
West, Ellen Wren sued him for criminal libel.

Hardy was arrested on 26 October 1950, granted £500 bail
and ordered to appear in court the following morning. He had to
assure the courts that his self-published novel would be withdrawn
from sale.

Ellen Wren claimed the book imputed that she had committed
adultery. She went into battle against Hardy with one of the most

prominent Catholic lawyers in the country, Jack Galbally, who argued in court that Hardy's novel was 'the foulest libel ever written'.

After six months Hardy won against Ellen Wren. His counsel countered that the character of John West was merely based on characteristics of businessman John Wren: 'If John West is not John Wren, then it follows that Nellie West is not meant to be Ellen Wren.' Some say that Hardy won by a legal accident, his victory based on technicality; in the end all that Ellen Wren had achieved was to give Hardy a bestseller and ensure that her life would be inextricably linked to Hardy's so-called fictional characters John and Nellie West forever.

Three-cornered Tussle

The three players in this political game of tit for tat shared a common bond—the Catholic Church.

Hardy was born into a large Catholic family in Bacchus Marsh in 1917. He left home aged thirteen and took any sort of job he could find. These early years among ordinary workers had a profound influence on Frank Hardy. He joined the Communist Party in 1937.

John Wren was what would have been known at the time as a 'tyke': a slum-dwelling, destitute 'mick', typical of a class who would not rise up the social ladder, always remaining on the outside of the law. Wren's type would spend their days gambling, drinking, hanging around the streets, eking out a poor and unsatisfying existence. In Wren's Collingwood the local football team, the 'mighty Magpies', offered the community a symbol of hopeful defiance. The more the rest of Melbourne despised 'the Maggies', the more the locals rallied defiantly behind them.

Daniel Mannix was Irish-born. He was a street-wise, politically savvy Catholic priest from the old school. He cut his teeth in Ireland in the years just before World War I, at a troubled time when the IRA was making yet another determined push against the occupying army of the English. Mannix was fifty years old when he was appointed to the Melbourne diocese in 1913. He was soon embroiled in the argument over conscription that rent Australian society down the middle during the war years. Mannix was immovable in his opposition to conscription. He saw in Melbourne the same established order that had denied the Irish their basic rights in his homeland. He saw the poverty, poor housing, exclusion from employment, poor educational opportunities and cycle of defeat that repeated itself over and over again—and among his flock he saw the same cannon-fodder expected to march again to the beat of an English drum. Believing that Britain was fighting a 'sordid trade war', Mannix would not readily hand his people over to fight in another war for the English.

In reality, the three men wanted essentially the same thing: to see their people, the ordinary working men and women who lived condemned to the slums, be allowed the opportunity to pick themselves up and make a decent life in a fair society with equality of opportunity. Hardy saw communism as the answer; Mannix saw the example of Christ and the demise of English power; Wren saw pounds, shillings and pence.

Wren made his opportunity from the weakness of his class; the gamblers, petty crooks, drinkers and fighters. While the rich sat smoking their cigars in 'establishment' clubs and watched the horses race by, the ordinary punter was excluded from their party. Wren offered the working class a chance to participate. He began SP book-making in Collingwood, allowing poor working-class punters to bet as little as they could afford. Before long Wren had several 'shops' operating. He bought up properties around him in Collingwood, creating a network of tenants who would allow punters through their homes to place a bet with his illegal SPs but closed their doors when the police came calling. John Wren used the small and winding alleyways of inner-city Melbourne to keep the law at bay. He used his tenants as a barricade against arrest. Wren became a sort of Robin Hood figure, who took from the poor, moved the money around and gave back to the poor again, making himself richer and richer along the way.

John Wren was buying his way up the social ladder. He became a confidant of the Archbishop and the two men held sway over the same flock; where Mannix looked after their spiritual wellbeing, Wren took care of the secular. Wren was not really a crook, but he did skim closely to the edge of the law—he was at worst a fixer, at best an entrepreneur. If he had been born across the river from Collingwood, in the leafy suburbs of Kew or Hawthorn, he would have been called a businessman, but he would surely not have been born a Catholic.

Wren eventually left his days of SP bookmaking behind him; he invested in racehorses, owned three racetracks, and built Festival Hall for boxing and wrestling matches. He ran cinemas and newspapers, making him possibly the biggest provider of entertainment in Victoria at that time. By the 1950s Wren had risen to a position of great influence, but was largely kept away from the seat of real power, the world of politics. It was there that Mannix excelled.

However, there was one political machine that threatened the influence of the Church—communism, and The Movement was determined to distance the Labor Party from Soviet influence, even if it meant destroying the party in the meantime.

Alongside the furore that accompanied Hardy's *Power Without Glory* court case Prime Minister Menzies mounted one last attack on the Communist Party; like Stanley Bruce before him he wanted to destroy the power of the trade unions, so he banned the party. Facing a double-dissolution election campaign, Menzies pushed the supposed links between federal Labor and the communists consistently throughout his campaign. Menzies won government, although a referendum held to change the constitution and allow him to outlaw the party was lost.

The End of a Soviet Dream

Hardy was the quintessential Australian yarn-spinner. He made a name for himself as a teller of tall tales, which he called 'Billy Borker' yarns; he published a great number of books, and lived to see a television program based upon his *Power Without Glory* go to air. The program left the public in no doubt who the character of West was meant to portray, but by the time it went to air in 1970 it was far too late to embarrass anyone anymore. In fact the program served to make the character West appear as a lovable rogue, which is probably how Wren could be most accurately portrayed—if Hardy had been really attempting to portray him after all.

Newspaper advertisement advocating the destruction of the Communist Party at the September 1951 referendum

Although most Australians were cautious of communism Menzies' cause was lost. Australians voted for freedom of association in the face of repression by government decree.

Wren was much admired; remembered for his generosity and a genuine interest in the well-being of the poor in his patch, and as a passionate supporter of the Collingwood Football Club. Iconic player Lou Richards remembered Wren's generosity when the Magpies won the 1953 Grand Final against Melbourne. After the game Wren walked into the club dressing room and handed over a prize of £1000 to be split up among the players.

Mannix fought the good fight long and hard. He was a man of great humility, yet he could stand among kings. Every day he would walk from his grand mansion 'Raheen' on the eastern side of the Yarra River, across through the west, through Collingwood to St Patrick's cathedral in the city. He walked through his patch, among his people. During the conscription debates of World War I Mannix, accused of disloyalty, replied, 'If I put Australia and Ireland before the Empire, it is not that I love England less, but because I love Australia and Ireland more.' Mannix was loved by his people in return.

In Frank's Own Words

Frank Hardy's words go some way to examining the level of public debate in Australia, and the attitude to World War I, conscription and the continued struggle of the Irish against the English. Hardy saw acutely how the class struggle was played out, and then how the struggle for power among all the factions of the left, including the influence of the Catholic Church, inevitably trampled on the aspirations of the 'true believers'.

In *Power Without Glory*, after the character of John West had been insulted by an Irish priest over his small contribution to the Easter collection, Hardy described Reverend Doctor Daniel Malone's [Mannix] response:

> News of the insult to John West was not long in reaching Doctor Malone. Archbishop Conn told him it was a further example of the irresponsible Sinn Fein spirit that was becoming rampant in Victoria, even among the clergy. The old Archbishop was worried that he might lose the Church's biggest patron.
>
> Malone was also worried that John West might withdraw financial aid from the Church, but the incident appealed to his Irish sense of humour. Secretly he found it possible to chuckle at the very thought of it. However, he regretted that John West had been insulted—for political reasons. Daniel Malone's main political principle was Home Rule for Ireland, but his training and experience had taught him that the Church must have political influence; and he hadn't taken too long to realise that in Australia its prospects lay with the Labor Party. He had a long-range plan in which John West featured prominently. The Irish priest had chosen an inappropriate time to be sarcastic.[16]

Malone paid West a visit at his home. West received him coolly, insisting that the Irish priest be removed. Malone agreed, and the priest was transferred to the country. Still indignant over the slight to his generosity to the Church, West attacked Malone:

> 'I never forget an insult, Your Grace. I know I was insulted because of this Irish business. I was insulted because I am a patriot and want England to win the war ... I don't like the attitude the Church has been taking towards the war effort in the past few weeks. You and the clergy must remember that if England is beaten, we are all beaten. Anything that holds back the war effort is treason.'
>
> 'Those are strong words, Mr West. After all, England is not herself blameless. But many of the clergy and laity think as you do. They are free to do as their conscience dictates.'

Hardy continued to give background to the 'troubles' in Ireland:

> The British troops suppressed the Irish Rebellion, but support for the
> rebels ricocheted around the world. In Australia, the Irish movement,
> which had bubbled beneath the surface for decades, boiled over; and
> Doctor Daniel Malone emerged as its leader.

Hardy described Malone addressing a meeting in the Melbourne
Town Hall organised to raise financial aid for Ireland:

> 'Your generosity to-night and in the days to follow will bring comfort
> to those poor people who are crouching amidst the charred ruins of
> O'Connell Street, and this meeting and your unbounded sympathy
> will give heart and hope to all those Irishmen, living and dead—
> because patriotism is not buried in the grave—who love Ireland, and
> who, even in Ireland's darkest hour, despair not of the future of their
> country.'

Hardy is portraying the leader of Melbourne's Catholic community
as a traitor to England, a seditionist at heart:

> 'Our loyalty is freely questioned. The answer is that Irishmen are
> as loyal to the Empire to which fortunately or unfortunately, they
> belong, as self-respecting people could be under the circumstances.
> I, at all events, am free to confess that down in the hearts of Irish
> people and their descendants is a wealth of loyalty that the British
> Empire has never deserved or won … those depths of loyalty in Irish
> hearts never will be sounded, that the rich affection never will be
> won, until England grants that measure of self-government that we
> are here to-night to plead for and demand.'

Hardy throws his character of Member of Parliament Frank Ashton
(read Frank Anstey MHR) into the anti-conscription furnace, and
watches him catch fire:

> 'It is the agitators who make revolutions. Revolutions spring from the
> very hearts of the people; these men [unions] are the leaders of the
> people, and because of that the enemies of the people fear them.' [17]

Through the mouth of Ashton, Hardy turns his wrath on wartime prime minister Billy Hughes:

'The reason why conscription is advocated 'ere is because the workers are more advanced, more militant, and more united than anywhere else. The working class of Australia has become an example to the whole world. I 'ope, deep in me 'eart, that all the workers will realise that the reason for the illegal call up and demand for conscription is to lead men to the slaughter to make a fat man's holiday. This is a war for markets and trade and cannot benefit the working man in any way. Hughes can only march to victory over the corpses of the Unions who 'ave given him place and power, and over the bodies of men with whom he 'as worked and associated for many long years, 'E can only march to victory over the dead bodies of young Australian workers. The Australian working class will give its answer to Hughes! Hughes will fail.' [18]

And on the referendum over conscription he did.

Hardy digs his writer's pen even deeper into his character of John West: he makes West's daughter Mary (read Mary Wren) into a dedicated, died-in-the-wool communist. West rails at her:

'No daughter of mine will be a Communist! You'll cease to associate with these people or get out of my house!'

'I'm sorry, father; but I can't go back on my principles.'

'Principles!' he shouted, pounding the table. 'You call it principles. They should all be put in jail! Nothing is sacred to them. They're trying to stir up trouble. they will destroy our way of life.'

'Yes, and replace it with a decent way of life.'

In the form of this novel Frank Hardy laid bare the resentment the hard left had for the Church and The Movement, which would eventually split Labor apart.

Hardy moved little distance from the identities his so-called fictional characters were portraying. The names he gave to his characters were easy to translate–John Wren became John West; Johnson Street Collingwood, Jackson Street Carringbush; Premier Thomas Bent, Premier Thomas Bond; Bagville Street, Sackville Street;

'Snoopy' Tanner, 'Squizzy' Taylor; Malone, Mannix and so on. Hardy steered as close as he dared and was hit with a libel suit anyway.

Where *Power* reads as fact, it must be remembered that much of it is fiction, but the views expressed by Hardy, as spoken through his characters, did express views widely held by both left and right at the time.

The Arrival of Egon Kisch

Hardy described the arrival of alleged communist intellectual Egon Kisch in Australia through the eyes of his character Mary West (see also page 285):

> When Kisch arrived, Mary was one of more than two hundred people who went on board the ship on which Kisch was 'interned' shouting: 'We want Kisch! Kisch must land!'
>
> Over the heads of the crowd she saw him. His bronzed, rugged face suggested toughness and emotional intensity, fierce sincerity and energy. The quizzical eyes glinted with humour; his gaze would penetrate the outer shell of things, she felt.
>
> Next day she was at the wharf again with hundreds of other people. The liner was set to sail, taking Kisch to Sydney. As it began to move, Kisch appeared at the deck rail. All eyes turned upwards. Cheering began; even the sailors on the English warships, there for the Melbourne Centenary celebrations, joined in.
>
> 'We want Kisch!' the crowd shouted.
>
> 'I want you!' Kisch shouted back.
>
> Then the crowd gasped. Kisch had climbed up on to the rail. 'God!' someone said. 'He's going to jump!'
>
> Suddenly Kisch leapt. He hurtled twenty feet to the wharf, where he lay in a heap.

Kisch broke one leg and was carried back on board the ship, which steamed off, bound for Sydney.

Like so many other events described in *Power Without Glory*, this story was true. Such truths make it a battle to separate facts from fiction, and the story of John and Nellie West inevitably became the story of John and Ellen Wren no matter where the real truth lay.

Ellen Wren knew that, but even the usually unbeatable lawyer Frank Galbally was not able to win that battle for her.

The Art of Protest

Melbourne-born artist Noel Counihan was a genial fellow—of good humour, a passionate Swans supporter, a tireless artist whose works expressed a lifelong commitment to his socialist principles. There can be no doubt that this dedication to social justice, as he saw it, was forged in the lessons he had learned at his mother's knee. She knew the defeat that came from disappointment and thwarted ambition, and worked hard to ensure that her sons would have every opportunity to make something of their lives and the most of their talents.

His father was a commercial traveller for ladies' undergarments; his mother was a milliner. His father was Catholic, his mother Protestant; they had married in secret, defying the Church. The marriage soon proved to be a mistake and his father took to the bottle, often beating his mother when the drink took over. Counihan remembered having to care for her as she lay unconscious on the kitchen floor. Priests visited his mother when his father was away travelling, and pressured her to convert to Catholicism, about her two boys' education, and their commitment to the Church. Annoyed by the persistent interference of the priests in their lives, Counihan's mother developed a lifelong resentment of the Catholic Church.

She had ambitions for her son Noel and saved enough money to send him to Caulfield Grammar School for one year. It was there that his teachers noticed his skill at drawing. They suggested he apply to the National Gallery of Victoria Art School and he was fortunate to be accepted when he was still only sixteen years old.

Social-realist artist Noel Counihan in his studio
(Photograph by Julie Millowick)

The people have an answer: War or peace, London
Linocut by Noel Counihan, 1950
(National Gallery of Australia, Canberra)

After Caulfield Grammar, Counihan worked for a year in the warehouse of the company that employed his father, attending drawing classes at the gallery school at night. He started at the gallery school one year later, in 1930, but was soon disillusioned by the conservative tonal-realist approach that was promoted by the director, Bernard Hall, and teacher, Charles Wheeler.

The art school did, however, thrust Counihan into a maelstrom of 'radical' Melbourne's cultural life. Noel was quickly drawn into the life of the young bohemian, a life filled with exciting ideas, political discussions and youthful notions of socialism. He mixed with the leading young artists of his generation. A turning point came when he was invited to share a studio with other artists, modernists Roy Dalgarno and Nutter Buzzacot, on the corner of William and Little Collins Streets in Melbourne. Several other artists had their studios in this famous building where Norman Lindsay had also painted in his youth.

The Melbourne scene, at that time, was an exciting milieu of artists, writers, musicians, trade unionists, radical academics, doctors and lawyers, which centred on the radical magazine *Stream*. Counihan met writers, Marxists, booksellers, poets and other artists—Adrian Lawlor, William Frater and Arnold Shore among them. Through them Counihan was introduced to the Friends of the Soviet Union and it was there that he came in contact with revolutionary activists from all over Europe—Greeks, Russians, Polish Jews, Yugoslavs and fiery Italian communists. He read Marx and

Engels, studied *Wage, Labour and Capital* and his world was instantly changed. Counihan adopted the *Manifesto* and rejected the Catholic Church forever.

An epiphany came for Counihan when he led the workers in the Flinders Street warehouse, where he was still working during the day, to stand up to their employers against low wages and unpaid overtime. Counihan was still only eighteen years old when he took on the bosses—and was sacked for his efforts. When he informed his parents of the outcome of his efforts to help the workers his father flew into a violent rage, casting Noel's most prized possessions, his books and magazines, into the fire. Noel Counihan left home.

He moved into the Worker's Art Club, sleeping on the floor in a room above a shoe shop in Royal Lane. He was about to experience life lived at the edge, the life of the unemployed in a country descending into economic depression. These years were possibly the most influential on the young, impressionable artist. He discovered his major theme: his observation of the plight of the dispossessed, the homeless, the poor and the hungry; and the unstoppable greed of capital dismissive of humanity were the images that stuck with him all his life, and he returned to this theme again and again.

In 1933 he was arrested and sentenced to three months' imprisonment for his part in a protest against police suppression of the unemployed; Counihan had addressed a street protest from an iron cage on the back of a truck, defying the police until they managed to break the cage open. He spent three days on remand in Pentridge until he was released on bail.

He had his first exhibition of drawings, portraits and caricatures at the Soho Gallery in Melbourne's Block Arcade in 1933, and as a result was commissioned to provide caricatures on a regular basis for the *Argus* weekend supplement.

Travelling in New South Wales in 1935–36, making a few pounds drawing portraits of local citizens in country towns, he met the refugee artists Vassilief and Bergner in Sydney. Their personal experience of war, hunger, despair and dislocation was the genesis of Counihan's lifelong commitment to the struggle of humankind

Boy in helmet
Screenprint by Noel Counihan, 1968
(National Gallery of Australia, Canberra)

against repression and the stupidity of war. He was never to depart from the humanitarian ideals formed at this young age.

He took an active part in the anti-war movement, protesting at the rise of fascism in Italy and Germany in the years leading to World War II. He was invited to the Broken Hill School of Mines where he made a series of drawings on miners, exhibited at the school in 1937. He was to return to this theme with a series of powerful lino-prints of Wonthaggi coal miners in 1947.

He was involved in the establishment of the Contemporary Art Society in 1938, which formed as a rebuttal of Federal Attorney General Robert Menzies' attempt to establish the Australian Academy of Art. This would have established a hierarchy of state-accepted artists responsible with conserving traditional academic standards in art.

Counihan began his professional career drawing political cartoons for various Australian newspapers in the 1930s and produced caricatures for the *Bulletin*. He drew for Melbourne's *Table Talk* and the *Sun News-Pictorial* magazine; his first left-wing political cartoons were published in the Communist Party newspaper *Worker's Weekly* and *Worker's Voice*. In the years 1947–48 he drew caricatures of trotting drivers for the weekly sporting paper the *Trotter*, which was edited by Frank Hardy, who was also working on his novel *Power Without Glory* at the same time.

Counihan travelled to Eastern Europe and England in 1949, working in London until he returned to Australia in 1952. He had gained a certain notoriety among the publishers of the international socialist left and had cartoons published in Polish and Hungarian papers. In London he was asked to draw a weekly caricature of prominent political figures and political cartoons for the conservative paper the *Daily Mail*. Counihan disliked the right-wing editorial bias of this paper and declined; he was still contracted to provide caricatures for the *Mail*, but he saved his cartoons for the left-wing press. After he returned to Melbourne Counihan worked as staff artist for the Victorian Communist party weekly paper the *Guardian* until the late 1950s when his growing commitment to painting pushed his cartooning into the background.

On Bakery Hill
Oil painting by Noel Counihan, 1958
(Ballarat Gold Museum. Reproduced with permission, the Estate of Mrs P Counihan)

Counihan was a member of a group of politically motivated artists which included painters such as Albert Tucker and Yosl Bergner. Known in the 1950s and 1960s as social-realists, their work reflected their wartime experience. Counihan observed the world around him, and he represented what he saw with the passion of the committed socialist. His paintings—of working men and women at home, struggling to survive, struggling against one another or in the street, waiting for the march to begin, waiting for their lives to change; and the political process, on the steps of Parliament House, in the party room or in the pub—were acutely observed snapshots of human behaviour.

He continually sought out the struggle in the frailty of humanity at odds with established power. His later works reflect this. *The Laughing Christ* is an 'indictment on the suffering that Christian capitalism has imposed upon mankind'.[19] The powerful series of *The Boy in the Helmet* comments on the stupidity of the Vietnam War, while the beach paintings series *The Good Life* comments on 'the comfortable materialistic vulgarity of the consumer society from which the boys were recruited for Vietnam, a society which profits from Vietnam'. [20] Noel Counihan was an artist whose lifelong commitment to social-political comment never wavered. He observed a nation struggling to make sense of its troubled past, and reconciling its history with the hedonistic pleasures of antipodean existence at odds with the world. He saw a modern world of opportunity denied, of growing inequality, where 'big capital' enjoyed profits won by the blood of its own young, and made his life's work a mirror, in protest, to this world.

Revisiting Eureka

Almost a century after the event, several contemporary artists revisited the theme of Eureka. The battle at the stockade became a motif able to express the spirit of political dissent, and positive action, against repression. On the surface Eureka could be interpreted as a purely historical theme, while the subtle anarchy in the contemporary re-working of its message could serve as an allegory for left-wing dissent.

Counihan painted a large 8 × 6 ft canvas to commemorate the centenary of the Eureka Stockade. He avoided the usual clichéd battle scene, but rather concentrated on the miners gathered at the point of protest on Bakery Hill. The painting reflects Counihan's concern for the humanity of the moment, how great events impact on smaller lives. The painting *On Bakery Hill* reflects the prints he had produced while in England of protesters and 'ban-the-bomb' marches. *The Age* critic considered the work to be 'quite the most important historical painting to be executed in this country [Australia] for many years'. Fellow artist William Dargie, although rather more politically conservative than Counihan, tried in vain to have the painting purchased by the Commonwealth Art Advisory Board for the national collection, but it would appear that Counihan's political history may have stood in the way. Today the painting hangs in the Gold Museum adjacent to Ballarat's historic mining village Sovereign Hill.

A Bird's-eye View

William Edwin Pidgeon was born in Paddington, New South Wales in 1909. WEP, as he became known, was descended from Irish migrants

Bottles are handed out burning hot—the necks of two bottles are knocked together! Contents are drunk in colonial style. Look out! the roof, sides and all fall in! An enormous mass of flame and smoke arises with a roaring sound. Sparks are carried far, far into the air, and what was once the *Eureka Hotel* is now a mass of burning embers!
The entire diggings in a state of extreme excitement. The diggers are lords and masters of Ballaarat; and the prestige of the Camp is gone for ever.

Left: The *Australian Women's Weekly* cover by William E Pidgeon (WEP), published 23 January 1952
Right: Linocut by William E Pidgeon, from a special edition of Carboni's *Eureka Stockade* published by Sunnybrook Press in 1944
(*La Trobe University Library, Bendigo Collection. Reproduced with permission, the Pidgeon Family Estate*)

who had lived in County Wexford, in the shadow of Vinegar Hill. Although staunchly loyal to the Crown, one ancestor, an over-zealous Orangeman named Richard Pidgeon, was imprisoned for three months for the illegal arrest and detention of a suspected Catholic rebel.

WEP had little formal art education, spending only six months at JS Watkins Art School and a few months at Sydney Technical College. At the age of sixteen he began work as a cadet artist for the *Sunday News*. A couple of years later he joined the *Guardian* and stayed until they were taken over by Sun Newspapers, at the outbreak of the depression. He was sacked for the way he painted noses, which always looked a bit like his own. He freelanced through the depression years and also worked for the Labor newspaper the *World*.

WEP soon became one of the most popular cartoonists in the Sydney papers alongside Jimmy Bancks, creator of the popular strip 'Ginger Meggs', with whom he had a lifelong friendship.

When the *World* was sold WEP was asked by George Warnecke, an editor for Frank Packer's Consolidated Press, to create a dummy for a new magazine to be called *The Australian Women's Weekly*. WEP worked on *The Australian Women's Weekly*, contributing hundreds of cover designs and illustrations, until January 1949 when he resigned to concentrate on painting. He was not lost to the popular papers, however, as he continued to freelance for Australian Consolidated Press throughout the 1950s.

WEP had been appointed as Packer's official war correspondent, and was already a household name when he joined the troops in the Pacific theatre during World War II. His wartime paintings are unique in their humanity. Not for WEP the great scenes of heroic battle; rather, he drew the common experience of the ordinary soldier waiting at the front line, in the camp or in training. His wartime paintings show young Aussie blokes, as mates, together against the world. With characteristic good humour WEP showed the self-deprecating larrikinism of the Australian character; in his drawings of the lithe muscular bodies of young Australian men stripped of their uniforms to survive the tropical heat, he shows the raw power of man at war. WEP showed few men as heroes; what he did was show all men together working as one body for one cause. WEP conjured the archetypal Australian character, resemblant of Lawson or Paterson; while he may have been working half a century after them, he was, in essence, working with the same raw material—the Aussie bloke in adversity.

Linocut from Carboni's Eureka Stockade, published 1944

(La Trobe University Library, Bendigo Collection. Reproduced with permission, the Pidgeon Family Estate)

In 1944 gallery director Hal Missingham was asked to curate an exhibition of art from the forces to be toured throughout Australia. William Edwin Pidgeon won several of the prizes, not for battle scenes, or gallant acts of heroism and derring-do, but for simple observations of men going about their duty.

His painting *Interior, Transport Plane Evacuating Wounded*, which won him first prize, was a fine example of his point of view. Other artists represented in the exhibition were Noel Counihan, Charles Bush, Donald Friend, Roy Dalgarno and Ray Crooke.

Ground Staff, Morotai
Watercolour by William E Pidgeon, 1945
This painting was first reproduced in *The Australian Women's Weekly*, 21 April 1945.
(Courtesy: Viscopy and the Pidgeon Family Estate)

WEP returned to the theme of the ordinary man in adversity with his illustrations for a centenary edition of Raphaello Carboni's *Eureka Stockade*, published in 1942, which also included a foreword by Labor leader Dr Evatt.

WEP's linocuts bear a striking similarity to Counihan's prints of Wonthaggi miners. While some may consider that one work feeds from the other, it must be remembered that both artists came from the discipline of the illustrated magazines and practised an art form steeped in a long tradition of 'black-and-white' Australian illustration. They had both learned the power of a good contrasting graphic image and employed the technique to dramatic effect.

WEP was not a radical; he did not try to right the world's wrongs with his work. His numerous covers for *The Australian Women's Weekly* entertained, his portrait paintings (he won the Archibald Prize three times) observed carefully and made astute comment on the personality of his sitter. In the *Eureka Stockade* prints he shows how much he was moved by the emotive power of the Eureka story, this story that is pivotal in the passage of Australian history, and whose retelling is at the core of a century of left-wing dissent. WEP is one more artist who embraced this theme of the great struggle of the ordinary man against his oppressors in its unique Australian setting.

'The Happening Days', cartoon by Bruce Petty
Published in *Petty's Australia Fair*, 1967

CULTURE WARS

THE POP REVOLUTION AND THE LOSS OF INNOCENCE

'LET STALK STRINE'
Shout! Shout! Knock Yourself Out!

Just ten years after the end of World War II the world witnessed another explosion almost as loud as Hiroshima, only this time noone suffered—only social mores were destroyed, the established order of things turned upside down, and for the next fifty years it looked as if teenagers were to rule the world, and why not? The adult world had made a pretty sorry mess of it before them.

When a Memphis white boy who moved and sounded like a black man leapt onto the world stage, he brought an end to the day of the crooner and the era of the pop idol had begun. With a sneering curl to his lip and a lock of long, black hair defiantly caressing his forehead, American singer Elvis Presley thrust his pelvis and trembled his knees and fired the first salvo in the pop revolution.

From Presley's 'Jailhouse Rock' to Bill Haley's 'Rock Around the Clock', Jerry Lee Lewis' 'Great Balls of Fire' to Lennon and McCartney's 'Love Me Do', the first few post-war decades were alive to 'jumpin-jive' and nothing could stop the juggernaut of American-styled pop culture.

Australia, like a sponge, just soaked it all up. With a local media and conservative government still desperately tied to mother England and the 'Bulldog Breed', the introduction of television to Australia in 1956 opened the floodgates and the country was literally

The Discovery of Art
By Molnar, published in *Sydney Morning Herald*, 4 February 1961
(National Library of Australia Collection)

swamped with an American vision. Flickering boxes glowed in the corner of lounge rooms across Australia and sang out into the dark 'M-I-C–K-E-Y–M-O-U-S-E'.

Australia was seduced by the glamorous world of American television; it offered the viewer a gloriously happy world of opportunity, equality and personal freedom. It was a world where a humble farm boy could become the leader of the nation, where through hard work and good ideas any common person could transform into anything they wanted to be. It was a world where there was no class born to rule–it was only money, and good looks, that mattered. Australians were transfixed, and they were caught between the constraints of the old order and the promise of the new.

'The Wild One'

In 1956 a young university student from the leafy suburbs of Sydney combed his blond hair into a cowlick, put on a leopard skin tie, brushed his blue suede shoes and leapt onto the stage screaming 'SHOUT! SHOUT! Knock Yourself Out!', 'HE-E-E-E-Y Everybody'–and Australia joined the rock'n'roll revolution.

Australian-born, of an Irish Catholic background, Johnny O'Keefe epitomised the spirit of rebellious youth. Having established himself on the local scene, Johnny O'Keefe and his backing band the Dee Jays had their first break as the warm-up act to Bill Haley's 1957 tour of Australia. O'Keefe made his first record, *You Hit the Wrong Note Billygoat*, with a song given to him by Haley. *Billygoat* may not have been a smash hit for O'Keefe but he was not deterred by the lack of immediate success; by sheer persistence he forced himself on concert promoter Lee Gordon.

O'Keefe released a studio EP, to which audience sounds were added later; *Shakin' the Stadium* was released as the 'live' recording of O'Keefe's support for Buddy Holly's 1958 tour. As a result, Australia's first home-grown hit of the rock'n'roll era 'The Wild One' was the feature song on the EP. Holly's drummer Jerry Allison took the song home to the US where he recorded it with a James Cagney–sounding voice and it became a hit. By popular demand Buddy Holly was then forced to sing O'Keefe's song at every concert.

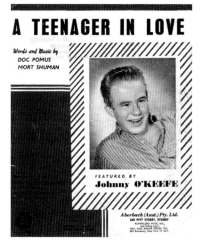

Song sheet featuring 'The Wild One', Johnny O'Keefe, Australia's first king of rock'n'roll

Australian-born of Irish Catholic background, O'Keefe became the voice, and the face, of youthful exuberance when the ABC chose him to lead their foray into youth-oriented television with the pop program *Six O'Clock Rock* in 1959.

O'Keefe's antics may be seen as a parody of the leaders of the American pack—Presley, Haley and Holly—but O'Keefe's was an Australian voice, his was an Australian face, and he became the first of an endless parade of Aussie rock idols. O'Keefe took the American sound of youthful rebellion, gave it an Aussie accent and exported it back to the world.

When in 1959 Australian television decided to broadcast programs marketed at a teenage audience similar to *American Bandstand*, Frank Packer's Nine Network chose as its host a Mr Nice Guy, a Dick Clark doppelganger in the guise of the bespectacled Brian Henderson, while the ABC copied Britain's *6.05 Special* and put *Six O'Clock Rock* to air. While the ABC featured O'Keefe and the Dee Jays as the resident band they, as cautious as ever, employed the services of an attractive American girl, Ricky Merriman, as host. Within six weeks O'Keefe had taken over. 'The Wild One' became the face of Australian rock'n'roll. He first entered the Australian charts in 1958, at the same time as a country singer from Queensland had a number-one hit with a novelty song about a thirsty cane cutter.

A Pub With No Beer

David Gordon Kirkpatrick, also known as Slim Dusty, recorded the classic paean to the thirsty drinker 'The Pub With No Beer' in 1957. The lyrics had been adapted by composer Gordon Parsons from a poem published in the *North Queensland Register* by Irish-born cane cutter Dan Sheahan. Sheahan had been told by the publican in his favourite watering hole that there was no beer left after American soldiers had drunk the Day Dawn Hotel at Ingham completely dry in one night of revelry. Forced to accept a glass of wine as substitute, Sheahan sat himself down in a corner of the bar and penned the plaintive words to 'A Pub Without Beer'.

Slim Dusty saw the poem published in the *Register*, rearranged the words a little and set it to music, and a classic was born. The song is filled with archetypal characters—swaggies, blacksmiths, stockman, barman and boss—even a thirsty dog on the veranda. Parsons and Dusty had conjured up an image as old as Henry Lawson and dropped it into the popular vernacular. First released as a 78 rpm single, 'The Pub With No Beer' was the first Australian-made hit single and the first to win a gold record, and still remains the highest-selling Australian single of all time. It reached number 1 on the Irish charts, where it stayed for ten weeks, and number 3 in Britain.

While the Americans may have sung the blues from the south, Australians continued to set their own stories to music. Australian songwriter Geoff Mack wrote the lyrics to a song called 'I've Been Everywhere, Man', which became a hit for local lad Lucky Starr in 1959.

It was one of the first songs since Jack O'Hagan wrote 'On the Road to Gundagai' in 1922 that featured Australian place names without any embarrassment or the need to ape Americanisms. Three years later American country star Hank Snow had a hit with the same song after American and Canadian place names replaced the Oodnadatta track et al.

Even with this success at home, the biggest problem for Australian culture was that the traffic was almost entirely one way—out. Every singer, songwriter, actor, dancer, poet, painter or tinpot philosopher who had earned his or her stripes in the land of Oz had to be tested on foreign shores, and the great diaspora of Australian talent that had begun at the turn of the century with Melba, Streeton, Lawson and Paterson, among countless others, turned into a steady stream headed for England. Coming the other way were the Yanks, ready to take over our broadcast media; the ten-pound Poms, who underwrote the pop sound of the sixties; the Kiwis, who gave us more thespians than we could poke a stick at; and the 'reffos' who brought European culture with a capital 'K'. Under the weight of this cultural emigration Australia could either lose its own voice or accept all comers and adapt it to a new sound—the voice of multiculturalism. Aussies decided to adapt, and any newcomer with talent and a passion for success was adopted instantly and joined the pantheon of Australian heroes.

The cultural revolution had begun. No longer were Australians expected to sound like BBC Poms on the radio and Strine accents soon became the norm. By the end of the sixties Australian 'Kulture' was universally accepted in all its multitude of voices.

Strike Me Lucky!

One of the naughtiest of those voices had been the Sydney-born Dutch Jew who became Australia's favourite black sheep. Born Harry van der Sluys, the son of a cigar merchant, he adopted the stage name of Roy Rene and the character of Mo MacCackie of MacCackie Mansions, then with his mate 'Stiffy', straight-man Nat Phillips, set out to terrorise polite society.

Beginning as a vaudeville act at the age of fourteen, Mo and Stiffy worked the boards until Nat's death in 1928. Although Mo then worked with a number of partners, it was his arrival on the radio airwaves in 1940 that made him a nationwide success. His crackling voice filled with double entendre and salacious innuendo, titillated and scandalised; the naughtier he became the bigger his audience grew. In his day Roy Rene was one of the most popular characters on broadcast radio. His catch phrase was 'Strike Me Lucky' and this became the title of the Ken Hall film made in 1934, which was unfortunately not a great success for Mo.

Although he repeated his stage character on the silver screen, where with his film wife he operated a 'Jewish Home for Bankrupt Bookmakers' Children', with all of the children bearing Mo's trademark large semitic nose and unshaven cheeks, the humour of his stage act that relied so much on ad lib and split-second reaction was missing on film.

Roy Rene's biographer Max Harris wrote of Mo on stage:

> There he would be, leering, spitting, expostulating, and celebrating every ugly vulgarity to be found in a society rich only in inhibitions, self-delusions and respectable hypocrisies. You can laugh at the grotesque in front of you, he seemed to be saying, 'laugh at the sub-human stage Jew, but he is you and I'm going to prove it.' And he did. He and his audiences laughed at the very worst in themselves.

Harry van der Sluys, a.k.a. 'Mo' MacCackie.
(National Archives of Australia)

Mo died in 1953, but he left a legacy for others who followed. Mo looked inside himself, he exposed his own flaws, carrying his audience along with him until they too laughed with him at similar flaws they recognised within themselves.

It was this same sort of self-reflection, although with a barbed-wire tongue, that has seen the success of a housewife from Moonee Ponds (aka Dame Edna Everage), whose rise to megastardom began around the time of Mo's departure from the stage.

The Antipodeans

At the end of World War II Australia opened its doors, welcoming migrants from all over war-ravaged Europe. Boatloads of Britons arrived alongside thousands of war-weary displaced Europeans, all longing for a better, safer life in the sun.

John O'Grady, a Sydney-born pharmacist who had seen service in New Guinea and after the war among the Pacific Islands, returned to Australia, gave away the dispensing desk for his typewriter and pounded out one of the funniest novels of its time. Using the pseudonym of Nino Culotta, O'Grady told the story of a cultured, well-educated northern Italian journalist on commission to Australia to report stories of interest to Italians at home.

Culotta, who spoke very good English, arrived in Australia only to discover that he could not understand anything anyone said to him and that very few Australians could understand him either.

His book *They're a Weird Mob*, which sold over 300,000 copies and was made into a film, was primarily about Sydney. It starred Italian actor Walter Chiari as Nino, and the archetypal Aussie bloke Chips Rafferty also starred alongside a virtual march past of every Aussie who had ever trod the boards, including a cameo performance by Melbourne's own favourite son, television personality Graham Kennedy.

They're a Weird Mob is essentially a look at Australian culture, the strange qualities of Australian English and the curious quality of Australian mateship. At first, Nino is baffled by what he encounters and makes many hilarious linguistic mistakes, yet he finds his feet among a team of builder's labourers. O'Grady makes some interesting observations through Nino's eyes. He observes the simple unspoken equality among Australians at work. He wrote that Nino 'liked the way it was between his workmates Pat and Joe, that although Joe was the boss … Pat was no servant'. He asked himself, 'Could it be that in Australia there were no masters and servants as we knew them? Or was this case unusual?'[21]

On the train returning from work one day soon after he arrives Nino is sidelined by a drunken old bigot typical of the 'White Australia' xenophobe; an old digger who hates anyone he does not understand. The drunk is verbally attacking a group of southern Italians, a group of short, stocky 'Meridionali' most unlike the tall, fair-headed Nino, who came from the north of Italy around Milano— even Nino does not like the 'Meridionali' very much himself.

The old digger turns to Nino, thinking that he is another Australian, and begins to berate the migrant family: 'Trouble with this country, there's too many dagoes in it. Takin' the bread and butter outa the mouths of our wives an' children. Can't even speak English. Don' wanna speak English … this is our country. We fought fer this country didn' we? Wot do we wanna let that mob in fer?'[22] Ever the

gentleman, Nino explains the situation to the family in his native
tongue, which further confuses
the drunken digger, then before
a fight breaks out Nino 'bumped
him on the top of his head' rendering him harmless, then heads off
in search of a policeman.

Nino decides to find a wife
and, without any knowledge of
the often slow and embarrassing
process of Australian mating,
sees a couple of likely lasses in a
cafe, makes his choice and begins
to woo her. A few weeks later the
lass of his choice, Kay, takes Nino
to meet her father, played in the
film by Chips Rafferty. The con-

Dust jacket, hard-back edition,
They're A Weird Mob, published
by Ure Smith, Sydney, 1957

versation at their first meeting goes as follows:

> Kay's dad. 'H'm. Dago ain't yer?'
> Nino: 'No. I'm Italian.'
> 'Dago. Yer bigger than most... but yer still a Dago.'
> 'You should be pleased.'
> 'Pleased. Why?'
> 'You have a picture of one on your wall. In the place of honour.' [Nino
> pointed at a portrait of the Pope].
> 'The Pope?'
> 'Yes [the Pope]. We are both Italians. If I am a Dago so is he. So are most
> of the College of Cardinals.'
> [Kay's father looked at Nino with a degree of excitement in his eyes]:
> 'H'm. Reckon we'll ever have an Australian Pope?'
> [Nino replied]: 'It is possible. If Kay has a son, perhaps he will be the
> first.'
> 'Cripes. Don't think much of yerself do yer. Born in a tent?'
> 'The founder of the Church was born in a stable.'[23]

Nino finishes his story; summarising what he has learned of the Australian way of life, he writes:

> … [the Australian] works hard with much cursing and swearing, and is most unhappy when he has no work to do. He loves beer and tobacco, and impassioned arguments. He is kind and generous and abusive. He will swear at you, and call you insulting names, and love you like a brother. He is without malice. He will fight you with skill and ferocity and buy you a beer immediately afterwards. He is a man of many contradictions, but his confidence and self-sufficing are inspiring …
>
> There is no better way of life in the world than that of the Australian. I firmly believe this. The grumbling, growling, cursing, profane, laughing, beer-drinking, abusive, loyal-to-his-mates Australian is one of the few free men left on this earth. He fears no one, crawls to no one, bludges on no one, and acknowledges no master.[24]

Let Stalk Strine

A small book written by the improbably named Professor Afferbeck Lauder (Professor of Strine at the University of Sinny) was published in 1965. Titled *Let Stalk Strine*, it was the first attempt since CJ Dennis's *Sentimental Bloke* to examine the Australian argot. The brainchild of Melbourne-born artist and graphic designer Alistair Morrison (aka Prof Lauder), *Let Stalk Strine* may not have been taken all that seriously by the world of academia but it began a serious attempt by a vast army of cultural anarchists intent on speaking with an Australian voice. A new generation of Australian commentators began the seriously enjoyable, hilarious and often laughable task of making sense of popular culture.

In the introduction to his book the professor recalled an incident reported in the *Sydney Morning Herald* on 30 November 1964 as the inspiration for his research. Visiting English writer Monica Dickens was at a book-signing in a Sydney shop when a woman handed her a copy of her latest book to be autographed and said, 'Emma Chisit.' Monica Dickens duly signed the book: 'To Emma Chisit'. Handing the book back to her, the perplexed admirer enquired in stronger voice, 'No. Emma Chisit?' It then dawned on the English author that the persistent customer was actually speaking another language, albeit one that may have had its roots in the Queen's native tongue but had grown apart in the heat of the southern sun.

On reading this article Morrison had a kind of epiphany. He realised that there was no Strine dictionary available for visitors, 'stewnce', 'new Strines' or any others who could only speak the Queen's English. He set about bringing together a collection of commonly used phrases and placed them in the context of a typical conversation to help novices to Strine become familiar

Let Stalk Strine, published 1965
Intent on complete anonymity, author, designer and artist, Alistair Morrison, illustrated his own book under the pseudonym of the artist 'Al Terago'.

with the strangely slewed patterns of this antipodean tongue.

Back to the Future

In the fifties a group of young Australian artists milling around influential Melbourne solicitor John Reed and his wife Sunday took a collective and conscious decision to ignore the direction of American modernism and created a uniquely Australian style, which was labelled Antipodean Art. It was an art movement that had the energy of the fauves, the vigour of the expressionists, yet a narrative style that echoed the Heidelberg School.

The Antipodean painters–Sidney Nolan, Arthur Boyd, Albert Tucker, Russell Drysdale, Donald Friend and Sali Herman–took the Australian rural landscape as the leif motif and emblazoned it with epic tales of colonial history. Together they explored all the great themes: Gallipoli, the Great War, Burke and Wills, the gold rush and Eureka, the struggle of the Depression, World War II.

In the Library at 'Heide', Templestowe, Melbourne: John Reed,
Sidney Nolan and Sunday Reed
Photograph by Albert Tucker, c.1942
(National Library of Australia. by Permission, Barbara Tucker)

They took the great myths and gave them an Australian setting: Christ tempted in an Australian landscape; Greek gods given black faces; Moses leading the multitude through a tangled landscape devastated by gold mining; Ned Kelly set against a flat theatrical backdrop, the landscape reduced to patterns and gestures, an illustrated tale as visual abstraction. These artists defined Australia for the modern generation. Theirs was the vision of Lawson for the modern age, and like Lawson they venerated the struggle of the underdog.

The Australian painters eschewed the American abstract expressionist style emanating from New York. They consciously sought to examine Australian stories without reference to any other culture. When they were criticised for being parochial, their themes rooted

Sunday Evening
Oil on asbestos cement sheet by Russell Drysdale, 1941
(Art Gallery of New South Wales Collection)

in an Australian regional narrative, Tucker rejoined with: 'What is abstraction but New York regionalism.'

Tucker spent much of World War II in Heidelberg Repatriation Hospital. Although he was not an official war artist some works from this period examined, on the surface, the impact of American soldiers on leave in Australian cities; his subtext was the decay of society losing the battle against capitalism, militarism and the excesses of the modern age. A series of works titled 'Images of Modern Evil' show grotesque 'soldiers' grappling with 'modern girls' represented simply by fantastic breasts and monstrous lips. The works suggest a loss of innocence, society's surrender to an uninhibited world where morality has been abandoned in the face of wartime destruction and capitalist greed. Although Tucker had for a short time been a member of the Socialist Party, unlike Counihan, Tucker believed that art was an expression of the individual and he would not accede to the demands of the left who would determine

Victory Girls
Oil on cardboard by Albert Tucker, 1943
(National Gallery of Australia Collection)

what art should say on behalf of 'the people'. Tucker argued publicly with Counihan over this point and abandoned the socialist left in pursuit of his own artistic freedom. Championing the cause of the individualism of the artist, in a parody of the socialist mantra, Tucker declared, 'Intellectuals of the world unite, you have nothing to lose but your brains!'

Sidney Nolan, the son of Irish Catholic immigrants, was born with a working-class chip on his shoulder. Nolan explored the 'big' stories where the little man was called to make a stand: from Ned Kelly to Burke and Wills, Eureka to Gallipoli, Nolan defined these stories for a modern age. He made the image of Ned Kelly his icon; his vision of the 'black-helmetted' Ned is inescapable, a universally Australian symbol of the spirit of rebellion. Ned may have been a bad boy, but Nolan made him a working-class hero, Nolan's art forgiving him his flaws.

Just like Nolan's helmetted Kellys, Drysdale's paintings have become iconographic images of the Australian character. Two paintings in particular, *Sunday Evening* (page 319) and *The Cricket Match*, are regarded as among the best-known pictures in Australia.

This group of so-called 'antipodean artists' rejected the Heidelberg style of a charming, sunbathed, rural Australian idyll in parody of European arcadia, and sought to portray their reality in paintings of ordinary life set against a sunburnt, drought-stricken, burnt-out backdrop; a landscape 'alien to man, harsh, weird, spacious and vacant, given over to the oddities and whimsies of nature, fit only for heroes and clowns, saints, exiles and primitive men'.[25] *Sunday Evening* epitomises Drysdale's vision of this 'real Australia' in the middle of the twentieth century. His *Cricket Match* was painted on commission from English publisher Walter Hutchinson, who wanted a painting of an Australian cricket match to complement the English

Sidney Nolan with his painting *Ned Kelly and Horse*
(Australian Archives Collection)

pictures in his private collection—the National Collection of British Sports and Pastimes. When the painting was delivered to London Hutchinson was sorely disappointed. He rejected Drysdale's image, cabled Melbourne and sacked his agent Leonard Voss Smith, who had first suggested Drysdale for the task. Hutchinson had hoped, at the very least, for a painting of a cricket match played beneath some towering gums, a colonial vision of English life abroad, but instead Drysdale painted two young blokes playing against a dun-coloured pub wall in a dusty, dirty, hot and lifeless outback streetscape; an image instantly recognisable to all Australians, but no doubt a mystery to most Poms.

In *Cricket Match* Drysdale painted the heart of Australian experience and the Poms rejected this vision. Upon learning that Drysdale was considered to be an important Australian artist, Hutchinson reinstated Voss Smith but the painting was still sent back 'to the colonies'.

Death of the American Dream

Before his untimely death in a motel room at Thirroul on the New South Wales south coast in 1992, Brett Whiteley had been the enfant terrible of the Australian art world. Notorious for his addiction to heroin, yet regarded as the greatest artist of his generation, he left a body of work that is both daring in its vision and expressive of the Australian rural and inner urban landscapes. Where Whiteley may have assimilated the panorama of Drysdale's palette, he gave it a harbour view.

In 1967 he was in New York on a Harkness Foundation Scholarship, living at the infamous Chelsea Hotel alongside other artists and musicians where he was both fascinated by and fearful of the fast-moving pace of the city and the excesses of America, its preoccupation with power, money, violence and death.

Like most of his generation, Whiteley became increasingly concerned about the destructive conduct of the Vietnam War and conceived of a painting that would force political change. He believed

Brett Whiteley at work in the studio
Photograph by Greg Weight, 1972
(National Library of Australia)

322

he could paint a work so large and so powerful that it would bring about peace. Rather naively it would seem, he believed that his painting would be so convincing in its imagery that upon seeing it the American government would stop the war and pull their troops out of Vietnam.

Whiteley was unconsciously attempting a *Guernica* for his own time; maybe his intention was not so naive after all, as the Americans draped blue covers over a tapestry of Picasso's *Guernica*, where it hangs in the United Nations building in New York, when they were promoting their cause for their second escapade into the Gulf. They, like Whiteley, were also convinced that a painting can change the world's attitude to war.

Whiteley's *The American Dream* is a vast work, on eighteen wooden panels twenty-two metres in length. The painting begins peacefully with a sunburst on the left and finishes on the right with the blue Pacific Ocean, waves splashing on an island paradise. Towards the centre his imagery descends into chaos. Whiteley collaged images taken from news magazines; he installed flashing lights and wrote tiny heartfelt messages, which added to the visual cacophony of the centre panels.

In this explosive painting Whiteley envisaged the direction the world was headed; he was convinced that the inevitable result of the escalating and pointless conflict in Vietnam would be nuclear annihilation. In explanation Whiteley wrote of the 'almost seeable MADNESS that ran through most factors of American life', of 'a stark and unnecessary *cerebral* violence to which [he] was totally unaccustomed'.

After working on *The American Dream* for almost a year, his New York gallery, Marlborough-Gerson, refused to show it. Sick from experimentation with alcohol and drugs, disillusioned by the apparent failure of the work, Whiteley left New York and headed for Fiji. He took refuge from the brutality of the western world in a paradise of his own imagination.

America took no notice. The troops stayed their course. Vietnam fought on. The war was won, or lost, depending which side you were on. Australia followed blindly.

THE HIGH COST OF VIETNAM

The First Casualties of Menzies' Undeclared War

Although the Australian government had committed military advisors to assist the right-wing government of South Vietnam in July 1962 and a contingent of air force personnel in 1964, the Liberal government led by Sir Robert Menzies refused to admit that Australia was involved in a war—until 30 June 1965, with what appears to have been a rush of blood to the head while at a dinner held in the Australian Club in London. In answering a question about Australia's troop deployment to Vietnam Menzies declared: 'We are at war. Make no mistake about it!'

Back in Australia federal opposition leader Arthur 'Cocky' Caldwell demanded to be told exactly who Australia was at war with: 'Is it North Vietnam or China as well?' Given the Australian Liberal Party's, and Menzies' in particular, long-held aversion to communism and their fear of the so-called 'yellow peril', it could have been assumed that Australia was going to be at war with all of communist Asia. Caldwell railed against Menzies: 'If we are at war why have neither the parliament nor the people of Australia been

Labor's Dr Jim Cairns addresses anti-Vietnam protestors.
(Australian War Memorial)

324

told clearly and frankly why we are at war, what are the objectives of the war, and what sacrifices are expected of the nation, as well as of conscripted youths?'

Caldwell accused Menzies of imparting information abroad, 12,000 miles from his homeland, while in the company of wealthy, elderly and politically sympathetic men and women, that he had not been prepared to tell the Australian people.

On 14 November 1965 two Australian army advisors were killed in action against the Vietcong at Tra Bong. The first conscript to die was twenty-one-year-old South Australian Errol Noack, who was reportedly shot by a Vietnamese sniper as he bent down to refill his water bottle at the junction of two creeks. Some have suggested that Noack was actually killed by 'friendly fire', shot by a rifleman from another company unaware that the Australians were in the same district while on a joint US–Australian operation against Vietcong 'insurgents' near Saigon on Cracker Night, 24 May 1966.

Noack's death was the catalyst for continued resistance to the discriminatory method of conscription by young Australians and the movement against the war growing within the community at large.

In the beginning most protests against Australia's involvement in the Vietnam conflict came from student organisations, left-wing unionists and card-carrying communist sympathisers. Once the real cost of the war, shown in the wasted lives of young Australians, began to be felt at home the protest against Menzies' undeclared war escalated into a dull roar, until the moratorium movement led by Labor politician Dr Jim Cairns proved unstoppable.

When the first conscripts were flown out to Vietnam from the RAAF base at Richmond in New South Wales on 19 April 1966, protesters were prevented from gaining access to the base. Four days earlier protesters had been arrested when 2000 anti-Vietnam demonstrators had converged on Sydney's Garden Island naval base, having marched from Martin Place. The authorities were not prepared to allow the voice of protest to be heard too loudly and closed down access to Richmond base ahead of the arrival of the demonstrators.

Protest Takes a Leap Forward

Opposition leader Caldwell was shot in the face by a gunman as he left an anti-conscription rally at Mosman Town Hall on 21 June 1966. Nineteen-year-old loner Peter Kocan levelled a sawn-off rifle at the window of Caldwell's car and pulled the trigger. The window deflected the bullet in its path and shattered, striking Caldwell in the face with shards of broken glass; the bullet intended to silence the opposition leader had simply lodged in the lapel of his coat. Kocan was sentenced to life imprisonment. Released after ten years, he subsequently made a successful career as a novelist.

On 21 October 1966 dissident protesters among a crowd of 750,000 who had turned out to welcome American president Lyndon Baines Johnson to Australia attacked his motorcade as it passed along St Kilda Road. Australian prime minister Harold Holt, who had replaced Menzies in January, had previously announced that Australia would 'go all the way with LBJ'. Holt's unilateral commitment of the Australian people in support of American ambitions in Asia proved too much for some protesters, who broke through the extensive police barricade and pelted the president's limousine with paint bombs while chanting a different mantra: 'LBJ, LBJ, how many kids did you kill today?'

When protesters lay on the road in front of his car as it passed through Sydney, the premier Robert Askin told the driver 'to run over the bastards', such was the disregard that conservative politicians felt for the heartfelt opinions of their own citizens. It was no wonder that those opposed to the government in power felt the need to express themselves so dramatically. Polite political representation held no sway, personal protest by noncompliance had no effect; only mass demonstration could force the government to take notice. After all, Australia was a democracy and most Australians still believed that the government was elected to represent the wishes of the people—not the other way around. To get the conservative politicians to listen took a long time and many suffered the full might of the law in the meantime.

However, the law did not stop the steady march of protest.

On 23 December 1966 Sydney school teacher William Wright, claiming he had been forcibly abducted from his home and inducted into the army against his will was granted exemption from military conscription on the grounds of conscientious objection.

One hundred and fourteen were arrested when the Queensland police attacked 3500 students and staff from the University of Queensland, demonstrating against a requirement by the government to apply for and be granted a permit before any public meeting could be held in the city of Brisbane. The conservative right-wing government of National Party leader, Kingaroy peanut farmer Johannes Bjelke-Petersen, had enacted the law effectively repressing any political protest in the state of Queensland. But his laws did not stop the voice of dissent in that state.

While the war in Vietnam continued to escalate, taking its toll of lives lost on all sides, the protest movement spread to all states and territories. In Melbourne twenty-one-year-old John Zarb was gaoled for two years for refusing to obey his call-up notice. Zarb, the first conscript to be prosecuted under the newly amended National Service Act, claimed that he was not a pacifist and was prepared to do his military training, he just objected to the war in Vietnam and regarded Australia's involvement as unjust.

One of the most prominent of the draft resistors was Sydney journalist Simon Townsend. Taking the decision to become an objector to the war, he told television broadcaster Peter Thompson forty years later in an interview on the ABC program *Talking Heads*, that he believed that 'the war was wrong and conscription for that war was wrong', adding that he would do the same thing under the same circumstances today.

As a twenty year old, on the cusp of a career in journalism, Townsend objected to his conscription and soon found himself in court. Working in the media, he was ideally placed to draw attention to himself. He became the most public face of conscientious objection and for that he was to suffer the vengeance of the law. He was arrested and spent a month in Long Bay gaol. He faced a court martial and was detained at Ingleburn Army Camp, put on a bread and water subsistence ration, and subjected to sleep deprivation for

Left: Protestors march through Melbourne demanding the release of John Zarb.
(La Trobe Picture Collection, State Library of Victoria)

Right: Mild-mannered reporter Simon Townsend became the public face of the anti-conscription movement when he was incarcerated at Ingleburn Army Camp and put on a bread and water ration.
(La Trobe Picture Collection, State Library of Victoria. with permission, the Herald Sun Newspaper)

the period of the court martial. Even in the face of this 'bastardisation' Townsend remained true to his course and insisted that it was his intention to disobey any military orders he was given—at any time. All the while he was in detention a crowd of placard waving supporters demonstrated outside the court.

On 4 July 1969, a crowd of 3000 protesters chanting 'Ho Chi Minh, Ho Chi Minh' stormed the gates of the US consulate in Melbourne. The police blocking the road to the consulate were well prepared as there had been a similar attempt to storm the grounds the previous year. The police waded into the protestors with batons while they fought back with flour bombs and stones, throwing firecrackers at the hooves of the police horses. Thirty people were arrested in that unseemly fracas.

Activist Geoff Mullen also ran foul of the law. He had registered for National Service as was required of all twenty year olds, but decided that he would voice his protest to the war by refusing to attend army medical examinations, first in February and later in August 1968. In November 1967 he had written to the Department of Labour and National Service advising of his intention to refuse; for this he was fined and gaoled for twenty-nine days in February 1969. On his release he wrote articles for the *Tribune* and the *Sydney Morning Herald* outlining his opposition to conscription.

I am in gaol and I suppose all the official records will say I am a criminal. I might, of course, plead that I have a moral duty to oppose conscription while at the same time the government has the legal duty to imprison me.

In this way I might see myself, and be seen, as a moral young man who takes gaol and suffering upon himself to forge a way to a better Australia. But this is not so. I don't really give a bugger about moral or legal systems, governments, religions, better worlds, 'pie in the sky' or anything like that. I want solely to live my life without interference or interfering, now. And to my mind, conscription is always an unreasonable interference with any man's life. Not even 'freedom and democracy' can justify the taking of a conscript's freedom ...

If I cannot fight in Vietnam, I cannot for the same reasons implicitly approve the war by taking non-combatant status nor indeed can I continue to tolerate this iniquitous system of conscription and argue that mine is a special case that should obtain exemption for me. The Vietnam War and conscription are not only wrong for me but for all Australians. For my own case, I henceforth refuse to recognise any government legislation that is unjust and I disaffiliate myself from any such laws ...

This act in no way constitutes disloyalty to Australia. In doing so I am more patriotic than any of those merchants of death in Canberra. In opposing conscription and our aggression in Vietnam, I am doing my utmost that Australia should not become a nation of slaves or barbarians.

Former Australian Test captain Lindsay Hassett draws a marble from the National Service Ballot.

Called the 'Lottery of Death', it beggars belief why a national sporting hero would give credibility to such a divisive issue as military conscription out of a Tattersall's barrel.
(La Trobe Picture Collection, State Library of Victoria)

Just before he was sent to prison Mullen issued a statement, which reads in part:

I refuse to be conscripted as I consider conscription is the first step towards a totalitarian state. If there be any difference between Australia and the communist regimes that we hate, it should be that Australia shows some respect for individual liberties. Conscription narrows and for some obliterates this difference.

Soon after his release, in an article published in the *Sydney Morning Herald* on 30 March 1969, he wrote:

Conscription … harms Australians far more than Asians. It is first of all opposed to any concept of democratic freedom. If a government exists to protect the liberty of its citizens, then surely conscription is inconsistent with this notion. One hardly preserves a person's freedom by taking it away. This seems so obvious to me, and yet it is incomprehensible to many Australians. I see my own task as two-fold: first to maintain my own integrity and second to re-affirm to others the importance of their own dignity and rights.

Mullen continued in his resistance and was eventually sentenced to two years' gaol for resisting the draft. Mullen's imprisonment pushed the conscription issue to the front pages. Conscription, alongside Australia's involvement in Vietnam, became a major election issue in 1972; both helped to usher in the reformist Whitlam Labor government.

Just a Turn to the Left

On 8 February 1967 a new Labor opposition leader, the urbane Sydney lawyer Gough Whitlam, took the helm of the federal Labor Party after Arthur Caldwell stood down. Caldwell had failed to win power at three elections and had not sought re-election as leader of the party.

Whitlam easily defeated Dr Jim Cairns and Frank Crean, who had also stood, then appointed Lance Barnard as his deputy. Whitlam soon set about to make his mark on Australian politics. His agenda was for wide-reaching social reform; he promised an end to conscription, the end to Australia's involvement in the Vietnam War, land rights for indigenous Australians, removal of fees from university education, establishment of a universal public health system, meaningful engagement with Asia, equality of opportunity for women and a renaissance for Australian culture.

'It's Time!'

Whitlam stormed home to victory in the election of 1972. After twenty-three years in opposition the federal Labor Party finally dislodged the Liberal-Country Party from the seat of government and changed the face of the nation, almost overnight. Whitlam had gone to the polls under the slogan 'It's Time!' and a majority of voters agreed.

Within a week of taking office Whitlam and Barnard moved with lightning speed. Even before the rest of the cabinet had been appointed the foundations of reform were put in place. Australia began by recognising the nation status of China—while still in opposition Whitlam had been the first Australian politician to visit China since the communist revolution in 1949, when he crossed over the border from Hong Kong into the People's Republic in July 1971. The Labor government abolished conscription, released draft resistors from gaol and began the repatriation of troops from Vietnam. The equal pay case was reopened, and action was taken to preserve land rights for Aborigines, among other social reforms. The Whitlam government had in its first weeks responded to the demands of the Australian nation for reform, acting on many

Two songs, considered Australian anthems, were written out of dissatisfaction with the legacy of the Vietnam conflict. Both give voice to the sense of abandonment felt by the Vietnam veteran when confronted with the bureaucratic indifference of a government blind to their needs, and a population resentful of their service.

Khe Sanh

Written by Don Walker, recorded by Cold Chisel

I left my heart to the sappers round
    Khe Sanh
And my soul was sold with my
    cigarettes to the blackmarket man
I've had the Vietnam cold turkey
From the ocean to the Silver City
And it's only other vets could
    understand

About the long-forgotten dockside
    guarantees
How there were no V-Day heroes in
    1973
How we sailed into Sydney Harbour
Saw an old friend but couldn't kiss her
She was lined, and I was home to the
    lucky land

And she was like so many more from
    that time on
Their lives were all so empty, till they
    found their chosen one
And their legs were often open
But their minds were always closed
And their hearts were held in fast
    suburban chains
And the legal pads were yellow, hours
    long, paypacket lean
And the telex writers clattered where
    the gunships once had been
But the car parks made me jumpy
And I never stopped the dreams
Or the growing need for speed and
    novocaine

So I worked across the country end
    to end
Tried to find a place to settle down,
    where my mixed-up life could mend
Held a job on an oil rig
Flying choppers when I could
But the nightlife nearly drove me
    round the bend

And I've travelled round the world
    from year to year
And each one found me aimless, one
    more year the more for wear
And I've been back to South East Asia
But the answer sure ain't there
But I'm drifting north, to check things
    out again

You know the last plane out of
    Sydney's almost gone
Only seven flying hours, and I'll be
    landing in Hong Kong
There ain't nothing like the kisses
From a jaded Chinese princess
I'm gonna hit some Hong Kong
    mattress all night long

Well the last plane out of Sydney's
    almost gone
Yeah the last plane out of Sydney's
    almost gone
And it's really got me worried
I'm goin' nowhere and I'm in a hurry
And the last plane out of Sydney's
    almost gone

of those issues that had caused so much angst for the previous government.

Australia entered a new era of proud nationalism, also referred to as 'ockerism'. Still tied to the British Crown, Whitlam moved to change this relationship with Britain, which itself was aligning with a united Europe, in effect abandoning its old colonies to their own fate. With the stroke of a pen Australians ceased to be British subjects and became Australian citizens; their relationship had changed overnight. Australians were to become foreigners in their own mother country and were forced to visit the land of their own queen through gates marked 'aliens', while citizens of the European Union, many from countries once considered to be the enemy of the Commonwealth, marched in unchecked.

The British queen also became the Queen of Australia and the country was forced to forge a new relationship within its own region with a uniquely foreign personage as its head of state.

In contrast to the way Australians have always honoured their gallant fighting men and women, when Whitlam brought the troops home they were met with indifference, and at times outright hostility. Set apart from the Anzac legend by the politicisation of the war, returning troops, whether conscript or regular, had become symbolic of compliance with a government deaf and blind to the will of its people. The troops represented Australia's undeclared involvement in what Caldwell had previously described as a 'filthy and unwinnable war'. They represented the dishonesty of the government and bore the brunt of community disgust with the war, considered to be its compliant perpetrators. The returning troops represented Australia's blindly obsequious support for American imperialism in Asia and America's fearful rage against communist expansion.

No matter that the people of Vietnam had democratically chosen a communist for the leader of their country; for the Americans, and for British business interests who wished to maintain governance over their Asian territories, the socialist menace had to be stopped in Vietnam before the rest of Asia followed suit. The west had seen the map of Asia like an hourglass and imagined the communist Chinese

I Was Only Nineteen (A Walk in the Light Green)
Written by John Schumann, recorded by Redgum

Mum and Dad and Denny saw the passing-out parade at Puckapunyal
It was a long march from cadets.
The sixth battalion was the next to tour, and it was me who drew the card.
We did Canungra, Shoalwater before we left.

And Townsville lined the footpaths as we marched down to the quay
This clipping from the paper shows us young and strong and clean.
And there's me in my slouch hat with my SLR and greens.
God help me, I was only nineteen.

From Vung Tau, riding Chinooks, to the dust at Nui Dat
I'd been in and out of choppers now for months.
But we made our tents a home, VB and pinups on the lockers
And an Asian orange sunset through the scrub.

And can you tell me, doctor, why I still can't get to sleep?
And night-time's just a jungle dark and a barking M16?
And what's this rash that comes and goes, can you tell me what it means?
God help me, I was only nineteen.

A four-week operation when each step could mean your last one on two legs
It was a war within yourself.
But you wouldn't let your mates down till they had you dusted off
So you closed your eyes and thought about something else.

Then someone yelled 'Contact!' and the bloke behind me swore
We hooked in there for hours, then a Godalmighty roar
Frankie kicked a mine the day that mankind kicked the moon,
God help me, he was going home in June.

I can still see Frankie, drinking tinnies in the Grand Hotel
On a thirty-six-hour rec leave in Vung Tau
And I can still hear Frankie, lying screaming in the jungle
Till the morphine came and killed the bloody row.

And the Anzac legends didn't mention mud and blood and tears
And the stories that my father told me never seemed quite real.
I caught some pieces in my back that I didn't even feel
God help me, I was only nineteen.
And can you tell me, doctor, why I still can't get to sleep?
And why the Channel Seven chopper chills me to my feet?
And what's this rash that comes and goes, can you tell me what it means?
God help me, I was only nineteen.

slowly seeping down, drawn south by the force of gravity until they occupied all territories across the equatorial region. From the days of Sir Henry Parkes and his vision of a 'White Australia', conservative politicians have feared this gravitational flow of the so-called 'yellow peril'. When Menzies first committed troops he was acting to prevent this, his greatest fear, the takeover of the region by communist forces—once they had taken Asia it was then only a short hop across the islands to turn Australia completely red.

No Parade for the Vietnam Vets

Upon their return the troops were not feted as had been their fathers, and their grandfathers, before them. The Australian public had excised Vietnam from their minds. It was neither a glorious nor a just war, and the western alliance had been forced to abandon their cause without victory. The people of Vietnam had won; they had reclaimed their own version of democracy, fighting with sticks and unrelenting determination against the mightiest firepower ever unleashed. All that had been achieved was the deaths of thousands of innocent citizens caught up in the middle of a senseless military excursion. Of the 59,000 Aussies who served in Vietnam, 508 were killed and 3131 wounded. Of the 9,000,000 Americans who served, 58,000 went home in body bags, 303,000 were wounded and 75,000 disabled.

The actions of the Liberal-Country Party coalition government caused Australian society to be riven apart, supporters set against dissenters, the right set against the left in a battle of the streets that eventually brought the conservative government undone.

Yet Vietnam still remains a cause of dissent. Too many changes were made in its name, too many young Australians caught in the milieu of political activism to allow that fervour to dissipate. Although Australia had seen dissent in its streets, democracy had been tested and the nation had met the challenge.

Inevitably, the passage of time healed the rift in the community; the heroic deeds of the Australians who fought and died in the jungles of Vietnam have at last been allowed their own chapter in the Anzac legend.

THE POP WIZARDS OF OZ
'We're off to see the Wizard'

An irreverent, satirical, anti-establishment magazine rolled off the presses and hit the streets of Sydney for the first time on April Fool's Day 1963. OZ magazine was the brainchild of students Richard Neville, editor of the University of New South Wales magazine *Tharunka*; Richard Walsh, editor of Sydney University's *Honi Soit*, and artist Martin Sharp. Neville and Walsh wanted to launch their own magazine and enlisted the talents of Martin Sharp and fellow art students Gary Shead and John Firth-Smith as co-contributors.

Fully intending to challenge establishment conventions, from the very first issue OZ offended the sensitivities of the authorities. They tackled the government on issues such as conscription, were vehement in their opposition to the Vietnam War, questioned public mores over contraception and abortion and experimented with obliquely promoted illegal smoking substances. Every establishment figure was fair game for OZ, politicians, the Church, royalty, Uncle Tom Cobbly and all. In fact, OZ was a prime tall-poppy cutter, bringing the pompous, the patronising, the petulant and the deceitful politician to ridicule in the public gaze.

The first issue coincided with a visit to Australia by Queen Elizabeth in March 1963. OZ took pot shots at the royal tour, the tour where Prime Minister Robert Menzies had made the fawning remark, 'I did but see her passing by, and yet I love her till I die.' Sharp drew a caricature of the queen with a smiling mask tied over her face, Neville wrote a parody of the various mishaps of

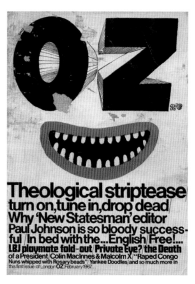

London *OZ*, Issue No. 1
(Private Collection)

336

the Royal Tour and highlighted the less than overwhelming reception afforded the queen by revising the so-called truth printed in the dailies under the heading DEPARTMENT OF FACT. The initial print run of 6000 copies sold out within three hours of it hitting the streets and Richard Walsh immediately ordered a reprint. OZ had hit the ground running.

OZ also launched Martin Sharp into the public eye and his first major exhibition held at Sydney's Clune Gallery in 1965 was a sell-out success. Soon after, Sharp trod the well-worn antipodean trail and headed for London. He stayed for a while with Richard Neville's sister in Knightsbridge, then moved to a house in Chelsea when he found a good studio space. Living downstairs was fellow Australian expat Germaine Greer, who was writing *The Female Eunuch*, the book that brought her fame, at the same time. It was there that he met guitar legend Eric Clapton, and by chance gave him the lyrics to a poem he had written. Clapton returned some time later with a new recording, a single with 'Born Under a Bad Sign' on the A side, Sharp's 'Tales of Brave Ulysses' on the B. Sharp was then commissioned to design the album covers for Cream, the short-lived but profoundly influential rock-blues band Clapton led, backed by bassist Jack Bruce and frenetic drummer Ginger Baker. With this entrée into the world of psychedelic rock Sharp produced several of the gems of the period, including a classic poster for Bob Dylan, posters for Cream and for Britain's answer to Dylan, Donovan.

Sharp was riding a wave of popular success and soon helped to establish OZ magazine in London. The first issue was published in February 1967 and the magazine continued, despite its legal battles, until forty-eight issues later it ceased publication, in 1973.

In June 1971 London publishers Felix Dennis (a poet, art student and layabout musician whose publishing enterprises have made him one of Britain's richest men today), Jim Anderson and Richard Neville faced court at London's Old Bailey, charged with 'conspiracy to corrupt the morals of young children and other persons'. Had they been charged with obscenity they would have faced a maximum penalty of a £100 fine or six months' imprisonment. The prosecution, incensed by what it saw as an attack on British morality by colonial pot-heads and 'scrofulous' hippies, resurrected an archaic law that had no upper limit of either fine or sentence.

The offensive material in question was published in the 'School Kids Issue', an issue of OZ that featured contributions of artwork and writing from school children. In this issue fifteen-year-old schoolboy Vivian Berger adapted a Robert Crumb cartoon by adding a collage of the head and scarf of easily-recognised, and much-loved, English newspaper cartoon character Rupert Bear to the American underground comic artist Crumb's drawing. The resulting collage showed an over-excited Rupert violating an unconscious naked female.

A parade of respected artists, art critics, academics, poets and cultural commentators were hauled before the court to offer opinion in what was to become the longest conspiracy trial in English legal history. The OZ editors were defended by John Mortimer, who later made his reputation as the creator of the popular 'grumpy old man' of 'the Bailey' Horace Rumpole. (The claret-swilling barrister was played in the television series 'Rumpole of the Bailey' by expatriate Australian actor Leo McKern. In the strangely circular world of celebrity it was Leo McKern who also portrayed the character Dad Rudd in the 1995 film adaptation of George Whaley's play *On Our Selection*, in which McKern played opposite Dame Joan Sutherland, who played Ma Rudd.)

In a surprisingly mature statement in defence of his artwork, Berger told the court that he was 'portraying obscenity' but not actually 'being obscene [him]self'. He said that he had deliberately set out to shock an older generation (an attitude well within OZ Australia's modus operandi) and added as a qualifier that 'if the news covers a war or shows a picture of war, then ... they are portraying obscenity–the obscenity of war. But they are not themselves creating that obscenity, because it is the people who are fighting the war that are creating that obscenity. The obscenity is in the action, not in the reporting of it. For example, I consider that the act of corporal punishment is an obscenity. I do not consider that the act of reporting or writing about corporal punishment is obscene'.

At the conclusion of the trial the boys from OZ were refused bail, kept in prison for seven days, given enforced haircuts, and emerged to face the judge. Found guilty they were sentenced to prison for terms ranging from nine to fifteen months. Both Neville and Anderson faced deportation, Dennis was considered to be less intelligent by the judge and received a lighter term. All were subsequently quashed on appeal. Dennis sued for libel.

The OZ trial came at a time when the public were beginning to tire of the excesses of the psychedelic underground movement. Woodstock and the sexual revolution had made its mark but the caravan was already moving on. Germaine Greer simply accused the magazine of 'naive untimeliness'.

OZ magazine had kicked down the door of polite student activism and tapped into the desire for informed dissent and social activism. Like English comedian Peter Cook's *Private Eye*, on which OZ had originally styled itself, OZ treated the serious world of politics as a wonderful joke and brought the antics of the high and mighty into scrutiny and ridicule. Although it only lasted a few short years OZ had laid the groundwork for many other satirists who followed, out from underground and into the mainstream.

The Female Eunuch

The journey from Star-of-the-Sea convent in the Melbourne beachside suburb of Gardenvale to King's Road Chelsea, via Melbourne, Sydney and Cambridge Universities, was one of self-discovery for Germaine Greer.

When she first arrived in Sydney to work towards a Master's degree she joined with the Sydney Push, a group of intellectuals and radical libertarian anarchists. Unlike the usual card-carrying Melbourne intellectual aesthete arguing endlessly about art, truth and beauty, the Push sought only the 'truth'.

In the company of the Push Greer realised: 'I was already an anarchist. I just didn't know why I was an anarchist. [The Push] put me in touch with the basic texts and I found out what the internal logic was about how I felt and thought.'

On graduation from Cambridge she moved to London where she contributed to Peter Cook's *Private Eye*, and as 'Dr G' to *London OZ* magazine, guest editing issue No. 29.

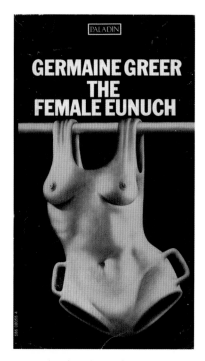

Original jacket-design for Germaine Greer's internationally influential discourse on female emancipation, *The Female Eunuch*. Paperback edition, published by Paladin in 1970 *(Author's Collection)*

Everyone digs the idea of the new female militancy so long as all it does is demand things from men. Rejecting that workshop mentality, *OZ* argues that if anything will free women, it will be their own peculiar force.

While distancing herself from an unfortunate marriage Greer wrote *The Female Eunuch*, a seminal book that instantly became essential reading for modern feminists. When it hit the bookstores in 1970 it sold out immediately, becoming an international bestseller, translated into eight languages.

The Female Eunuch challenged the role of the traditional suburban nuclear family, claiming that through it women have no chance of reaching their true potential. She claimed that the male-dominated structures of traditional society have destroyed the opportunities for women to fulfil themselves spiritually, academically, professionally and sexually:

> A eunuch is any person who has been castrated. The female eunuch is the woman who has been castrated in order to function as the feminine stereotype. That is, the glamorous, supermenial who is expected to be all things to all men, and nothing to herself.

Greer suggested that women should burn their bras as a gesture of female emancipation. She suggested that the brassiere was a symbol of subjugation. Thousands of women around the world gathered in public places thrusting their brassieres into flaming braziers, symbolically announcing their liberation. At a formal dinner at the female-only Newnham College, Cambridge, as silence was called for speeches, Greer, fully engrossed in the conversation in which she was engaged, could be heard across the hall. In her loud, still Australian-accented voice, she was explaining to others at her table that:

> ... there could be no liberation for women, no matter how highly educated, as long as we were required to cram our breasts into bras constructed like mini-Vesuviuses, two stitched white cantilevered cones which bore no resemblance to the female anatomy. The willingly suffered discomfort of the Sixties bra, she opined vigorously, was a hideous symbol of male oppression.

Greer has never kept any idea, however outrageous or confronting, to herself. She has published widely on most social issues, including sexual liberation, female emancipation, and the menopause, and even compiled a coffee-table book in appreciation of the beauty of pre-pubescent boys. No matter what barbs are slung at her, she remains one of the most influential female voices of the twentieth century—*The Eunuch Female* is a cornerstone of the women's liberation movement.

She has, however, distanced herself from the unnecessarily demonstrative act of bra-burning, suggesting that to take this action too literally would be to make it appear as a compulsory action, therefore becoming an oppression within itself.

In 2001, Greer proposed a treaty with Aboriginal Australia, suggesting that the country be declared an Aboriginal Republic, circumventing the difficulties Australia seemed to be having with the Crown and the constitutionality of the foreign monarch. Prime Minister John Howard described her as elitist, a term he used regularly to attack anyone who thinks deeper than himself, when she criticised Australians for being 'too relaxed to give a damn' about anything. They were both probably right.

The Nosy Ferret

An independent journal of opinion began publication in Melbourne in 1972, taking over former finance editor of the *Sydney Morning*

Herald Tom Fitzgerald's independent *Nation*, a fortnightly paper that Frank Packer had once vowed to 'snuff out'. Fitzgerald wrote: 'Frank Packer says he'll snuff us out. Our little candle to his great sun, but they can't bear even that feeble ray of other light.' Just as his paper merged to become *Nation Review* in July 1972, Fitzgerald wrote:

> The liberal and radical strains in Australian intellectual life, though substantial in number, are always struggling to have a vehicle of communication … whatever the reasons for the difficulties they are persistent and liberals and radicals, without sinking their differences, must love one another or die as an articulate force in this country.

Nation Review was a paper of radical, intellectual and independent opinion. It had moved beyond the undergraduate, underground subversiveness of *OZ* and entered the mainstream, an intelligent, irreverent, influential and at times seriously funny political and social commentator. Journalists, artists and cartoonists, from all sides (mostly left) contributed to *Nation Review*; one of the young artists who began his cartooning career with *Nation Review* was Melbourne art student Michael Leunig. While Leunig was enrolled at Swinburne Film and Television School he began contributing cartoons to underground publications, eventually landing a job at the short-lived *Newsday*. When *Newsday* folded he began to draw for *Nation Review*, where his quirky drawing style and wry observations of human foibles and aspirations soon made him a favourite among those leaning to the left.

Michael had been conscripted in one of the Vietnam ballots while he was still at university but registered as a conscientious objector because of his personal beliefs. Michael Leunig's ethical standards, philosophical attitudes and simple humanitarianism are self-evident in all his works; he wears his heart on his metaphorical sleeve and never shies away from expressing his opinion, even in the face of strong and repeated criticism from those whom he offends—and Leunig offends repeatedly. In fact, he could be classed as a serial offender, and society is all the better for it.

Leunig has assumed a mantle as the voice of the little man. His 'little man' is one of the enduring characters he uses to carry a message of hope; his little man observes the world at large, and the world within. Leunig's other characters, Mr Curly and Vasco Pajama, also stem from his days at *Nation Review* and represent unwavering hope and curiosity about the world; another is a little wandering duck, Leunig's symbol of innocence.

Leunig has published more than twenty books of drawings, poems and prayers, but it is his regular contributions to the *Age* newspaper that have kept him in the public eye and brought his ever-increasingly vitriolic opinions on matters political under daily scrutiny.

An Innocent at Home

In 2006 Leunig was the subject of an unfortunate hoax when a member of the satirical ABC television program 'The Chaser' submitted one of his cartoons to the Iranian government–controlled newspaper *Hamshahri*. The paper had announced a competition for the most offensive Holocaust cartoon as revenge for the publication of several cartoons lampooning the prophet Mohammed in a Danish newspaper.

Leunig's original cartoon was deemed offensive by Michael Gawenda, then editor of the *Age*, who refused to publish it when it was submitted in 2002. The cartoon showed a little man, his swag over his shoulder, standing at the gates of Auschwitz prison camp, above which the words 'Work Brings Freedom' are written. A second panel depicts the same gates; the heading says Israel 2002 and shows an Israeli soldier at the gates, over which the words 'War Brings Peace' are written.

The depiction of the gates has real poignancy for Holocaust survivors, and for the Jewish people at large, as it was the words 'Arbeit mach Frei' that were wrought in iron over the gates of the concentration camps of the Third Reich, gates through which few ever walked to their freedom. Their journey was usually only one way—to their inevitable deaths.

Leunig cartoon published in *The Age* on Anzac Day, 1995
(Reproduced with Permission)

Although the cartoon angered the Jewish community, a survey taken by the ABC's *Media Watch* showed that most people believe in the notion of freedom of expression and that it should have been published.

The entry of Leunig's cartoon was originally taken as genuine by *Hamshahri* but deleted from their website after Leunig contacted them and requested that it be removed. Ted Lapkin, policy director of the Australia-Israel Jewish Affairs Council, commented:

> The thing we need to remember is that the cartoon which was sent in—even though not by Leunig—would fit perfectly within the terms of the competition run by the Iranian newspaper. Leunig can play the martyr as much as he wants. But the fact remains that no one has put out a fatwa calling for his death. His cartoons have offended the Jewish community—but contrast the reaction here to the Middle East, where they are rampaging the streets over cartoons.

Leunig claimed that his cartoon was simply an anti-war cartoon; the Jews point out that he has never created an anti-war cartoon that has attacked the Palestinian view. Given the violent response across the Arab world to the Danish press, it has probably been a wise move. It appears that the pen may truly be mightier than the sword—fewer people die from ink than 'lead-poisoning', yet the cartoon drawings seem to have a greater impact on the nation's leaders than a hundred deaths in battle or the mass protest of its citizens.

Leunig was relentless in his mockery of Australian prime minister John Howard and his dalliance with the armed forces of the United States of America in their excursion into Iraq. He lampooned Howard's jingoistic breast-beating, Howard's obsession with Anzac mythology and his obsequious fawning at the feet of George W Bush.

Leunig has upset the Catholic Church, nursing mothers, the RSL, the left, the right and the centre; no human activity is safe from the acute clarity of his observation, but he is no bile-filled monster. Leunig is a quiet, unassuming, nature-loving, gentle man who envisages a world at peace; he sees nations united truly in a brotherhood of man—and ducks.

An Innocent Abroad

London's *Time Out* magazine described the opening shot of Australia's film renaissance *The Adventures of Barry McKenzie* as 'unappealing spinoff from the *Private Eye* comic strip, chronicling the adventures, with and without his Aunt Edna, of a loud-mouthed, sex-crazed innocent from Oz newly arrived in Earl's Court. The odd amusing incident, but mostly spoiled by sheer repetitiveness and the unmodulated top-of-the-voice vulgarity sought at all costs'.

While this review is probably spot-on, the 'Poms' unused to the subtlety of contemporary Australian humour seemed to have been watching a different movie to the one thousands of Aussie blokes and sheilas saw when it was released in 1972.

The Australian film renaissance had begun under the patronage of former Liberal prime minister John Gorton, a curious conservative with a taste for the arts. Under Whitlam the nation found

The Adventures of

Barry McKenzie

BARRY CROCKER •BARRY HUMPHRIES •PETER COOK •SPIKE MILLIGAN

SHAMELESS SAGA OF YOUNG AUSSIE IN POMMYLAND

(M)15+ RECOMMENDED FOR MATURE
AUDIENCES 15 YEARS AND OVER

Video cover for the film *The Adventures of Barry McKenzie,* based on Barry Humphries' *Private Eye* comic-strip creation about the innocent Aussie abroad—'Bazza'.

its own voice. Australian culture had looked in the mirror and no longer saw a second-class English culture, but an Aussie one; it reflected the raw voice of the ocker, and Australia announced to the world—in a broad Strine accent—that the age of the ocker had arrived. 'You little bewty!'

Bazza McKenzie had first appeared in the English satirical magazine *Private Eye*. Written by Barry Humphries and illustrated by Nicholas Garland, together they had conjured up the image of a gauche innocent abroad, a lantern-jawed, wide-eyed boy from the bush, dressed in his double-breasted suit (his clean undies on in case he was knocked down by a bus) and a broad Akubra pulled down over his eyes. Bazza had his Qantas bag filled with essential items (cans of Fosters) and had flown to London to see the world, desperately in search of a root.

Bazza is an innocent abroad; he seems to channel the spirit of an earlier author, Steele Rudd's (aka Arthur Hoey Davis), rustic character Dave Rudd, always eager to please, never seeing the bad in anyone. He has a naivete, is uncomfortable around women, suspicious of 'poofs', and at ease with his mates. Bazza could be considered almost 'a sandwich short of a picnic' but he is nobody's fool; he just believes that everything will be 'jakes', that in the company of his cobbers, as long as he can 'sink a few tubes', 'she'll be right mate!'

Produced by broadcaster, journalist, advertising guru and one of Australia's 'Living Treasures' Phillip Adams AO, *The Adventures of Barry McKenzie* stars his creator Barry Humphries as plain Edna Everage, before she received imperial honours. Peter Cook and Spike

346

Milligan also starred, and there were several cameo performances by a number of at that time undiscovered stars of the Australian screen, including walk-ons by John Clarke and Dick Bentley, an expat actor who had also shared the BBC microphone with Jimmy Edwards and Peter Sellers (his most unforgettable character was the morose Ron in the BBC radio program 'The Glums').

Humphries may have established his alter ego Edna with her biting denunciation of suburban Australian mediocrity, but he lovingly adorns the set with images reflecting a true affection for the icons of Australian ordinariness. When our Bazza enters the Earl's Court flat of his mate Curly the room is literally adorned with Australiana: a reproduction of a Sidney Nolan *Ned Kelly* is pinned to the wall; a tea towel printed with native flora is draped over a tray spread with gifts from 'home', vegemite and lamingtons; spare 'grundies' on a washing line are rigged up over the kitchen sink. Humphries has exploited the symbolism of Australiana and the easy recognition that accompanies the sight of these 'sacred' relics on screen is curiously satisfying.

Not so Innocent Anymore

Australian film has played a central role in the creation of an independent culture, showing Australian stories with Australian characters and Australian values. Film is a mirror of society and as such has a powerful influence on the hearts and minds of the people. Film is used as popular entertainment and because of this can be used to communicate the most esoteric of messages.

The first feature-length movie made in Australia, Harry Southwell's 1920 film *The Kelly Gang*, and its remake in 1922, were initially banned by the censors, fearing it would evoke audience sympathy with the outlaws. No matter that Kelly had been hanged forty years earlier; the authorities were still afraid of public empathy for the rebellious Australian-born Irishman.

Few films over the years have had the impact of some 'little-man' movies produced towards the end of the last century, *The Castle* (1997) pre-eminent among them. Others such as *Reckless Kelly* (1993), *The Bank* (2001) and *The Man Who Sued God* (2003) have all explored the same theme–the common man against the big end of town, David versus Goliath.

These films are the twentieth-century versions of classic bush yarns; the 'Dad and Dave' stories created by Steele Rudd. Like Lawson and Paterson, Rudd's yarns have hapless characters, rural rustics who are constantly at the mercy of the big landholders, the banks or the unpredictability of the weather. His characters 'Dad and Dave' are born of convict stock and their families kept in their place by the 'top-end-of-the-bush'–the squatters.

David vs Goliath: 'The Castle'

Working Dog Productions' (Santo Cilauro, Tom Gleisner, Jane Kennedy and Rob Sitch) simple film *The Castle* is the tale of a family man joined in battle against the government and big business. Daryl Kerrigan, played by the ubiquitous Michael Caton, is a tow-truck driver, an ordinary bloke who is the much-loved head of a much-loving family, happy with their lot. They live in an ordinary house, under a span of high-voltage power lines, right next to the runway

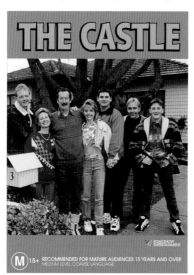

The Castle—a classic tale of working-class hero Daryl Kerrigan and his fight against the big end of town

(Permission, Working Dog Productions)

of an international airport. They are happy, content to scrounge bits and pieces, and have made for themselves their own private paradise–their Castle. No matter how ordinary and architecturally style-defying their house, they have done it by themselves and are well pleased—until they receive a notice in the mail ordering them to move out, their home having been compulsorily acquired for a runway extension.

Daryl refuses to comply and leads the fight against the airport corporation, taking them all the way to the High Court. Initially he engages the services of local

348

solicitor Dennis Denuto (Tiriel Mora), the only tertiary-qualified person he knows apart from his daughter, played by Sophie Lee, who has qualified as a hairdresser at TAFE. Denuto is completely baffled by the court. In his closing remarks he defines his opposition to the acquisition as being against the principles of the Australian constitution. The judge asks him, 'Which part?' Unable to say precisely what he means, as he actually has no idea at all, he replies, 'It's the vibe. It's the vibe of the thing.'

In effect Denuto is right. It is his belief, as it is Kerrigan's, that all Australians are protected by the government simply because they are Australians. It doesn't matter what is actually written down; they believe implicitly that 'every man's home is his castle', and that government can not take the family's home from them. They believed in the common sense of all Australia, the law, the land, society and community–the vibe. They do not reckon on big business, where all of that stands for nought–it's only the money that matters.

Breaking the Bank

In Don Watson and John Clarke's script for *The Bank* they also set an ordinary man against big business. Country boy Jim Doyle, played by David Wenham, is a computer whiz on the very cutting edge of fractal technology who infiltrates the inner sanctum of corporate banking and engineers the biggest stock-market crash in history. He acts in retribution for the callous eviction of a failing small-town tourist operator that resulted in the drowning death of the man's son.

Jim Doyle manipulates the computer program he has built for Centabank, convincing the board that he can predict the ebb and flow of stock movements, engineering massive profits for the bank by what would appear to be a confidence trick wholeheartedly approved by the bank. However, there is a twist in this tale. A vengeful Doyle brings the bank to its knees by causing the program to fail at a crucial moment, diverting the expected windfall from the bank into an untraceable account. The little man had his day after all.

Seriously Reckless

Curiously named Australian actor Yahoo Serious took the myth of the Kelly Gang and created a delightful comedy replete with every possible Aussie icon imaginable in his film *Reckless Kelly*, first screened in 1993. From kangaroos in the bath to cockies screeching overhead, Serious created a Kelly Gang with a history almost older than Dreamtime. His Kellys are connected by Aboriginal ancestry, and have ownership of Reckless Island, which has been sold by a Sydney-based banking corporation to a Japanese consortium who are about to tow the island to the Sea of Japan.

Serious takes on the banks, and he takes a swipe at the government's attitude to native title and an Australian republic. There are so many social themes and obvious sight gags in *Reckless Kelly* that it is a truly didactic comedy that leaves no Australian icon unscathed.

When Serious's Ned Kelly confronts Sir John, the head of the bank (played by Hugo Weaving) in his Sydney office there is a moment of pure 'republican' joy as Kelly cuts the Union Jack from the Australian flag hanging on Sir John's wall and replaces it with a green and gold kangaroo, cut from a towelling bar mat. In darkened cinemas all across the country the audience spontaneously applauded this action. Here Kelly (Serious) gives voice to the latent desire of most Australians to be left alone to take charge of their own affairs without deference to any foreign authority, no matter how benign.

Yahoo Serious's dedication in the film reads: 'This film is dedicated to the irreverent spirit of a great Australian outlaw who championed the rights of the individual against the oppression of authority–Ned Kelly. Born–1855. Hanged–1880'. David versus Goliath again.

Billy Connolly Sues God

When Scottish actor and comedian Billy Connolly took the role of the hapless fisherman whose boat was destroyed by lightning in *The Man Who Sued God*, he joined ubiquitous Australian actors Colin Thiele and Judy Davis in yet another story of the little man against the big end of town. This time it was the little man against

God. Having been told by his insurance company that he would receive nothing in compensation for the loss of his boat—lightning is classified as 'an act of God'—Connolly attempts to sue the Church as the representative of God on earth.

In a hilariously clever argument, Connolly and the representatives of the church have to prove respectively that God does or does not exist, therefore denying or agreeing to the insurance company's point of view.

Once again the little man triumphs over big business; this time big business also includes big religion. In a country such as Australia where the spiritual is clearly kept separate from the secular, and the relevance of any god has always played second fiddle to almost every other concern, the film relishes the success of the little Aussie [Scottish] battler.

Like Connolly's hero, *The Castle*'s Kerrigans are not Steele Rudd's rural rustics; both typify the little Aussie battler, salt-of-the earth Aussies, at ease, even 'relaxed and comfortable' until their hallowed home comes under threat. In each story, whether the Kerrigans, Wenham's avenging banker, Serious's Kelly or Connolly's fisherman, their home (or boat) is the centre of their being, the core of family life that gives each man meaning. Under threat each man becomes a Nietzschean 'Superman', and stands equal to any in defence of his rights.

What a Proposition

Released in 2006, the film *The Proposition*, directed by David Hillcoat from a screenplay by Nick Cave, has taken the genre of the classic Australian saga full circle.

When the renaissance of Australian cinema began with *Barry McKenzie* in 1972, film-makers explored the rich vein that was Australian literature. Just as the antipodean painters had taken Australian stories as their theme, so too did the film-makers. From *My Brilliant Career* to *The Devil's Playground*, Australian film told every story it could get its hands on. The goldfields were brought to life with Brian Brown as Peter Lalor, *Twenty Thousand Horsemen* recalled the last great cavalry charge at Beersheba. In *Gallipoli*, David

Williamson rewrote the landing at Gallipoli in a devastating film starring Mel Gibson and Mark Lee, whose death in the closing scene is one of the most poignant images in contemporary Australian cinema. Williamson showed that the Anzac story can be told and retold; its power as a myth of the common man proving his worth against the cupidity of the ruling classes endures because so little has changed. From Helen Morse as *Caddie* to Paul Hogan as Mick Dundee, Australian cinema has looked at the nation's roots and laid them bare.

The Proposition blows away the last bit of good soil and scorches the roots until they burn. *The Proposition* is a brutally honest film that sets the traditions of colonial England against the burnt-out outback. Cave has taken the classic bushranger myth, mixed in a dash of Irish rebellion, queen, country and the bonds of family against all odds, and served up a dish filled with revenge that is best served scorchingly hot.

From Ray Winston's portrayal of the loyal but introspective Englishman charged with the administration of a colonial outpost set on the edge of hell, to Guy Pearce's troubled outlaw given the choice between the lives of two brothers, *The Proposition* returns to Irish roots for its premise, the struggle for freedom. Added to that are contemporary attitudes to treatment of indigenous Australians and the brutalisation of everyman by an unforgiving environment governed by absent authority.

At the end of the film Danny Huston's bushranger character is tracked down and shot by his brother. Guy Pearce has agreed to the proposition to save the life of a younger brother facing execution for the murder and rape of a family of settlers in exchange for the life of the older outlaw. Huston dies quietly gazing at a glorious outback sunset, his soul granted freedom by his death in what he alone could see as a sun-kissed paradise.

The English Crown could hold his 'Irish rebel heart' prisoner no more.

SORRY!
The Birth of a Black Nation

Even though Australia's indigenous population was not counted among the national figures and had no rights to vote for the governance of their own land, by the 1950s the voice of Black Australia was beginning to make itself known. A few indigenes had made their presence felt in white society: Aboriginal men had fought alongside other Australians on the battlefields of World War II; the central desert artist Albert Namatjira had bridged the centuries painting his own land with a European vision; and sportsmen and women were readily accepted among the nation's elite—after all, anyone who could win glory in a sports-obsessed nation was more than equal.

Positive action by some governments saw an increasing enrolment by Aboriginal students in higher education, unwittingly sowing the seeds for a new generation of black activism. Yet there remained many mysteries surrounding a culture few whites had ever taken any notice of, save for a few dot-pattern-decorated ashtrays or the arrival of Jimmy Sharman's boxing tent at the local agricultural show. For most white Australians, black Australians simply did not come into their sphere at all. In the era of social awareness that was the hallmark of the 1960 and 1970s this was, inevitably, to change.

In the feature film *Jedda* (1955), Australian film-maker Charles Chauvel set about to change common perceptions of Aboriginal culture, to question conservative attitudes on the concept of assimilation—a system of evolutionary genocide that would slowly see the black nation disappear altogether—when he chose a daring theme for the first film to be shot in Australia in colour. Conceived at a time when Aboriginal issues rarely made any positive news, Chauvel had difficulty attracting any funding at all. Few investors were keen to put their money into a film about Aborigines especially with unknown Aboriginal actors cast in leading roles.

Chauvel was forced to establish his own production company to finance the film and on release it achieved international acclaim, being the first Australian film to be shown at the prestigious Cannes Film Festival.

The opening title states: 'To cast this picture the producer went to the primitive Aborigine race of Australia and now introduces NARLA KUNOTH as Jedda, a girl of the Arunta tribe and ROBERT TUDEWALLI, a man of the Tiwi tribe as Marbuk. In this film many people of the Northern Territory of Australia are reliving their roles. The story of Jedda is founded on fact.'

Chauvel tells the story of Jedda, a young Aboriginal girl brought up in a white society. Her mother died in childbirth and Jedda is taken into the white household of outback station owner Sarah McMann, who has suffered the loss of her own baby girl. Jedda becomes a substitute child and is brought up by McMann as a white girl. Sarah teaches her to read, clothes her in white girl's dresses and tries to convince her that she had left the world of the 'savage' behind.

However, Jedda is drawn to the life of her own people who live and work on McMann's station. Jedda longs to accompany them when they go walkabout. One of the film's more dramatic scenes shows Jedda practising the piano while her people are conducting a corroboree outside; the two sounds clash and Jedda begins to pound at the piano until she almost loses her 'western' composure. Jedda is lost between two worlds and soon is attracted to Marbuck, a 'wild' Aboriginal man who kidnaps her, taking her back to his people. Marbuck is rejected for having broken 'an unbreakable tribal law'; he has taken a woman from a different skin tribe and is sung to death as punishment. The last scene shows Marbuck, driven mad by the tribal singing, falling to his death with Jedda in his arms.

Chauvel created a parody of *Romeo and Juliet* and placed it against the glorious backdrop of the Northern Territory. His 'star-crossed lovers' were not simply defying a code of family honour, but were defying the entrenched attitudes of a nation still committed to the idea of a white Australia. Chauvel also held up a mirror to Aboriginal culture as it too grappled with the validity of its own traditions in the modern world.

'Terra Nullius', Not Likely!

In 1963 student activist Charles Perkins led a group of fellow students on an American-style freedom ride through Aboriginal communities across rural areas to focus on the substandard living conditions of most indigenous Australians. Although there were many in the white community who regarded any Aboriginal protest as communist-inspired sedition, Perkins did become the well-mannered face of indigenous protest, able to bridge the gap between black and white. Perkins also became the first indigenous head of a federal government department when he was appointed as permanent head of the Department of Aboriginal Affairs in 1981.

There were others in the Aboriginal community who took a far less conciliatory line in making demands for a better future and inclusion in Australian affairs. In 1966 a Gurindji man, Vincent Lingiari, led a walkout of 200 Aboriginal stockmen and their families from Vesty's (British Pastoral Company) cattle stations at Newcastle Waters and Wave Hill, 600 kilometres south of Darwin.

They were protesting at the appalling conditions in which they were expected to live; their wages and benefits were fixed, with only a specified amount of both money and goods allowed, and government benefits were paid to the pastoral company on their behalf, not directly to the workers themselves.

Lingiari and his co-workers established their own settlement at Wattie Creek and struggled for the next seven years to gain freehold to their traditional lands.

Charles Perkins
Photograph by Robert McFarlane, 1967

In a pensive mood, Aboriginal student activist Charles Perkins sits on the bus on his way to university.
(National Library of Australia. By Permission, Robert McFarlane)

They wrote to the United Nations asking for intervention based on the UN charter, stating that no people should be discriminated against because of race or colour. The letter read in part:

> Our tribal lands have been taken from us and handed over to big pastoral companies. We have received only inadequate compensation for this. However, compensation is not the point, our people want to have a say in controlling and working the land ... On the big cattle stations of the Territory our people work long hours doing skilled, hard and often dangerous work mustering, branding and injecting cattle for a miserable $6.60 a week.
>
> This is happening in a country which is really ours and where even the poorest white man receives nearly $40 a week and usually lives in a comfortable home.
>
> Most of our people live in humpies without even the minimum hygiene facilities. Their diet consists of the poorest parts of meat, tea, flour and sugar ... we are fighting for our very existence as a people.

Although the appeal to the United Nations was unsuccessful their continued struggle led to the establishment of the Commonwealth Land Rights Act (NT) 1970, which eventually saw the granting of freehold title over 3250 square kilometres of tribal land to the Gurindji people. They were also granted veto over mining and development rights on their land.

Just Say 'Yes'

On 27 May 1967 the biggest ever 'Yes' vote recorded in a national referendum ushered in a new era for Australia's indigenous people. 90.8 per cent of all Australians voted in favour of the federal government taking control of Aboriginal affairs, granted the power to make laws for Aborigines living in the States, and the inclusion of Aborigines, for the first time, on the national census.

Faith Bandler, New South Wales 'Yes vote' campaign director, urged the federal government to act immediately and declare discrimination illegal. She told the government that they had to realise 'that the overwhelming "yes" vote means that the people of Australia have told them to get on and do the job'.

Vincent Lingiari
Photograph by Michael Jensen, 1966
Vincent Lingiari with Aboriginal elders at the camp
they established at Wattie Creek
(National Library of Australia)

Aboriginal people were preparing to take their place in Australian society and were prepared to embarrass any recalcitrant government too slow to act on their behalf. At a bicentennial re-enactment of Cook's landing held at Sydney's Kurnell Beach in 1970, a group of Aborigines held their own ceremony to acknowledge this as a 'day of mourning', on the site of the old Aborigines Protection Board at La Perouse at the other end of Botany Bay.

In 1971 the Aboriginal Advancement League appealed to the United Nations for assistance in their claim for land rights, seeking six billion dollars in compensation.

The McMahon Liberal government virtually denied land rights to Aboriginals when it announced its Aboriginal policy on 26 January 1972. The government would allow only limited tenure to Aboriginal communities who were able to demonstrate an appropriate commercial or social use for the land, as any admission of land rights would have threatened the economic future of the mining and pastoral interests who had assumed control of much of outback and north-western Australia—and of course mining would be allowed on any Aboriginal reserve.

On the afternoon of that Australia Day–Invasion Day–1972, young Aboriginal activists pitched a tent on the lawns in front of Parliament House, Canberra and established the Aboriginal Tent Embassy. Whereas a new Parliament House has been built further up the hill, behind the original Parliament building, the tent embassy has remained in the same place for more than thirty years, its protest a constant reminder to parliamentarians of the continued struggle of indigenous Australians for equality of opportunity in their own land.

At Wattie Creek in 1975 Prime Minister Gough Whitlam had the honour of handing over to Vincent Lingiari a title which had been purchased from Vesty's by the Aboriginal Land Fund Commission. Whitlam spoke to the Gurindji people: 'I want to give back to you formally, in Aboriginal and Australian law, ownership of this land of your fathers. Vincent Lingiari, I solemnly hand to you these deeds as proof in Australian law that these lands belong to the Gurindji people.'

After this short speech Whitlam bent to the ground and scooped up a handful of dry soil. He poured it into Lingiari's open palm as he said, 'I put into your hands this piece of the earth itself as a sign that we restore them to you and your children forever.' Vincent Lingiari responded: 'We are all right now. We are friendly, we all mates.'

A 'Murray' Man Named Eddie

'[Our land] … it was handed down from generation to generation, they knew by the boundary lines and markers. There was a certain tree, or stones, heaps of rocks, different trees. They knew exactly where the place was.'
– *Eddie Mabo*

Eddie Mabo, a young Torres Strait Islander, who for a youthful indiscretion had been exiled from his home on Mer Island (in the Murray Island group), was working as a gardener in the grounds of James Cook University in Townsville, where he came under the influence of local trade unions and sympathetic members of the Communist Party.

Eddie (born Edward Koiki Sambo on Mer Island in 1936 but had taken the name of his uncle Benny Mabo who brought him up) joined in with university life. Although he was not enrolled he began to sit in on classes and read books in the library, especially those written by white anthropologists who thought they knew the history and customs of 'his' people.

In conversation with several professors over lunch one day in 1974, Eddie was talking about his home on Mer Island. Professors Loos and Reynolds were surprised to hear Mabo talk about the island as if it were his, as if he owned it. They had the difficult task of explaining to Eddie that the land did not belong to him, or any other of the Mabo family, but to the Crown.

In 1981 a Land Rights Conference was held at James Cook University where Mabo spoke to the delegates. He could not accept this idea of Crown ownership over land he clearly believed was his, by inheritance.

A lawyer attending the conference suggested that the Murray Islanders should challenge the claim of 'terra nullius' in the High Court. Although the arguments presented were powerful and convincing, Justice Moynihan declared that as Eddie was not the son of Benny he had no right to inherit Mabo land.

With increasing bad health Mabo virtually gave up the fight, retiring to Murray Island to fish and paint. But the case continued.

In January 1992 Mabo died, five months before the High Court reversed the decision previously handed down by Justice Moynihan, announcing that 'Moynihan's decision that Mabo wasn't the rightful heir was irrelevant because the decision that came out was that native title existed and it was up to the Aboriginal or Islander people to determine who owned what land'.

Treaty

The voice of dissent on behalf of the Aboriginal people had grown apace. The Aboriginal rock band Yothu Yindi had a hit record with a single titled 'Treaty' in 1991, a dance hit that voiced the nation's

Ceremony around the campfire at the Aboriginal Tent Embassy, Canberra,
demonstrating against the visit of American President George W Bush in 2003

Photograph by Benjamin Rushton

(National Library of Australia)

dissatisfaction with the pace of change. The sound of polit-rock, Midnight Oil, had a hit a few years earlier titled 'Beds Are Burning' in which they questioned how white Australia could be so comfortable when there was so much inequality in their own backyard. Aboriginal faces were seen regularly in the mainstream media, on the sporting field, on television and on the dance and theatre stage, and commanded extraordinary attention in the nation's art galleries. The black nation had made the transition from curiosity to the mainstream and by their achievements had made the white nation sit up and pay full attention.

However, there was still much to be done. Just as the Mabo decision was being handed down in favour of land rights Aborigines stormed the old Parliament House in Canberra, marking the twentieth anniversary of the tent embassy on the grounds opposite. An Aboriginal barrister from the Redfern legal service, Paul Coe, presented a 'Declaration of Aboriginal Sovereignty' to Chris Tickner,

Minister for Aboriginal Affairs, claiming Australia for Aboriginal people on the grounds that 'they had never surrendered or acquiesced in [their] claim to these lands or territories'. Aboriginal poet Kevin Gilbert announced that his people would not wait another decade for land rights: 'We will spread dissent and discord, and prove that white Australians do not hold a sovereign title. It is a defective title because we never surrendered our land.'

The so-named Mabo decision challenged the prevailing orthodoxy that Aborigines had no concept of land ownership—hence 'terra nullius'. It also challenged the rights of industrialists, mining and pastoralist companies who continued to exploit the resources of the land, ignoring those dispossessed by their activities.

Conservative governments, alongside a hysterical media, claimed that Aboriginal people, buoyed by the High Court decision, would attempt to reclaim three-quarters of all Australian land, dispossessing the generations of Europeans and others, who had enjoyed the benefits of white settlement. Some politicians even suggested that Aboriginals would take away the suburban homes occupied by white families, claiming prior rights to the land on which they had built their lives. This did not happen. By and large, it seems that urbanised Aborigines have been content in the acknowledgement of tribal lands without threatening the freehold of their neighbours; rural Aborigines living in remote areas of Queensland, Western Australia and the Northern Territory have successfully pursued land claims, in most cases allowing for commercial operations to continue. Even Ayer's Rock's name was changed to the traditional name Uluru and the nation did not crack apart.

When Sorry Still Seems to be the Hardest Word

At the closing ceremony of the Sydney Olympic Games in August 2000 a public protest by Australian polit-rock band Midnight Oil was beamed to more than a billion people worldwide. The Oils came onto the stage dressed in black tracksuits with the words 'Sorry' stencilled all over them. As lead singer Peter Garrett punched the air, screaming into his microphone looking as if he would burst a blood vessel, as is his style, the Oils almost tore the stadium down

LOVE MEANS NEVER HAVING TO SAY YOU'RE **SORRY**

Silk-screen poster created by the Guerrilla Girls Poster Workshop, published by Red Planet, 1999
(La Trobe Picture Collection, State Library of Victoria)

as they ripped into their political anthem 'Beds Are Burning'.

Aboriginal rock group Yothu Yindi followed with 'Treaty', another song critical of John Howard and his federal government's refusal to deal appropriately with the question of reconciliation, the stolen generation and his refusal to say 'Sorry' for the iniquities towards black Australia by white Australia in the past.

In what should have been Howard's triumphal moment he was forced to sit there, the rest of the world looking on as the entire audience screamed their approval of the Oils, and Mandawuy Yunupingu and Yothu Yindi, and their dissatisfaction with the prime minister.

Just saying 'Sorry' is a gesture the prime minister could have easily made, but he continually refused to utter this simple word. He refused to make any apology for the actions of past generations. His attitude may have some validity; after all, few Australians living today can actually be blamed for the actions of their forebears. Australian-born citizens cannot simply pack up and go anywhere else; there is nowhere for them to go. Most Australians, black, white or brindle, acknowledge that they all have to live together and simply seek a gesture from the elected leader of their democratic land to say 'Sorry' on behalf of them all. For a seemingly petulant John Howard 'Sorry' seemed to be the hardest word.

At the same Games Aboriginal athlete Cathy Freeman carried the hearts and hopes of all Australians when she ran for gold in the women's 400-metre race. The earlier decision to award Freeman the honour of lighting the Olympic flame was criticised by many for being patronising and too politically correct. Freeman was not the biggest name in the Australian sporting arena and she had also been openly critical of Howard's refusal to say 'Sorry' on behalf of the nation for the colonists' treatment of her people, but Cathy won her race, and won easily, although the entire nation had watched in terror, their hearts in their mouths, when she lagged behind earlier in the race—but triumph she did.

If the power of the people can lift any athlete's performance, Cathy Freeman was carried to the tape on the sheer will for her to win by all of Australia on that night. Her win represented all that Howard refused to say, and on the night when he should have been standing proud before the eyes of the entire world he was diminished. Diminished by the efforts of a young Aboriginal woman and the lyrics of a couple of rock bands.

A Black Arm-band View

In response to an inquiry into the forced removal of Aboriginal children from their families a report entitled 'Bringing Them Home' was tabled in Parliament in 1998. The report cast light on the practice of forced assimilation of Aboriginal children into the white community. The removed children became known as the 'Stolen Generation'. The acknowledgement by Australians of European origin of this once common practice has gone some way to acknowledge the hurt done to the Aboriginal people.

The response of Prime Minister John Howard to any questioning of the actions of Australia's colonial past in the treatment of the indigenous population has been to accuse his critics of wanting to take a 'black arm-band' view of Australia's history.

While Prime Minister Howard would not deny that the indigenous population could have been treated better by white settlers, he refused to offer even a symbolic gesture. In spite of his refusal the Australian people voted with their feet in support of the Aboriginal people. A thousand 'Sorry Books', an initiative by popular author Bryce Courtenay and Hazel Hawke, former wife of ex-Prime Minister RJ Hawke, were placed in communities across the nation; thousands joined in a 'Journey of Healing'. The first held in May

On 28 May 2000 Australians in their tens of thousands joined in the Reconciliation Corroboree March across Sydney Harbour Bridge, giving voice to that which Prime Minister John Howard Would not say—'Sorry'.

(Photograph by Rick Stevens. With permission Fairfax Photos)

1999 saw the Sydney Harbour Bridge blocked end-to-end by 'Sorry' Australian citizens. Around the nation Australians had shown their disappointment in the Howard government over this issue—but to no avail. Howard responded by shutting down ATSIC (Aboriginal and Torres Strait Islander Commission), claiming it was unworkable and that it did not represent the voice of the majority of Aboriginal people.

The sole voice of national Aboriginal leadership was silenced.

Former prime minister Malcolm Fraser, patron of the National Sorry Day Committee, issued a press release on 27 April 2005, which read in part:

> The attempt to separate 'practical' from 'symbolic' reconciliation seems to mean that the government will not acknowledge past wrongs, and will not accept any obligation to redress the effects of unjust treatment. But it is only possible to share responsibility to answer a problem once agreement has been reached on each party's responsibility for causing the problem ...
>
> If either the Liberal Party or the Labor Party were prepared to argue genuinely for a new relationship between indigenous and non-indigenous Australians, based on justice and healing, they would attract many from the middle ground who feel unrepresented by the Canberra political processes, and who would be ready to support policies that genuinely advance Aboriginal reconciliation and wellbeing.

A CAUSE WORTH LOSING
Who Mentioned the Word Republic?

For more than a century Australians have argued back and forth over two issues. Both would make little change to the way the country functions; both would make an enormous impact on the way the nation feels about itself–the flag and the republic.

Few Australians argue for real revolutionary change. When Germaine Greer accused Australians of being just too lazy to do anything about such issues she was attempting to jolt Australia out of its complacence.

The issues are just not important enough to get too upset over them, yet they did come to the fore as the nation looked towards celebrating the unification of the Colonies into the Federated Australian Commonwealth. After the first century of nationhood it seemed an appropriate time for an examination of the changes made in that first 100 years and what its future direction should be.

Barry Jones MP (Deputy Chairman of the People's Constitutional Convention held in the Old Parliament House Canberra, 2–13 February 1998) takes a measured view of the proceedings.
Photograph by Louise Seselja
(National Library of Australia)

A majority of Australians from all sides of politics, not withstanding social, ethnic or economic demography, agreed that the time of the constitutional monarch was over and that Australia should at last become a republic.

Liberal Party leader John Howard did not agree. No doubt honouring the fawning poetry of his hero Sir Robert Menzies, Howard could not envisage the queen passing by either; he seemed to wish that she could remain on the throne for ever. However, during the 2006 Commonwealth Games in Melbourne, after a desultory appearance by 'Her Maj' at the opening ceremony, Howard did allow himself the reflection that he could not see the position of monarch, as the Australian head of state, lasting longer than the lifetime of the present incumbent. Given that her mother lasted longer than a century, was Howard suggesting that Australia could become a republic in 2026, at the very earliest, and hopefully not within his own expected lifetime? Then he would not have to deal with the issue at all.

He would not allow himself to be disloyal to the English queen. When defending his reactionary position to the republican debate, Howard was often quoted: 'If the thing isn't broke, why fix it?' Most Australians can't be bothered to disagree; after all, what does it matter who sits on our throne? The regal position has so little relevance to everyday life, why bother about it, it's just a bit of pomp and ceremony anyway. If this is the case, why do so many defend the position so vehemently, and why did Howard frame the point of reference for the Republican Convention held in Canberra's Old Parliament House in 2002 in such a way that the model taken to the 2002 Referendum on the Republic would be voted against by the majority of Australians who desired a different outcome?

Keating's View

Before Howard came to power Prime Minister Paul Keating announced his government's decision to begin the process of creating an Australian Federal Republic in the House of Representatives on 7 June 1995:

> It is the government's view that Australia's head of state should be an Australian and that Australia should become a republic by the year 2001 ...
>
> Many Australians have come to favour a republic. Just as many, perhaps, now believe it is inevitable.
>
> Many may regret the prospect of change and be unsure about the means by which it can be achieved, but recognise that sooner or later we must have an Australian as our head of state. That one small step would make Australia a republic ...

A True Blue Country Boy

Australian country singer John Williamson has argued the case for the Australian republic and the redesign of the nation's flag for more than twenty years. Like so many millions of other Australians he is passionate in his desire to see the nation's banners celebrating our island home without deference to the United Kingdom:

Singer John Williamson's design for a 'True Blue' Aussie flag
(© John Williamson. Reproduced with permission)

> If my dream of purely Australian flags is seen to be anti-British then I am sorely misunderstood. Our British heritage is securely placed in Australia's hereafter. The State names, Queensland, New South Wales, Victoria, and main streets in our cities, George Street, Elizabeth Street, Edward Street etc, will always preserve the fact that the Australian nation was founded by the British monarchy.
>
> Not to mention the hundreds of towns and suburbs named after the same in the British Isles. I believe that those who cling to the monarchy and the Union Jack are no different (comparatively) from those in the late nineteenth century who objected to the then proposed federation and the change from the Union Jack to a British ensign.
>
> In other words, there is no doubt in my mind that a republic is inevitable as is a purely Australian flag.

Williamson, who has been banned from performing in some RSL clubs because of his song 'A Flag of Our Own', has created the design shown above as his suggestion for a new standard. He says:

> Like two boomerangs, the sweep of the legs and tail of the launching kangaroo can be recognised at a great distance. The four-million-year-old marsupial symbolises our ancient island continent. And finally, a kangaroo cannot go backwards.

In contrast to this argument John Howard stated on conclusion of the Sydney Olympics that the huge enthusiasm shown for the Australian flag had killed any move to change the flag and dump the Union Jack from its corner. Rather than go forward, it would appear that Howard's kangaroo *can* go backwards.

Governments can wait for opinion to force their hand, or they can lead. They can wait for the world to change and respond as necessity demands, or they can see the way the world is going and point the way ...

We are approaching the twenty-first century and the centenary of our nationhood. As never before we are making our own way in our region and the world. For us the world is going—and we are going—in a way which makes our having the British monarch as our head of state increasingly anomalous ...

The 1890s conventions were proponents of change; they were concerned with one question—how to create from the separate Australian colonies one indissoluble Commonwealth of Australia. So would any convention on the republic need to be a proponent of the republic, and concerned only with one issue—the best means by which the people of the Commonwealth of Australia can have an Australian as their head of state.

The meaning of the changes [proposed by Labor] are simple and, we believe, irresistible—as simple and irresistible as the idea of a Commonwealth of Australia was to the Australians of a century ago.

The meaning then was a nation united in common cause for the common good. A nation which gave expression to the lives we lead together on this continent, the experience and hopes we share as Australians.

The meaning now is still a product of that founding sentiment—it is that we are all Australians. We share a continent. We share a past, a present and a future. And our head of state should be one of us.

John Howard who was federal opposition leader at that time replied the following day:

I want to say first, on behalf of the Coalition, that this is an important debate. Although the question of the constitutional structure of Australia is not something that weighs heavily upon Australians as they go about their daily lives, although the question of whether or not Australia becomes a republic will have no bearing on our standard of living and our capacity to economically penetrate the fast-growing

Cartoon by Cathy Wilcox published in *The Age*, 1997
(Reproduced with permission)

Asia-Pacific region, nonetheless, the constitutional future of our nation is a matter of great importance ...

This debate is not about who is the better Australian. There are decent, passionate, loyal Australians on both sides of this argument. The overwhelming issue—indeed, I believe the great test, the great answer and the great issue—is what system of government will best deliver a united, stable and tolerant Australian nation.

Let me say that the interests of eighteen and a half million Australians are more important than the identity of one. Our view is a fundamentally democratic view. We believe the people of Australia cannot be involved enough in deciding the future of our constitution. With an issue as critical and as important as this, there cannot be too much democracy ...

The Australian constitution is no more Paul Keating's constitution than it is mine. All Australians should have an equal say in its future and in our country's future. The Prime Minister [Keating] believes that any involvement by the Australian people is too much involvement. He believes you should be involved only in the final stage and that you should be asked merely to adjudicate on his question about your constitution, rather than allow you to be part of the creation of any change if that is what you want. That is why the only way to properly handle this matter is through the people's convention of the Coalition.

On attaining office Howard lived up to his word and a people's convention was held. Opinion leaders from all walks of life were invited to Canberra in 1999 and spent five days attempting to agree on a model to be put to the people. The only drawback was that Howard would not allow the question of a direct vote for a president to be a part of any proposed model; he desired a political appointment chosen by Parliament.

When the referendum was put to the people they responded by voting 55 per cent against and 45 per cent in favour of the model. The Australian people had, on the one hand, showed their distrust of parliament, while on the other voted against their desired position of an Australian republic.

President of the Australian Republican Movement, Sydney banker Malcolm Turnbull, who later joined Howard in Parliament as Liberal member for Wentworth, declared on hearing the result of the poll: 'This was the day that Howard had broken the nation's heart.'

The issue did not go away. Australians just went about their business and decided to wait. There was no urgency, they were not apathetic, but recognised there is no sense getting too excited about something that seems irrelevant to them anyway and will eventually come about by an evolutionary process that won't cause them to go to any effort at all.

It seems to be that this state of affairs should suit most Australians right down to the ground.

JUST SAYING NO

This was the day that Howard had broken the nation's heart.
– Malcolm Turnbull 1999

The referendum to alter the Australian Constitution to establish the Commonwealth of Australia as a republic failed to gather a majority of votes in favour, even though it was well recognised before the question was put that the majority of Australians wanted to make the change—of the 11,785,000 registered Australian voters, the majority, 6,410,787, voted against achieving their own goal. Why?

The answer is quite simple. Prime Minister John Howard, a constitutional monarchist muddied the waters. The question put to the Australian people read like this:

> A proposed law: To alter the Constitution to establish the Commonwealth of Australia as a republic with the Queen and Governor-General being replaced by a President appointed by a two-thirds majority of the members of the Commonwealth Parliament.

It was the last dozen words of this proposed alteration to the Constitution that had voters hitting the 'No' button. What Australians wanted was to be able to vote for the people's president, to be able to make a popular choice. No doubt they had hoped for a cast of worthwhile, intelligent, well-meaning, visionary, deserving candidates who would capture the public imagination—and there were a score of names being bandied about at the time which did just that. What the nation didn't want was to have Canberra choose another party-hack, or unemployed Royal, or green-baggy-cap-wearing cricketing hero, or semi-retired media magnate, or overtly generous contributor to party fund-raising attempting to buy themselves into the top job in the nation. No! We wanted to choose our own, and if we chose Bert Newton, then so be it. At least he would have been our Bert. The truth is that if Barry Humphries, a.k.a Dame Edna Everage, had stood for President the nation probably would have voted with a resounding 'Yes', just for fun, as long as Sir Les Patterson was allowed to have a go at the job every now and then as well. At least Dame Edna already has regal pretensions and is comfortable on the world-stage with royalty and commoners alike. [Isn't it a pity that Graeme Kennedy has passed on, he was already known as 'The King'].

What the nation voted against was Canberra, as once again Australians showed their mistrust of high-office, and of those in authority who presume to speak for all of us.

The 'Yes' campaign was lead by Malcolm Turnbull in the vanguard. Although divided in detail the 'Yes' side brought together old opponents who as elder statesmen presented a united front in favour of Australia becoming a republic: Malcolm Fraser and Gough Whitlam gave joint statements in favour, and were joined by many other prominent Australians in endorsing a 'Yes' vote, leading the 'No' side to brand republicans as an 'elite', led by politicians and not the people and out of touch with the wishes of ordinary Australians. It appears that they were right, because the question did not allow for a popular vote, the result simply reflected a vote against politicians, and not actually in favour of Her Majesty.

British political journalist Bill Deedes, who observed the media circus prior to the referendum, wrote in *The Daily Telegraph*, 8 November 1999: 'I have rarely attended elections in any country, certainly not a democratic one, in which newspapers have displayed more shameless bias. One and all, they determined that Australians should have a republic and they used every device towards that end.' With the weight of the combined Australian media behind the 'Yes' movement how could they possibly lose? The answer lay in the question, and the reality that Australians can be a rather self-flagellating lot. If they can't have their own way they would rather be denied their prize. As one media commentator said many years ago: 'Remember, Australia rhymes with failure'. It is often failure that Australians honour. So, the republic could wait, and wait it has.

What the nation ended up with was the end of the debate. Now nobody mentions the republic anymore, except on January 26, when the media gets itself into a lather and runs the old 'Shall we change our flag?' debate up the virtual flagpole, and increasing numbers of journalists question the veracity of the nation celebrating a day when all that happened was the English turned up, ran the Union Jack up a tree, and declared Australia an empty land. Arthur Phillip seemingly ignored the groups of natives watching them as they began their colonial occupation of this land they dubbed 'terra nullias'– belonging to no-one–while claiming it from south to north for the British monarch, mad-king 'Georgie-Porgie'.

Who speaks for us?

The only politicians in recent years to truly capture the spirit of the whole nation have been Prime Ministers Keating and Rudd: Keating's Redfern speech (10 December 1992 at the Australian launch of the International Year of the World's Indigenous People), where he outlined his vision for reconciliation and reparation:

> . . . the starting point might be to recognise that the problem starts with us non-Aboriginal Australians. It begins, I think, with that act of recognition.
> Recognition that it was we who did the dispossessing.
> We took the traditional lands and smashed the traditional way of life.
> We brought the diseases. The alcohol. We committed the murders.
> We took the children from their mothers.
> We practised discrimination and exclusion.
> It was our ignorance and our prejudice.
> And our failure to imagine these things being done to us.
> With some noble exceptions, we failed to make the most basic human response and enter into their hearts and minds.
> We failed to ask–how would I feel if this were done to me?
> As a consequence, we failed to see that what we were doing degraded all of us.
> If we needed a reminder of this, we received it this year. . . it might help us if we non-Aboriginal Australians imagined ourselves dispossessed of land we had lived on for fifty thousand years –and then imagined ourselves told that it had never been ours.
> Imagine if ours was the oldest culture in the world and we were told that it was worthless.

Imagine if we had resisted this settlement, suffered and died in the defence of our land, and then were told in history books that we had given up without a fight.

Imagine if non-Aboriginal Australians had served their country in peace and war and were then ignored in history books.

Imagine if our feats on sporting fields had inspired admiration and patriotism and yet did nothing to diminish prejudice.

Imagine if our spiritual life was denied and ridiculed.

Imagine if we had suffered the injustice and then were blamed for it.

It seems to me that if we can imagine the injustice we can imagine its opposite.

And we can have justice.

Sorry

After almost a decade of Liberal-conservative government with Prime Minister John Howard setting the agenda for public debate, repeatedly refusing to make a symbolic gesture in acknowledgement of the harm done to Australia's first people, it took a Labor leader, Queenslander Kevin Rudd, to make an apology to the 'forgotten Australians' in a speech broadcast to the nation from the forecourt of the national parliament in Canberra on 13 February 2008. A huge crowd had gathered, including indigenes from across the nation. Some had travelled more than a week from remote communities in the far north and the west to be present at what was to be for them a special day, a turning-point for Aboriginal Australians. Two hundred years since James Cook had claimed possession of the eastern seaboard in the name of the British monarch, it was another white-fellah who stood before them and made that long-denied gesture of reparation when he simply said 'Sorry'.

Then, Liberal leader, one-time president of the Australian Republican Movement, Malcolm Turnbull broke down in tears as he acknowledged the harm done to Aboriginal children placed in the care of the white-man's institutions. Rudd said 'Sorry':

Sorry that as children you were taken from your families and placed in institutions where often you were abused. As a nation we must now reflect on those who did not receive proper care. Robbed of your families, robbed of your homeland, regarded not as innocent children, but regarded instead as a source of child labour. To those of you who were told you were orphans, brought here without your parents' knowledge or consent, we acknowledge the lies you were told, the lies told to your mothers, fathers and the pain these lies have caused for a lifetime.'

In recognition of the difficulties faced in later life by many who had suffered, he acknowledged: 'If you hurt a child a harmed adult will often result.'

Malcolm Turnbull added: 'Any nation that does not protect its children does not deserve to be called a nation', and to those of the stolen generation gathered before him he added: 'This nation did not care enough for you.'

This was the apology that the nation had been waiting for.

It was the simple statement that Howard could not allow himself to say. He appeared to believe that by admitting the past he would become responsible for it, maintaining that as he had not perpetrated the harm himself, nor had his generation, he had no reason to say sorry. To do so would implicate the Crown, as the figurehead, that could be held to ransom in reparation of past wrongs—that Elizabeth could be held to pay for the wrongs done in the name of her crazy great-grandfather George—all the Aboriginal folk wanted was a gesture.

Prime Minister Kevin Rudd described the moment as an opportunity for 'the nation to turn a new page in Australia's history by righting the wrongs of the past and so moving forward with confidence in the future.'

Former Prime Minister Keating had recognised the need for all Australians to acknowledge the 'sins' of a collective past, and to find a way for the nation to go forward together as one. In contrast, when he became prime minister, John Howard allowed Pauline Hanson, a disaffected former liberal party member from Ipswich in Queensland, to try and move the country sideways with her redneck 'common-sense' in defence of the rights of the whites, against all comers. Since then the nation has descended into indecorous squabbling about indigenous issues, the Intervention, migration, detention centres, the *Tampa*, boat-people–the whole unedifying face of national debate about who we are is summed up in this extraordinary statement to the Australian parliament by John Howard in December 2001: 'We will decide who comes to this country and the circumstances in which they come.' As if he had any right to deny others that which his forebears had assumed for him. Howard declared those who championed a revison of white history, who, in examining the dispossesion of indigenes at the hands of European settlers were taking a 'black arm-band' view of Australia's past. Almost as a precursor to Abbott's inflamatory comments of Australia Day 2012 he believed that we could all just 'move on', that that was then, this is now–and there is nothing to be gained by apologising for it.

Melbourne writer Jenny Sinclair, in response to Howard's declaration of exclusion, began to dig into her own family tree and came to this conclusion:

> Having found that I come from what once would have been called pioneer stock, should I be proud or ashamed of what may have been done in my name, for their children and their children's children? Would it have been better to spring from newcomers than such unreconstructed colonials? I suspect it's people like me John Howard means when he says 'we decide who comes here' but I don't want to be part of his 'we'.
>
> I side with the black armbands, the sorry people, the ones who admit that harm was done, is being done, and would like, in their incoherent, possibly ineffectual way, to make things better. At least to try.
>
> Our views–there is no single view–are not negative. They're realist. They struggle with what is, what must be addressed. I'd rather wear a black armband to remind me of the past and future than be part of a whitewash over rotting foundations. In the end, it will be the artists and writers, the historians and truth-tellers with black armbands, who help heal the soul of this nation.'

She concluded her thoughts with:

> …some small old town not far away, across the worn-down landscape
> of ancient weathered volcanos—is where I'd like to die, magpies
> carolling outside the walls of my room as I drift off to sleep.[26]

Maybe that's the real test of who you are: not where you are born at
random, but where you choose to die.

What is January 26?

Many Indigenous Australians call it 'Invasion Day', the day they
lost their land. Most Australians used to think it was just the day
the British arrived. As long as Aussies got a public holiday who
really cared what is was for? In the old-days, before Howard, the
day was used for naturalisation ceremonies when new citizens were
welcomed to join the nation. There were usually a few half-serious
celebrations where blokes in badly made redcoat uniforms pushed
a surf-boat onto a beach somewhere and ran a British flag up a
gum-tree; all to the rattle of a kettle-drum and a couple of 'God save
the Queen's'.

New Australians lined up in town and country parks, or dusty
civic centres across the nation; and with their hands over their
hearts the new citizens were welcomed into the Australian family.
However, since 1999 this day has seen political manipulation to
make it an invocation of national pride and as a celebration of all
things 'Aussie'. It has grown like topsy, while in many corners there
are those in the community who do not enjoy the hubris, or the
American-style flag-waving patriotism that accompanies it.

Big politics has a lot to answer for in shaping the direction of
national debate when determining how Australians feel about
themselves, their new neighbours at home, and in the south-Asian
region as a whole. The remnant of colonialism is still at the heart
of Australian experience and until that yoke is cast off the debate
about the nature of Australian-ness will continue. The issue of the
flag will come up every January 26, the republic will be discussed on
late-night political talk-shows for a day or two, and as now happens
every year a group of flag-wearing white-boys will have a crack at

a few new-comers, forgetting that they themselves, or at least their parents, or grandparents, were new to this land not so long ago. When Paul Keating said: 'We failed to ask–how would I feel if this were done to me?' he also cut to the very heart of the debate about migration: how would it feel if it were done to you?

On 26 January 2012, the day that Labor Prime Minister Julia Gillard lost her shoe in a dramatic reprise of Russian Agent Eva Petrov's loss of footwear during her dramatic capture by KGB agents in Darwin in 1954; Gillard was hurried away from a presentation of bravery awards at the Lobby Restaurant in Canberra when Aboriginal activists gathered angrily outside the popular Canberra eating-house, banging on the plate glass windows in protest at Opposition leader Tony Abbott's comments about the tent-embassy that had stood on the lawns opposite the Australian Parliament for forty years. It was reported to the Aboriginal activists manning the tent embassy that he thought it should be pulled down (well, that's what they believed, he insists that he just said that 'we should move on'). The Aboriginal and Torres Strait Islanders who manned the embassy believe they have a right to show their anger at the Australian government, and Abbott–a constitutional monarchist–in particular, especially on 'Invasion Day'.

An editorial comment published in The Age the following day, headed 'Australians all did not rejoice' commented:

> ...January 26, 2012, is already an unusually memorable Australia Day, for all the wrong reasons. It starkly reminded the nation of divisors that have not yet been resolved, and it did so at a time of renewed agitation to recognise indigenous people in the constitution. Some may see the day's events as an obstacle to that overdue change; on the contrary, they should be a spur to bring it about.

Martin Flanagan, in his article published in the *Saturday Age*, 28 January 2012, titled 'Why we need to find a new date for Australia Day' wrote:

> What happened in Canberra on Thursday was doubly unfortunate. The image, on Australia Day, of an Australian prime minister being

bundled towards her car looking harassed in response to a perceived threat by a group of Aboriginal protestors has history stamped all over it.'

The question is not whether January 26 is the best date for Australia Day. The question is whether we could possibly have arrived at a worst date. The tragedy is that we need not have put ourselves in this position. January 26, the date when Captain Arthur Phillip raised the British flag at Sydney Cove, was originally celebrated as Anniversary Day or Foundation Day. Oh that it still were.

Even so, 20 years ago, Australia Day was not the event that it is now. It was ramped up during the culture wars of the Howard years. Its invigoration was part of the crude triumphalism that accompanied Pauline Hanson being let off the leash [and anyone who denies the damage that did Australia in other countries, particularly in Asia, is a fool or a knave] and the appointment of revisionist historian Keith Windschuttle to the board of the ABC.

Politically, one of Howard's greatest successes was to sell his brand of nationalism to the young, but it was not the act of a statesman since it left us with a national day that annually calls up our deepest and most abiding division.

… At some point, Australians are going to have to bite the bullet and consider celebrating Australia Day on another date. Anzac Day has been suggested. Anzac Day has its own myth and power–perhaps too much since it has become a giant historical blur [with a fair dash of Howardian hubris thrown in–Author's annotation].

Flanagan proposed January 22; a day that celebrates the end of the Battle for Australia, as it became known, at Kokoda in 1943. This was a battle fought by Australians, including Indigenous Australians, in defence of our own country. No Poms, nor Yanks, just Aussies fighting for themselves, to protect their families in defense of their nation, and not a Royal among them.

Can't Get Enough of Those Royals

The British Royal family is a serious soap opera. Manufactured by itself and presented via an obsequious media to a gullible public who week by week devour the titillating tales of the most dysfunctional family in the land, the Royals act out a Regal *Days of Their Lives*, like *Desperate Housewives*, where the seven deadly sins are grist to their mill.

Yet Australians can't get enough of them. The monarch pops in every decade or so, a handsome prince and his beautiful bride may fly by and the Australian media falls to its knees desperate for a tit-bit, a photo opportunity, a suspect baby-bump, a moment of vexation, a sucking of toes, or a loopy Windsor talking to a stick of asparagus, a salacious divorce, an adulterous affair, a racist remark or an 'annus horribilus'.

Diana Spencer, the 'People's Princess' will never die. She continues to smile at us from the covers of weekly magazines lined up at the supermarket checkout. She will never age, she will always be there—for us, our Princess. She has escaped the royal soap opera and has become an ideal. Virtuous in extremis, forever lovely in her untimely demise.

What of her Danish counterpart? Mary Donaldson, an Australian lass, a Tasmanian born of Scottish migrant parentage, who married the Crown Prince of a foreign land whom she met in a pub in Sydney. She has become a Royal. No Australian citizen could ever expect to achieve the same exalted position marrying into the family of our own monarch: this would simply not be possible.

Europe is at one, while the old colonies, especially those so insecure in their national identity that they are unable to cast off the anachronism of a 'mother country', a mother who no longer welcomes her 'colonial' children as equal to her neighbours still hanker for her love. Does mother reciprocate?

Well, yes she does. On 2 January 2012 The Age announced: 'Queen's special gift for John Howard:—Not since Sir Robert Menzies has the monarchy bestowed such approbation on an Australian politician.

John Howard's 11-year prime ministership and his dogged adherence to a constitutional monarchy have earned him entree into an exclusive club with a capped living membership of just 24 after Buckingham

Palace announced yesterday he had been appointed a member of the Order of merit.

Only Menzies' Knight of the Order of the Thistle, an honour the Liberal Party founder received in 1963 carries more royal kudos.

Curiously, the citation reads: 'It is given to such persons, subjects of Our Crown, as may have rendered exceptionally meritorious services in Our Crown services or towards the advancement of the Arts, Learning, Literature and science or such other exceptional service as We see fit to recognize'.

Australians such as John Howard are no longer subjects of the Crown but citizens of Australia. Australians ceased to be subjects to any regent in 1972 after Britain had joined with the European Common Market, cutting many of its family ties with its former colonies.

When Labor leader Gough Whitlam came to the prime minister-ship his government dispensed with Imperial honours. However, it stands to reason that John Winston Howard, who was dubbed by 'Dubbya', President GW Bush, as 'The Man Of Steel' may as well receive his pretty gong from Britain's Queen Elizabeth II, aka Queen of Australia, in recognition of his meritorious services in 'defeating the republicans'.

The Bendigo Art Gallery, when staging an exhibition in March 2012 of photographs and fashion worn by a former American actress and later Princess Grace of Monaco, was very excited about the impending visit to the central Victorian goldfields city of another royal person. A lead story on the front page of the *Bendigo Advertiser*, 29 December 2011, announced in very bold type: 'Princess Charlene of Monaco Set for Royal Visit'. Who? Who is Princess Charlene? A South-African born lass who recently married a Prince, that's who.

Bendigo and nearby Castlemaine had its fair share of royals popping in and out in 2011: 'Prince William toured flood-affected areas in April and Danish Crown Prince Frederick visited [nearby] Castlemaine last month,' the newspaper reported, 'the visit of Princess Charlene will be the third royal visit in 12 months'.

The director of the Bendigo Art Gallery, Ms Karen Quinlan, added: 'Within the exhibition we hope to move you a little closer to

Cartoon by Michael Leunig
Melbourne-based artist and social commentator Michael Leunig is one of those 'rogues' and 'dreamers' who diligently 'pokes a big stick' at the pretensions of Australian society. This cartoon, published in *The Age* during the heat of one of Australia's many debates on the issue of a new flag, showed his suggestion for the new design: Leunig offered a flag made of corrugated iron.
(Courtesy Michael Leunig and the Melbourne Age *newspaper)*

the person, the classic style, her timeless elegance and ultimately I hope to enhance our understanding of this 20th century iconic woman whom we admire and still love.'

Like Diana, Princess of Wales, Grace Kelly also remains forever young. What hope the republic when the monarchists have all the glamorous icons?

Whither the Flag

Another flag, which represented the burgeoning federation of Australian Colonies into on Commonwealth, known as the Federation flag, was very popular and it was expected that it would be adopted as the first national flag of Australia. The problem with the Federation flag was it bore a similarity with the flag of the Southern

Cross, with the white pointed stars of the southern constellation positioned on a blue ground just like the digger's banner flown at Eureka fifty years earlier. The Eureka flag represented dissent and notions of republicanism. In consequence the Federation flag was simply unacceptable.

The debate about the national flag continues, although under current national leadership all such discussions have largely diss-appeared from the political agenda, yet commentators such as Suzy Freeman-Greene writing in *The Age* on 4 February 2012 continue to express their dismay at displays of rampant nationalism and hope for change:

> Amid pride and prejudice, it's time for a new flag:–Whenever I see a flag worn as a cape, I can't help thinking of those Cronulla crusaders shouting, 'We grew here, you flew here' or 'Aussie, Aussie, Aussie, oi, oi, oi'.
>
> I grew up watching flags fly from poles, not shoulders. The first time I saw them draped on bodies en masse was in footage of the December 2005 Cronulla beach riots.
>
> . . . The Howard government worked steadfastly to put the flag centre stage, fostering a feel-good nationalism in response to that gloomy black-armband mob. And we have embraced America's in-your-face patriotism and fondness for public emoting–even as we wave a flag that includes the Union Jack.
>
> . . . Whereas once we had lively discussions about changing the flag, or questioning the flag-waving, such talk is now labelled 'un-Australian'. . . Witness the bumper-sticker with a picture of the flag that reads: 'Support it. Or f--- off'.
>
> . . . I'm not f---ing off, but I reckon we deserve a better flag. The most prominent feature of our current one is the British Union Jack–a symbol of colonial oppression to most indigenous Australian, and its dominant position on the flag can send a subliminal message that Australian-ness is linked to British ancestry.

Russell Kennedy, Melbourne graphic designer and Monash University lecturer, created his vision of a new flag for Australia in 1999. Today it is recognised as the Reconciliation flag and has been

given to every secondary school in Victoria to be flown on special days that honour Australia's indigenes. This flag, featuring the red, black and gold of the Aboriginal flag, a striking graphic leaping kangaroo and the stars of the Southern Cross is a most beautiful design that ticks all the boxes when proposed as an alternative design to the current British Naval Ensign.

Do Australians deserve better? As song-writer, singer and national icon John Williamson has said: '... there is no doubt in my mind that a republic is inevitable as is a purely Australian flag.' More than two hundred years since Arthur Phillip raised the Union Flag at Botany Bay, more than a century since federation, almost half-a-century since Britain cut its ties to the colonies, it would appear that in spite of a proclivity to vote against their own desires a majority of Australians believe they at least deserve the right to determine their own icons by popular vote.

Maybe the time has come when all Australians, no matter from whence they come, should embrace their common destiny, to promote their community to the world as a truly independent nation, and come together as one.

Australians all, let us rejoice, 'beneath our southern cross'.

BIBLIOGRAPHY

Baker, DWA, *Days of Wrath: A Life of John Dunmore Lang*, Melbourne University Press, Melbourne, 1985

Bomford, Janette M, *That Dangerous and Persuasive Woman: Vida Goldstein*, Melbourne University Press, Melbourne, 1993

Craig, William, *My Adventures on the Australian Goldfields*, Cassell & Co., London, 1853

Clarke, CMH, *Select Documents in Australian History, 1851–1900*, Angus and Robertson, Sydney, 1955

Crowley, FK, *Modern Australia in Documents: 1901–1939, Vol. 1*, Wren Publishing, Melbourne, 1973

Culotta, Nino, *They're a Weird Mob*, Ure Smith Pty Limited, Sydney, first published 1957

Dimmack, Max, *Noel Counihan*, Melbourne University Press, Melbourne, 1974

Hardy, Frank J, *Power Without Glory*, first published by the author in 1950

Headon, David & Perkins, Elizabeth, *Our First Republicans: Lang, Harpur, Deniehy*, The Federation Press, Leichhardt, 1998

Howitt, William, *Land, Labour & Gold, or Two Years in Victora with Visits to Sydney and Van Diemen's Land*, Lowden, Kilmore, Victoria, 1972, first published 1855

Hughes, Robert, *The Fatal Shore*, Collins Harvill, London, 1987

Lauder, Afferbeck [aka Morrison], *Let Stalk Strine*, Ure Smith Pty Ltd, Sydney, first published 1965

Lawrence, DH, *Kangaroo*, Penguin Books, Ringwood, Victoria, Australia, 1986

Margery, Susan, *Unbridling the Tongues of Women–A Biography of Catherine Helen Spence*, Hale & Ironmonger, Sydney, 1985

Moore, Andrew, *The Secret Army and the Premier: Conservative Paramilitary Organisations in New South Wales, 1930–32*, New South Wales University Press, Kensington, 1989

Oldfield, Audrey, *The Great Republic of the Southern Seas: Republicans in Nineteenth Century Australia*, Hale & Ironmonger, Alexandria, 1999

Serle, Geoffrey, *The Golden Age. A History of the Colony of Victoria, 1851–1861*, Melbourne University Press, Melbourne, 1963

Smith, Bernard, *Australian Painting, 1788–1960*, Oxford University Press, Melbourne, 1962

PICTURE CREDITS

Page 233:
Photograph at left:
John Simpson Kirkpatrick and his
donkey, Gallipoli, 1915, National Library
of Australia

Photograph at right:
Private AJ Currie (left) and 202 Private
John Simpson Kirkpatrick. Both of the
3rd Field Ambulance, in Blackboy Camp
in Western Australia. The skeleton was
used for instructional purposes and is
wearing a slouch hat.
Australian War Memorial (A03116)

Page 245:
Will Dyson
Fatalist
Charcoal with wash on paper 1917
52.7 × 66.1 cm
Australian War Memorial (ART02224)

Page 249:
Norman Lindsay (1879–1969)
Pollice Verso 1904
Pen and Indian ink
45.7 × 58.7 cm irreg. (image); 47.6 × 60.6
cm (sheet)
Felton Bequest, 1907
National Gallery of Victoria, Melbourne

Page 298:
Noel Counihan (1913–1986)
The people have an answer 1950
Linocut, printed in black ink, from one
block 27.8 x14.4 cm
Kenion Press Ltd, printer
Gift of Doon Stone, 1978
National Gallery of Australia, Canberra

Page 300:
Noel Counihan (1913–1986)
Boy in helmet 1968
Silkscreen, printed in black ink, from
one screen 71.2 × 52.0 cm
Norman O'Connor, printer
National Gallery of Australia, Canberra

Page 303–4:
Sir Sidney Nolan
Eureka Stockade
Foyer, mural for the Reserve Bank of
Australia, Melbourne, 1973
Photographed by Wolfgang Sievers
National Library of Australia

Page 368:
Tru Blu Flag. Reproduced by permission
of John Williamson

Australian War Memorial:
p. 218	Portrait of Harry 'Breaker' Morant, A05311
p. 224	Rally Round the Flag, ARTV05143
p. 227	Anti-conscription Leaflet, RC0036
p. 233	Bunbury PO1446.001. Pvte Curry and 202 Pvte John Simpson Kirkpatrick, AO3116
p. 245	Dyson, 'Fatalist', ART02224
p. 253	Two airmen in front of *Chloe*, VIC1723
p. 260	Tanunda, SA, PO1738.003
p. 234	Dr Jim Cairns, Anti-Vietnam, P00671.014

NOTES

1 R Hughes, *The Fatal Shore*,
   Collins Harvill, London, 1987,
   p. 190

2 Craig, *My Adventures on the
   Australian Goldfields*, Cassell &
   Co., London, 1853, p. 43

3 W Howitt, *Land, Labour & Gold*,
   Lowden, Kilmore, Vic, 1972,
   Letter XIV, 1 March 1853,
   pp. 250–1

4 G Serle, *The Golden Age: A
   History of the Colony of Victoria,
   1851–1861*. Melbourne University
   Press, Melbourne, 1963, p. 260

5 CMH Clarke, *Select Documents
   in Australian History, 1851–1900*,
   Angus and Robertson, Sydney,
   1955, p. 341

6 This unpublished, seditious
   note was written by JD Lang
   in a private notebook. Lang
   papers, vol. I, MSML A221, p89,
   7 July 1845, Mitchell Library,
   Sydney

7 CMH Clarke, op cit, p. 566

8 G Serle, op cit, p. 251

9 Transcription from Emily Nuttall
   Thorne–'Clontarf', an account
   of the attempted assassination
   of Prince Alfred, Duke of
   Edinburgh, at Clontarf on
   12 March 1868, MLMSS 6100,
   State Library of New South Wales

10 From Sir Roland Hill (1795–1879),
   British social reformer, founder of
   the Penny Post

11 S. Margery, *Unbridling the
   Tongues of Women–A Biography
   of Catherine Helen Spence*, Hale &
   Ironmonger, Sydney, 1985, p. 179

12 ibid, p. 163

13 DH Lawrence, *Kangaroo*, Penguin
   Books, Ringwood, Vic, 1986, p. 106

14 ibid, p208

15 ibid, p219

16 F Hardy, *Power Without Glory*,
   first published in 1950, p. 273

17 ibid, p. 281

18 ibid, loc cit

19 M Dimmack, *Noel Counihan*.
   Melbourne University Press,
   Melbourne, 1974, p35

20 ibid, p59

21 N Culotta, *They're A Weird Mob*,
   Ure Smith Pty Ltd, Sydney, 1957,
   p. 40

22 ibid, p. 185

23 ibid, p. 200

24 ibid, p. 204

25 B Smith, *Australian Painting,
   1788–1960*, Oxford University
   Press, Melbourne, 1962, p. 251

26 www.wetink.com.au/assets/pdfs/
   reads/Issue_6/Thecircumstances.
   pdf

ACKNOWLEDGEMENTS

Thanks to Don Walker for permission to reproduce the lyrics to *Khe Sanh*, a hit for the band Cold Chisel, now an anthem; and to John Schumann for the lyrics to *I Was Only Nineteen (A walk in the light green)* an Australian classic from Redgum.

Thanks also to John Williamson for the use of his *Tru Blu* flag; Bruce Petty for his cartoons on pages 230 and 246; Michael Leunig for his on pages 234 and 235; and Cathy Wilcox for hers on page 251.

Thanks also to photographers John Elliott, Robert MacFarlane, Julie Millowick, Ben Rushton and Greg Weight; my son Julian for his photographs of the 'Sacred Flame' on page 248; photography student at La Trobe University, Bendigo, School of Visual Arts & Design, Karl Henry, for his photograph on the same page; Working Dog Productions for their permission to reproduce images from *The Castle*; and Dr Anne Beggs-Sunter, of Ballarat University, who read the story on Peter Lalor and offered some helpful advice.

I would also like to thank the staff of the following institutions who continue to provide an excellent service in tracking down and preparing picture files ready for reproduction: The National Library, Canberra, National Portrait Gallery, Canberra; La Trobe Picture Collection, State Library of Victoria; State Library of New South Wales; State Library of Queensland; State Library of South Australia; State Library of Tasmania; Northern Territory Images; Library of the City of Woollongong; Gold Coast Library Picture Collection; National Library of Ireland; University of Glasgow; Art Gallery of New South Wales; National Gallery of Victoria; National Gallery of Australia, Canberra; Art Gallery of Western Australia; Bendigo Art Gallery; Ballarat Fine Art Gallery; Australian War Memorial, Canberra; Castlemaine Art Gallery & Historical Museum.

Nancy Cazneux; Mick and Pat Counihan; Peter Pidgeon; Maria Prendergast; Martin Sharp; Gary Shead; Barbara Tucker and Wendy Whiteley have been most helpful in permitting me to use the artworks and photographs created by the artists Cazneux, Counihan, Sharp, Shead, Tucker, WEP and Whiteley. In each case they have read my early drafts and offered some very helpful, and timely, insights into the lives of these important artists.

Once again I would like to acknowledge the constant forebearance of my wife Christine, who, this time joined me on a fact-finding mission around Ireland; tramping over 'Vinegar Hill', then through the rain on the search for the home of Peter Lalor. She has seen the inside of a lot of museums and historic homes on her 'holidays'.

INDEX